Go-home Bay—on the Georgian Bay of Lake Huron

The Saint Lawrence
[Canada]

Its Basin and Border-Lands

Samuel Edward Dawson

HERITAGE BOOKS
2019

HERITAGE BOOKS
AN IMPRINT OF HERITAGE BOOKS, INC.

Books, CDs, and more—Worldwide

For our listing of thousands of titles see our website
at
www.HeritageBooks.com

A Facsimile Reprint
Published 2019 by
HERITAGE BOOKS, INC.
Publishing Division
5810 Ruatan Street
Berwyn Heights, Md. 20740

Originally published
Toronto, Canada
1905

Copyright © 2003 Heritage Books

— Publisher's Notice —
In reprints such as this, it is often not possible to remove blemishes from the original. We feel the contents of this book warrant its reissue despite these blemishes and hope you will agree and read it with pleasure.

International Standard Book Number
Paperbound: 978-0-7884-2252-2

TO THE RIGHT HONOURABLE

SIR WILFRID LAURIER

P.C., G.C.M.G., D.C.L., ETC.

PRIME MINISTER OF THE DOMINION OF CANADA,

THE FOREMOST REPRESENTATIVE IN THE PRESENT DAY OF THE PEOPLE WHOSE DEEDS ARE RECORDED HEREIN; WHO, BY THEIR COURAGE AND ENDURANCE, WON TO CIVILIZATION THE WILDERNESS OF THE GREAT TRANSVERSE VALLEY OF THE CONTINENT AND ITS BORDER LANDS,

THIS BOOK IS, BY KIND PERMISSION, RESPECTFULLY

DEDICATED

PREFACE

IN the following pages an attempt has been made to set forth in order the chief facts relating to the discovery and exploration of the northeastern part of the continent of North America. It is the nearest to Europe, and has an interest of its own, inasmuch as it was the first part of the main continent to be reached from the Old World.

No attempts to penetrate beyond the sea coast of this region have been recorded, until the Cartier voyages opened up the Gulf and the River St. Lawrence as a broad waterway leading to the mysterious West, or, as often called in the language of that day, to the East. The limits of exploration remained for sixty years after Cartier at the site of the present city of Montreal, eighty-six miles above the head of tide water. The foundation of Quebec by Champlain in 1608 initiated a new series of explorations. These extended over the whole basin of the St. Lawrence and over the water-parting into the basin of the Mississippi contiguous to it. The story is full of geographic and historic interest, and abounds with romantic adventure. This also forms a part of our theme.

To narrate intelligibly the achievements of these explorers, it is necessary, incidentally, to dwell upon the geography of these regions. Following up the avenue of " the River of Canada," the French pioneers outflanked the barrier of the Alleghenies, " the endless mountains " which so long retarded discovery at the south. They passed readily up into the great fresh-water seas in the centre of the continent and over the portages at the heads of their tributaries into the adjoining basins at the north, the west, and the south, unlocking all the river communications of the interior. Reference must also frequently be made to that confederacy of astute and politic savages which, seated on the water-parting of the

St. Lawrence, Ohio, Susquehanna, and Hudson rivers, held for a hundred years the balance between the English and French nations and stamped its impress on the destiny of the continent.

Nor is it possible to present the subject without dwelling upon the progressive occupation of those immense territories, where the steam whistle has replaced the war-whoop, and where great cities have grown up on the portages; where the enormous silences of inland oceans, once scarcely ruffled by the wary dip of the paddles of some war party gliding upon its bloody errand, now resound to the blare of gigantic and demonstrative whalebacks, or of steam tugs towing long trains of loaded barges. These are themes worthy of more adequate presentment than they can receive within the limits of a single volume. They are subjects of never-ending interest, for when the New World was discovered the Old World itself had recently been reborn, and, alive to all new influences, regarded the new continent with a newly awakened curiosity and a pardonable credulity—for what might not be possible in a world unknown to Aristotle and Ptolemy!

Ottawa, December, 1904.

CONTENTS

PAGE

LIST OF ILLUSTRATIONS xix

GEOGRAPHICAL SKETCH

Newfoundland—Acadia—The St. Lawrence Basin . . xxiii

CHAPTER I

INTRODUCTORY

Early charts—Estimation of longitude and latitude—Revival of Greek science—Geography in the Dark Ages—Geography at the era of the Renaissance—Columbus—Discoveries of the Portuguese—Legendary islands of the Atlantic—Behaim's globe—Rapid extension of exploration 1

CHAPTER II

JOHN CABOT'S FIRST VOYAGE—DISCOVERY

Discovery of the mainland—Previous attempts of Bristol sailors—Cabot at Bristol—First voyage—Cathay the objective point—Variation of the compass in 1497—Nature of the country found—Cape Breton the landfall—La Cosa's map—Cape Race the key to North American geography—John Cabot's testimony—Sebastian Cabot's testimony—Historic importance of the question 13

CHAPTER III

JOHN CABOT'S SECOND VOYAGE—DISAPPOINTMENT

John Cabot's brief triumph—New letters patent—Expedition on a large scale—Merchandise for Cathay—Sebastian Cabot's experience—His subsequent career—First record of ice—Extent of the coasting—Robert Thorne's evidence—First and second voyages contrasted—Misconceptions as to Sebastian Cabot—His service in Spain and return to England—Neglect of English historians . 35

CONTENTS

CHAPTER IV

THE CORTE-REALS AND PORTUGUESE DISCOVERY

PAGE

The Golden era of Portugal—The Corte-Real family—First expedition under Gaspar Corte-Real to the North—The different voyages confused—Second expedition of Gaspar Corte-Real to the West and Northwest—A slave coast in America—Gaspar Corte-Real does not return—Unsuccessful efforts of his brothers to learn his fate—Maps of Cantino and Reinel 47

CHAPTER V

MYTHICAL PRE-COLUMBIAN DISCOVERIES

Discovery of America easy in theory—Claimed for all western nations—Claims of the Portuguese—of the Azoreans—of the Basques—of the Bretons—of the Normans—Atlas of Andrea Bianco—Stokafixa—Origin of the name Labrador—of the name Bacallaos—Beothiks (Red Indians) of Newfoundland—Fishing vessels, Breton, Portuguese, Basque, early on the coast 59

CHAPTER VI

PRIVATE ADVENTURERS—CABOT TO CARTIER

The Cabot patents superseded—English adventurers with Azorean partners—Slow development of English fisheries—Sebastian Cabot not concerned in English enterprises—John Rut's voyage—Voyage of Master Hore and the lawyers—Bretons and Normans flock to the fisheries—Prominence of the Portuguese in early days—Fagundez—Breton and Portuguese names on coast—Earliest voyages of French and Spanish Basques 74

CHAPTER VII

THE VOYAGE OF VERRAZANO

Disbelief in the continuity of the American coast—Francis I. seeks a share in the New World—Commencement of national navies—French corsairs prey on Spanish commerce—Juan Verrazano—Engaged to lead an expedition

CONTENTS

for France—He sails to the West—Extent of his voyage—His own account to the King—Unreasonable doubts of its authenticity—The sea of Verrazano—He sails on another expedition and is not heard of again—Juan Verrazano a different person from Juan Florin, who was hanged by the Spaniards **87**

CHAPTER VIII

THE VOYAGE OF STEPHEN GOMEZ

Gomez a Portuguese pilot in the service of Spain—He deserts Magellan—Engaged by Charles V. to search for a central opening to the South Sea—Sails in the winter of 1524-25—Extent of his exploration—Carries back a cargo of slaves—The coast of Acadia examined from the Penobscot eastward—The Bay of Fundy—The Gut of Canso—The Island of St. John—Cape Breton—Cape Smoky—Cape North—The Bay of the Bretons . . **98**

CHAPTER IX

RESULTS OF EXPLORATION UP TO JACQUES CARTIER'S FIRST VOYAGE

Atlantic seaboard completely explored—Viegas' map—Defects of the early maps—The Gulf of St. Lawrence unknown—Philippe de Chabot, Seigneur de Brion—Cartier selected to explore for a western passage to Asia—Cartier's birth and previous life **114**

CHAPTER X

CARTIER'S FIRST VOYAGE, 1534

Sources of information—"Relation Originale"—Departure from St. Malo—Arrival at Bonavista—Coast blocked with field ice—Strait of Belle-Isle—Course inside the Gulf—Arrival at Blanc Sablon; the first point of the present province of Quebec—Inner coasts of Labrador and Newfoundland—Discovery of the Magdalen group—North coast of Prince Edward Island supposed to be mainland—Coast of New Brunswick at Miramichi—Chaleur Bay—Gaspé—Anticosti—Return to St. Malo. NOTE—The birds mentioned by Cartier **121**

CONTENTS

CHAPTER XI

CARTIER'S SECOND VOYAGE, 1535-36

Second expedition commissioned—Cartier sails May 19, 1535—Rendezvous at Blanc Sablon—Course through the Gulf—Arrives at the kingdom of Saguenay—Indian interpreters at home—Grand river of Hochelaga reached—Pushes on to Canada—The three kingdoms—Arrives at Stadacona—Beauty of the country—The lord of Canada—Winter quarters chosen—Proceeds to Hochelaga—Indian jugglery—Passes Ochelay—Reception at Hochelaga—Productions of the country—Cartier's religious service—His view from the mountain (Montreal)—Return to Stadacona—Winter quarters on the St. Charles—Winter sufferings—Scurvy—Despair of the crew—The wonderful tree of healing—Arrival of spring—Departure for St. Malo—Donnacona and his chiefs carried off—Newfoundland proved to be an island . . 151

CHAPTER XII

SOME DISPUTED POINTS OF CARTIER'S VOYAGES

The Indian nations of the St. Lawrence valley—Algonquins—Huron-Iroquois—The healing tree, Ameda—The chaplains of Cartier's expeditions—Etymology of the word Canada—The Ste. Croix of Cartier's winter quarters . 179

CHAPTER XIII

CARTIER'S THIRD VOYAGE—ROBERVAL—1541-43

Delay of Cartier's third expedition—Cartier commissioned, October, 1540—Disgrace of Admiral Chabot de Brion—Cartier's commission revoked—New commission places Roberval in command—Cartier sails in May, 1541—Roberval's delays—Jealousy of Spain—Cartier establishes himself at Cap Rouge—Revisits Hochelaga—Examines the Lachine Rapids—Indian distrust—Roberval sails in April, 1542—Cartier encounters him in St. Johns harbour—Cartier sails away to France and Roberval proceeds up the river—Roberval establishes his winter quarters—His harsh rule—His incompetence—Visits Hochelaga—Return to France in 1543—The story of Marguerite and the Isle of Demons—Cartier's life and character. NOTE—Cartographical results of the Cartier Voyages 192

CONTENTS

CHAPTER XIV

CARTIER TO CHAMPLAIN

PAGE

Private traders in the Gulf and River—Cartier's discoveries shown in the maps reproduced in the "Bibliotheca Lindesiana"—The Cabot map of A. D. 1544—Jean Allefonsce—Breton and Norman fishermen and traders—Neglect of the French Court—Basques upon the coast—Decline of Portugal—English enterprise aroused—Sir Humphrey Gilbert's expedition—English begin to enter the Gulf—La Roche's expedition—Convicts abandoned on Sable Island—Legend of the Franciscan monk . . 215

CHAPTER XV

SAMUEL DE CHAMPLAIN

Critical point of Canadian history, A. D. 1600—Chauvin builds a trading post at Tadoussac—Pont-Gravé—De Chastes—Samuel de Champlain enters upon his life work—His family and previous history—First arrival in Canada—At Tadoussac—He goes up the river to the sites of Quebec and Montreal—Returns to Tadoussac and explores the lower river—The Sieur Prevert's marvellous reports—Champlain returns to France—Death of De Chastes—De Monts takes his place and is commissioned Lieutenant Governor for the King—Opposition of the merchants—Character of De Monts—De Monts sails for Acadia, 1604—Champlain joins the expedition and explores the Acadian coasts—Lescarbot—Basin of Annapolis Royal—St. John harbour and river—Settlement at Ste. Croix—Poutrincourt—Colony removed to Port Royal—L'Ordre de Bon-Temps—Commercial jealousy thwarts De Monts' plans—Poutrincourt's family clings to Acadia. NOTES—Meaning of the name Acadia—Annapolis Basin—Settlement at St. Sauveur—Early English voyages to the New England coast 231

CHAPTER XVI

CHAMPLAIN IN QUEBEC

Champlain the founder of Canada—Settlement at Quebec in 1608—First winter at Quebec—War between Algonquins and Iroquois—Necessity of siding with the Algonquins—War party against the Mohawks—Lake Champlain discovered—Defeat of the Iroquois—Second conflict, at the

Richelieu—Assassination of Henry IV., the patron of Champlain and De Monts—Champlain in 1611 goes to the Sault—Makes a clearing on the site of the city of Montreal—He meets the Indians of the Ottawa and lake regions—Champlain returns to France—Continued hostility of merchants—Company reorganised—Champlain arrives at the Sault—Proceeds up the Ottawa River to find the Northern Sea—Narrow escape at the Chute à Blondeau—The site of the present capital described—Arrives at Allumette Island—Vignau's falsehoods exposed—Disappointment of Champlain—He returns to France—Conciliates opposition and brings out Recollet missionaries 253

CHAPTER XVII

CHAMPLAIN IN ONTARIO

Champlain goes up the Ottawa—His course by Lake Nipissing and French River into Lake Huron—The Huron nation—The Huron territory—The great war-party assembles—Route down the Otonabee and Trent—Lake Ontario crossed—The Iroquois territory—Terror inspired by Iroquois among surrounding nations—Champlain and the Hurons assault an Onondaga town without success—Retreat—War-party breaks up and Champlain unable to reach Quebec—He visits the country between Kingston and Ottawa—Returns to Huron country and winters there—Visits the Tobacco nation and the Ottawas—Returns to Quebec in May, 1616—Extent of Champlain's explorations in Canada—Religious differences—Huguenots and Jesuits—Moderation and constancy of Champlain 273

CHAPTER XVIII

EXPLORATION OF THE WEST, FROM CHAMPLAIN TO THE DISPERSION OF THE HURONS

Explorers trained under Champlain continue the work—Physical features of the country favour exploration—Interpreters and traders lead the way—Adventures of Etienne Brulé—Recollet missionaries commence their labours—Assistance of the Jesuits invited—Missionaries established in the Huron country—They visit the Neutral nation—Quebec taken by the English—Champlain and most of the colonists carried to England—Canada re-

CONTENTS xv

PAGE

stored to France—Return of Champlain—Jesuits the only missionaries allowed to return—Nicollet starts to discover the Great South Sea—Jesuits resume missions to the Hurons—Michilimackinac—Lake Michigan discovered—Green Bay or Baie des Puants—The Winnebago nation of Dakota stock—Nicollet reaches the water-parting of the Mississippi basin—Jesuit mission to the Hurons—St. Mary on the Wye—Sault Ste. Marie visited by the Jesuits—The Lake system begins to be understood—Brébœuf among the Neutrals—Premonitions of martyrdom—Destruction of the Huron nation 289

CHAPTER XIX

EXPLORATION RESUMED AND POSSESSION TAKEN FOR FRANCE

The Huron country abandoned—Fear of the Iroquois—Jesuits and Huron converts retire to Quebec—Desolation and massacre extend over the West—Peace, in 1654, permits resumption of the fur trade—Missions resumed—Radisson and Chouart—Radisson among the Iroquois—Radisson and Chouart on Lake Michigan—Pass Sault Ste. Marie into Lake Superior—Make a trading post at Chequamegon Bay—Explore the country over the water-parting—Return to Three Rivers—Second expedition of Chouart and Radisson—They resolve to discover the Sea of the North—Go up to Lake Superior to Chequamegon Bay—They are conducted by Cree Indians to Hudson's Bay—Return and subsequent adventures—Father Ménard perishes south of Lake Superior—Father Allouez founds a mission at Chequamegon Bay and on Lake Michigan—De Tracy and Talon arrive in Canada—Iroquois sue for peace—The route by Lake Ontario opened—The Sulpicians commence to establish missions—Expedition of Dollier and Galinée—They find an earthly paradise on Lake Erie—Return by Michilimackinac—St. Lusson is sent to the Sault Ste. Marie and takes ceremonial possession for France 312

CHAPTER XX

JOLLIET AND LA SALLE—THE MISSISSIPPI VALLEY UNVEILED

All westward routes opened—Louis Jolliet and Father Marquette—They start for the Mississippi—Fox and Wisconsin portage—Arrive at the prairie region—The Mississippi reached—Paddle down as far as the Arkansas—

Return by the Chicago portage—Marquette remains on Lake Michigan—Jolliet goes down to Quebec—His maps and papers lost—Death of Marquette—St. Ignace de Michilimackinac—Robert Cavelier de La Salle—His post at Lachine—Starts with Galinée and Dollier, but separates from them—Discovers the Ohio—Controversy about the discovery of the Mississippi—Arrival of Frontenac—La Salle's western schemes supported by Frontenac—The first step, Fort Frontenac—Henri de Tonty—La Salle at Niagara—He builds the *Griffon* for the upper lakes—Loss of the *Griffon*—La Salle's indomitable spirit struggles against disaster—Overcomes all obstacles—Fort Crèvecœur destroyed—La Salle reaches the Mississippi—Goes down to the Gulf of Mexico and takes possession for France 341

CHAPTER XXI

HENNEPIN AND DULHUT—WESTERN EXPLORATION CONTINUED

Mississippi and St. Lawrence divide south of Lake Superior—Wild rice region—The Dakota nation reached—Hennepin on the Illinois—He reaches the Mississippi—His pretended discoveries—His captivity among the Sioux—Weeping Indians—Rescue by Dulhut—Mendacity of Hennepin—Daniel de Greysolon, Sieur Dulhut arrives in Canada—He establishes himself at the head of Lake Superior—His adventurous life—His explorations to the extreme western limit of the St. Lawrence valley . . 363

CHAPTER XXII

EXPLORATION TO THE NORTH AND EAST

Champlain's early attempt to reach the Sea of the North—The quest continued—Chief routes from Canada to Hudson's Bay—Expedition of De Troyes—Father Buteux killed on the St. Maurice—Unrecognised devotion of the missionaries to the North and East—Lake St. John discovered—Fathers Druillettes and Dablon start for Hudson's Bay—They turn back at Lake Nekouba—Talon sends Father Albanel—He reaches Hudson's Bay—Finds the English flag there—Injustice of the Governor of Canada to Chouart and Radisson—They transfer their services to England—Lead Gillam's expedition to Rupert's River—Father Albanel's second journey—Taken prisoner by the English—Chouart and Radisson return

CONTENTS xvii
PAGE

to their allegiance—Radisson founds a French fort on the Bay—He turns English again and captures it—Jolliet at Hudson's Bay—The Traite de Tadoussac—The Labrador wilderness—The missionaries on its southern border—The desolate plateau—The Grand Falls discovered . . 375

CHAPTER XXIII

OCCUPATION OF THE ST. LAWRENCE VALLEY

Close of the era of discovery—Physiography of the continent favours French and retards English exploration—The Iroquois bar the route by the lower lakes—Great warfeast at Montreal—Iroquois opposition ceases—Expedition to the interior of Labrador—Rumours of the Grand Falls stimulate the efforts of explorers—Remarkable exploration of A. P. Low for the Geological Survey of Canada—The grim territory traversed in two directions—The occupation of the valley of the St. Lawrence on the far west—Headquarters of the great fur companies on Lake Superior—Course of occupation along the southern water-parting—Lowness of the divide of Lakes Michigan, Erie, and Ontario—Divides of Lake Champlain, the Connecticut, the Chaudière, and the St. John—Arrival of the loyalists and English settlement of Ontario and Acadia 401

CHAPTER XXIV

OCCUPATION OF THE ATLANTIC COAST

The history of the French settlements in Acadia—Vicissitudes of English and French Conquest—Alexander, La Tour, and Charnisay—Nicholas Denys—Port Royal (Annapolis) repeatedly changes masters—It becomes nominally English—Settlements on the St. John River and Prince Edward Island—Settlement at Halifax—Deportation of the Acadian French—Anticosti—The Island of Newfoundland—Exploration and settlement impeded by Government—Cormack's expedition—The interior opened up by a railway 415

APPENDIX

LIST OF THE CHIEF WORKS CONSULTED OR REFERRED TO . . 429

INDEX 443

ILLUSTRATIONS

1. Go-Home Bay; Georgian Bay of Lake Huron . . . . *Frontispiece*
2. Extract from Martin Behaim's Globe *Facing page* 8
3. The Cabot Tower at Bristol . . " 18
4. The Key Point of North American Geography — Fig. 1, Ruysch Map, A. D. 1508—C. de Portogesi. Fig. 2, King Map, A. D. 1502—Cape Raso. Fig. 3, Cape Race, A. D. 1900 . . . . . " 28
5. Juan de La Cosa's Map, A. D. 1500 " 30
6. Extract from Sebastian Cabot's Map of 1544, showing the point of Cape Breton as the landfall. Fig. 4 . . . . *Page* 32
7. Robert Thorne's Map, A. D. 1527. Fig. 5 . . . . " 41
8. Sebastian Cabot—From a contemporaneous portrait, last owned by Richard Biddle; destroyed by fire in 1845 . . . . *Facing page* 44
9. The Cantino Map, A. D. 1501-2. Fig. 6 . . . . *Page* 54
10. Pedro Reinel's Map, A. D. 1505. Fig. 7 . . . . *Facing page* 57

ILLUSTRATIONS

11. Ribeiro's Map, A. D. 1529, . . . *Facing page* 80
12. Cape Blomidon—at the entrance of the Basin of Minas . . . . . " 106
13. View on the Gut of Canso . . . " 110
14. Gaspar Viegas' Map, A. D. 1534. Fig. 8 . . . . *Page* 115
15. Portrait of Jacques Cartier . . . *Facing page* 120
16. The Great Bird Rock, from an Admiralty Chart. Fig. 9 . . . *Page* 134
17. The Magdalen Group, true shape. Fig. 10 . . . . " 136
18. Deadman's Island (Alezay), from an Admiralty Chart. Fig. 11 . " 138
19. Representations of the Magdalen Group on early maps. Fig. 12 . " 139
20. Plan of Hochelaga—from Ramusio *Facing page* 168
21. Cartographical results of the Cartier Voyages. A—Harleyan World Map, circa A. D. 1536. C—Desceliers' World Map, A. D. 1550 . . . . " 214
22. The Sebastian Cabot Map of A. D. 1544 . . . . " 216
23. View of Tadoussac . . . . . . " 232
24. Champlain's Chart of Tadoussac Harbour . . . . " 234
25. Champlain's Map of Sault St. Louis and site of the city of Montreal . . . . " 236
26. Digby Gut—The entrance to Annapolis (Port Royal) Basin . . " 246
27. Portrait of Champlain . . . . . " 252

ILLUSTRATIONS xxi

28. Champlain's Map of Quebec Basin *Facing page* 254
29. Defeat of the Iroquois on Lake Champlain . . . . " 260
30. Running the Sault St. Louis in the present day . . . . " 264
31. Chaudière Falls at Ottawa . . . . " 266
32. Entrance to French River . . . " 272
33. Onondaga Fort attacked by Champlain and the Hurons . . . . " 278
34. Barrie; on Lake Simcoe in the Huron Territory . . . . . " 282
35. Shadowy River—Muskoka . . . " 290
36. Site of St. Mary on the Wye—The central point of the Huron Mission . . . . " 308
37. Fort of the Gentlemen of the Seminary at Montreal . . . . . " 330
38. The Earthly Paradise of Dollier and Galinée . . . . " 334
39. Paul de Chomedey, Sieur de Maisonneuve; founder of Montreal " 342
40. Map of Strait of Michilimackinac . *Page* 349
41. Falls of Niagara. . . . . *Facing page* 356
42. Map showing the interlacing of the head-waters of the St. Lawrence, Mississippi, and Red River of the North . . . . " 364
43. Grand Discharge Rapids, Lake St. John . . . . " 382
44. Quebec about A. D. 1700 . . . . " 402
45. Quaint Conceptions of Canada in 1715 . . . . " 408

ILLUSTRATIONS

46. The Town and Fortifications of Montreal in the 18th century, from an old engraving . . . *Facing page* 412
47. View from the site of the Old French Fort at Port Royal, looking across the Annapolis Basin " 416
48. Panorama of Sault Ste. Marie . . " 426

GEOGRAPHICAL SKETCH

ALTHOUGH in such a work as this it is frequently necessary to dwell from time to time upon the geography of the country, it will be convenient to review in one general survey the physical features of the entire region discovered by the men whose deeds are recorded. The characteristics of the Atlantic border region first presented to the early sailors differ much from those of the interior valley, and to that region it is necessary first to direct the attention of the reader. Much of the extreme northeastern part of the continent where it stretches far across the ocean towards Europe is still comparatively unknown. Until the last ten years the interior of Labrador was a great blank upon our maps, and little was known even of the interior of the island of Newfoundland until the opening of the railway a few years ago.

The portion of the Atlantic coast which falls within the scope of this volume extends through seventeen degrees of latitude, from the mouth of the Penobscot in Maine to Cape Chidley on Hudson's Strait, the northern point of Labrador. Of the Atlantic Labrador very little can be said. Along its stern front rise cliffs, abruptly from the sea, at Cape Chidley 1500 feet high, and 2000 feet 50 miles further south. The bays and inlets in this rocky barrier and the surf-lashed islands which fringe the coast afford shelter, but it is a forbidding coast, and the region behind the steep barrier of cliffs is unknown.

Nearest to Europe is the oldest colony of England, the island of

NEWFOUNDLAND

It has an area of 42,000 square miles—considerably larger than the united areas of Ireland and Wales. Its coast is most profoundly indented by the sea, so much so that, for a long time after its discovery, it appeared on all the maps as a group of islands. The bays reach from 30 to 50 miles inland; in its whole circumference it is studded with harbours affording unlimited shelter to the fishing craft on the coast. The shape of the island is roughly an equilateral triangle—the extreme distance from north to south being 317, and from west to east 316 miles.

The coasts are rocky and forbidding, even in the bays, and along the Atlantic they present for long stretches a rampart of rock from 200 to 400 feet high. The entrance to the harbour of St. John's is by a cleft only a half mile wide. The harbour is one of the best in America, deep and perfectly landlocked. A range of mountains 2000 feet high extends along the greater part of the west coast, but is fringed in most places with a band, a few miles wide, of low shore. The interior is a low, undulating tableland, with moors covered with moss and patches of low trees, and with marshes and innumerable lakes and ponds. Along the river valleys and the lakes there are extensive regions of excellent land with fine timber. Many detached peaks, locally called "tolts," rise abruptly from the plain.

Three large rivers extend almost across the island. Two of them, the Gander and the Exploits, rise in the southwest and flow northeast, and the third, the Humber, rises in the northeast and flows southwest. The rivers abound with fish—salmon and trout; the coasts and bays swarm with codfish; and large herds of caribou migrate spring and fall through the centre of the island. Copper and iron are mined, and coal is found, though the deposits are not worked. Fish, lobsters, oils, and minerals are the chief exports, and provide a livelihood for the population which fringes the eastern and southern coasts. The west coast has been kept vacant by the French claims, happily disposed of by a treaty recently ratified.

NOVA SCOTIA

The Province of Nova Scotia is a peninsula, and, politically, it also includes the island of Cape Breton, separated

GEOGRAPHICAL SKETCH xxv

from it by the deep Gut, or Strait of Canso, only three-quarters of a mile wide at its narrowest part, at which place a bridge is projected. The peninsula is 268 miles long, with a width of 60 to 100 miles, and the island is 108 miles long; but in width is very irregular, for the interior of the island is occupied by the Bras d'Or, an arm of the sea. The area of the whole province is 20,600 square miles.

The Atlantic coast is low, but rocky. It abounds in excellent harbours; that of Halifax is accounted to be among the finest in the world. The coast facing the Bay of Fundy is high and steep, because of a mountain ridge running close to the shore. A remarkable gap opens at Digby and admits the largest vessels into Annapolis Basin, an excellent landlocked harbour, the only one of note on that coast. The Basin of Minas opens out from the Bay of Fundy, and extends sixty miles into the land with a breadth of twenty miles. The entrance is remarkable for the bold headlands on either side. Cape d'Or and Cape Chignecto belong to the Cobequid mountain range, and Cape Split and Cape Blomidon are the bluff terminations of the ranges which shut in the Annapolis River.

The interior of the peninsula is of moderate height and abounds with lakes. The side facing the Atlantic is less fertile than the parts facing the inner bays. Two ranges of mountains, known as the North and South Mountain, bound the valley of the Annapolis River, and the Cobequid Mountains extend from Cape Chignecto, on the Bay of Fundy, through the peninsula to Cape Canso on the Atlantic.

CAPE BRETON

This beautiful island is worthy of note because of the Bras d'Or, a remarkable loch which occupies its centre. Two ranges of mountains open at an angle from the southwest to form a basin communicating with the ocean by two narrow passages on the northeast. Large ships can pass into it and moor close to the shores. The western range is the higher, and, as a tableland 1200 feet high, is prolonged to a promontory, steep on both sides, and ending in the bold headlands of Cape North and Cape St. Lawrence. The chief town is Sydney, where are large coal mines. The old harbour of Louisbourg is being again frequented, not as of old by ships of war, but by collier steamers. The island is underlaid by coal seams, which crop out at the east, south, and southwest shores. A narrow isthmus only a mile wide separates the Bras d'Or from the entrance of the Strait of Canso.

NEW BRUNSWICK

The Bay of Fundy is a remarkable arm of the North Atlantic, extending 180 miles towards the Gulf of St. Lawrence, and separating the peninsula of Nova Scotia from the Province of New Brunswick. Into this deep funnel the tides sweep on a broad front and gather force and height, as the shores close in, until they form a bore five feet four inches high. The tidal wave increases in swiftness, from three miles an hour at Cape Sable, to seven at the head of the bay. The rivers are all tidal, and at ebb present immense flats of red mud, through which the fresh water trickles to the sea; but suddenly, at flow, they become wide brimming streams. Rich dyked meadowland surrounds the head of the bay and all its branches.

The broad estuary of the Penobscot River, crowded with islands, is the Rio do Gamas of the old Portuguese maps and the Norumbegue of later years. It is the western boundary, on the sea coast, of the region treated of in this volume, and is the true boundary between the English and French colonies; though Canada has been negotiated out of the country between it and the St. Croix in one of the many diplomatic surrenders which have shorn her ample proportions.

At the St. Croix River is the present boundary between Canada and the State of Maine. The country is rugged and the shore is low, but rocky, and continues the same

GEOGRAPHICAL SKETCH xxvii

for some distance eastward along the New Brunswick coast. The Province of New Brunswick is almost square, being 230 miles from north to south, and 200 miles from east to west. It extends over an area of 28,200 square miles, and, for the most part, is a plain originally densely forested. It is now largely settled and cleared, especially along the rivers, but large portions of the interior are still a wilderness, the cherished resort of sportsmen.

New Brunswick in its general aspect is a rolling plain, furrowed by numberless river courses, which, in the interior, have cut deeply into the softer rocks and have formed wide valleys—flooded by the spring freshets, but productive meadows for the rest of the year. The River St. John is the chief feature of the Province. It drains one-half of it and a goodly portion of the State of Maine. It is navigable without a break as far as Grand Falls, 216 miles from its mouth. Its course is north and south, and its numerous affluents touch at their sources all the rivers which water the remaining half of the Province. The Miramichi and Richibucto are important rivers, flowing directly into the Gulf of St. Lawrence; the Nipisiquit and Restigouche flow into Chaleur Bay. These are the chief streams, and with their many affluents cover the country with a network of flowing waters. Dividing ridges of highlands separate the basin of the streams draining into the Gulf from a narrow strip along the Bay of Fundy and from the basin of the St. John.

THE ST. LAWRENCE BASIN

The St. Lawrence basin is a great transverse valley 530,000 square miles in area leading from the Atlantic Ocean to the heart of the continent, and commanding all the avenues of communication throughout its whole extent. It is not only possible, but it was in old days usual, to pass in canoes from St. Lawrence waters to Hudson's Bay, to the Gulf of Mexico, and into the Mackenzie River, draining into the Arctic Ocean. The headwaters

xxviii GEOGRAPHICAL SKETCH

of the Peace and Liard rivers, tributaries of the Mackenzie, rise close to the sources of the Fraser and Yukon, flowing into the Pacific Ocean, and the Saskatchewan and Athabasca lead up close to the chief passes of the Rocky Mountains. Though canoes are not carried across the last divide, the St. Lawrence basin is the gateway of access to all these river systems.

The length of the River St. Lawrence, if measured from the open ocean at the Strait of Belle-Isle to the head of Lake Superior, is 2388 miles, and the largest ocean steamships may pass up 986 miles to the city of Montreal. Beyond that, canals, in the aggregate 71 miles long, open up 1402 miles of inland navigation through the river and lakes.

The width of the river proper is on an average a mile and three-quarters. Its narrowest points are at Detroit and Quebec. It is generally deep. The shallowest places are the expansions of Lake St. Peter, below Montreal, and Lake St. Clair, above Detroit. Deep channels have been dredged at these localities, and the canals admit of the passage of craft drawing fourteen feet of water.

The basin of the St. Lawrence lies chiefly north of the river, for all its great tributaries flow from that direction. It is separated on the north by a low divide from the basin of Hudson's Bay. Myriads of lakes are the perennial sources of the countless streams which swell the flood of the "River of Canada," and sustain its volume throughout the year.

While the basin of the St. Lawrence system extends to the headwaters of all its tributaries, the valley of the river in a narrower sense has a character of its own, since it is level and largely alluvial and of more recent geological age. The Archæan nucleus of the continent, known as Laurentian, bounds it all the length of its northern border. This is a plateau 1000 to 1600 feet in height, at varying distances from the river, but never very far away. The lofty and precipitous northern shore of Lake Superior belongs to the Laurentian system, and it continues along the north shore of Lake Huron and extends over

GEOGRAPHICAL SKETCH   xxix

the northern part of the Province of Ontario. It crosses the Ottawa thirty miles above Ottawa city, and is visible on the far horizon from the river valley as a range of rounded mountains. Over the southern margin of this plateau the innumerable feeders of the river fall in rapids or cascades, representing a wealth of energy only realised since the recent application of hydraulic power to the generation of the electrical forces. All along the river from Montreal the range of mountains may be seen, far away, but coming gradually closer until Quebec is reached. At Cape Tourmente, twenty miles below Quebec, these highlands come out on the river as a mountain 1919 feet high. They follow on along the shore past the mouth of the Saguenay, rising to 2547 feet at Les Éboulements, and 1800 feet on the Saguenay. They retreat on the lower river and continue at varying distances in rear of the Labrador coast to the Strait of Belle-Isle.

On the southern side the valley is invaded by an extension of the Appalachian system, known as the Green and White Mountains, in Vermont and New Hampshire respectively. This range enters the valley near Lake Memphremagog, and passes through the eastern townships of Quebec Province. It forms a mountain background for a long distance below the city of Quebec, and at Matane comes out on the southern shore. The mountains continue thence along the south shore and form the rough tableland of Gaspé. In their course they occasionally rise to 3700 and 4000 feet. The average height on the peninsula of Gaspé is 3000 feet. These ranges of highlands bound the valley of the river on both sides.

To the west the St. Lawrence basin is bounded by the sub-basin of Lake Winnipeg, which approaches to a distance of 60 miles from Lake Superior. The divide is 1000 feet high, but the distance is not great, though the portages are heavy. On the south the divide separating the basin of the Mississippi and the sub-basin of the Ohio from that of the St. Lawrence is low and obscure, and reaches very close to the southern shores of the Great Lakes. That is the feature which gives to the great river its special importance in unlocking the communications of the inner continent. East of Lake Ontario the water-parting passes more southward and sweeps round the heads of Lakes George and Champlain, from whence it turns abruptly to the north to exclude the head of the Connecticut River a little south of Lake Memphremagog. The White Mountains and the highlands at the sources of the Kennebec, Penobscot, and St. John mark out the remainder of the divide by very strong features

THE LAKES

The St. Lawrence River is remarkable for the great number of expansions in its course. Apart from the Great Lakes, there are on its lower waters Lakes St. Francis, St. Louis, and St. Peter, but the great inland seas of the upper river are unique, for they cover a total area of 98,510 square miles. They occupy the inner basin of the continent, and yet from Lake Superior, the last of the series, to tide water at Three Rivers, halfway between Quebec and Montreal, is a fall of only 602 feet in the whole course of 1500 miles. Their depth is very great, and in two of them reaches below the sea level. Superior is 900 feet, Huron 500, Michigan 1000, and Ontario 412 feet deep. Lake Erie is shallow, for its average depth is only 90 feet.

We may now consider this great river more closely, and it will be convenient to follow the flow of its waters. Its source is the St. Louis River, a stream rising in the cramped watershed west of Lake Superior, where the Mississippi and Winnipeg divides press within 60 to 100 miles of the Lake basin. At its mouth is the brand-new but very important city of Duluth—a recent creation of centring railways, not of the river, which is chiefly important as a harbour, for it is not navigable for more than 20 miles.

Lake Superior is the uppermost of all the St. Lawrence lakes, and the largest, although few rivers of magnitude contribute to its volume. It is 420 miles long and

GEOGRAPHICAL SKETCH xxxi

80 miles in average breadth. Its area is 31,240 miles, but the area of the basin in which it rests is surprisingly small, for the water-parting of Hudson's Bay approaches close to its northern shore. The basin extends to the north to enclose Lake Nipigon, and, turning westward at the head of Lake Nipigon, it encounters the water-parting of the Winnipeg sub-basin. The divide of this latter basin reaches to within 60 miles of the western shore of Lake Superior, and touches on the south the water-parting of the Mississippi.

The north shore of Lake Superior is rugged and lofty. The country gives promise of mineral production only. Lake Nipigon is very deep, and its whole area is studded with islands. The coast of Lake Superior retains its character as it turns to the southwest. Thunder Cape marks Thunder Bay, surrounded by cliffs 1000 feet high, where Port Arthur and Fort William carry on the Canadian trade of the lake. The Kaministiquia River falls in at Fort William.

The south shore of the lake and the extreme western end, where the Mississippi basin reaches close, is not so high. Bluffs of sandstone, worn by the waves into picturesque forms, or sandy beaches, are its chief characteristics. Keweenaw Point is a promontory 20 miles wide, stretching 60 miles into the lake. Portage Lake, at its base, extends nearly all the way across, and this old canoe short cut, supplemented by a ship canal, saves 120 miles of dangerous coasting round the Point. The Pictured Rocks are the most attractive feature of the south shore. They are perpendicular sandstone bluffs, 50 to 200 feet high, worn into fantastic forms of castle, chapel, or portal, and stained in all shades of brown, yellow, and grey, with occasional blues and greens, by the minerals abounding in the vicinity. From the Pictured Rocks to the Sault the coast is sandy. At Sault St. Mary the lake discharges in rapids, which are overcome by canals, one on each side, each consisting of one lock larger and longer than any other lock in the world. At this point the St. Lawrence is known as the St. Mary's River, and drops, at the Rapids, 22 feet in a quarter of a mile. It is the only noticeable drop in level until Niagara is reached. Lakes Huron, Michigan, and Erie are one many-armed sea, indenting in vast bays some of the most productive territory in the world.

The St. Mary's River requires continual dredging, as it passes through Hay Lake and Mud Lake, to keep sufficient depth in the channels for the very large craft now navigating the upper lakes. At Detour—the easternmost extremity of northern Michigan, almost exactly on the parallel of 46° N.—two great routes diverge. The traveller may either continue east into Lake Huron or turn (as the name suggests) west and then southwards through the Straits of Michilimackinac into Lake Michigan. It is a cardinal point, for the great Laurentian backbone of Canada here strikes directly to the eastwards following the north shore of Lake Huron. It cuts across the base of the peninsula of Ontario, crosses the Ottawa River 30 miles above Ottawa city, and, passing 30 miles in rear of Montreal, emerges upon the river 20 miles below Quebec. The junction of the three great lakes at Detour is in summer one of the most interesting and beautiful spots in the whole valley—the blue sky, and the clear water reflecting it, and the wooded islands on the far margin of the sea-like expanse make a striking scene of natural beauty enhanced by the human interest of the occasional smoke of huge lake craft wending their diverging ways on the far horizon.

Lake Michigan is 345 miles long by 58 miles wide, and covers an area of 25,590 square miles. It is the deepest of the lakes, and its bottom is 400 feet below the level of the sea. Its most remarkable feature is Green Bay,—a corruption of Grand Bay,—but known in early history as Baie des Puants, or simply as La Baie. The Bay reaches far into the country, and receives the Menomonee and Fox rivers from the interior of the present State of Wisconsin. The route by the Fox River, through Lake Winnebago and into the Wisconsin River, was Jolliet's route to discover the Mississippi. At Chicago the Mississippi sends up the Des Plaines River, one of its tributaries, to within 9 miles of the lake shore, and the waters of the two great basins are now continuous by means of a canal. The country is level and the lake shores are clay bluffs of very moderate height, washed down into sand dunes and sandy beaches at the southern end of the lake, where the waves have full sweep from the north. The St. Joseph River—a tortuous stream draining northern Indiana and southern Michigan—falls in on the southeast side, but the basins of the Mississippi and Ohio approach so near that there are few affluents of importance.

Lake Huron covers an area of 23,780 square miles. It is 400 miles long, with an average breadth of 70 miles. The water is deep and very clear. The north shore is high and rocky, and the Archæan rocks extend down the coast of Georgian Bay, giving that region physical characteristics very different from the other lakes, and even from the rest of the lake shore. At the north the Manitoulin Islands and the long promontory of Cabot Head separate the Georgian Bay and the North Channel, and that part of it is studded with islands. It is a region of wonderful beauty. In Georgian Bay alone the islands have been estimated to exceed thirty thousand in number. The rest of the lake is free from islands, and the shores sink into clay bluffs from the level land as do those of the other lakes, excepting Superior. The peninsula of Michigan is enclosed between Lakes Huron and Michigan, and on the Huron side it is deeply indented by Saginaw Bay,—the widest and stormiest part of the lake,—where the traveller may be out of sight of land and easily believe himself upon the ocean.

The St. Lawrence leaving Lake Huron is called the St. Clair River, and leads into Lake St. Clair, a shallow lake 25 miles long and 20 miles wide, where dredging is necessary to maintain in the channels sufficient draught for large vessels. From Lake St. Clair it passes, as the Detroit River, into Lake Erie through a channel requiring constant dredging.

xxxiv GEOGRAPHICAL SKETCH

Lake Erie is 250 miles long, with an average width of 38 miles. It is a shallow lake, especially at its western end. The average depth over its whole area of 10,030 miles is only 90 feet. The shores of the lake are level and low, and the region is one of unparalleled fertility. The sub-basin of the Ohio approaches the south shore of Lake Erie closer and closer as it extends eastwards, until at Chautauqua Lake the distance is only 6 miles. Large cities, Toledo, Cleveland, Erie, Buffalo, are on the south shore, for the great basins of the Mississippi and St. Lawrence there exchange their traffic by the most direct route east and west.

Under the name Niagara River the St. Lawrence thence pursues its course to Lake Ontario, a distance of 33 miles. Here occurs a drop in the elevation of the whole country over an escarpment extending across the peninsula of Ontario to Cabot Head, projecting into Lake Huron. From the upper to the lower plain the whole river—the discharge of the four upper lakes—precipitates itself in one leap at Niagara Falls at the estimated rate of seven thousand tons a second. The river flows evenly, though fast, past Grand Island, when it unites into a stream two and a half miles wide, and rushes swiftly down in foaming rapids an incline of 55 feet to the edge of the fall. There it is divided by Goat Island. One part, called the American Fall, drops 167 feet with a straight crest line of 1080 feet, and the other, the Canadian or Horseshoe Fall, with a crest line 3010 feet in length, in an immense concave curve drops 158 feet into the gorge below. Lengthened description would be superfluous in these days of universal travel and innumerable guide books.

The original line of the escarpment where it crossed the river was in remote ages 7 miles lower down, at Queenston Heights, and the river has worn its way backwards and cut out for itself a gorge 200 feet deep, in which it foams its impetuous way through rapids and whirlpools down another declivity of 111 feet to the level of Lake Ontario, 240 feet above tide water.

GEOGRAPHICAL SKETCH xxxv

Lake Ontario—the last of the series—is 190 miles long by 40 miles (average) wide. Its average depth is 412 feet, and it covers an area of 7330 miles. The shores are low, as in the case of the other lower lakes, not rising above the surface of the lake more than 50 to 100 feet. A remarkable peninsula on the north shore shuts in the tranquil landlocked Bay of Quinté. Toronto, the second city of the Dominion, is on this lake at the beginning of an old portage route to Georgian Bay. Hamilton is an important city at the head of the lake, and Kingston (the Fort Frontenac of the Indian wars) is at its outlet. Rochester is on the southern shore at the mouth of the Genesee (the river of the Senecas), and Oswego at the end of the Mohawk portage route. At the eastern end the river encloses in its narrowing channel the islands known as the Thousand Islands. Then assuming its proper name, it flows as the St. Lawrence to the sea. It loses the 240 feet of level from the lake in a series of rapids until it reaches tide water.

The St. Lawrence (River of Canada, or Cataraqui of old books) is a stately river of clear and bright water flowing from one to three miles in width in its course to Quebec between low banks formerly densely forested, but now cleared and very fertile. Near Prescott, 119 miles above Montreal, the rapids commence. The Galops, Rapide Plat, and Long Sault are the first group; after which follows Lake St. Francis, an expanse of tranquil water 38 miles long. Then follow in quick succession the Coteau, Cedars, and Cascades Rapids to Lake St. Louis, 15 miles long; after which the final and most formidable of the series, the Sault St. Louis, drops the river down 45 feet to Montreal. The 12 remaining feet are accounted for by the current St. Mary, at Montreal, and the 86 miles to Three Rivers, where the tide is reached. All these rapids are run in descending from Niagara to Quebec by large steamers carrying hundreds of passengers.

At Montreal is the commercial centre of the country—the natural point of exchange, the end of ocean navigation, and the beginning of inland navigation, where the

Lachine canal commences the series of upward steps. The step which overcomes Niagara is the Welland canal, from Port Dalhousie on Lake Ontario to Port Colborne on Lake Erie, and the final step is the Sault Ste. Marie canal. This series of canals is the great stairway to the heart of the continent, and a stream of vessels drawing 14 feet is constantly passing up to return by the more exhilarating method of running down hill.

The river from Montreal to Quebec flows quietly through a very level valley and an almost continuous settlement on both sides. As it expands to form Lake St. Peter it becomes shallower, and much dredging has been done to enable ocean vessels drawing $27\frac{1}{2}$ feet to reach Montreal. The tide is first felt at Three Rivers, and at a place called the Richelieu large vessels wait for high tide to pass through. This place must not be confounded with the Richelieu River. It is named from an island where Champlain built a post and called it Richelieu Island. As the river nears Quebec, mountains begin to close in on both sides over the level valley. Opposite Quebec the river forms a deep basin—one of the great harbours of the world, though so far from the ocean. The mountains close round in a great amphitheatre, and Cape Diamond crowned with fortifications rises steep over the city. The St. Lawrence now takes on a new character. It becomes a tidal river. The tides rise 16 feet, and the largest ships pass up and down with them. The Island of Orleans at first obscures the width, but beyond it the river rapidly widens, and where the Saguenay falls in it is 25 miles across. The water, which is brackish and undrinkable 30 miles below Quebec, is salt at the mouth of the Saguenay.

It is impossible within the limits of this sketch to mention, even in the briefest way, all the rivers tributary to the St. Lawrence. The tributaries to Lake Superior are small streams on the southern watershed, and on the north the Nipigon River is the only one of importance. The Menomonee and Fox rivers of Green Bay and the St. Joseph and Grand rivers on the east side are the

GEOGRAPHICAL SKETCH xxxvii

principal feeders of Lake Michigan. Lake Huron, despite its wide area, has no great river falling into it. The eastern watershed of the peninsula of Michigan is not wide enough to beget great rivers, and the watershed at the north is also very narrow. The chief affluents are from the Province of Ontario—the French River, discharging Lake Nipissing, the drainage of the Muskoka Lakes, and the Severn River, draining Lake Simcoe. The Thames, one of the largest rivers of the peninsula of Ontario, drains into the shallow Lake St. Clair.

The water-parting of the Ohio approaches so close to Lake Erie that its feeders from the south are small in volume. The largest are the Maumee and the Sandusky. On the north shore the Grand River drains into it a large part of the Ontario peninsula. Lake Ontario has the Genesee and the Oswego rivers as its largest feeders from the south, and on the north the Trent draws into it the waters from the lakes east of Lake Simcoe and south of the Ottawa basin. It is not the magnitude, but the number, of the streams which swells the volume of the St. Lawrence as it passes through its lake expansions, and the stately river flows out of its great settling basins deep and broad, in a clear and transparent flood.

Eastward of Lake Huron the basin of the St. Lawrence broadens out on the north and from thence come its great tributaries. Chief of all is the Ottawa, a river 780 miles long, and draining an area of 80,000 square miles. It rises in the Grand Lake Victoria, and, after a circuitous course through many small lakes, reaches Lake Temiscaming, whence it flows eastward to make, at its junction with the St. Lawrence, the delta island on which stands the city of Montreal. It is a broad and deep river expanding into lakes; not a quiet stream, though there are long stretches of tranquil water, but vexed with rapids; and at the city of Ottawa dropping 40 feet over the Chaudière Falls. Its darker water joins the bright blue St. Lawrence at an acute angle and flows side by side, clearly distinguishable until the tide is reached in Lake St. Peter.

Many other rivers flow in from the north; for the northland, with its innumerable lakes, is the fertile mother of streams, and though none equals the Ottawa, many are of large volume. The St. Maurice is 300 miles long, and joins the main river at Three Rivers—a turbulent stream which, 25 miles above that city, flings itself into a chasm 150 feet deep as the Shawinigan Falls. The Batiscan, the St. Anne, and the Jacques Cartier join the great river before it reaches Quebec. Below that city the sullen waters of the Saguenay silently add their volume, black with the shadows of its grim gateway, and leading up 60 miles an estuary deep enough to float the largest battleship before relaxing its sternness at the appropriately named Ha! Ha! Bay.

Eastward of the Saguenay are many large rivers flowing in from the Quebec Labrador—a convenient name used to denote that part of the main Labrador coast which drains into the River and Gulf of St. Lawrence. Chief among them are the Betsiamites, the twin rivers Outarde and Manicouagan, the St. John, the Moisic, and a hundred others—turbulent streams foaming down from the interior wilderness plateau.

On its southern shore the tributaries of the St. Lawrence, with one exception, are not large; for the watersheds of the Hudson, the Connecticut, the Kennebec, the Penobscot, and the St. John press hard upon the basin of the great river. But between the Mohawk (a tributary of the Hudson) and the Connecticut the St. Lawrence reaches far into the south by the water of Lake Champlain and Lake George, which discharge northwards by the beautiful river Richelieu—a long stretch of navigable water of great commercial importance before the era of railways, and always the gateway of military attack and defence on the south. Other streams of importance are the St. Francis, the Yamaska, the Chaudière, the lower Du Loup, until the valley of the Matapedia is reached, which leads behind the mountains of Gaspé into Chaleur Bay.

The axis of the St. Lawrence valley does not lie east

GEOGRAPHICAL SKETCH xxxix

and west. From the Straits of Belle-Isle in lat. 52° it leads southwest to Detroit in lat. 42°; then, turning to the northwest, it attains at Lake Nipigon a height of 50° N., so that the form of a gigantic " V " is roughly traced in its course. This indicates a great variety of climatic conditions, modified also by the influences of large bodies of water; and from the region of grapes and peaches on Lake Erie one may pass to the stern and barren shores of Belle-Isle. The climate of the valley is, speaking generally, continental—a region of cold winters and warm summers—where winter passes suddenly into summer without any hesitating spring, and where the autumn (or fall, as the natives properly call it) delays long before it yields the heat stored in its ample treasures of waters, and a summer warmth of long days, quick and energetic—for maize and tobacco and melons ripen at Quebec and Sault Ste. Marie. The Tobacco nation of the Hurons were so named by the French discoverers from the quality of their tobacco grown on the eastern shores of Lake Huron, and Cartier describes, with wondering curiosity, the maize used as food at Quebec and Montreal.

The peculiar " V " shaped course of the main river valley is due to the fact that the primary Laurentian nucleus of the continent is of that shape, and, along its edge, in an alluvial valley resting on Silurian rocks, the river flows and expands into broad lakes. It is a broad generalization, but to describe it more in detail would unduly lengthen this sketch. All the valley was clothed with forest when it was discovered, and the level and fertile fields which now support a large population have been wrested from the wilderness by the axe of the early settlers.

The characteristics of the Laurentian country, which forms and feeds the great river from the north, are very marked. It is a plateau, two or three hundred miles wide, of ancient hills or mountains 1000 to 1600 feet above the sea, rounded in form by the immense lapse of ages, and forest-clad to their summits. Myriads of lakes, connected by countless mazes of streams, gather up the waters which flow down to the lower level in rapids and falls along the entire edge of the valley. At the heads of the streams and their tributaries the waters interlock so that, in the early days of the colony, the Indians would pass from one to the other, and bring their furs to market by the Ottawa, St. Maurice, or Saguenay, according as one or the other was free from hostile Indians.

Such are the broad general features of the region with which this volume is concerned. Imperfect as this sketch is, it may be of assistance in explaining the incidental geographical notices scattered throughout the narrative.

THE ST. LAWRENCE BASIN

CHAPTER I

INTRODUCTORY

THE subject of the present volume is the discovery and exploration of the northeast coast of North America and of the great transverse valley of the St. Lawrence which searches the continent to its very heart. It is limited to regions still subject to the British Crown, exclusive of those territories north of Hudson's Strait, which can more conveniently be treated under the heading of Arctic geography. The theme is thus limited, not because of any intermingling of political ideas with a question of geographical history, but because the great features of the Bay of Fundy and the Gulf of St. Lawrence mark off a region easily separable from the remaining coast, and distinguished by peculiar and striking characteristics. After following the discovery and exploration of the coast, the exploration of the basin of the St. Lawrence River, and its expansions of inland fresh-water seas, will be followed up to the waterpartings of the tributaries of Hudson's Bay on the north and west, and of the Mississippi and other streams draining into the Gulf of Mexico and the main Atlantic Ocean on the south. In this part of the work it will be necessary to take into consideration those portions of the western United States which belong to the great basin.

Besides the difficulties proper to historical investigation, such inquiries as these present additional difficulties in documents, such as maps and charts, quasi-scientific in their nature, but drawn up under widely erroneous notions. Much of the confusion which has been introduced into the history of American discovery is due to efforts to treat these cartographical documents with the minute seriousness due only to the careful production of modern scientific research. The early cartographers embodied in their works the mythology of their day. The unknown interiors of continental masses were filled up with legends and pictorial illustrations drawn from sacred and profane history. We may see upon them Prester John with his mitre, the Queen of Sheba, and the three Kings of the East. Gog and Magog are shut up in the far north behind a chain of mountains waiting for the time appointed in Ezekiel xxxix. for their irruption, and Jerusalem, adorned with towered structures, is set, according to the prophets, in the centre of the whole earth. Then there are strange monsters portrayed in all seriousness—men with pigs' heads, men with only one foot, men with ears large enough to cover their bodies, and, even in the sea, are strange mythical creatures like the *remora,* a fish six inches long which has the power to stop a ship under full sail. It requires discursive reading to understand all these allusions. When, on an important map made in Jacques Cartier's time, we see pigmies drawn up with bows and arrows in deadly conflict with an army of cranes in the region surrounding the present capital of Canada, we know that the cartographer thought he was portraying a part of Tartary. The discovery of America was a very gradual process, and outside of Spain, Portugal, and Italy it attracted, for a long time, very little attention. English literature is unconscious of Cabot, Columbus, and Vespucci until A. D. 1553, when Richard Eden began to write.

Then again we must take into account the fact that these old maps are drawn to magnetic meridians, while ours are always drawn to the true meridian. This principle alters the lie of a coast and the direction of a course and the neglect of considering it has been the cause of much controversy. Thus the course from Cape Race to Cape Breton is laid down on the oldest maps on

INTRODUCTORY

a due west line, and in the contemporary description these points are plainly said to lie east and west. So they do by compass, but the true course is more nearly west-southwest, for Cape Breton is in lat. 45° 57', and Cape Race in lat. 46° 39', and there is a drop of 42 miles to the south in that short stretch of coast. The coast line on La Cosa's map thus explained becomes intelligible. It will be seen, later on, how seriously a long course across the ocean is affected by magnetic variation, but attention is now directed to its effect in distorting the coast lines.

Determinations of latitude were not easily made from the deck of a vessel with the imperfect instruments of that period; but when made on firm land they were fairly accurate. Nevertheless it is a fact that, in the earlier maps, the Antilles are laid down eight degrees too far north, being all placed north of the tropic, instead of being all south of it. Longitudes are, however, far astray, for, before chronometers, it was only on rare occasions that longitude could be determined with the least degree of accuracy. On the northeast coast of America the longitudes were from fourteen to twenty degrees out of the way, but in estimating longitudes in the Eastern Hemisphere the Spanish and Portuguese experts differed to the extent of forty-six degrees. The subject is further complicated by the different estimations of the circumference of the earth and the consequent length of a degree. Translating all these differences into our standard nautical miles, it will appear that a degree upon the equator of Columbus was 45.33 miles, of Ptolemy 50 miles, of current opinion in Spain (in A. D. 1500), 53.33 miles, of the Badajos convention and of Champlain, 56 miles. When, therefore, we transfer distances from early maps to our maps made with degrees of 60 nautical miles, we shall go astray if we do not make the necessary compensations.

Finally the old maps abound in errors of spelling, and of transcription and translation, where a cartographer or engraver is following the copy of a language he does not understand. Only slowly, and with occasional relapses, did geographical science struggle to its present perfection. Only slowly did the popular mind go back to the science of the Greeks, and as slowly did modern science pass beyond it.

That the earth is spherical is a belief which, in the fourth century before Christ, was generally accepted by the Greeks. Their astronomers observed in eclipses of the moon that the shadow of the earth is circular and the phenomena attending the appearance or disappearance on the horizon of arriving and departing ships were familiar to a sea-faring people. This belief was held in a thoroughly scientific manner. Latitudes were determined by the shadow of the gnomon, and attempts were made to measure the circumference of the earth, with results which became the basis of calculation for the sailors who discovered America.

In the decay and destruction of the old civilisation and the confusion, long protracted, which attended the migration and settlement of the new nations, the geographical science of the Greeks was lost, and very crude and erroneous notions prevailed generally in Europe. The study of geography first revived among the Arabs; for the works of the Greek philosophers were translated into Arabic, and schools of geography flourished at Bagdad and Cordova in the ninth century of our era. The works of the Arabian geographers were translated into Latin, and in that way the writings of the Greek philosophers again became known in the West. In the eleventh and twelfth centuries the dawn of reviving literature and science in Europe appeared with the founding of the great universities and the rise of the philosophy of the schools.

To allude to many of those scholars who, in the seclusion of a cloister, kept the lamp of learning alight during the Dark Ages would lead too far afield. Friar Roger Bacon in his " Opus Majus " (1267) and Cardinal d'Ailly, in his " Imago Mundi " (1410), are the two who had the most influence in geography; for Bacon's views, as presented and reinforced in d'Ailly's work, were the

INTRODUCTORY 5

chief springs of the convictions of Columbus. The great sailors of the fifteenth and sixteenth centuries were not direct students of the Greek and Arab science; but derived their knowledge indirectly through the writings of the great scholars of the Middle Ages which, being in Latin, were then open to all. That the belief in the sphericity of the earth had not been lost, but, on the contrary, was generally accepted by the learned, is manifest in Dante's Divine Comedy. Without hesitation he assumes it and makes Virgil conduct him down, through the earth, to the centre of gravity, where Lucifer is fixed, as it was impossible he could fall lower. From that point Dante ascends, with his guide, to the surface of the earth in the opposite hemisphere, where he sees, for the first time, the constellation of the Southern Cross. Dante had studied at the great universities of Europe, and the state of geographic and astronomic knowledge at that time is reflected in his poem. Grotesque as is the idea of having to turn head over heels in the centre of the earth, which they of course had to do in order to ascend, it is of interest in showing that the conception of the earth as a sphere was firmly grasped, and that gravitation towards the centre of the earth was recognised as pervading all nature. The treatise on the astrolabe, which Chaucer compiled for the use of his little son Lewis, also shows that the study of astronomy in its practical application to latitude and longitude was a favourite one among the learned in England in the fourteenth century.

Two centuries, very nearly, elapsed from Dante to Columbus, and in them had occurred the stir of thought caused by the popularisation of ancient learning and science consequent upon the invention of the art of printing. Then was the very height of the Renaissance, and the great cities of the south of Europe became centres of keen interest in geographical science. In this interest popes and princes shared to such an extent that these studies became the fashion among courtiers, while the daring and skilful sailors of the maritime cites of Italy and of Portugal, Catalonia and Minorca were extending the bounds of discovery into all seas. It is difficult to realise at the present time how little England counted for in all this stir of maritime extension, and yet it was an English ship and an English crew which first touched the continent of America, though the moving spirit and captain commanding was an Italian, born in Genoa and trained in Venice.

It may seem surprising that the Western Ocean was first crossed at its widest part; but the surprise will disappear upon a comparison of the different conditions of navigation in the North and South Atlantic. Columbus sailed in the region of the trade winds and, throughout the whole voyage, the weather was fair and the wind constant on the ship's quarter. He was in the great equatorial current, and the drift of the ocean was with him on his western course. It was fair-weather sailing, and the constant favouring conditions themselves alarmed the common sailors, for they thought they had reached a region where the winds never blew back towards Spain. In the North Atlantic it is far different. North of lat. 40° the drift of the ocean is towards Europe, and the prevailing winds are from the west. Westward from Ireland to America is one of the most unquiet regions of ocean in the world, and a vessel on a westward course in those latitudes will have to contend, not only with adverse winds and broken weather, but with frequent and dense fogs. Therefore it was that, although in the north the continents draw together and the degrees of longitude are much shorter, the efforts made from Bristol were baffled until the success of Columbus had demonstrated the existence of land within reach across the ocean.

It does not lie within the scope of this volume to dwell upon the voyages of Columbus or upon the Bulls of partition and the treaties which are supposed to have divided the world between Spain and Portugal. It is important, however, to observe that as the sailors of that day had no means of ascertaining longitudes excepting by dead reckoning, it could and did happen that the line of partition, settled in 1494 between Spain and Portugal at

INTRODUCTORY

Tordesillas, was supposed to cut the coast of North America at what is now Nova Scotia. After some hesitation on the part of Spain, all the coast of the maritime provinces of Canada and of Newfoundland were, under these documents, tacitly conceded to Portugal. The present volume then will deal only incidentally with Spanish voyages or Spanish maps. It is with Portuguese and French sailors and with their maps it will be most concerned; for, although the English under the leading of Cabot first discovered the coast of North America from Labrador to Cape Hatteras, they did not follow up the discovery by such occupation as would give them a title under international law; nor did they even attempt it until over one hundred years had elapsed, and prior occupation had established the French title to that portion of North America now known as Canada.

The circumstances which led up to the discovery of America cannot be fully explained without some reference to the groups of islands in mid-ocean which were the outposts of Spain and Portugal in their maritime enterprises. The Canary Islands are only sixty-five miles from the coast of Africa. They were known to the Carthaginians and Romans as the Fortunate Islands, and Ptolemy fixed there his first meridian of longitude. They had been forgotten, but in the thirteenth century were occupied by the Genoese and at the opening of the fifteenth century were conquered by Norman adventurers who held them under Spanish protection. They were for Spain the point of departure for the New World, and ships bound to the West Indies reached there the regions of the favouring trade winds, and could refit if necessary. They were little connected with the discoveries on the northeast coast of America. They are chiefly interesting because, during the seventeenth and eighteenth centuries, the first meridian of longitude for most of the European nations passed through Ferro (Hierro), a small island, the most western of the group.

The other groups belonged to Portugal and had been colonised by active and energetic settlers seasoned by long familiarity with the hazards of the ocean. The Cape de Verde Islands are in lat. 16° N. They are 300 miles from Africa and were of great assistance to the Portuguese sailors on their way to the East Indies. The names of two of them, Fogo and Bonavista (Boavista), repeated on the east coast of Newfoundland, mark the presence of Portuguese there at an early date. Fogo (fire) is an appropriate name for an island with an active volcano, but on the coast of Newfoundland it is evidently a reminiscence, as is also Bonavista. The Madeira Islands were rediscovered about A. D. 1420. Columbus married a daughter of Perestrello, a distinguished sailor for Prince Henry of Portugal and coloniser of Porto Santo, one of the group. He resided for a time on the island, and his son Diego was born there. There also, by Perestrello's papers and charts (which he had access to), all the secrets of the Portuguese discoveries were opened to him, and on the strand 560 miles from the mainland of Europe the billows of the great Western Ocean washed up strange fragments from the hidden and mysterious world beyond.

Furthest to the west and north, in the latitude of Lisbon and 850 miles from the continent of Europe, is the group of the Azores, rediscovered and colonised by the Portuguese in A. D. 1431-32. On the island of Fayal in this group resided for some time Martin Behaim, one of the great navigators and geographers of the age of discovery. He married the daughter of Job de Huertar, who colonised it in 1466, and in 1489 he had a son born there. He spent much of his life in Portugal and the Azores, although he was born at Nuremburg. While Columbus was at sea on his first voyage of discovery Behaim was in Nuremburg, and he constructed a globe which he presented to the city. It is still preserved there and is one of the most important historical monuments extant. All inquiries concerning the early history of America should be preceded by a careful study of Behaim's globe, for on it is the contour of the eastern coast of Asia based on accounts of Marco Polo, and the

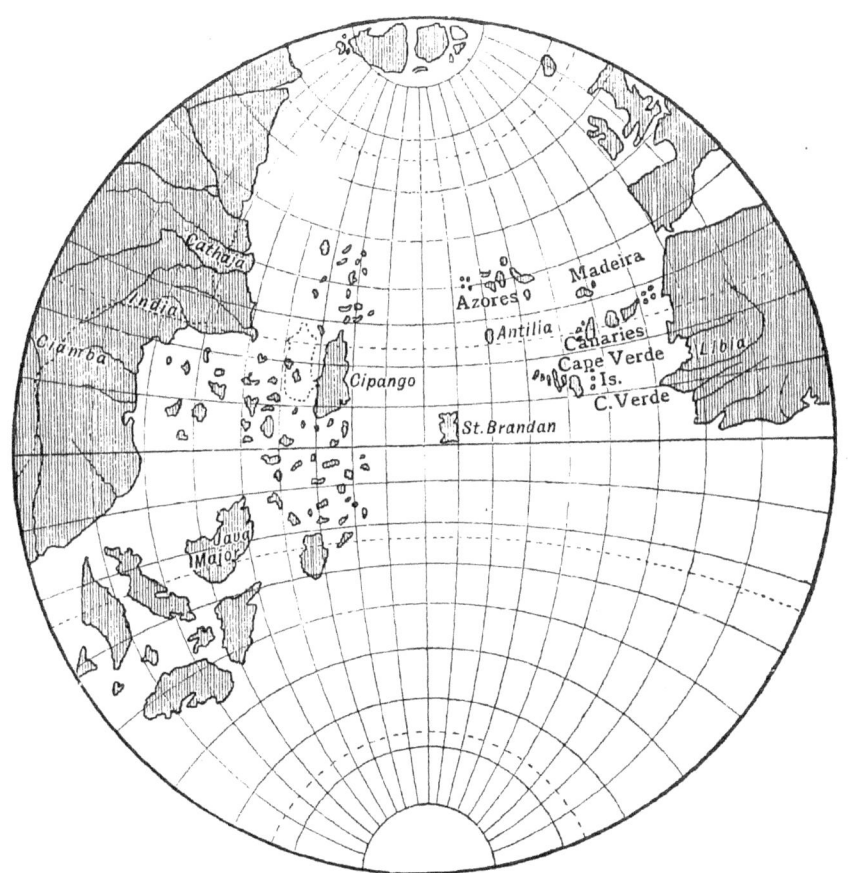

Martin Behaim's Globe. A.D. 1492
(The Atlantic coast omitting the legends)

INTRODUCTORY 9

earliest maps of America adopted these outlines to fill in the undiscovered portions of the coast line of the west.

While these actually existing island outposts upon the Western Ocean strongly assisted in the discovery of the Western World, there were many islands non-existent, save in the imagination, which nevertheless stimulated the efforts of the sailors of that age. The old maps contain many imaginary islands, and, while their positions often change on the maps, the legendary associations of some of them were of special interest to the south and of others to the north of Europe. Antilia was laid down on almost all charts in the latitude of the Strait of Gibraltar. It was sometimes confounded (as in the legends on Behaim's globe) with the island of the Seven Cities. Both were firmly believed in by the learned as well as the unlearned in Spain and Portugal. The name of the former persists to this day in the Greater and Lesser Antilles of the West Indies. The latter island was believed to be the refuge of seven bishops who, with their flocks, fled, after the defeat of Don Roderick, from the fury of the Moors. Later the name was transferred to the mainland of America and to a region northeast from Mexico. Two other islands, Isle Maida and Isle Verde, are found on all old charts and in Faden's Atlas, published as late as 1776, Mayda Island is laid down in long. 20° W., and Green Island in long. 24° W.

These islands appealed to Mediterranean sailors. The imagination of the northern people was stirred by legends of the island of St. Brandan and of Brazil. The imaginary island of O'Brazil may be found in Jeffrey's American Atlas (published in 1776) west of Cape Clear in long. 17° 35' W. The legend of St. Brandan is Celtic and is of very old date. The Saint was accompanied, on his voyage to the Island of the Saints, by St. Malo of Brittany, known in Normandy as St. Maelou, whose beautiful church is one of the chief ornaments of Rouen. Martin Behaim (a German by birth) placed the island far to the south, but it was usually supposed to lie west from Ireland. He gave the date of the voyage as A. D. 565. It may be found on maps as late as 1755. The legends relating to the adventurous expeditions of these two Saints are very numerous and interesting. Tennyson's poem " The Voyage of Maeldune " is one of them. Maeldune found the island and one of Brandan's companions upon it.

The island of Brasil, O'Brazil, or Bresil is a persistent, but more mysterious, island; for the etymology of the name is unknown. It is probably a corruption of the name of an Oriental dye-wood yielding a rich red colour, and, when such wood was brought from South America, the land (first called Santa Cruz) where it was found was named Brazil. The word is used by Chaucer in the sense of a dye, and the island of Brazil may be " the crimson island " seen by strained imagination in the crimson sunsets of the stormy North Atlantic. No legends are attached to it, but from A. D. 1480 to the year of Cabot's voyage the Bristol people had been trying to find it. It was usually laid down as west and north of Ireland and so it is found on Behaim's globe. We may safely dismiss as mythical all that has been claimed for Basque discoveries in America prior to Columbus and Cabot. They are vague and legendary statements, based on no records or authorities of any weight. Some writers cite Andrea Bianco's Atlas (A. D. 1436) in proof; for they find in it an island " Scorafixa or Stokafixa," as they think in the northwest Atlantic which they take to signify *stockfish* and to lie in the position of Newfoundland. Others have attempted to show a similiarity between the Basque and American languages, but without success, and it has been said that Cabot found the " Basque word bacallaos " in use for codfish on the Newfoundland coast. These statements will be fully discussed in later chapters. The voyage of Skolno (for the king of Denmark) to the Labrador coast in 1476 is also apocryphal.

The globe of Behaim, then, is of the utmost importance in American history. It is a contemporary graphic record by a sailor and geographer of the first rank, who was mixed up, theoretically and practically, with the maritime enterprises of the age. It shows clearly that it was not a surprise to learned scholars or skilled mariners in Europe when Columbus found land across the Western Ocean. A greater problem presented itself later when men began to see that the land found was not Cathay and that there existed a barrier continental mass unsuspected and undreamed of, which shut off direct communication with Asia. Against this barrier the sailors of western Europe were to strive for two hundred years more, and their efforts were continued in that passionate search for a northwest passage which has calmed down only in our own time.

In the earliest documents of discovery every land found in the West was supposed to be an island more or less large—an island in an archipelago which we see on Behaim's globe guarding the eastern coast of Asia. These coalesced into a continent as the coast was more narrowly searched. Sebastian Cabot wrote to Ramusio that he verily believed that all the north part of America is divided into islands. He was right, as any map of that region will show, but he had not reckoned upon a barrier of ice. He seems to have suspected the existence of an opening somewhere in the region of Bacallaos, and Stephen Gomez certainly did. That suspicion it was the task of Jacques Cartier to justify and, although he did not find a passage to the Great South Sea, he found an avenue into the very heart of the continent through the most wonderful system of waterways in the world.

Although Balboa, Cortes, and Pizarro demonstrated that at the south, America was separate from Asia, it was confidently believed until much later times that, on the north, Asia was continuous with the northern part of America, and that the Great South Sea washed the southern shore of this immensely prolonged joint continent. In the royal commission to Cartier this belief is plainly apparent. Jean Allefonse, the pilot of Roberval, wrote that "these lands (Canada) belong to Tartary," and are a "continuation of Asia," and his belief is embodied in the maps of the French school of cartography. The early explorers persistently reiterate that "hawks" were found; as if that fact had some bearing on their discoveries. Hawks are not characteristic specially of the northern parts of America, but when we read in Marco Polo that Kublai Khan took 10,000 falconers on his hunting expeditions with gerfalcons and other hawks in great numbers we can guess what the minds of the old navigators were dwelling upon.

And so for a hundred and fifty years the French sought unwearying for the gateway of the west. Cartier sailed up the St. Lawrence to Montreal and heard stories of great seas a few weeks' journey westward—nay, at Hochelaga, from the top of Mount Royal, he saw with his own eyes the glimmer of Lake St. Louis and the Lake of Two Mountains; and he might well have wondered whether the way to Cathay led by the west over the one, or by the southwest over the other. Champlain, lured by the same hope, followed up the Ottawa in a bark canoe, and was brought by his Indian guides to the Mer Douce—the fresh-water sea of Lake Huron. The same dream distracted the cares of the missionary on the shores of Lake Superior, harassed by the perverse malignity of his savage flock; it inspired the saintly Marquette and the tireless Jolliet on their lonely journey down the unknown Mississippi, wondering as they paddled whether it fell into the Gulf of Mexico or into the Vermilion Sea; and still, at the present day, a suburb of the busy city of Montreal re-echoes the same quest in its name *Lachine,* and recalls the memory of an indomitable spirit, a ruined fortune, and a tragic death.

CHAPTER II

JOHN CABOT'S FIRST VOYAGE—DISCOVERY

CANADA, in the strict sense of the word, consists of the ancient Province of Quebec, which, in 1791, was divided into the provinces of Upper and Lower Canada. In 1841 these were reunited into one province. Of that Canada Jacques Cartier was the discoverer. As Egypt depends upon the River Nile and is inseparable from it in thought, so that Canada —old Canada—is inseparable from the River St. Lawrence and its lake expansions, and upon the waters of that great river Jacques Cartier, a Breton of St. Malo, was the first European to sail. On July 1, 1867, the British provinces, excepting Newfoundland, were confederated and merged into one Dominion. This, with its after accretions, is the Canada now existing; and of Canada so constituted John Cabot was the discoverer; for in 1497 he landed upon the shore of one of its eastern provinces and in that and the following year he sailed along its Atlantic seaboard, as well as along the outer coasts of Newfoundland.

The circumstances of this momentous discovery were well known in the time of Queen Elizabeth, and some of them are recorded by Hakluyt, but in the contemporary annals of England there are only scanty notices of them. For one hundred years the English thought little of their discoveries across the ocean, and did not take enough interest in them to claim exclusive rights. In the meantime other nations also entered upon them and when, two hundred years after the primary discovery, a struggle arose among the colonising nations for these western lands, the diplomatists of the other nations either challenged the fact of any discovery by England, or accepted it only for the barren and icy regions of Northern Labrador, or Greenland. It was Richard Biddle of Pittsburg, Pennsylvania, who re-opened the whole question in a work based upon documentary authorities and first printed at Philadelphia in 1831. He wrote with great originality and independent research, but new and most important material has since his time been brought to light, during the long controversy which was inaugurated by his stimulating book.

There are now between seventy and eighty millions of English-speaking people in North America; but the early history of the continent must be sought in Spanish, Portuguese, and Italian literature. The first ship to touch the mainland of the Western World was an English ship; but the main proofs of that fact must be gleaned from the archives of Southern Europe. The testimony is more weighty for that reason, since it is not coloured by national pride, and it is impartial, because it is unconscious. The intellectual as well as the commercial prominence of the Italian people is emphasised by the facts that Columbus, a Genoese, discovered America for Spain; John Cabot, a Genoese-Venetian, discovered the mainland for England; Juan Verrazano, a Florentine, created a claim for France by his voyage along the coast of the Northern United States and Acadia; and the whole Western World was named America after another Florentine, Amerigo Vespucci.

In those days Bristol was, in all England, second only to London in importance. Wealthy merchants carried on extensive trade with the northern parts of Europe and especially with Iceland. There was, in truth, more maritime enterprise in Bristol than in any other part of the realm. The trade in codfish was very large on account of the numerous fast days of the church, and it centred at Bristol. Recent scepticism has thrown doubt upon the recorded voyage of Columbus from Bristol to Iceland in 1477; but even if that story be entirely false, it is of very early invention, and is sufficient to establish the importance of Bristol as the key-point of northern commerce. It is not smooth-water sailing in these northern

JOHN CABOT'S FIRST VOYAGE 15

seas, and in the west of England a hardy breed of mariners was trained, who were the predecessors of the fishermen of the Banks of Newfoundland. We read of many attempts of Bristol sailors before A. D. 1497 to discover the secret of the Western Ocean, and one expedition, made in 1480, under command of Captain Thlyde, was out for nine weeks. It was a most determined attempt, but, although Thlyde is described in contemporary annals as the most scientific mariner in all England, the west winds were too much for him, and he was driven back, in September, to shelter on the west coast of Ireland. In the seven years immediately preceding Cabot's voyage two or three attempts were made every year to discover the island of Brasil. There is in fact one solitary pointed crag in that part of the ocean, and it first appears as Rockall on the charts about A. D. 1600. It is 260 miles northwest from Ireland—a sheer cliff of black granite, white at top with sea birds; only 100 yards in circumference at its base, but surrounded by a bank of considerable extent, the resort of innumerable codfish. There is evidence to show that within 200 or 300 years an exposed sandbank existed round the rock, but it could never have been the Crimson Island—Brasil—of the Bristol sailor's quest.

At what time John Cabot arrived in Bristol is not definitely known. He was Genoese by birth, but had been naturalised in Venice after fifteen years' residence, and he came with his wife and three sons into a community prepared for any maritime enterprise. To the tales of the island of Brandan and Brasil in the North he could add the legends of Antilia and the Seven Cities of more southern latitudes. He added also, what was far more important, the experience of one trained in the wide-extended commerce of Venice, and a firm belief in the rotundity of the earth and all which that implied. Of his three sons, Sebastian only is heard of again. He rose to eminent positions in the naval service, first of Spain and then of England.

News of the success of Columbus in 1492 spread over Europe, and incited the emulation of Cabot. He was an

Italian stranger, poor and without friends. The Bristol merchants may have lent him influence at court to attract the attention of Henry VII., but that monarch remembered the application of Bartholomew Columbus, and was ready enough to approve of an enterprise which, without cost to himself, might result in extending his power. It is worthy of note that the petition to the king was in the names of John Cabot, citizen of Venice, and his sons Lewis, Sebastian, and Sancius. There was no other name upon it. Letters patent were granted, dated March 5, 1496, and were made out to John Cabot and his sons alone. The letters gave " full and free authority &c., of navigation to all parts, countries and seas of the east, west, and north, under our banners, flags, and ensigns." The King did not authorise any discovery to the south; for there the Spaniards were in occupation. The Cabots were empowered to sail " with five ships or vessels of whatever burden or quality soever they be, and with as many mariners or men as they will have with them in the said ships *upon their own proper costs and charges;* to seek out, discover, and find whatsoever islands, countries, regions or provinces of the heathens or infidels, in whatever part of the world they be, which before this time have been unknown to all Christians." The letters patent then go on to grant the right to fly the English flag over such new lands and " conquer, occupy and possess as vassals or governors, &c., &c.," and to acquire " for us the dominion, title, and jurisdiction over those towns, castles, islands, and mainlands so discovered." It is further stipulated that all arrivals from discovered lands shall be confined to the port of Bristol, and that one-fifth of the whole profits shall be reserved to the King's use. On the other hand all goods imported from the new lands are to be free of duty, and the Cabots are to have a monopoly of the trade therewith. Finally, the King enjoins his subjects to give to the grantees " all favour and help as well in arming the ships or vessels, as in supplying them with stores and victuals *to be paid for by their own money."* The King was

JOHN CABOT'S FIRST VOYAGE 17

very careful not to risk anything. The Cabots had the risk, and the King was to have one-fifth of the profits. The chief advantage of the letters patent was to give official status to the voyage, and to enable Cabot to take possession, under the protection of England, of any country he might discover.

Cabot's movements at once attracted the attention of Dr. de Puebla, the Spanish ambassador at London; and he wrote to inform his master, Ferdinand of Aragon, of the proposed voyage. This letter is not extant, but its contents may be gathered from the King's reply. This is dated March 28, 1496, and was written from Tortosa in Aragon; so that de Puebla's letter must have been written before the letters patent were actually issued. Cabot could not have been very long in England, for the ambassador wrote "that a person like Columbus had come to England to engage the King in a similar enterprise to that of the Indies, but without prejudice to Spain or Portugal." The King replied that "he was at liberty, but that it could not be done without infringing upon the rights of those nations," thus implying that he understood the Bull of partition to apply to the whole of the regions across the ocean. We learn from another despatch that Cabot had been previously in Lisbon and Seville seeking aid for his enterprise, without success. He must have had difficulty also in Bristol, for he could only fit out one small vessel, although the patent permitted him to take five. He was, indeed, as both the Spanish ambassadors wrote, "one like Columbus," poor, visionary, skilful, daring, persevering, and boastful. Of the trials and disappointments he experienced we know nothing, while the rebuffs of Columbus are the theme of many volumes. Spain gave Columbus and his posterity honours and rewards, but Cabot sank into an unknown and unhonoured grave, and the millions upon millions of English for whom he pre-empted the continent of the West decreed to his memory, after four hundred years of neglect, only the small memorial tower on Brandon Hill at Bristol. Honour to the Bristol people who assisted him in 1497, and honour to those who commemorated him in 1897, but greater honour to Spain, that even in her day of humiliation she could yet care for the remains of Columbus, and that his descendants are still grandees of her sadly shrunken empire.

The neglect of the English people does not derogate from the merit of John Cabot's discovery. It is a fact to be remembered that Cabot touched the continent of America thirteen months before Columbus saw the mainland at the Boca del Sierpe, on the coast of Venezuela. Many of the details are known to us now, from the letters of some intelligent foreigners then resident in England, and other important documents which have, in recent years, come to light. A spirited controversy preceded the celebration of the four hundredth anniversary of the discovery; and in its course these new facts and documents have been thoroughly sifted and placed beyond all danger of ever again being obscured.

Early in the month of May, 1497, Cabot sailed from Bristol on his lonely voyage. If we may believe Barrett's "History of Bristol," his ship was called the *Matthew*. Barrett copied from older records not now in existence. The rest of his statement is confirmed by independent evidence, and that he, or anyone else, should falsify a record to insert so unessential a matter as the name of a ship does not appear to be a reasonable supposition. She was a very small vessel, and carried only eighteen of a crew.

The objective point of the voyage was Cathay (Northern China), of which province Cambaluc (Pekin) was the chief city and the residence of the Grand Khan. The localities will be found on Behaim's globe, the particular descriptions are in Marco Polo's travels. That was the country which Cabot reported on his return that he had found. In those days, when longitude could only be known by dead reckoning, it was the custom to make the latitude sure in familiar waters, before turning to the wide ocean. So Columbus, in 1492, first went to the Canaries to take his western departure for Zipango. Again, on

The Cabot Tower at Bristol

JOHN CABOT'S FIRST VOYAGE 19

his third voyage, when he set out to discover the land to the south he had heard of in Hispaniola, he made his southing to the Cape Verde Islands and struck directly west from there. A similar reason would induce Cabot to turn north upon the outer coast of Ireland, until, having got the supposed latitude of his objective point, he struck for it across the ocean. If his destination had been to the north, the familiar course to Iceland, inside the channel and north of Ireland, would have taken him well on his way. How far up the west coast of Ireland he sailed we do not know. It may have been to Blacksod Bay in lat. 54° N., as assumed by a very competent authority. It could not have been farther north. It is recorded in connection with Ruysch's map, in the Ptolemy of 1508, that the ship Ruysch sailed in turned to the west in lat. 53° N. There can be no doubt as to Cabot's course. The letters make that abundantly clear.

It was west. But what is west? or rather, what did the sailors of that day mean by west? It was then always west by compass. We may be sure of that, and also that their compasses were the same as ours. When Columbus sailed west from the Canaries he dropped 240 miles south to his landfall at Guanahani, and, again, in his third voyage, when he sailed west from the Cape Verde Islands in lat. 14° 53' N. he struck land at the south coast of Trinidad in lat. 10° N., having dropped 293 miles to the south. He followed his compass, though he was sailing in a region of clear skies, where the stars came out brightly every night. Cabot, on the contrary, was sailing in latitudes of adverse winds and dense and protracted fogs. Of necessity he followed his compass, for how otherwise could he retrace his course over the grey measureless waste of ocean, where he might not be able for days to get an observation of the sun, or to see the stars by night? It was not a new thing that the needle should deviate from the North Star. That had already been observed, and, all over the west of Europe, the deviation was recognized as about one point east of north.

What was new was western variation—the crossing over of the needle from east to west. That indicated to those who first saw it that they had entered into a sphere of unknown conditions. In sailing westward from Ireland, Cabot very soon ran into a region where, on a western course, the curves of magnetic variation are very rapidly traversed. He would, of necessity, in latitudes so far north, experience a variation double that recorded by Columbus. This was a condition of which he could have had no previous knowledge. Columbus had been the first to notice the phenomenon in a region of slight variation, but in the North Atlantic Cabot would have found it increase steadily throughout the whole distance, until he reached the American coast. Here then is an additional and very strong reason why he had to follow his compass. On our charts, made to the true meridian, Labrador is west from Ireland, but on a magnetic meridian it is far to the north of west. The question of magnetic variation was soon grappled with and calculated upon by sailors, and we are able to form an approximate of what it was in 1492. We have, even in Pedro Reinel's map of 1505, positive evidence of what it was on the northeast coast of America at that time, for on his map is a secondary staff pointing true north, and marked with truer latitudes than those on the line which marks the magnetic meridian. It was somewhat less than it is now; but an average variation of 12° 45′ would have carried Cabot south of Cape Race, and by the course steered the landfall of Cabot is indicated as not only south of Labrador, but south of Newfoundland. Those, therefore, who decide the question from the study of a modern globe or a Mercator chart must be misled; for these are drawn to the true meridian, while Cabot was always sailing on a magnetic course, ever swerving to the south. Labrador on a Mercator chart is opposite Ireland on a true west course. For that very reason, if for no other, Labrador was not the landfall. If Cabot started from 53° N. his landfall was, of necessity, far to the south of it when he arrived upon the coast of America, where the

JOHN CABOT'S FIRST VOYAGE 21

variation was over two points. We must thoroughly recognise these facts before we can profitably follow the charts and courses of the early navigators. They are nowhere more clearly explained than by Champlain. He says: "The early navigators, who sailed to parts of New France (Canada) in the west, thought they would not be more astray in going thither, than when going to the Azores, or other places near France, where the variation is almost insensible in navigation, and where the pilots have no other compasses than those of France set to northeast, and representing the true meridian there. And so, when sailing continually toward the west and wishing to keep on a certain latitude, they would shape their course straight towards the west by their compass, thinking they were sailing on the parallel they wished to go upon. But, continuing on in a straight line, and not in a circle, like all parallel lines on the globe, after a long distance, when in sight of land they sometimes found themselves three, four, or five degrees more southerly than necessary, and thus they were deceived in their latitude and reckoning, . . . and thus, as the meridian changed, the points of the compass changed, and consequently the course. It is then most necessary to know the meridian, and the variation of the magnetic needle, and it is of service for all pilots sailing round the world, and especially at the north and south, where the greatest variations of the magnetic needle occur, and also where the circles of longitude are smaller, since their error would be the greater if they did not know the variation of the magnetic needle."

No better authority than Champlain could be cited. He was a master sailor in theory and practice, and for thirty years sailed backward and forward between the English Channel and the Gulf of St. Lawrence. The whole treatise on this subject will be found translated from Champlain's Voyages in the Transactions of the Royal Society of Canada for 1894 as Appendix A to a paper on the Cabot voyages.

These considerations may seem tedious; but they are

all important in the study of the early voyages. They are laws written in the book of Nature, and cannot be realised in the atmosphere of libraries. One look into the binnacle of a west-bound ship and one glance at the headlight and at the North Star will clear away the misconceptions which have obscured the subject, and have caused no little waste of time and ink. One such glance will show why every west-bound course must, of necessity, be a diagonal to the south.

We have it on record that the voyage was not a smooth one. Land was found on June 24, and, if the date of sailing, given as " early in May," be fixed as the 5th, it would have lasted fifty days. He " wandered for a long time, and at length hit upon land." There was not likely to be much straight sailing in such a voyage, and Cabot must have fought his way with great perseverance. With fair wind and weather it is recorded, in A. D. 1583, that the voyage might be made in twenty-two days or even less. The indications of the letters are that Cabot had neither.

The contemporary accounts give some particulars of the place where John Cabot first touched land. " The land is excellent and the climate temperate, suggesting that brasil and silk grow there." Brasil is a tropical dyewood, then extensively used, and imported from the East. Silk culture was an industry of warm climates. " The sea is full of fish, which are not only taken in a net, but also with a basket; a stone being fastened to it in order to keep it in the water." This is a point strongly made: " they took so many fish that this kingdom will no longer have need of Iceland; from which country there is an immense trade in the fish they call stock-fish." This information is recorded as taken direct from the lips of John Cabot himself. No human being was seen, but Cabot judged there were inhabitants " from certain snares spread to take game, and a needle for making nets, and some notched trees which he found." Such are the special marks recorded to identify the spot where Cabot landed. That the " tides are slack " may be said of the

JOHN CABOT'S FIRST VOYAGE 23

whole Atlantic coast, but there can be no question as to the nature of the country found, for the same writer in another letter calls them "fertile islands."

Cabot did not remain long. Although "he saw no man," he did not go far into the country. His crew was small, and "being in doubt he came back to the ship." Nor did he see anyone on the coast along which he sailed in returning, "but he did not wish to land lest he should lose time, for he was in want of provisions."

The aim of the expedition had been achieved. Land had been found to the west. They were sure that it was "the mainland of the country of the Grand Cam," just what they had expected to find. This first voyage was a simple reconnoitring expedition, in a small unarmed vessel, with a crew of only eighteen men. Cabot took possession of the country by hoisting the flag of England, as he was empowered to do by the letters patent, and then returned. Being a Venetian he hoisted also the flag of St. Mark, for which he had no warrant. He was certainly back in London on August 10, 1497, and there is highly probable ground for believing that August 6 was the day he arrived at Bristol. His voyage to the landfall had occupied from fifty to fifty-three days. The return voyage was made in forty-three days, but Raimondo da Soncino reported to his master, the Duke of Milan, "now that they know where to go, they say the voyage thither will not occupy more than fifteen days after leaving Ibernia (Ireland)." After making the landfall he coasted, according to one report, along the land for three hundred leagues. This is one of the difficulties in the narrative, for there was not time for so long a coasting voyage, and it conflicts with the prompt return enforced by the scarcity of provisions. It is clear that he coasted along the south of Newfoundland as he returned. That, in a straight line, is 316 miles. He followed the coast which, however, could hardly have lengthened his course to so great a degree.

In view of the prevailing influence of the English language on the North American continent the landfall of Cabot assumes great historic interest, for, excepting the Northmen in the tenth century, the handful of Englishmen on his little vessel were the first Europeans to touch the mainland of the Western World. After long controversy the smoke has cleared away, and an intelligent opinion upon the subject may be readily formed. Three localities only call for serious consideration. Taking them in order from the north they are, first:

Some point on the coast of Labrador from lat. 53° to Cape Chidley. The more the physical characteristics of this coast are known the more it is seen to be absolutely irreconcilable with the mild climate and semi-tropical conditions described in the contemporary records. The following passage from a work written by one familiar with the coast (published in A. D. 1900) will show the contrast:

"The climate is rigorous in the extreme. The snow lies from September to June. In winter the whole coast is blocked with ice-fields, drifting from Baffin's Bay and other outlets of the Arctic Ocean, while in summer the glittering icebergs, stranded or floating, impart a stern beauty to its storm-beaten shore. Perhaps no country on the face of the globe is less attractive as an abode of civilised man. Much of the surface of the country is covered with low mountains and barren plateaus, on which are vast plains of moss interspersed with rocks and boulders. At the heads of the bays and fiords only, is there a large growth of timber, and along the margin of some of the rivers, patches of cultivable land are to be found. The Atlantic coast of Labrador is a grim and terrible wilderness, but having many scenes of awe-inspiring beauty." That is Labrador in A. D. 1900. What it was in A. D. 1534, Jacques Cartier reported on his first voyage, as recorded in Hakluyt's quaint version:

"If the soil were as good as the harboroughs are, it were a great commoditee; but it is not to be called the new *Land* but rather *stones* and wilde cragges, and a place fit for wilde beasts, for in all the North Land I did not see a cart-load of good earth; yet went I on shoare in many

JOHN CABOT'S FIRST VOYAGE 25

places, and in the Iland of White Sand there is nothing else but mosse and small thornes scattered here and there withered and dry. To be sure, I beleeve that this was the land that God allotted to Caine." This was said of the coast of Labrador, inside of the Strait of Belle-Isle, and from lat. 51° southwards. The contemporary account of John Cabot and his companions, recorded in the letter of the Milanese envoy, dated December 18, 1497, was: " And they say that there the land is excellent and the climate temperate, suggesting that brasil and silk grow there."

The theory of a landfall in Labrador is still copied from book to book, and the voyages, which can no longer be disputed, are explained so as to thrust the English on a barren and inclement coast far to the north. When Biddle revived the question in 1833 the documents had not come to light which reveal the true landfall. They have been found since in the archives of foreign countries— the La Cosa map of 1500, the Cabot map of 1544, the documents at Simancas and Venice. These are decisive evidences which have rewarded the research of scholars since Biddle's time. Then the coast of Labrador was unfrequented, and its interior was a blank on the maps and one might safely affirm almost anything concerning it; but in the present state of geographical knowledge that is no longer possible. The British Admiralty Pilot, referring to the coast southward from Cape St. Lewis, in 52° 30', to a point within the Strait of Belle-Isle, describes it, as Jacques Cartier did, consisting of bare granite hills, rising abruptly about 700 feet from the sea level. The water is said to be deep and navigation not intricate, " but the frequent fogs, the heavy easterly swell rolled in from the Atlantic, and the icebergs, which are almost always drifting along with the current from the northward, all contribute in making the condition of the coast hazardous to vessels." Belle-Isle is in 52°, so to strike Labrador the landfall is, of necessity, placed north of 53°. In Dr. Grenfell's " Vikings of To-day " is a characteristic picture of the coast between 53° and 54°. On July 13 he crossed from Belle-Isle to the mainland, and he says: " By mid-day we ventured to make a start and headed direct for Cape Charles, close inside the island of Belle-Isle. As we brought the hills and steep cliffs of Labrador into view we found there was still much snow in the gulfs and crevices; while it was necessary carefully to thread our way among the numbers of icebergs, which, up to this very week, had been blocking the straits."

Again the landfall described by Cabot was remarkable for its abundance of fish. The date was June 24, old style, which, in that century, would be equivalent to July 3 of the present calendar; but it was proved before the Commission of the Fishery clauses of the Treaty of Washington, in 1877, that the fish do not set in upon the coast at lat. 53° 24′ until July 12, and, farther north, until August. The cause which determines the movement of the fish is the ice thrown upon the coast by the Arctic current; but Cabot makes no mention of ice or of icebergs upon this voyage, although they are a striking feature of his second voyage. John Cabot could not possibly have been upon the coast of Labrador without meeting many icebergs, for we read in the Admiralty Sailing Directions, " Icebergs may be encountered all the year round, but are most numerous from June till August." June 24, old style, is just the time of year when the imposing procession of icebergs, passing southwards, is densest, and when stranded bergs most frequently obstruct the harbours all along the Labrador coast, from the Strait of Belle-Isle northward.

Passing southward, the second locality, cited as the landfall of the first English voyage across the western ocean, is Cape Bonavista, on the east coast of Newfoundland. This idea has nothing to suggest it but the similarity of sound to the words *prima vista*. It has not the transcendent impossibility of Labrador; but it is excluded by the documents. It is fatal to the theory that neither it, nor any other name, is found on the east coast of Newfoundland on La Cosa's map. It is evident from that map that, when Cabot arrived at Cape Race, the Cape of England (Cavo de Inglaterra), he struck home for England without turning up along the east coast.

Moreover, the name is not found among the names upon the east coast, shown in the earlier maps after La Cosa's. In Visconte de Maiollo's map of A. D. 1527, the name *ben posta* occurs, but it is not until A. D. 1534 upon Viegas' map (Portuguese) that the name is found, and it is there spelled Boāvista, though pronounced Bonavista, after the rules of the Portuguese language. As will appear in a succeeding chapter, the east coast of Newfoundland was discovered and named by the Portuguese. The first mention of a landfall at Bonavista is as late as A. D. 1625, on a printed English map, known as Mason's, and on a French manuscript map, of the same year, by Dupont of Dieppe. Much importance is attached to what is called an "immemorial tradition" on the coast; but as there were no settlers there for a hundred years, there was no material to create and continue a tradition. The name Bonavista ("happy sight," as it is translated), may have suggested the tradition, but the name was doubtless given from some fancied resemblance to a familiar home island in the Cape Verde group.

The third, and most southern, point claimed as Cabot's landfall is Cape Breton. To this locality both circumstantial evidence and positive testimony plainly point. The country around is one of the most beautiful regions in North America. Its summer climate corresponds to John Cabot's description. "The summers of Cape Breton," writes an Englishman who resided there for many years, "challenge comparison with those of any country within the temperate regions of the world. During all that time there are, perhaps, not more than ten foggy days in any part of the island, except along the southern coast, between the Gut of Canso and Scatari. Bright, sunny days, with balmy westerly winds, follow each other in succession week after week, while the mid-day heats are often tempered by cool, refreshing sea-breezes." The eastern coast of the island was renowned for its abundant fisheries, and became the resort of English, French,

Spanish and Portuguese fishermen from the earliest times of discovery. From the year 1504 it was the favourite fishing ground of the Bretons; and Cape Breton is one of the earliest names on the maps; while the adjacent sea, bounded by the coasts of Newfoundland and Nova Scotia, was called the Bay of the Bretons. The easternmost point of the island—the very cape itself—is wave-washed and rocky; for a narrow barrier of primordial rock protects the carboniferous basin from the wash of the open Atlantic. It is, as appears on La Cosa's map, on the line of magnetic west from Cabot's point of departure and thus, in every way, fulfils the conditions described. It is also the only point of the island which the geography of the coast permits to be a primary landfall; moreover, it is the first place ever named as the landfall; for it is called *Prima tierra vista* (first land seen), on the map of 1544, compiled with data received from Sebastian Cabot. All other landfalls were devised subsequently to this first mention,—they are hypotheses of later times.

There is, in fact, positive evidence for Cape Breton, and for no other spot on the Atlantic coast. Pedro de Ayala, Spanish ambassador at London, wrote to the sovereigns of Spain, on July 25, 1498 (before Cabot had returned from his second voyage), that he had obtained from him a chart and would send it to them. In the year 1500 the king of Spain employed Juan de La Cosa, a celebrated pilot, who had been a companion of Columbus, to make for him a map of the world, and this very map, after many vicissitudes, was, in 1853, restored to the archives of Spain. It is worthy of the closest attention, not only from the celebrity of its compiler, but because it is the earliest map extant showing any part of the New World. It was completed in October, 1500, six years before the death of Columbus. From the first it was an authoritative public map, and now it is the venerated treasure of the Naval Museum at Madrid. A tracing of the North American portion of the map is given at page 30. It is drawn to compass bearings, and the trend of the coast

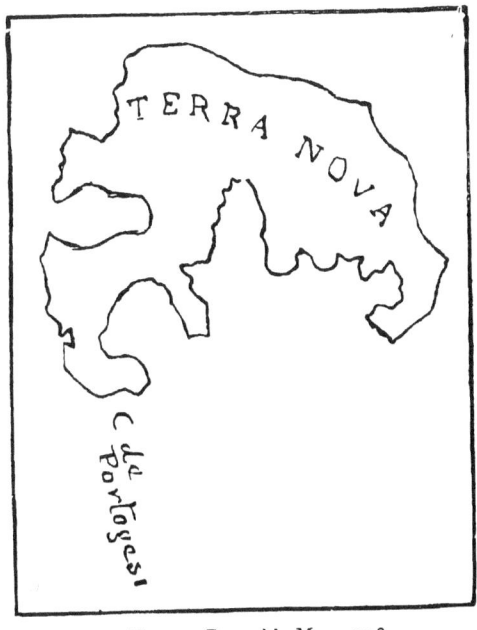

Fig. 1. Ruysch's Map, 1508

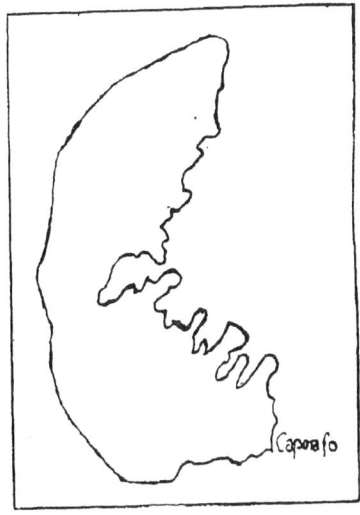

Fig. 2. King Map, 1502

Fig. 3. Cape Race, A.D. 1900

The Key Point of North American Geography

JOHN CABOT'S FIRST VOYAGE

upon the true meridian inclines towards the south by the whole extent of the variation of the needle. No mistake is possible about the date, for it is on the map itself, and is A. D. 1500. No Englishmen had been upon the coast but the Cabots. Therefore, when we find upon it "Mar descubierto por les Yngleses" (Sea discovered by the English), we may be sure that in compiling the map for the king of Spain, La Cosa availed himself of John Cabot's map, sent to the same king by Pedro de Ayala, his ambassador in England. The English discoveries are marked by English flags for a certain distance along the northeast coast of the continent, and the Spanish discoveries are marked by Spanish flags upon the West India islands to the south. The only names on the northern continental coast are the names on the "sea discovered by the English"—necessarily Cabot's names.

The salient point on the map is that remarkable headland, Cape Race, which, since the discovery of the continent, has been the great landmark of all mariners sailing on the Western Ocean. It stands on La Cosa's map looking across the unbroken ocean waste, in A. D. 1500, as it does still on a Mercator chart, facing the projecting coast of South America, then just discovered. It is called *Cavo de Ynglaterra* (Cape of England); for it is the last point of the New World looking towards England. On Ruysch's map it is called C. de Portogesi, see Fig. 1 (Portuguese Cape); but on the King map, A. D. 1502, it is called Capo Raso, see Fig. 2, and, ever since, as Cape Raso, Rasso, Razo or Race, the name has expressed the physical character of the locality. The figure 3, page 28, is a reproduction of a photograph in the Canadian Marine Department, taken at some happily quiet moment. The English form "Race" obscures the meaning. It is the "flat cape"—worn smooth in its aeonian resistance to the Atlantic surf. It is the first permanent name on the continental coast of North America.

We need not discuss the longitudes of any of these early maps, for longitudes could not be correctly ascertained in those days. It is evident, from the position of the Azores, that the longitude of this map is 25° out. It has already been observed that, up to A. D. 1520, the latitudes of the Antilles are almost 8° too far north, and this plainly appears in La Cosa's map, for Cuba and Hispaniola are entirely north of the tropic instead of being entirely south of it. The map is not graduated, but the distance between the equator and the tropic gives a measure by which we may see that the latitude of Cape Race is too high to the same extent that the latitude of Cuba is too high, and it is also pertinent to observe that Cape Race is at the same distance from the equator as Bristol.

On the east side of Newfoundland, north of Cape Race, there are no names, the coast line is hypothetical, but from Cape Race westward the coast is named, and the last name to the west, *Cavo descubierto*, reveals the secret of the first landfall on the continent of America. As plainly as words can express it that point is Discovery Cape. It corresponds with the *Prima tierra vista* of the Sebastian Cabot map of 1544 and is the east point of Cape Breton.

The moment this is apprehended, everything becomes clear. All the evidence falls into line. Ayala, with John Cabot's chart before his eyes, wrote (July 25, 1498) to King Ferdinand that the land found was "at the end of that which belongs to your Highness by the convention with Portugal" (*i. e.*, the Treaty of Tordesillas), and we know the line of demarcation was held to cut the Nova Scotia coast at the equivalent of our meridian of 60°, and close to Cape Breton. Those who frequent the coast know that in June, July, and August Cape Race is seldom seen. The southeast corner of Newfoundland is wrapped in fog for twenty-four days out of thirty. Appendix C of a paper in the Transactions of the Royal Society of Canada for 1897 is a table compiled from the records of the lighthouse keeper at Cape Race for the month of June in four successive years 1894-1897, establishing that fact, if indeed, so patent a fact in physical geography

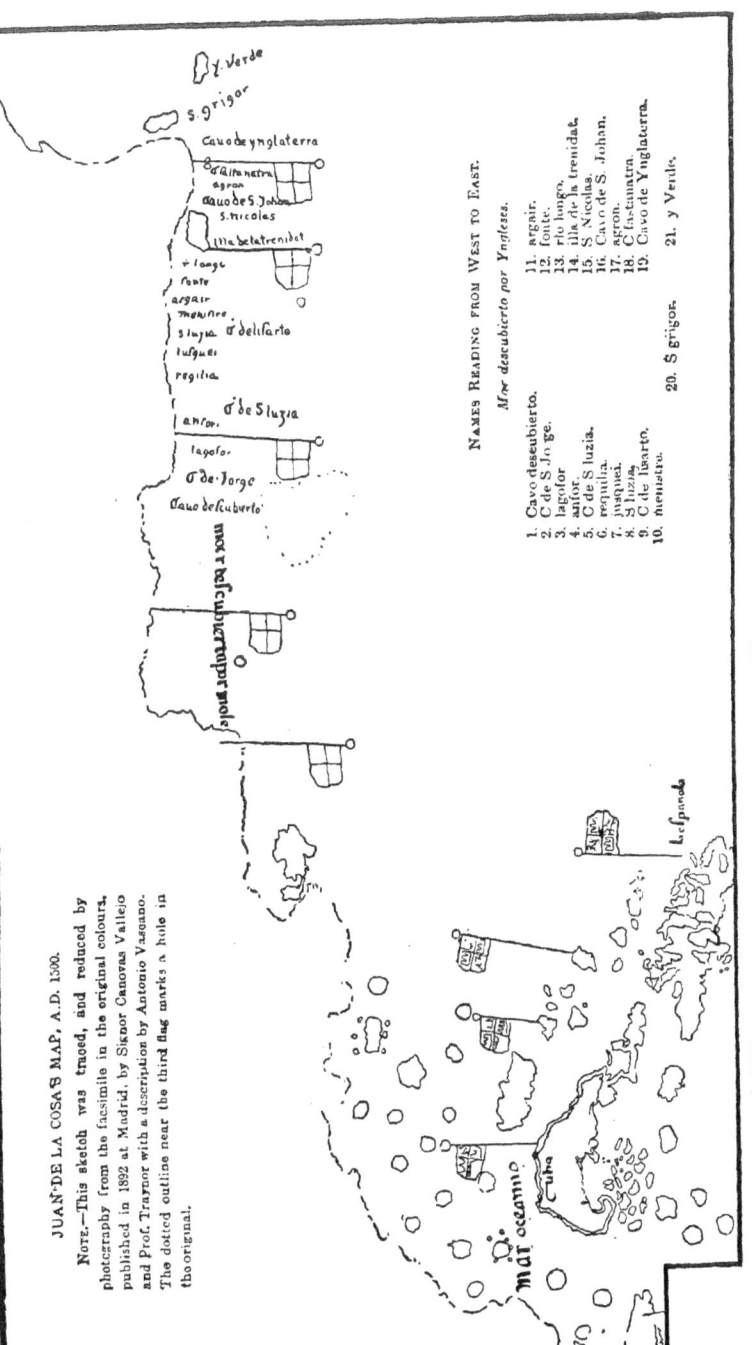

North American portion of Juan de la Cosa's Map, A.D. 1500

JOHN CABOT'S FIRST VOYAGE 31

needed establishing. Passing Cape Race in foggy weather Cabot continued on his western course and could not fail therefore to arrive at Cape Breton. There, as we know from the contemporary letters, he did not stay, but, being short of provisions, he returned at once. In returning he coasted and named the south coast of Newfoundland, and took his departure for England from the Cape of England (Cape Race). The reason the return voyage took 43 days is thus apparent.

Such is the testimony of John Cabot to the discoveries of the English, embodied in a contemporaneous map made for the King of Spain by the master and owner of the flagship of Columbus on his first voyage in 1492 and the pilot of his fleet. The testimony of Cabot's son, Sebastian, is contained in a world-map, dated 1544, of which the copy in the National Library at Paris is the only one known to exist. It is a printed map and was found as recently as A. D. 1843. The information given upon it is partly by numbered legends on the map itself, and partly by legends, in Spanish and Latin versions, printed separately and attached to it—forming one document with it. The map has been the occasion of much controversy. The American portion of it is given in Chap. XIV, and its chronological place, A. D. 1544, must be borne in mind, because it has sometimes been taken to be a map of Sebastian Cabot's own discoveries. After a long controversy it is now admitted that, while Sebastian Cabot may not have drawn the map, he at least contributed to the materials upon which it was constructed, and that, among other things, the information concerning northeast America was contributed by him.

Figure 4 is a tracing from a photographic enlargement of the original map, and on it the words *Prima tierra vista* indicate that the landfall—the *Cavo descubierto*—was on the east point of Cape Breton Island. Of the two points shown the words refer to the easternmost, and indeed Cape North could not have been discovered first, for the land around is too high to be passed unobserved, and the course would require to be abruptly changed to reach it. Legend No. 8, upon the map of 1544, refers to the first voyage and states that the land was first found on June 24, 1494, now recognised as a misprint for 1497. An island was discovered the same day lying opposite and close to the landfall, which they called St. John, because it was St. John the Baptist's day. Then follows in the Latin text a full point, and the next word, *Hujus,* begins with a capital letter. The rest of the

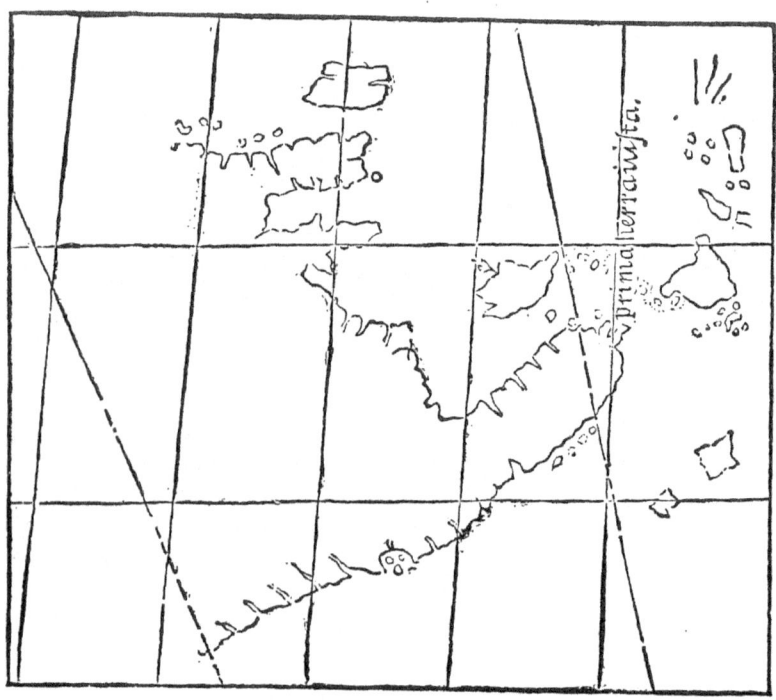

Fig. 4. Extract from the Sebastian Cabot Map of A. D. 1544; showing the point of Cape Breton as the Landfall

legend refers to the whole region of the north, and various particulars are given of the country, the people, the bears and other animals, the birds, and the fish. Much confusion has arisen from reading this legend, as if it formed part of a special description of the island, instead of a general description of an extensive region, characterized by the two bears drawn upon the map, which the discoveries of forty succeeding years, and especially those of Cartier, had made known. The Magdalen group of islands discovered by Cartier in the Gulf of St. Lawrence are marked, by error, "island of St. John," although they do not lie near, or opposite, the landfall and could not be discovered on the same day.

The scope of this volume will not admit of further discussion. Those who care to follow the question further may do so in the books and papers mentioned at the end of this volume. The Island of Cape Breton must be carefully distinguished from the cape itself, from which it was named. The region was not known as an island, and is shown on the map for a hundred years as a part of the peninsula of Nova Scotia. The Gut of Canso, dividing it from the mainland, is only 4518 feet across at its narrowest part—not so wide as the East River at New York, for the Brooklyn bridge is 5989 feet; nor so wide as the St. Lawrence, for the Victoria bridge at Montreal is 9184 feet long.

Let it not be thought that this event is unworthy of the time devoted to its elucidation. That the English were the first to tread the soil of the continent of the New World is a fact of supreme historic importance. For almost a century they neglected, and undervalued their new acquisition. Silent as to the momentous achievement of Cabot, their annals were crowded with the ephemeral doings of men whose names and deeds might well have passed into oblivion. Nevertheless, when they came to the New World, they did not come as interlopers. They did not come with a title only to rocky and uninhabitable wastes of ice and storm. They came as of right to the regions best adapted to develop a strong industrial civilisation. Not to the relaxing climate of dreamy islands in southern seas, but to those temperate latitudes where the European races attain their highest level. When the forest wilderness of Cape Breton listened to the voices of Cabot's little company, it was the first faint whisper of the mighty flood of English speech which was destined to overflow the continent, to the shores of another ocean, far-distant and undreamed of for many years.

CHAPTER III

CABOT'S SECOND VOYAGE—DISAPPOINTMENT

KING HENRY VII., although cautious and not subject to enthusiasms of any kind, was elated at the success of the first voyage; for a great success it appeared to be. On August 10 he granted from the Privy Purse a reward of ten pounds " to hym that founde the new isle." Not a large sum, for King Henry VII. was " not prodigal "; but it represented many times that amount in these days. On December 13, 1497, he granted to John Cabot a pension of twenty pounds a year, charged upon the customs revenue of the port of Bristol. Pending preparations prospects were in truth most promising, for " the country of the Grand Cam " had been reached, and what that signified Marco Polo had taught to Europe. The expedition had reached Cathay, of which empire the capital was Cambaluc (Pekin), the winter residence of the Grand Khan, a city " twenty-four miles square and admirably built "; the emporium of an amount and variety of merchandise so vast that Marco Polo found it beyond his powers of description. There, he wrote, were " to be seen, in wonderful abundance, the precious stones, the pearls, the silks and the diverse perfumes of the east. Scarce a day passes that there does not arrive nearly a thousand waggons laden with silk, of which they make admirable stuffs in the city." There was no shadow of doubt but that Asia had been reached. La Cosa filled up on his map the unexplored gap between the discoveries of Cabot and Columbus with conjectural outlines from the eastern coast of Asia. The Cantino map (A. D.

1502) inscribed upon Greenland the legend *ponta d'Asia* and added "it is believed that this is the extremity of Asia." Ruysch's map (A. D. 1508) showed the supposed connection—Terra Nova, an extension of Northern Asia, Cathay, Tebet, Bangala, and Quinsay forming one continent with it, and the great river Polisacus (Hoang Ho) falling into the *Sinus Plisacus* of the great ocean; in which, far to the south, were the Antilles and South America shown as islands. Other maps might be cited, but these are sufficient to show the current belief. What a prospect for trade was opened up by this Italian adventurer! His previous attempts in Seville and Lisbon to obtain aid for an expedition, in more northern latitudes than Columbus had sailed in, had failed, and it had taken him twelve months to equip one little vessel, and get together a crew of eighteen men to make this attempt. "A foreigner and poor, he would not have been believed if his crew, who were nearly all English of Bristol, had not testified that what he said was true." We read also that Cabot was " of gentle disposition " and he must have been a man of great patience and resolution; " another," we are informed, " like Columbus "; and, though naturalised in Venice, he was in another respect like Columbus, for he was born in Genoa. It is worthy of note that although he had resided fifteen years in Venice to qualify him for naturalisation, Cabot was evidently unknown to the Venetian representative in London, or to his two brothers in Venice, Alvise and Francesco Pasqualigo, with whom he corresponded.

Then came the short hour of John Cabot's triumph and, for a time, he was lionised in London. The King, miserly though he was, " granted him money to amuse himself with." He was " called the Great Admiral " and " great honour was paid him." He " went about dressed in silk " and made promises of lands in his new domains. To a Burgundian who was with him he promised an island, and he promised another to a Genoese friend. Two poor friars, who were to go on the next voyage, were to have bishoprics. The Bristol merchants took up the

CABOT'S SECOND VOYAGE 37

enterprise warmly, and Cabot went back to Bristol to his wife and family; for there the next expedition also was to be fitted out. Additional letters patent were issued by the King, not cancelling or traversing the former letters, but giving to John Cabot the additional and exceptional power to take any six ships suitable for the proposed expedition, in any port of the kingdom, together with such accessories as were necessary, paying for them such a price as the King would pay, if they were taken for the royal service. In these letters Cabot's sons were not mentioned.

During the winter of 1497-98 preparations went on and others joined in the enterprise. The King assisted by advancing loans to those who fitted out ships. The following sums are on record: "To Lanslot Thirkill of London, twenty pounds; to Thomas Thirkill, thirty pounds; to Thomas Bradley, thirty pounds; and forty pounds five shillings to John Carter" for the same object. There is no record of the day of sailing of the expedition, but it was early in May. The observant letter-writers whose reports we have been quoting now desert us, and few details can be gleaned elsewhere. Dr. de Puebla, the senior Spanish Ambassador, wrote to the Spanish monarchs, at the end of July, that the expedition had sailed and that the King had sent five armed ships. From a chronicle quoted by Hakluyt we gather that divers merchants of London ventured small stocks of goods, and that there were three or four small ships that went in company laden with merchandise "such as coarse cloth, caps, laces, points, and other trifles." This is a practical commentary on the report given by Cabot and his sailors concerning the character of the land found. It is incredible that such consignments should be made to countries like Labrador or Greenland. The English merchants risked their money upon the productiveness of the "new found land." De Ayala, the second Spanish Ambassador, writing at the same time, adds that the fleet was provisioned for one year, and that, at the date of the letter (July 25) one of the ships, on board of which was a certain friar Bull, had been driven back to Ireland in distress. The chronicle, cited in Hakluyt, adds that the fleet "so departed from Bristowe (Bristol) in the beginning of May; of whom in this Mayor's time (October 28, 1498) returned no tidings"; and of that expedition, so full of hope and promise, no tidings are to be found in the annals of England to this day. John Cabot disappears, and his memory was nearly lost forever. His sons Lewis and Sancius are heard of no more, and although Sir George Peckham, in Hakluyt's Voyages, says that "a fair haven in Newfoundland is to this day (A. D. 1583) known and called Sancius' haven," no such haven can be found on any map, or exists now upon the island. Placentia, which some have supposed to be the haven intended, is named for a Basque town in the district of Vizcaya. His son Sebastian, however, became an important person in the history of maritime discovery. It is easy to see that an expedition with such aims and based upon such expectations must have failed, and that all concerned in it must have been miserably disappointed; but the details of disaster will never be known.

It is not probable that the younger Cabot was among the eighteen men on the first voyage with his father, but he did take part in the second voyage. We have not only his own statement, but every indication points to his having seen the new lands with his own eyes. He described to Peter Martyr the icebergs of the north (seen, not on an expedition with eighteen men, but on an expedition with three hundred men) and the bears which swam and caught fish in the sea. These are strange experiences, not likely to be invented or even repeated at second hand. Moreover King Ferdinand, himself, wrote to Sebastian Cabot (September 13, 1512) and the "navigation to the Bacallaos" is mentioned in the letter, in a way to prove that it was the cause of the invitation to enter the service of Spain. Ferdinand of Aragon was not a prince easily deceived, or one to be deceived with impunity. That Sebastian said he had been there is not, on any theory

CABOT'S SECOND VOYAGE

concerning his veracity, to be taken as proof that he had not been there. It would indeed be strange if a young man of capacity and intelligence, as he most certainly was, did not take part in an expedition of such magnitude, sailing with such éclat under Royal auspices, and with his father in command.

Nothing is on record concerning him for fourteen years after until, in May, 1512, in the following reign, his name appears in the public accounts as receiving twenty shillings for making a map of Gascony and Guyenne to be used in a campaign in the south of France concerted between Henry VIII. and Ferdinand of Aragon. Later in the same year he entered the service of the Spanish King and removed to Seville with his wife and family, where he was appointed to the rank of captain, and was subsequently advanced to be pilot major with very important functions in the naval service of Spain. What knowledge we possess of the results of the second voyage is mainly derived from the statements of Sebastian Cabot as recorded in the works of Spanish and Italian authors, especially from Peter Martyr, Ramusio, and Gomara. Sidelights and confirmations may be gathered from many other sources, but it is remarkable that all our information concerning the second voyage upon which English diplomacy chiefly relied in making claims in the New World should be drawn, not from the records of England, but from foreign sources. The historic value of these accounts and the character of Sebastian Cabot have been of late discussed so thoroughly that it is unnecessary to enter into further details.

Peter Martyr (in the sixth book of his third Decade), gives an account of Sebastian Cabot's expedition from information received from his own lips; but it has been overlooked that the account is only incidental to another inquiry. The passage has been too frequently read only in extract and, to apprehend its true bearing, it must be read with the context. Martyr is really discussing the equatorial current. He observes that the sea flows from east to west, and, not knowing of the Gulf

Stream, he is speculating as to what becomes of the overflow. He discusses various theories, and at last reaches that which supposes the overflow to return to the north. He is not satisfied with that either, for he says those who have sailed on the northern seas affirm that the sea flows to the west there also, though not so swiftly. Then he goes on to say that "these northern seas have been searched by one Sebastian Cabot," an intimate friend then with him at Seville, and continues by reporting what he had heard from Cabot's own lips bearing upon the difficulty present in his mind, which done, he says: ". But it shall suffice to have said that much of the gulfs and straits and of Sebastian Cabot. Let us now, therefore, return to the Spaniards." That is, return to the main subject of his work, of which these Cabot notes were an incident or a digression. Bearing this in mind—remembering that Martyr was not concerning himself with the doings of the English,—we may see why no mention of John Cabot is made, without supposing Sebastian Cabot to have been a liar. We learn from the "Decades" that it was a large expedition, with three hundred men. That one note marks it as a description of the second voyage. The son Sebastian seems to arrogate to himself the whole inception and conduct of the enterprise. He "fyrst with three hundred men, directed his course so farre towards the North Pole that, even in the moneth of July, he founde monstrous heapes of ise swymming on the sea, and, in manner, continuall daylight; yet sawe he land in that tract free from ise. Thus, seeing such heapes of ise before hym, he was enforced to turne his sayles and folowe the west, so coastynge styll by the shore, that he was thereby brought so farre into the south by reason of the land bending so much southwarde that it was almost equall in latitude with the sea called Fretum Herculanaum." This means, in short, that he sailed first to the coast of Labrador, where he pushed his way north among the icebergs, as far as he could go, and then he turned south and coasted along shore nearly as far as the latitude of the Strait of Gibraltar. All of this

CABOT'S SECOND VOYAGE

is in accord with the physical geography of the coast. Robert Thorne, an English merchant, residing in Seville, sent privately to King Henry VIII., in 1527, a rough sketch of a map in order to show the King his rightful claim, by prior discovery, to a large part of the American coast. Robert Thorne's father had been upon an expedition to that coast. The

Fig. 5. Robert Thorne's Map, A. D. 1527

family was of Bristol, and Robert Thorne himself was much concerned with shipping. At Seville he was in a position to know Sebastian Cabot, and Seville was then the centre of western discovery. His map has, fortunately, been preserved in Hakluyt's "Divers Voyages," and the inscription on it, *Terra hac ab Anglis prima fuit inventa*, marks the coast from the extreme north of Labrador to a latitude as far south as Lisbon; thus confirming Peter Martyr's report of Sebastian Cabot's statement. Another proof that this voyage was the second of the Cabot voyages is the fact that the fleet was victualled for a year, whereas, the contemporary evidence proved, beyond a doubt, that the little vessel of the first voyage had to return for want of provisions, and was absent only ninety-three days. Moreover, there is no mention made of ice in the accounts of the first voyage, and in all accounts of the second ice and icebergs are strongly emphasised characteristics. Still another confirmation is that, inasmuch as the second expedition sailed early in May, provisioned for a year, and had not returned on October 28, there was abundant time to make the extensive explorations reported by Peter Martyr, while it is plainly evident that there was not time on the first voyage.

Gomara, in his "General History of the Indies," gives an account of the same voyage. His account appears to have been taken from the "Decades" of Martyr, though he adds some details from another source. He specifies 58° as the latitude reached in the north (Hebron, on the Labrador coast), and 38° on the south (Cape Henlopen, State of Delaware). These two accounts, the former published in 1516, when Cabot was in Seville, and the latter in 1552, after he had gone to live in England, confirm each other, and they also accord with the physical geography of the coast of Labrador as it exists at the present day. "Considering the cold," writes Gomara, "and the forbidding nature of the country, he turned to the south, and passing the Baccalaos, he proceeded as far as 38°, returning thence to England."

The high latitude reached by the early sailors bears evidence to their wonderful skill and courage in navigating their little craft. Greely observes that the latitude 77° 45' N. attained by Baffin, in 1616, was unequalled in that sea for two hundred and thirty-six years. The latitude reached by Cabot is variously stated from 56° N. to 67° 30', but it is certain, from Ruysch's map, that some years before 1508 an expedition had reached the mouth of Hudson's Strait. Probably Ruysch, who had been to America on a Bristol vessel, was on this very expedition.

CABOT'S SECOND VOYAGE 43

Anyway, he appears to be drawing from his own experiences in the legend on his map. " Here a raging sea begins, here the compasses of ships do not hold their properties, and vessels having iron are not able to return." On the Hakluyt map, at the same locality, is inscribed " a furious overfall," and Davis, on his third voyage, in 1586, says " we passed a very great gulfe, the water whirling and roaring as it were the meeting of tides." These are unalterable physical facts which fix the locality beyond cavil. Admiral Markham, who was a passenger on the Canadian Government expedition in 1886, under Captain Gordon, remarked the commotion peculiar to Hudson's Strait. He " repeatedly observed comparatively large pieces of ice being swept with great velocity in opposite directions." Captain Gordon found the dip of the needle at the western end of the strait to be 80°. He had much difficulty because of the sluggishness of the compass, and, in singular conformity with Ruysch's note in A. D. 1508, records his opinion that the compasses of an iron ship passing through the strait would not work.

The main features of the voyage of 1498 are given in the above citations from contemporary writings. Certain characteristic indications demonstrate that the second voyage was actually made to the regions stated. The icebergs, the field ice, the polar bears, the fish, the continual daylight, and especially the casual observation that the natives possessed copper, are incidental notes which could not have been invented. Over the whole theatre of controversy it is unnecessary to go. Those who believe that the region of silk and brasil-wood of the first voyage was on the coast of Labrador between 53° and 60°, cannot be convinced by futher evidence. Sebastian Cabot had little further connection with exploration on the northeast coast of America. We learn from a letter, written in 1522, to his government by the Venetian ambassador to Spain, that Cabot told him that he had visited England in 1519, and that, while there, Cardinal Wolsey had proposed to fit out an expedition if he would command it, and that he had refused because he was in the service of Spain. It is more than probable that he told the truth about Bacallaos to Ferdinand of Aragon, that there was nothing there for Spain, and, if any passage to Cathay did exist, it was far to the north, and if passable, it would be within the demarcation line of Portugal. This was the opinion of Stephen Gomez also, later in 1525. Both, in all probability, suspected the existence of an opening by Hudson's Strait, but such a passage, if found, would be more injurious than beneficial to Spanish interests, which lay entirely in the latitudes near the equator. When Cabot, in his old age, went to occupy a high position in the naval service of England, he devoted his energies to the discovery of a passage to China by the northeast. He was deficient in candour and greedy of reputation, and like Columbus, he would take credit for himself at anybody's expense. He subordinated his father's merits as a discoverer to his own, and, therefore, his father has narrowly escaped complete oblivion; but it must be noted to his credit that in the only instance where information comes direct from himself, as in the legend attached to the map of 1544, he did mention his father, and gives precedence to his father's name. He was an intriguer in an age of intrigue, but to quote from a recent writer, "it is a monstrous improbability that a man without any advantages of birth, wealth or influential connections, a foreigner among two jealous nations, should be no geographer, and yet incessantly making maps for public departments; no cosmographer, and yet called on as an expert in important suits, and as a commissioner to determine the line of demarcation; that he should be no sailor, and the examiner and certificator of all the pilots of Spain, or no man of science, and the censor of the chair of cosmography for the council of the Indies and the admiralty of Spain." To the English people he is important, mainly because he preserved the knowledge of the second and more extensive voyage, and promulgated it through Peter Martyr, Ramusio, Gomara, and

Sebastian Cabot

From a contemporaneous portrait last owned by Richard Biddle—destroyed by fire in 1845

CABOT'S SECOND VOYAGE 45

others, but John Cabot is the real discoverer, the real hero of both voyages, and to him alone the Bristol people have erected a monument. The eccentric and able Henry Stevens summed up the whole question in a short formula: " Sebastian Cabot—John Cabot=o." Whatever claims of priority England possesses on the American continent she owes to John Cabot. They are geographically summarised in Robert Thorne's rough sketch. It shows a discovery of the coast line from northern Labrador along the Acadian shores of the Dominion, and along the coast of the United States as far south as Chesapeake Bay. The facts are succinctly set forth in the writers quoted above. Those who care to enter more fully into the vexed questions of detail will find them set forth in the works enumerated in the list at the close of this volume.

The absolute silence of English chronicles concerning the return of this elaborately planned expedition tells of disappointment and pecuniary loss. There could not have been any great and overwhelming disaster; for that would have been recorded by the survivors; or if there had been no survivors, the catastrophe would have been so great that it could not have failed to find place in our annals. We know that one of the ships, at least, returned, for Launcelot Thirkill repaid, in 1501, the loan of thirty pounds, made to him by the King on March 22, 1498. No Cathay, no Cambaluc, nor Mangi, nor Zipango, were found. There was no outlet for "points" or "cloth" or "laces" among the fur-clad Esquimaux, or the half-naked Algonquin tribes of the more southern region. It must have been a collapse of all expectations, and there are vague indications of dissensions which, in cases of disappointed hope, are sure to arrive. Doubtless the fleet was scattered, and the ships came back, one by one, with survivors embittered against the Italian adventurer, who they would think had deceived them. In his address at the Cabot Commemoration, at Bristol, on June 24, 1897, the late Marquis of Dufferin and Ava brought to public notice, for the first time, some manuscript accounts of the collectors of customs at Bristol, in 1497, 1498, and 1499, which by the diligence of Mr. Edward Scott and the late Mr. Coote, both of the British Museum staff, had been discovered in the Chapter House of Westminster Abbey, and deciphered and translated. These prove that two years of John Cabot's pension of twenty pounds had been paid. The grant dated from Lady-day (March 25), 1497. The first year, therefore, had elapsed, and the second commenced to accrue before Cabot sailed in May, 1498. The accounts show that on September 29, 1499, there were two tallies in the treasury for twenty pounds, so that the second year's pension, ending with Lady-day (March 25), 1499, had been drawn. No later entry has been found, and nothing appears on the documents to indicate whether the money was paid to John Cabot, personally, or to his wife, or to his assigns, in his absence. And so the great admiral of a few months, who promised islands and bishoprics to his followers, passed out of English history. The English nation did not know the time of its opportunity, and had to win back with blood and treasure much of the territory it had thrown away. From those despised coasts of Bacallaos, for centuries, a large portion of the food of western Europe was drawn. Richer than the mines of Potosi, these treasures replaced themselves by a perennial reproduction. On the continent, in rear of the shores coasted by Cabot, have grown up the strength of the Northern States, and the promise of the Dominion of the north. That growth was not the work of princes or parliaments; it was the unconscious work of free communities of self-exiled emigrants, building better than they knew.

CHAPTER IV

THE CORTE-REALS AND PORTUGUESE DISCOVERY

IN A. D. 1500, and during the reign of King Emmanuel, called "The Fortunate," Portugal was at the summit of her greatness. She was the most enterprising maritime power in Europe, and the commerce of Europe crowded her ports. Emmanuel succeeded in 1495, and Vasco da Gama was sent in 1497 on his successful expedition to the East Indies. In 1500 Cabral chanced upon the discovery of the coast of Brazil, which thenceforth became a possession of Portugal, as it was east of the line of demarcation settled by the treaty of Tordesillas. The age corresponded, in Portuguese history, with the age of Elizabeth in England. The court was thronged with skilful and enterprising sailors from every land, and the noblemen of the country were competent and eager for maritime adventure. They, as well as the King, felt that a great opportunity had been lost in rejecting the proposals of Columbus. The idea of a passage to India by the west was not new to them, for a letter written from Florence in 1474, by Toscanelli to Fernan Martins, Canon at Lisbon, proves that such an idea had been in the mind of Alphonso V., then King. Portuguese sailors had discovered and occupied the Cape Verde Islands, Madeira, and the Azores, from which outposts on the Western Ocean new attempts at discovery were being incessantly made. The predecessor of Emmanuel (John II.) had been disposed to listen to Columbus, but had been dissuaded by the advice of his councillors. The reigning monarch, however, supported, if he did not instigate, a similar enterprise somewhat different in direction. There might be—probably was, so they thought—land in the north, falling within the Portuguese limits under the treaty; and a passage to the East Indies free from Spanish domination might in that way be attained.

Among the noble families of Portugal was that of Corte-Real, a name bestowed by one of the kings upon a gentleman adventurer, Vasqueanes da Costa, on account of the magnificence of his house or of his suite. One of his descendants was João Vaz Corte-Real, hereditary governor of Angra, one-half of the island of Terceira, one of the Azores. He had three sons; the eldest, Vasqueanes Corte-Real, became a royal councillor, comptroller of the King's household and captain-governor of the islands of Terceira and St. George of the Azores; the other sons were Miguel and Gaspar. From their close connection with this group, halfway across the Western Ocean, the family were from youth familiar with the sea and absorbed in maritime enterprises. Gaspar is described as a man "enterprising, valorous, and eager to gain honour." He had been an attached servant of the Duke of Beja, and when the Duke succeeded as King Emmanuel, Gaspar Corte-Real became a favourite courtier. He had made some previous attempt, it is not clear what, at western discovery; but it had not succeeded, and on May 12, 1500, the King commissioned him to make discoveries in the north and northwest, and gave him a grant of all the lands he might find. Some report of the Cabot voyages had doubtless reached Portugal, and the King would naturally be anxious to assert his right to the lands Cabot had intruded upon. The chronicles vary as to the share the King took in the expedition. It had the full royal authority, but much, if not all, of the expense was borne by the Corte-Reals. There were two voyages by Gaspar Corte-Real, in the latter of which he perished. These separate voyages have been for a long time confused, and that by many writers. They are distinguished by Kohl, but historical geography is indebted to Henry Harrisse for the discovery and publication of documents which clear up the whole question. As in the case of the voyages of Cabot, we are indebted

THE CORTE-REALS 49

mainly to the news letters of intelligent Italian envoys for what we know of the Corte-Real discoveries. A letter from Pietro Pasqualigo, Venetian ambassador, to his government and another to his brothers at Venice, a letter from Albert Cantino to the Duke of Ferrara, accompanied by a map to show the discoveries made, and short extracts from the histories of Antonio Galvano and Damian de Goes, are all the documents we can rely upon for details of the expeditions.

The first expedition sailed from Lisbon under command of Gaspar in the beginning of the summer of A. D. 1500, and with one ship, according to De Goes; but Galvano says he sailed from Terceira with two ships. The fact seems to be that the expedition touched at the family island in the Azores, and there a second ship probably joined. The direction sailed was north, and he came to a "cool region with great woods," to which he gave the name of Green Land (Terra Verde). This feature of "woods" marks the landfall of the first voyage as south of a definite latitude. It is applicable to any part of North America south of Labrador. On the Cantino map "woods" are plainly portrayed in the interior of the central land. This Terra Verde is not the Greenland of our maps, or of the Northmen of the tenth century, but the east coast of Newfoundland. According to Galvano Corte-Real reached a region lying in the latitude of 50° N. He found the inhabitants barbarous, and of a dark colour. For defence they used bows and arrows, and darts of wood with points hardened in the fire. They were dressed in skins of animals, and they lived in caves and huts. He coasted along the shores of the country. A letter from Albert Cantino to the Duke of Ferrara, dated October 17, 1501, is very important as confirming, from an independent source, the information given in the two letters of Pietro Pasqualigo, but, read at this distance of time, it appears to confuse together the voyages of 1500 and 1501. The commission to Gaspar Corte-Real was dated May 12, 1500, and, necessarily, was prior to his departure. Cantino writes of a voyage north for five months and then of a change of direction to northwest and west for three months, when land was found, to which must be added the time spent in coasting and returning. The confusion is evident, for it is certain that Corte-Real returned the same year from his first expedition. The first few sentences of Cantino's letter embody information concerning the first voyage, and then it passes on to repeat what he learned regarding the second. Pasqualigo, in both his letters, made distinct references to a previous voyage in 1500, but dwells on the details of the voyage of 1501. From Cantino's map we learn that Corte-Real went as far north as the southern point of Greenland. They found it a region of serrated mountains, and did not land. The cosmographers of the day considered it to be a point of Asia, and it is set down on the map as such. Corte-Real attempted to push farther northward, but was stopped by "enormous masses of frozen snow floating upon the sea [field ice], and moving under the influence of the waves." Then follows a touch in the narrative which proves that it is based on the report of men who had really seen the icebergs of the north. "Owing to the heat of the sun, sweet and clear water is melted on their summits, and descending, by small channels, formed by the water itself, it eats away at the base where it falls. The ships now being in want of water the boats were sent in, and in that way as much was taken as was needed." The fact of watering a ship at an iceberg on the ocean could not have been invented. Then he encountered "the frozen sea," probably large masses of field ice, and could go no farther north. He reached, says Ramusio, a place he named Rio Nevado, in lat. 60° N.—a river loaded with snow. This was probably Hudson's Strait. He returned in safety to Lisbon late in the year. His exploration of the eastern coast of Newfoundland was very complete, for the profiles on the earliest maps are more accurate than those of much later date, and he seems to have named many places on the coast. Thus, by A. D. 1500, the whole of the Atlantic coast of Newfoundland had been discovered—on the

THE CORTE-REALS

south by Cabot and on the east by Corte-Real, but it was by both supposed to be a part of the mainland. Besides this, both these navigators had gone north along the coast of Labrador, as far as Hudson's Strait, and Corte-Real had even reached Davis' Strait.

Gaspar Corte-Real sailed again from Lisbon on May 15, 1501. The expedition consisted of two ships,* and the King again gave his active concurrence. The course, however, was different, and land not before known to anyone, 2000 miles from Lisbon, was discovered to the west and northwest, evidently not the same land as on the former voyage. The accounts, in substance, are that, after finding land, they coasted to the north and found it continuous with that discovered on their previous voyage, only they could not go so far north because the ice was in greater quantity. They also thought that the new land was joined to the region discovered at the Antilles by the Spaniards. The country they describe corresponds to the coast of Acadia and the northern United States—they could find no end to it in either direction. It was wooded with very fine timber fit for masts of ships, and there were very large rivers, and " when they landed they found delicious fruits of various kinds and trees and pines of marvellous height and girth." It was a populous country. The natives were clad in skins and lived solely by hunting and fishing. They kidnapped a number of them. Fifty were in Corte-Real's own ship and seven were in the companion vessel which reached Lisbon safely between the 8th and 11th of October, 1501. It is important to take into account the different directions if we would understand this second voyage. It was not, says Pasqualigo,

---

* Like Kohl, I can find only two ships. Galvano, Cantino, Pasqualigo, and the Cantino map say two, and although it may be possible to argue from the dates of return that there were three, it is better to read the documents in a concurrent sense, where that can be done. Pasqualigo gives the date of return as October 9, and Cantino says it was October 11. All the references are to the same vessel.

"north as in the past year," but "northwest and west." Delaware Bay is true west from Lisbon, and, as in the cases of Cabot and Columbus, the tendencies bearing southwards on a western course of such a length as 2000 miles must also be considered. Pietro Pasqualigo wrote to his government, and to his brothers at Venice, accounts of the voyage heard from the sailors, and Alberto Cantino did the same for the Duke of Ferrara. They saw some of the kidnapped natives, and describe them as shapely in form and modest and gentle in manner, but dirty in their habits. They were marked with lines on their faces, and were clothed with skins of animals, chiefly otters. From the description, in which both correspondents agree, the captives could not have been Esquimaux, but may have been any of the Algonquin tribes of the American coast. Gaspar Corte-Real never returned. His vessel was doubtless the larger of the two, and he had sent his consort back, intending to explore the coast further. Whether he was wrecked or fell a victim to the resentment of the fellow tribesmen of his kidnapped captives was never known. One point of great interest is related by Pasqualigo. The sailors brought home a piece of a broken sword, gilded and of Italian make. He said also that "a native boy had two silver rings in his ears which, without doubt, seem to have been manufactured at Venice." Pasqualigo argued from that that the land discovered "must be the mainland [meaning Asia], because it is not possible that a ship could ever have reached that place without being heard of." He thought the articles had come overland. We recognise them as relics of Cabot's voyages.

Miguel Corte-Real could not be convinced of his brother's death. He had assisted in fitting out the expedition, and had even prepared a vessel to join the second one, but had been prevented, in the first instance, by royal orders and then by contrary winds. He obtained the King's consent and organised a search expedition of three vessels. They sailed from Lisbon on May 10, 1502, but nothing was ever heard again of the vessel in which

THE CORTE-REALS 53

Miguel sailed. They had arranged that in order to search the coast more thoroughly the vessels should separate and meet on August 20, at an appointed rendezvous. After waiting some time for Miguel's ship the other two returned without him to Lisbon. The King, grieved at the loss of his favourite, organised an expedition the following year (1503), but it returned without success. Then the eldest brother, Vasqueanes Corte-Real, the governor of Terceira, sought permission to organise another searching expedition. King Emmanuel, however, refused his consent. Thus closed this interesting chapter of maritime history.

The early geographical history of the maritime provinces of Canada is plainly written in the earliest Portuguese maps. From Cape Chidley at Hudson's Strait to the Bay of Fundy Portuguese sailors gave names, some of which have persisted to this day, though most have been overlaid by the subsequent activities of the Bretons, while of the names given by Cabot not one survives.

The earliest delineation of the northeast coast of America which we possess subsequent to that of Juan de la Cosa is the map which Albert Cantino had drawn by a cartographer in Lisbon to show the Corte-Real discoveries, and sent to the Duke of Ferrara, before November 19, 1502. The title is "Carta da navigar per le isole novamente trovate in le parte de l'India" (Sailing chart for the islands recently discovered in the regions of India). That cannot be pressed too far because, as pointed out by Harrisse, the map covers much more than the newly found regions. The upper part shows the results of the first voyage. Our present Greenland is seen at the top. Lower down is the east coast of Newfoundland, marked Terra del Rey de Portuguall. These coasts are not named, and they are drawn well to the east of the line of demarcation, which on the sketch is indicated by a dotted line. Beyond this, far to the west, but not to the south, is the coast of America found on the second voyage. There are names along the coast in the original, and much difference of opinion exists as to what is really indicated. The position of Cuba close to a point of land naturally suggests that the point is Florida, as on our present maps; but, on examination, it will be seen that not only Cuba, but every one of the Antilles is north of the line of the Tropic, whereas, in fact, the entire group is south of that line. The latitude is 10° out of the truth. If these islands be referred to their true latitude, and if

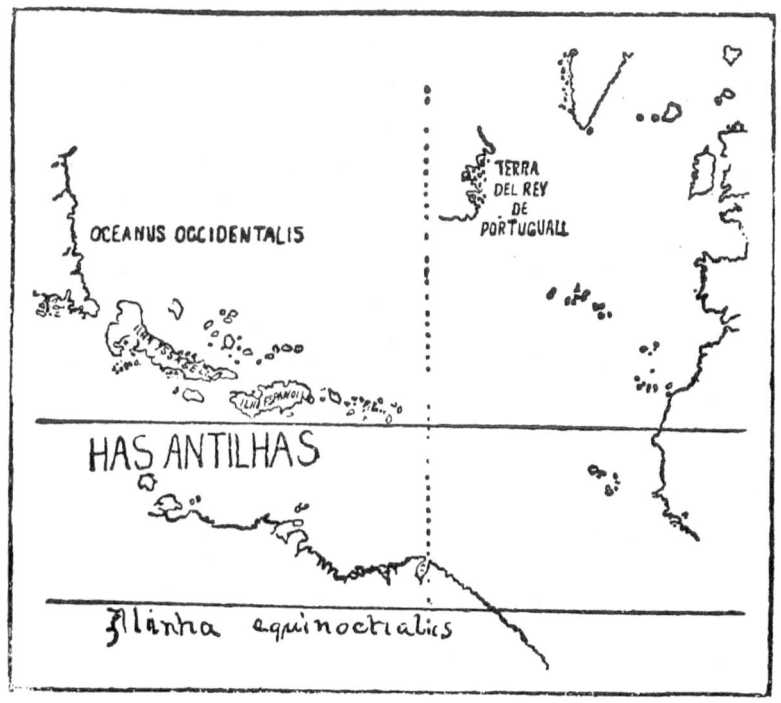

Fig. 6. Cantino Map, A. D. 1501-02

the land discovered be on a western course from Lisbon, as recorded by Pasqualigo, there will be a proper proportionate gap between the continental coast and the island of Cuba, and the point of land indicated will at once be seen to be Cape Hatteras, where the American coast bends plainly westward. The documents and the map will then harmonise, and there will be no need of hypotheses of "unknown navigators" to account for the

THE CORTE-REALS 55

names. This view is confirmed by referring to the European side of the map. The southern point of the American coast is opposite to the Strait of Gibraltar. Gibraltar and Cape Hatteras are both very nearly on the parallel of 35° N. It must be borne in mind that Corte-Real's own maps are not extant, and that Cantino had this map drawn for him by some unknown cartographer after the "cardes" (charts) of Corte-Real, or some of his sailors. The Azores are laid down as well as part of the coast of Europe and Africa, and a study of the map may reconcile some of the discrepancies of the different accounts as to distance. Cantino gives the distance as 2800 miles; Pasqualigo, writing to the Signiory of Venice, gives it at 1800 miles; but the following day writes his brother that it is 2000 miles. In those days longitude being calculated by dead reckoning, errors of great magnitude constantly occur on the early maps, but it has been pointed out that Corte-Real made his last departure from the Azores. Lisbon is nearly on the meridian of 10° W.—the Azores are on 30° W., and the mouth of Delaware Bay is 75° W. Sailing on that latitude degrees of longitude are forty-six geographical miles. The distance from Lisbon, his first departure, directly west to the mainland of America, is 2990 miles, but from the last departure, the Azores, it is 2070 miles. Italian miles are shorter than geographical miles, but the distances given should be and are proportionate.

The descriptions given afford conclusive evidence as to the region indicated. We learn that the land of 1501 was believed to be continuous with that discovered in the north in 1500. The nature of this coast should be noted. There were a "multitude of large rivers"—"a very great country"—"with delicious fruits"—"trees and pines of marvellous height and girth." Then Galvano says there were "so many mouths of rivers [bocas de rois] and harbours [abras] that the vessels of the search expedition of 1502 had to scatter along the coast." All these indicate, not the coast of Greenland, not of Labrador certainly, and not the coast of Newfoundland, where there are no large rivers of fresh water, but the coast of the northern United States and of Acadia up to a locality "where there is a very great abundance of salmon, herrings, cod [stockafis] and similar fish." On the principle of not invoking an unknown cause to account for anything where a known and sufficient agent exists, it is clearly more reasonable to think that these coasts were examined by some of the Corte-Real expeditions than to invoke the intervention of any unknown navigators.

The next map showing these discoveries at the north is a Portuguese chart of A. D. 1502 or 1504. Some names are given, and two of the five still persist on the coast. The landfall was evidently close to Conception Bay, and is marked Cabo de Concepicion. The Baya de Santa Cyria is the present Trinity Bay. Next to the north is Cabo de San Antonio, evidently the present Cape Bonavista. Then follows Rio de Rosa, Bonavista Bay, (for the name Bonavista does not appear upon the coast at so early a date). The next name, Ilha de Frey Luiz, still persists—distorted into Cape Freels. The last, *Baxos do medo,* is not a name, but a note, " dangerous shoal." It is near the north of Newfoundland. A little beyond that point the coast of Labrador trends away to the northwest, as in fact it does, and opposite is the coast of Greenland. The Strait of Belle-Isle was then, and for many years after, taken for a bay. From the accurate contour of this map it appears that the statement of Ramusio is correct—that Corte-Real went up as far as 60° N. to the Rio Nevado, the position of which is shown on later Portuguese maps. It will be observed that the coast of Newfoundland is continued south from Conception to what must be Cape Race, where it turns, but there is a line running west from Conception as a double coast line, the intention of which is not clear.

The most striking feature on the whole northeast coast of America is beyond question Cape Race. As has been shown, it appears on La Cosa's map as Cavo di Ynglaterra, but on what is known as the " King map," dated 1501 (figure 2), it is laid down—the only name—on a

THE CORTE-REALS

profile of the Newfoundland coast, beyond doubt taken from Corte-Real's explorations. The name Capo Raso (flat cape) is Portuguese, and figure 3 shows that it is an excellent summary of its physical characteristics.

Figure 7 is an extract from a chart of the Atlantic, made in 1504 or '05, by a celebrated Portuguese pilot —Pedro Reinel—who afterwards left Portugal and entered the service of Spain. It shows how thoroughly

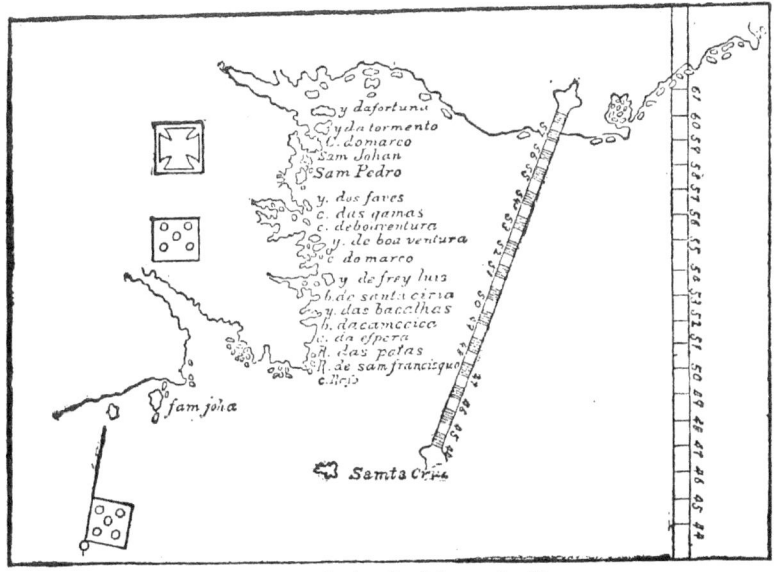

Fig. 7. Pedro Reinel's Map, A. D. 1505

the Portuguese had explored the east coast of Newfoundland at that early date. Three more names are upon it which survive under distorted forms, Rio de San Francisque (Cape St. Francis); C. da Espera (Cape Spear), and Isla dos Bacalhas (Bacalhao Island). Cape Bonavista is not marked, and it should be observed that the Island of Sam Johā (St. John) is laid down, and that it is opposite a point of the adjoining coast, which can be none other than Cape Breton. It was pointed out in a preceding chapter that Cabot's landfall of 1497 was marked by a single island, which he named St. John. Reinel has shown it plainly. This chart is also of prime importance, because, not only does the name C. Raso establish the early recognition of Cape Race,—the key point of the geography of the whole coast,—but it declares by the subsidiary staff pointing to the true north that the variation of the compass in that part of the Atlantic at that time was 21° W. If the latitude of Cape Race and Sam Johā are read to the true meridian on the inclined staff they will be found nearly correct. Cape Race is actually 46° 39′, and Scatari Island is 45° 50′. Thus early were the Atlantic shores of British North America discovered, while it was reserved to Jacques Cartier to open up, thirty years later, the great avenue to the west—the St. Lawrence valley.

CHAPTER V

MYTHICAL PRE-COLUMBIAN DISCOVERIES

ANYONE may see what an easy task it was to discover America if he will sit down in a library to study a good globe; and some writers, after proving that the Basques *could* have discovered America, suddenly assume that they did discover it, and then add that what the Basques found so easy in recent times was also easily practicable in times more remote. With equal appositeness a Portuguese writer observes that the Portuguese fishermen went as far as the Basque fishermen. That may be admitted, but it is no evidence that either reached Newfoundland before Cabot. Nothing seems easier on a globe. In fact, whoever started out at any time from the western shores of Europe to do it could not fail to hit America somewhere if he only stayed afloat and alive, and kept his vessel's head to any point between northwest and southwest. So we have disquisitions upon the nautical enterprises of the Phœnicians, the Carthaginians, the Greeks, the Romans, the Arabs, the Welsh, the Bretons, the Normans, and others, until it seems that every nation in Europe or Asia must have discovered America at some time or other before Columbus. It is not the object of the present volume to inquire into the marine of these nations which could, but did not, discover the western hemisphere. The voyages of the Northmen are of set purpose reserved from consideration in this volume, but it is germane to the present theme to discuss shortly those supposed discoveries on the northeastern coast of America which, it is claimed, had an influence upon the mind of Columbus and led up to the great public discovery which has transformed the world. It is only possible to discuss such of them as have taken on definite shape. "Immemorial traditions" do not admit of discussion; for whatsoever things men may choose to believe without evidence fall within the domain of faith. Besides, some of these "immemorial traditions" started up in quite recent times. They are "traditions" because they have no foundation capable of proof, and they are "immemorial" because no one knows who started them.

Many Portuguese writers are not content with the unquestioned achievements of their countrymen—of Gaspar Corte-Real, of Diaz, of Vasco da Gama, and the other great sailors who carried the flag of Portugal into all seas; they dispute, not only with England, but with Spain, priority in the discovery of America; and as their claims refer to the Atlantic seaboard of British America, they call for examination here. The only one which has been put forth in definite form is that, in A. D. 1464, João Vaz Corte-Real (the father of Gaspar), in conjunction with Alvaro Martins Homem, discovered the "Isle of Codfish," and that, in the same year, a royal grant for it was issued to them on condition that they would divide it between them. This claim appeared first in print in the "Historia Insulana" of Antonio Cordeiro, published in 1717. It was copied by Sir John Barrow in his "Chronological List of Voyages, London, 1818," as an established fact; and, from his work, it has been repeated. It has been put forward of late years with much ability by Ernesto do Canto and Luciano Cordeiro, and every little while it crops up as something new and important. The story has been carefully sifted and has been pronounced unfounded by Humboldt, Biddle, Winsor, Kohl, Harrisse, Major, Gaffarel, and almost all scholars of eminence, and it bears its refutation on its face. Martin Behaim spent many years in Portugal and at Fayal in the Azores, and he married the daughter of the governor of that island, but no hint of such a discovery exists upon his globe. If it were true that such a discovery had been made, it would certainly have been known also to the

MYTHICAL DISCOVERIES 61

King of Portugal, who is stated to have made the grant. Such knowledge could not have failed to come out in the endless disputes concerning the line of demarcation, during which all the eminent pilots of Spain and Portugal gave evidence. It would have won the case for Portugal, but it was never pleaded; nor did it come out in the defence of the suit of the heirs of Columbus against the Crown.

The Portuguese writers who advocate these claims cite a large number of documentary authorities, and so give them an appearance of documentary support. But when examined they all fade away into vague general statements or prove irrelevant to the question. It is true that there would be nothing extraordinary if a discovery had been made by João Vaz, seeing that he was addicted to nautical pursuits, and it is also true that Francesco de Souza might, perhaps, have mentioned such a voyage in a manuscript which was lost in the great earthquake at Lisbon, but that is not proof that there ever was such a voyage or that Souza did make such mention. Then the numerous grants cited as having been made are all prospective. They are for islands to be discovered; for the island of the Seven Cities " pretended to have been discovered," and for islands in directions unstated and which the documents show had not actually been discovered.

It might be said without reserve that all theories of discoveries on the northeast coast of America made for Portuguese sailors before Cabot and Gaspar Corte-Real have no foundation in fact. More recently the locality of a supposed pre-Columbian discovery of America has shifted to the Antilles and the South American continent. These are beyond the scope of the present work; but one consideration is fatal to them all. The court of Portugal in 1492 was the resort of the most skilled and active pilots in Europe, and nautical science was cultivated with the keenest interest. The proposals of Columbus were twice submitted to committees of experts on his council by the King and if these claims had any foundation it is impossible to imagine that there was no one in Portugal who knew of these early voyages, or could point out on the early charts those lands and names which have recently been taken to stand for portions of the western world. This question is now academic,—of interest to students of history and not of practical moment,—but then, at the end of the fifteenth century, it was burning in the hearts of men wakening up to the new learning, and we can never scan the charts of Andrea Bianco or others of his day with the eager curiosity of the daring seamen of Lisbon and the Atlantic Islands of Portugal; nor can we read as they could the archaisms and conventionalities of their methods of cartography. All the mass of citation piled up upon the question on the authority of Azorean documents and writers is not proof, nor even presumptive proof. On candid examination it leaves upon the mind the effect of disproof.

The voyages of the Basques have, strange to say, received, in proportion, more attention from Canadian writers than from the writers of Europe. The claims of the Portuguese have attracted little notice in Canada, though far more plausible. There is a romantic mystery enshrouding this inscrutable people in which all things become possible. In a collection of documents relating to the history of Canada published by the government of the Province of Quebec, among the earliest (No. 4), under the heading "Basques in the Gulf of St. Lawrence," is one to the effect that although "there are no records of the first voyages of the French there are nevertheless ample proofs that they made several voyages of great extent prior to the discoveries of the Portuguese and Spaniards." It continues, "the Basques and the Bretons have been for several centuries the only people who follow the whale and cod fisheries, and it is very remarkable that Sebastian Cabot when he discovered the coast of Labrador found there the name Bacallos which in the Basque language signifies codfish." This extract is said to be from an old manuscript without a date, although it is placed in the collection at A. D. 1497 to the confusion of the unwary reader.

MYTHICAL DISCOVERIES 63

That somebody, somewhere, and at some time, held such opinions is not important and hardly demands a position in the forefront of any collection of historical documents. The Basques and Bretons were early on the coasts of Canada, as will appear in the following chapter, and the fact is admitted by all; but that they were there before Cabot is disproved by the evidence of the greatest Basque sailor of the age of Columbus. In like manner we read in an important Canadian history that while Jacques Cartier is " generally regarded as the first who penetrated into the interior of Canada," that country had then been already known to the French, and that the Basques had, one hundred years before Columbus, not only discovered Newfoundland and its fishing banks, but Canada as well. Moreover, that a Basque sailor, familiar with the Newfoundland coasts, had imparted the information to Columbus.

Such statements as these tending to detract from the achievements of Columbus, Cabot, Cartier, and other great sailors should not be made excepting upon good evidence. They have often been disproved, nevertheless they are so incessantly repeated that we seem to be perilously near another " immemorial tradition " in Canada, and it is necessary in a volume concerning discoveries on the northeast coast of America to consider them once more.

During the six weary years of poverty and disappointment passed by Columbus while urging his proposals for the discovery of lands across the Atlantic; while his theories were examined and reported upon by commissions of men versed in all the nautical knowledge existing in Spain and Portugal, no one arose and said that Basque sailors had been fishing for a hundred years upon the coasts of Bacallaos in the far northwest across the ocean. If any sailors had been fishing there it was not for amusement; it must have been a commercial enterprise, and they had to dispose of their fish. They could not have kept the knowledge secret; for the vessels, of necessity, would have to frequent many ports to dispose of the immense quantities of their catch. Such treasures of ocean could no more have been kept secret then than the treasures of California or Australia in our day. Let it be supposed that they made the attempt to keep the secret to themselves. Juan de La Cosa was a Basque, one of themselves, born at Santoña on the Bay of Biscay, not only a sailor, but a ship owner. As owner and captain of the *Santa Maria* he chartered her to Columbus, and sailed in her on the memorable first voyage of 1492. In the year 1500 he was employed by the King, Ferdinand, to make a map of the world. This map is still extant, and upon those very coasts of British America, said to have been frequented by Basque sailors for a hundred years, he wrote for the King of Spain's own eye "Mar descubierto por les Yngleses" (Sea discovered by the English), and he placed English flags all along the northeast coast.

It is unquestioned that the Basques both of Spain and France were from early times the boldest seamen along the coasts of the Bay of Biscay and were skilled to dare the dangers of the most storm-vext region of the turbulent Western Ocean. It is not disputed that at the period now treated upon they were the most successful whale-hunters, and that they followed the whales far out to sea when, in the middle of the sixteenth century, they became scarce near the coast. It is quite true that they were capable of discovering America so far as seamanship is concerned, but that they did discover America is an assertion without any basis of proof.

As soon as the evidence, or what is called evidence, is examined, it fades away into that kind of assertion euphemistically called "immemorial tradition." These traditions were diligently inquired into by Martin Fernandez de Navarrete for his great collection of voyages and discoveries published in 1825-37 at Madrid under royal authority. He searched the records of San Sebastian and the ports of Guipuzcoa, and of the other Basque provinces, most thoroughly, and found no traces of Basque voyages until after the return of Stephen Gomez in 1526. He concluded, however, that from the year 1502 Basque,

MYTHICAL DISCOVERIES 65

conjointly with Breton fishermen, began to frequent the coasts of Newfoundland. A similar inquiry was made by Mr. (now Sir Clements) Markham. He visited every important town in the Basque provinces of Spain, from Cape Penas to the French frontier. The results were presented to the Zoölogical Society of London. He found that whales began to be scarce in the seventeenth century and then the whalers began to make long voyages. Mateas de Echeveste, who some suppose to have discovered Newfoundland before Columbus, did really frequent that coast, but his series of twenty-eight voyages began in the year 1545, and Columbus died in 1506.

The most definite form in which the Basque claim of priority appears is that Juan de Echaide, of San Sebastian, in the province of Guipuzcoa, discovered the Banks as well as the Island of Newfoundland at the end of the fourteenth century. No authority is found upon which the statement is based. This being accepted for fact, some proceed to confirm it by the surprising assertion that the "Canadian Indians would not trade with the French in any other language than Basque." Support for this grotesquely absurd statement is offered by references to "Pierre de l'Ancre," "Tableau de l'inconstance des mauvais anges," and to "Leonce Goyetche," "St. Jean de Luz Historique et pittoresque," Bayonne, 1856. Reference is also made to Father Lallemant (Jesuit Relations, A. D. 1626), who wrote: "The Indians [of Acadia] call the sun Jesus, and it is belived the Basques, who formerly frequented these places, introduced the name."

The preceding are claims on behalf of the Basques of Spain (Guipuzcoans), but similar claims are put forward for the French Basques of St. Jean de Luz, of Siboure, and of other Basque ports in the south of France. These are, if possible, vaguer still, and no name or approximate date is given. It is only that "there is reason to believe," or that "the respective writers believe that the Basques discovered Newfoundland one hundred years before the voyage of Columbus." The passage in the "Jugemens d'Oléron," sometimes referred to, is such a statement in the work "Les Us et Coutumes de la Mer," dated 1671, and is a note upon the text of the main work.

Margry (Navigations Françaises), without committing himself to their truth, dwells at length upon the claims of the French Basques; but gives only the usual traditions. He quotes from a manuscript memorial, purporting to have been presented, in 1710, by the merchants of St. Jean de Luz and of Siboure, in which it was set forth that, from time immemorial, the Basques of France had been whalers, and that they had gone westwards until they came upon the Banks of Newfoundland, and found a prodigious quantity of fish. This memorial is not authenticated by names, and gives no date to the time of discovery. No one disputes that the Basques of France also frequented the coasts of Newfoundland and Canada at a very early date. What remains to be proved is that they went there before A. D. 1501.

In connection with these theories, reference is sometimes made to the Atlas of Andrea Bianco, A. D. 1436. It was urged by Formaleoni, in 1783, and has been pressed, in connection with these mythical voyages anterior to Columbus, that, on the seventh sheet, is an island called "Scorafixa or Stokafixa," very far west in the Atlantic, and corresponding to the position of Newfoundland. An examination of the photographic fac-similes in the Lenox Library, New York, made with the kind permission of Mr. Eames, the learned librarian, does not confirm this statement. The place is not "far to the west of the Atlantic," but on the northwest corner of the map, and the edges of the map cut it. It is to the north of *Stilanda*, which is also cut by the edge, but which stands for the Shetlands, as is shown in the works on northern voyages, while the land to the north may be either the Faroe Islands, or Iceland. The name on the island is *ya Novercha stockfis*. To follow this inquiry further would lead to a discussion of the Zeni voyages. For our present purpose it is sufficient to say that both these lands (Novercha and Stilanda), are close to the coast of Nor-

MYTHICAL DISCOVERIES 67

way. The position of both absolutely excludes the western Atlantic, or the possibility of any portion of America being intended. These northern islands belonged to Norway, and were the sources of the supply of stockfish (cod) at that period. Lelewel, commenting upon the map, observes that "these [Novercha and Stockfis] are not two names, but a note to the effect that the stockfish exported from Norway is caught there."

The claims of the French of Dieppe do not call for remark in this volume, inasmuch as they have reference to the coast of South America, and to the adventures of Jean Cousin and Vincent Pinzon, his insubordinate lieutenant. The claim made for Skolno, the Polish pilot, in the services of Christian I. of Denmark, may also be passed over, for the voyage has no basis of authentic fact. The expeditions of Prince Madoc of Wales, with which Hakluyt opens his American Voyages, are supposed to relate to Florida, and the Welsh-speaking Indians are taken to be either the Tuscaroras, the Shawnees, or the Mandans. The subject is better left with the poets. The Zeni voyages are accepted by some, but their authenticity has not been maintained; and in any case, they can be most conveniently discussed in connection with the voyages of the Northmen, nor is it profitable to discuss what "unknown voyagers" may have done, save to remark that from all the indications existing, their field was in the southern regions discovered by Columbus.

A discussion of the early traces of Portuguese and Basque sailors upon these coasts leads, naturally, into an inquiry into the meaning of the two very early names, Labrador and Bacallaos. There is no completely satisfactory account of the origin of the name of Labrador. Its position varies on the earliest maps. Sometimes it is on the coast of Greenland, and sometimes on the present Labrador. The coast of Newfoundland, which in early maps is a part of the mainland, is at first Terra Corterealis, but the name Bacallaos is soon substituted. To the north of these names is Terra Laboratoris, Labrador, Lavrador, or Lavradore. Labrador is Spanish, and Lavrador is Portuguese, meaning an agricultural labourer, and to the present day in Mexico a peon, or field hand, is called a "labrador." In the letter of Pietro Pasqualigo to his brothers at Venice, dated October 19, 1501, he gives a description of seven of the natives, men, women, and children, who, only a few days before, had been brought to Lisbon by one of Corte-Real's vessels. Fifty others, he adds, are expected every hour to arrive on the other caravel. Cantino's letter to the Duke of Ferrara confirms this, and he states that he has "seen, touched and examined them," and that they are "bigger than our people, and with well formed limbs to correspond." Pasqualigo adds: "This most serene King hopes to derive very great profit from the new land, both from the wood for ships, of which they have need, and from the men, who *will be excellent for labour, and the best slaves that have hitherto been obtained.*" This recorded opinion of the King has, since Biddle's time, been generally accepted as the origin of the name; or the name was, at least, supposed to have been derived from this extensive kidnapping. Other navigators in the North, in later years, were content to take a few natives to train them as interpreters; but this voyage developed into a slaving voyage, hence the name "labourer's coast" was almost equivalent to "slave coast," and with reference to Corte-Real's voyage it was appropriate.

Many other etymologies have been suggested; but only one of them has any probable ground. Mr. Harrisse mentions a manuscript map at Wolfenbuttel, ascribed to A. D. 1534, which bears a legend, referred to the English discovery of Labrador, as follows: "And as the one who first gave notice of it was a labourer of the Azores they [the English] gave it the name." He quotes, in connection with this, a passage in the manuscript "Islario" of Alonzo de Santa Cruz. "It was called the land of Labrador, because he who gave notice and indication of it was a labourer from the Azores to the King of England when he sent on discovery Anthony Gabot [*sic*], an English pilot, and the father of Sebastian Gabot, at present Pilot-Major of your Majesty." To this may be added the fact recorded in the English records that, on March 19, 1501, King Henry VII. granted a new patent of discovery and exclusive trade, covering the same ground as that of John Cabot, to Richard Warde, Thomas Ashehurst, and John Thomas of Bristol, conjointly with João Fernandez. Francisco Fernandez, and João Gonzales of the Azores. It is also recorded that, on September 26, 1502, a pension of £10, during pleasure, was granted to Francis Fernandez and John Gonzales for services relating to the new lands, and the Portuguese writers say that documents in a law-suit exist in the Azores, to the effect that João Fernandez, *labourer,* of Terceira, went away in company with Pedro de Barcellos " to discover new lands," and was away for three years, and on his return found his property occupied by somebody else.

The dates of these documents are not given; but another Portuguese writer states that, in 1491-92, King John of Portugal commissioned Pedro de Barcellos and João Fernandez Lavrador to discover lands to the northwest. If they had found anything the same King John would have known it, and it would have modified his disappointment at the success of Columbus. He could not have failed to have put in an effective objection to the extensive claims of Columbus and of Spain. All the demarcation negotiations would have proceeded upon other lines. The advocates of the Azorean theory differ as to whether Lavrador was the family name or the name of the business of this discoverer. The name Lavrador was not given by Corte-Real, and is not on the Cantino map. It appears first on the King map of 1502—an unquestioned Portuguese map—and, in his latest book, " Terre Neuve," Mr. Harrisse conclusively argues that any connection of any English voyage with the name Labrador must be rejected. The name is on the Oliveriana map of 1503, on the Maggiolo map of 1511, and, though differing in location, soon became established on the maps.

The natives carried off by Corte-Real were not Esquimaux, but, from the descriptions given by the Italian letter writers, were Algonquins to the south, or Beothiks (commonly called Red Indians) of Newfoundland. These also were of Algonquin stock, and were probably akin to the Montagnais of the mainland. They were mercilessly slaughtered during the two following centuries by the Europeans of all nations, who resorted to the coasts for fish. None were spared; men, women, and children fared alike. The Beothiks retired into the wilderness fastnesses of the island, where they could live on the abundant supply of game and fish. Whenever they were seen by the whites they were shot. For two hundred years this wretched people were hunted to extermination, until, too late, the conscience of the English was aroused. No overtures could then induce the scattered families to hold any communication with the whites, whom they doubtless regarded as perfidious and malignant beings. Famine and disease reduced their numbers, until, some time in the year 1827, the remains of the last family were found at Red Indian Lake in the centre of the island. They died without making any sign for assistance to the white people, who would then gladly have done anything to relieve them. In 1819 a Beothik woman was captured and treated with great kindness. She was taught English, and called Mary March, from the month of her capture. Through her, attempts were made to win the confidence of her people, but she died of consumption the following year. A miniature portrait, drawn by the wife of the governor, is the only existing record of the type of a deeply injured race.

Taking all the evidence together it would seem that the theory generally accepted is the true one. The kidnapping of these poor people impressed all the chroniclers.

The name Bacallaos, applied in the early maps to Newfoundland and Acadia, has been the subject of very keen controversy. The initial difficulty arose from a sentence in the "Decades" of Peter Martyr, where he gives an account of Sebastian Cabot's voyage. He says, as if

MYTHICAL DISCOVERIES 71

reporting Cabot's statement: "Cabot himself named those lands Bacallaos, because, in the surrounding sea, he found a certain kind of large fishes resembling tunnies, so-called by the inhabitants, in such great multitudes that they sometimes impeded his ships." There is nothing said about Basques. Lescarbot imported the Basques into the question a hundred years later. The passage seems to state that Cabot found the "inhabitants" using the word *bacallaos* for a fish which swarmed on their coasts, and named the land from the word found in their mouths. Martyr, apparently, did not know anything more about these fishes than that they resembled tunnies (tinnos—thynnos), but at that time, and long before, the common people of Spain called the codfish, or haddock, of the north of Europe "bacallaos,"—the Romance equivalent of the Teutonic "stockfish." It is clear, however, that the word is pure Spanish, and that the equivalent Romance form had long been in use throughout the south of Europe; such a statement, if really made by Cabot, would have been equal to the admission that Spaniards had been there before him, whereas the whole purport of the communication was that he had been the first discoverer of the region. Careful consideration of the passage will suggest that what Cabot really said was that these swarming fish were the same as those which were used as food by the peasants of Spain, and called by them *bacallaos;* for Cabot was then living at Seville, and doubtless was speaking in Spanish. Such a statement would tend to magnify the importance of the country discovered. Martyr probably misunderstood, or forgot, the bearing of the word, and transferred to the people of Newfoundland the word long in use by the country people of Spain.

Again, we know that, upon the first voyage, "Cabot saw no man." The second voyage was also purely an English expedition, commissioned by the English Crown, and fitted out and manned by Englishmen. Cabot was not a Spaniard, but a resident in England, and it is impossible he would have given a Spanish name to the country he discovered for the King of England. With far greater probability Kohl asserts that the Portuguese gave the name; for it is first found on Pedro Reinel's map (1505) as *y dos Bocalhas,* in Portuguese form, and in Ruysch's map (1508) it appears in Latin (*insula Baccalauras*). Cabot did not go to Spain until 1512, after that map had been four years published. He was in charge of the official maps of Spain, and what he may have done was to adopt the name on the Spanish maps because it was characteristic of the region.

No argument or claim was ever put forward on account of this name *Bacallaos* until Lescarbot, in his " History of New France" (1612), sets out to explain the words Canada and " Bacalos." As to the first, he differs from Cartier; and is hopelessly wrong; and, as to the second, he says the name was given by the Basques of France (nos Basques), " who call a codfish *becaillos.*" He adds that the Acadian Indian name is apegé—it is now pegoo in Micmac, evidently the same word. If it be agreed that the Newfoundland Indians were not Micmacs, the vocabularies of Mary March show that their name was *bobboosoret,* and, therefore, as a matter of fact, it is not true that the Indian name was *bacallaos.* Lescarbot is a very lively writer, and must not be taken too seriously, when in his discursive moods.

The word bacallaos is a Romance word, found in all the Romance languages for dried codfish. The curing was formerly done by stretching on sticks and, in the north of Europe, *stockfish* is the expressive name; but the Mediterranean nations, who derive their languages from the Latin, express the same idea in derivative forms of the classic word *baculum,* or in post-classical use *baculus,* a stick. In Portuguese it is in the singular number bacalhao, in Spanish bacallao, in Italian baccalâ, in French bacaliau. The Basque word is bacaillaba, and is evidently a derivative from the Romance word. The Basques did not impose the names of their archaic tongue upon the nations around. Their name for oyster is the Spanish *ostra,* and their name for whale is the Spanish

MYTHICAL DISCOVERIES 73

balena; both Romance words. Others might be cited from Basque vocabularies, but these are sufficient to show that bacaillaba is not exceptional in its derivation.

No sooner were the northeastern waters of America made known by the voyages of Cabot and Corte-Real than Portuguese, Spanish, and Breton vessels thronged there for the cod fishery; and Basque vessels for cod fishing to a certain extent, and later for whaling. Nearly a hundred years passed, of trading and fishing along the coast, before there was a permanent settlement, and whatever the Indians may have known of European words could easily have been learned then. Father Lallemant, in the Jesuit Relations for 1626, as already observed, says the Acadian Indians call the sun Jesus, and that they learned it from the Basques. If so, they had a hundred years to learn it in without antedating Columbus. The same remark applies to Lescarbot's extravagant statement that so long and so intimate was the connection between the Basques and the Indians of Newfoundland and the Gulf shores, that the language of the latter was half Basque; and this expanded by another writer into a statement that the Indians would not trade in any other language.

Attempts have been made to set up a philological connection between the Basque and the American languages, but without success. After a long examination of the question, M. Julien Vinson recorded his conclusion that it is abundantly clear that no real relationship exists between them. The Basque belongs to the agglutinative type, and so do the American languages, but so also do the Japanese, the Manchu, and many other Asiatic groups. The subject cannot be followed further in the present work. If, before the lost continent Atlantis disappeared in the ocean, the Basques were the chief people of western Europe, and if they then came to America and founded the Huron-Iroquois group of nations, it is too long ago to detract from the fame of Cabot or Corte-Real or Columbus. It is a speculation of dreamland, and beyond the region of historical geography.

CHAPTER VI

PRIVATE ADVENTURERS—CABOT TO CARTIER

WITH the departure of the expedition of 1498, John Cabot and two of his sons—Lewis and Sancius—disappear from English history. Sebastian seems to have remained in England, and supported himself, as Columbus did for years, by drawing maps. He emerged from obscurity again in 1512, when he was employed by Henry VIII. to draw a map of Gascony and Guyenne, to be used for a campaign in the south of France, projected by the English and Spanish monarchs. The privileges granted to the Cabots were annulled by letters patent to others dated March 19, 1501. The Cabot grants are not mentioned by name; but a monopoly is granted to the new patentees with a warning to all other subjects of the King not to disturb them in their title and possession. A clause was added in the draft extending the same warning specially to any who might interfere with them under colour of any concession to any foreigner or foreigners made previously under the great seal. This clause stands on the record with a line drawn through it as if erased. It was not necessary—the Cabots were excluded by the general grant and prohibition, and the work of discovery was continued by others.

Although a few of the more enterprising of the merchants of Bristol followed up the voyages to the " new land," the real significance of Cabot's discovery was only slowly realised by the English nation. This is not surprising, because the English had at that time a large and steady trade for codfish with Iceland, for which they paid in manufactured goods. English vessels carried the dried fish to all the continental markets, and Bristol was

CABOT TO CARTIER 75

the chief emporium of a trade of very much more importance then than it afterwards became, for all Europe was Roman Catholic, and church fasts were numerous and better observed. Stockfish, or *bacalao*, was a staple food in great demand, and its price was high; nevertheless, those who ventured their stocks of "caps, laces, points, and other trifles" in Cabot's voyage, as they supposed to the rich country of Cathay, not only lost their money, but could see no prospect for a new outlet for English manufactures. Gradually it dawned upon them that in the seas swarming with codfish, not very much farther off than Iceland, they had treasures richer than the Spanish Indies. The west of England people took up the trade and undersold the Iceland fish so that the northern trade rapidly decayed in proportion as the Newfoundland trade increased. Difficulties were constantly arising also with the Danish Government, and the English fishermen in the northern seas were hampered by foreign imposts and regulations from which the Newfoundland fishing fleet was free. All this the English people, with characteristic slowness, took time to realise.

The patent of March 19, 1501, which annulled the Cabot patents, was granted to Richard Warde, Thomas Ashehurst, and John Thomas, of Bristol, with whom were associated João Fernandez, Francisco Fernandez, and João Gonzales of the Azores. On December 9, 1502, new letters patent were issued to some of the former holders; viz., to Thomas Ashehurst, João Fernandez, Francisco Fernandez, João Gonzales, and Hugh Elliott, granting very extensive powers and a monopoly for forty years. Patents cost King Henry nothing, and he took no share or risk himself. All expenses were borne by the patentees. The voyages made under these grants were at first led by the Portuguese; and we know at least of one voyage under the patent of 1502, for Robert Thorne of Seville, writing in 1527, to Dr. Leigh (the English Ambassador), says that his father sailed with Hugh Elliott. Of this voyage Robert

Thorne says that "if the mariners would then have been ruled and followed their pilot's minde, there is no doubt but the lands of the West Indies, from whence all the golde cometh, had been ours." Other voyages were made, for there is an entry in the public accounts, "to men of Bristol that founde Th'isle £5." That was on January 7, 1502, and on September 30, of the same year, there is another, "to the merchants of Bristol that have been in the Newe founde Launde, £20." There is an entry the following year (1503), on November 17, "to one that brought hawkes from the Newfounde Island, £1." The following spring (April 8, 1504,) a payment was made "to a preste that goeth to the New Islands, £2." In 1505 (August 25) is another entry showing that the voyages were still going on, "to Clays going to Richmond with wylde catts and popyngays of the Newfound Island for his costs 13/4," and on September 25 the men who brought them over are indicated—"to Portzugales that brought popyngais and catts of the mountaigne and other stuf to the Kinges grace, £5."

It has been supposed by a few writers that Sebastian Cabot was engaged upon some of these voyages, but there is no real ground for thinking so. All the experiences described by Martyr, Ramusio, Gomara, and the other early writers are fully covered by the two Cabot voyages in 1497 and 1498, and, in fact, the impression left by their narratives is that there was only one voyage, that upon which ice was encountered. Stress is laid upon a passage in Stow's Chronicle to the effect that in 1502 three men taken in the new-found islands were brought to the King. Hakluyt twice records the incident, first in his "Divers Voyages," as having occurred in 1501, but in his final work, "Principall Navigations," he changed the date, and assigned the capture of the men to the year in which William Purchas was Mayor, and to the fourteenth year of the King—that is, to the year 1498-99. Mr. Harrisse has collated these passages most convincingly, and if Hakluyt's authority be accepted, these natives must have been brought on

Cabot's second voyage. If, however, anyone should incline to accept the authority of Stow, Mr. Harrisse demonstrates that Cabot was not upon the voyage of 1502, because the new patent granted to Warde and the Portuguese was then in force, and he puts the matter beyond doubt by bringing forward, for the first time, a document proving that on September 25, 1502, the King granted a pension of £10 each, yearly, during pleasure, to Francisco Fernandez and João Gonzales, " in consideration of the true service which they have done unto us to our singular pleasure as captaines unto the newe founde lande." It was the Azoreans then who commanded in the expedition under the patent, and, moreover, as these same Azoreans were among the patentees of December, 1502, for a monopoly of forty years, there cannot be any way of including Sebastian Cabot in any voyage after that of 1498. That he was upon the voyage of 1498 we may be assured quite apart from his own statements, since Ferdinand of Aragon took him into the service of Spain because of his personal knowledge of Bacallaos.

The preceding considerations exclude also all possibility of an expedition in 1508, despatched by King Henry VII., and commanded by Sebastian Cabot. The argument for this rests mainly upon a manuscript report made by Marcantonio Contarini to the Signiory of Venice in 1536, twenty-seven years after the event. King Henry VII. was not one to fit out at his own cost another expedition of discovery, with three hundred men, and if he did so, there would, of necessity, be some trace of it in the public records or accounts. The conclusion of Kohl must be accepted as correct, " that there is nothing to show that Sebastian Cabot entered on a new enterprise for a long time; while others, stimulated by the fame of his discoveries, followed his track," or rather, let us add, his father's track.

Following up the traces of English enterprise on the northern coasts of America we come to an incidental remark of Richard Eden that Henry VIII. " furnished and sent forth certain ships under the governance of

Sebastian Cabot, yet living, and one Sir Thomas Perte, whose faint heart was the cause that voyage took none effect." The wording is peculiar, and taken with the context, it conveys the idea that, whatever expedition is referred to, it was abortive from the beginning and did not actually sail. The statement is repeated by later writers, but is controverted by the fact that at the time stated, about A. D. 1517, Cabot was high in office in Spain, where the following year he was made Grand Pilot. This is the voyage in which he is reported to have reached $67\frac{1}{2}°$ N., "where he found the sea open, on June 11"; and recent writers, still improving on that impossible feat, make him enter Hudson's Strait and pass into the Bay one hundred years before Hudson. As if that were not enough, he is made by some to pass up Fox Channel to $67\frac{1}{2}°$ until Sir Thomas Pert's faint heart failed him. So easy is it to sail ships on library globes, where the ice does not show! The Canadian Government sent expeditions into the Bay in 1884 and 1887, with steam vessels fitted specially for Arctic voyages and commanded by experienced sailors. It was a month later before they could enter the strait. The best commentary on this mythical voyage was made only four years after, in 1521, when the Livery Companies of London protested against being assessed for a voyage to the west, projected by King Henry VIII. and Cardinal Wolsey, to be conducted by Sebastian Cabot, who was to be brought from Spain. They protested that "it was a sore risk to jeopard five ships with men and goods, trusting to one man, called as we understand, Sebastyan, who as we here say, was never in that land hym self," but reports what he has heard his father and others say.

But all the while the west of England fishermen kept on sailing to Newfoundland in increasing numbers, so that in A. D. 1522 the Vice-Admiral Fitz William thought it necessary to send armed ships to the mouth of the channel to meet the returning vessels and protect them from French privateers. The competition of the French and Portuguese forced the English out of their old channels of trade and opened their eyes to the abundant treasures which John Cabot's discovery had placed at their disposal. Their neglect was a benefit to the world, for all shared in the exhaustless new food supply.

In 1527 King Henry VIII sent out an expedition, consisting of two ships, under John Rut. He was an officer of the incipient Royal Navy, and the object was to discover the regions of the Grand Khan by going further to the west. One of the ships was wrecked near the Straits of Belle-Isle, where, in lat. 53° N., they encountered "many great islands of ice," and durst go no further. These particulars are interesting, because 53° is the latitude, on Labrador, where some suppose Cabot to have made his landfall in 1497, and to have found a semi-tropical climate a month earlier in the year. The other vessel, the *Mary of Guilford,* then turned south and visited, on August 3, a "good haven in Newfoundland, called St. John, where they found eleven sails of Normandy, one of Brittany and two Portuguese barks, all a fishing." Rut continued on to the south, visiting and landing on the shores of Cape Breton, Nova Scotia, and New England, and returning to England in the beginning of October. He wrote a letter to the King from the harbour of St. John, on August 3, and sent it home by an English ship. It has been preserved by Purchas, and is the first letter on record sent to England from America. In the thirty-third year of Henry VIII, the first Act of Parliament was passed making mention of Newfoundland, called therein "Newland," and, as pointed out by Prowse, it is also the first English statute referring to America.

One of the English voyages during this period is the oddest on record. Master Hore, an enthusiastic gentleman geographer, persuaded some thirty gentlemen, mostly lawyers, " of the Innes of Court and of the Chancerie," to get up an expedition for discovery in the west. They sailed in 1536, and, after divers interesting observations, the provisions they brought with them gave out while they were on the shores of Newfoundland. Famine grew to such a height that one of the crew killed his mate while they were digging for roots. This being discovered, the captain assembled the crew and made "a notable oration," the heads of which Hakluyt records with much approval, pointing out the wickedness of eating each other, and exhorting them to repentance and to prayer for relief. The famine increased and they agreed "to cast lots who should be killed." The narrative goes on, "and such was the mercie of God that the same night there arrived a French ship in that port well furnished with vittaile." So they seized the French ship by a ruse, and, changing vessels, returned to England. These providential Frenchmen were sailors, and had come out, not for geographic study, but for a cargo of food, and did not need to eat each other on a coast where the sea swarms with fish, and the woods abound in game; so a few months afterwards they also arrived safely home, and made a claim on King Henry VIII. for damages, which he paid up liberally. This is the only naval expedition managed by lawyers to be found in the records of these coasts, and their experiences and rules of procedure were unique.

This entertaining episode leads up to the observation that the French, and especially the Bretons and Normans, recognised the value of the fisheries of Newfoundland and Acadia before the English, and in the sixteenth century exploited them to a far greater extent. On a Portuguese chart (1514-1520), to be seen at Munich, Cape Breton is laid down as the land discovered by the Bretons, and on Ribeiro's Spanish official chart the same region is inscribed "land of the Bretons." Cape Breton is called in Ramusio the "Cape of the Bretons," because they made it the central point of their fishery from the earliest period, as their operations extended chiefly along the Acadian coast and the south coast of Newfoundland. Indeed, we find the expanse of sea marked off by Cape Race and Cape Canso called, by Alonzo de Santa Cruz, the "Bay of the Bretons." The Bretons of St. Malo and the Normans of Dieppe were on the coast as early as

Ribeiro's Map, A.D. 1529

1504, the year after the last voyage of the Corte-Reals. The accounts of the voyage of Jean Denys of Honfleur, in 1506, and of Captain Velasco, often quoted from Charlevoix, are, says that historian, so confused and so much mixed up with fabulous matter as to be very doubtful. That is true as to Velasco, but Ramusio in "Discorso d'un Gran' Capitaine," refers to the voyage of Denys, and mentions the name of the pilot Gamart, and Harrisse found a MS. in the National Library at Paris with the following direction: "Let a note be made of the mark of my boats and barks which I leave in Newfoundland in the haven of Jean Denys 'called Rougenoust'" (the present Renews). The voyage in 1508 of Thomas Aubert in the ship *La Pensée,* owned by Ango of Dieppe, is well authenticated. He attempted to found a colony in Newfoundland, but it was unsuccessful. Several voyages seem to have been made, and Aubert was the first French captain to carry natives to France. It is recorded by Eusebius that in A. D. 1509, "Seven wild men were brought from that island (which is called the New Land) to Rouen with their canoe, clothing and weapons." The story, however, that Aubert in conjunction with Verrazano sailed eighty leagues up the St. Lawrence River and gave it that name has no foundation.

There are many incidental notices during the years intervening between 1504 and Cartier's first voyage which show that a large and increasing fishery was carried on in the new lands of the west from Breton and Norman ports. The most striking is a fact recorded by Navarrete that, in A. D. 1511, Queen Joanna of Spain commissioned Juan de Agramonte to go on a voyage to Bacallaos "to discover the secret of that country." Whether he really sailed or not is not known, but the fact that the French were then frequenting the coast is established by instructions given him to engage two pilots from Brittany "who are well acquainted with those parts." The same fact is established by the readiness with which the Emperor Charles in 1526 listened to the proposals of Nicholas Don, a Breton fisherman, who "had come upon new lands to the south of Bacallaos." Herrera records the conditions, no results followed, but the general admission of the special familiarity of the Breton sailors with that region is apparent.

The attempt made by Baron de Lery in A. D. 1517 does not rest on any solid basis, and it seems in itself problematical. Many recent histories contain reports of such an expedition, but Charlevoix simply notices it as a report incidental to the voyage of La Roche and refers it to A. D. 1508. The animals found on the island in later years were placed there by the Portuguese about A. D. 1553. This was related to Edward Haies in 1563 while Sir Humphrey Gilbert's expedition lay in St. John's harbour by a Portuguese sailor who was present when it was done. In 1523 a Captain Coo made prize of a Newfoundland fishing ship of Rouen, laden with fish and tackle, and in that year five vessels from La Rochelle went to Newfoundland. The French fishing fleet on that coast far exceeded that of the English and, in these early years, amounted to seventy or eighty sail, fitted out in all the chief ports in the north of France.

The Portuguese were, however, for a long time the most enterprising in developing the fisheries of the New Land, and their chief field of action was on the east coast. Representatives of the Corte-Real family held the hereditary title of "Governors of Terra Nova," until the direct line became extinct. It has been shown above that the first English voyages, after Cabot's second expedition, were led by Portuguese captains from the Azores. Very shortly afterwards a company was organised by the merchants of Terceira in the Azores and Aveiro and Vianna in Portugal for carrying on the fishery in an organised manner and establishing a colony. The business grew so rapidly that in 1506 King Emmanuel passed an edict that one-tenth of the profits of the fishing vessels from Newfoundland trading to Vianna and Aveiro should be paid to the Royal Customs. Nothing is recorded with any definiteness concerning these attempts at colonisation and, in fact, it is not probable

CABOT TO CARTIER 83

that they went beyond the erection of permanent fishing stages to be available year after year when the vessels went back in the spring. Still some serious efforts must have been made, and there are traces of an attempt to colonise Cape Breton from Vianna in 1525. Niganis, now Ingonish, is said by De Laet to have been a Portuguese settlement, and he states that the settlers moved away because of the cold. From Aveiro alone sixty vessels went every year to Newfoundland, and later, in 1550, the number increased to 150. From Mira, a town near Aveiro, or from the River Mira in the south of Portugal. Mira River and Mira Bay doubtless received their names, showing that the Portuguese had been active in Cape Breton at one time. They searched out the east coast of Newfoundland for convenient harbours, and explored the coast of Labrador in the track of Gaspar Corte-Real. Many names on the east coast, such as Cape Race (Raso) the flat cape, Cape Spear (Espera), Cape St. Francis (San Francisco), Cape Freels (Frey Luis), Fogo Island, Bonavista (Boā Vista), Bonaventure (Boā Ventura), Bacallhao Island, Conception Bay, Carbonear (Cape Carvoeiro), Fermeuse Harbour (Fermoso), still attest their presence in early days.

But while much credit must be conceded to the Portuguese explorers and fishermen in opening up, in conjunction with the Breton fishermen, the coasts of Newfoundland and Acadia, there is no ground for supposing that they had any knowledge of the St. Lawrence River, or of the Gulf, before Cartier's voyages. They were (after the Corte-Reals) fishermen visiting the coast annually for the cod fishery, and the Atlantic coasts had all the fish they could desire. It was trade, not knowledge, they were interested in, and although the Gulf also abounded in fish, the Atlantic coast abounded yet more. The maps of the time confirm this view. Stress has been laid upon a commission, granted A. D. 1521, to João Alvarez Fagundez, but the commission itself is the best answer to those who would extend it up the Gulf of St. Lawrence. The grant was described from the point where the line of demarcation of Tordesillas cut the coast " to the beginning of the land discovered by the Corte-Reals." These limits were never definite, but the line of demarcation was, on the maps, laid down to cut the coast of Nova Scotia. Fagundez' grant extended then from St. Pierre on the south coast of Newfoundland westwards, including Cape Breton and an indefinite part of Nova Scotia. It included the islands along the coast, most of which are known, *e. g.*, St. John, off the point of Cape Breton; St. Pierre, which still retains that name; the Archipelago of the eleven thousand virgins laid down on the old maps as in Fortune Bay; St. Cruz, which is off the Nova Scotia coast in all the old maps, and St. Ann's, on the maps of that time placed off the south coast of Newfoundland. The Archipelago of St. Pantaleon may be either of the groups on the same coast, now known as the Burgeo and the Ramea Islands. In Wytfliet's map the group of islands off that coast are called the Fagundez Islands, and Aguada Bay can be no other than Fortune Bay, which is distinguished also by the three islands, Great and Little Miquelon and St. Pierre, at its mouth. The map of Lazaro Luis (1563) on inspection refutes the theories attempted to be built upon it. The configuration of the gulf and river is from Cartier, and in another Portuguese map of similar type (Homem's) made in 1558 (five years later) Cartier's names are given.

The Spaniards did very little to develop the northeast coast, for it fell, as they thought, outside the limits of their sphere of influence; and, moreover, the West Indies and Gulf of Mexico occupied all their attention. It is on record that Ferdinand sent for Juan Dornelos in A. D. 1500 to plan an expedition which it is supposed was intended to find out what Cabot had discovered. The sequence of the summons is not known. Later, in 1511, when Queen Joanna commissioned Juan de Agramonte to prepare an expedition to the New Land, he was to found a colony there without infringing on the territory of Portugal. Only subjects of the Queen (Castilians) were to be taken, excepting the two Breton pilots. Of this project also no further records have survived. The subject must, however, have been constantly in the minds of the Spanish sovereigns, for the following year King Ferdinand invited Sebastian Cabot into his service, and he was meditating another expedition to the same region when he died in A. D. 1516. Doubtless there were fishing voyages of private merchants to the Banks, but we do not read of them, and the next attempt of the Government was not made until A. D. 1525, by the expedition of Stephen Gomez. It is worthy of note that in the negotiations for the treaty of Utrecht in 1712 the claims of the Spaniards upon the fisheries of Newfoundland were based upon ancient fishing rights of the Guipuzcoans, without mention of any other part of Spain.

Compared with the Bretons and Portuguese the Spanish Basques (Guipuzcoans and Viscayans) were late comers upon the coast, and that is borne out by the testimony of the Basques themselves, for whenever they pass from generalities to particulars, their dates are later than Stephen Gomez' voyage. A memorial in a lawsuit by the son of Martin de Echevete claims that his father was the first Spaniard to go to Newfoundland, and that his first voyage was made in A. D. 1545, after which he made twenty-eight voyages up to A. D. 1599. Again in A. D. 1561 in a suit for Church dues, in St. Sebastian, some of the witnesses were very old men, and they testified that the Newfoundland fisheries had been resorted to for only a few years before that time by vessels from that port, the chief port of Guipuzcoa. This confirms the memorial of Echevete. Others put the date back to A. D. 1540, but said that the fisheries were discovered in 1525, which was the year of Gomez' voyage. In 1697 evidence was taken at St. Sebastian concerning the assumption by the French of a right to exclude the Spaniards from the fisheries. One of the witnesses, a Biscayan captain, said that he had known Echaide, who died about 1650, being then eighty years old. The birth, then, of this sailor, who some suppose to have anticipated Columbus, was assigned to about A. D. 1570 by a fellow citizen giving his testimony in the city where both were born. These two are the only Basques who are named as discoverers.

CHAPTER VII

THE VOYAGE OF VERRAZANO

IT seemed, in the early days of discovery, a very irrational supposition that a barrier should extend almost from pole to pole, and shut off Europe from the coveted regions of the Eastern seas. Only by degrees did the truth dawn upon the minds of cosmographers and only with reluctance was it received at last. A village, now a suburb of Montreal, still bears the name "Lachine," telling of belief, as late as the end of the seventeenth century, in a waterway across Canada to Cathay, and the close of the nineteenth century witnessed the final efforts for a northwest passage thither. Western civilisation, chafing under so unreasonable a limitation, is at last cutting for itself the waterway which Nature denied; but for long years the old sailors made confident search up and down the opposing coast for the hidden secret. The belief of these early days was that the land they constantly encountered consisted of islands, through which passages must exist, and therefore we meet constantly the expression "discovery of new islands" when new portions of what we now know to be continental land were reached and reported.

Magellan had found a passage, but it was far to the south, and in 1526 Sebastian· Cabot sailed ostensibly for the same strait, but with the secret intention of searching for a nearer way. Indeed it has been conjectured with much plausibility that he had instructions from the Emperor so to do, and in that way they account for the remarkable fact that, although the expedition grievously miscarried, Cabot never lost the favour of the Emperor during the vexatious litigation which ensued. In truth Sebastian Cabot was a better courtier than sailor, and, when the captains under his command remonstrated that his course was too far to the west, he replied that he had a secret understanding with the Emperor about the course to be followed. For a while he thought he had found the long-sought passage in the La Plata River, and on the maps based on his report the width of that river is enormously exaggerated.

As has been shown, French vessels from the ports of Normandy and Brittany had frequented the coasts of Newfoundland and Acadia since 1504. Unconcerned with the Italian wars which absorbed the attentions and energies of the King and court of France, the merchants pursued their own course in developing the oversea fisheries. In A. D. 1515 Francis I. succeeded to the throne, and his marriage with Claude, the heiress of Bretagne, united that hitherto independent duchy to the crown of France. The formal union did not take place until A. D. 1532, and it was long before a common national sentiment welded the Breton duchy with the rest of the kingdom. Francis was a great patron of science and letters. A prince of his intelligence would in any event have felt the stimulus of the discoveries of the Spaniards in the New World; but a bitter rivalry with Charles V., who had competed successfully against him for the Imperial crown in A. D. 1519, brought on a struggle which lasted during his whole life, and the world beyond the ocean which was infusing new energy into his rival's kingdom excited his jealousy. What the Bretons and Normans had been doing in the West since 1504 had attracted no notice at the royal court. There was little in common between the brave and serious mariners and the equally brave but frivolous soldiers who thronged the court of the French king and poured out their life-blood like water upon the Italian plains.

It is necessary in treating of these times to remember that there were then no royal or national navies. Henry VII. of England made a beginning by building a large royal ship, but it was Henry VIII. who later instituted the Admiralty and royal dockyards and commenced to

VOYAGE OF VERRAZANO 89

make a distinct naval service. It was the same in France. The king had a few galleys and two or three large ships, and he was urged by some of his councillors to found a " sea army." Whenever vessels were wanted the king had to impress them from the merchants who owned them, in Dieppe, or Harfleur, Rochelle, St. Malo, or some other port. The words *armateur,* privateer, corsair, rover, when there were no public armed ships and no permanent naval service, connoted a very different group of ideas from that which they suggest at the present day. They were the only sea forces of their respective monarchs and they were countenanced, if not commissioned, by public authority; but, being volunteers, they paid for their own armament, and reimbursed themselves out of the commerce of the enemies of the state. The archives of Dieppe and Rochelle were destroyed in the bombardments which befell those cities, but it is on record that Jean Ango, a merchant prince of Dieppe, ravaged the Portuguese coast and blockaded Lisbon with his own ships alone. In the succeeding reign of Henry II. in 1555 the King ordered the Admiral Coligny to punish some outrages on French commerce by Flemish ships. It was done by a fleet of fishing ships of Dieppe. They chose their own captains and attacked and destroyed the Flemish fleet. There was no royal fleet to call upon and these fishermen were a volunteer sea army.

War broke out between Francis I. and Charles V. in A. D. 1521, and we learn from Herrera that French corsairs were pillaging the ships from India, as they arrived at the coast of Spain, until a squadron was raised by a levy upon the merchants to repel them. Similar harassing attacks continued in the following year, and the vessels returning from the West Indies had to wait at the Azores for a convoy. In 1523 Herrera chronicles the loss of the treasure ships sent by Cortez from Mexico to Charles V. It was a severe blow. The attack was made only ten leagues from Cape St. Vincent and only one Spanish ship escaped. The

French fleet consisted of six ships of La Rochelle, and thither they conducted their prizes and prisoners. The name of the commander is recorded as "Florin de La Rochelle." It is surprising that in the very same "Decade III." Herrera relates at length the voyage of discovery made in A. D. 1524, by Juan Verrazano in the service of France, without the least suspicion that he and Juan Florin or Florentin were the same person. No one thought of that for nearly two hundred years, until in 1723 Barcia said so. Then was a legitimate opportunity offered for a little of the superabundant scepticism which has characterised recent American history, but strangely enough, the identification has been very generally accepted.

Francis, says Herrera, persuaded by some of his subjects to follow the example of Charles V., for whom every day new lands were being discovered, resolved to send out a French expedition to those western lands which he thought "God had not created for Castilians solely." To this he was the more easily persuaded because the cosmographers of all nations believed there was a passage yet to be discovered, leading from the North Atlantic to the southern ocean of fabulous riches. Juan Verrazano (Giovanni da Verrazano), a Florentine of good family, was chosen as leader. He had been in the East Indies in 1517 and had resided at Cairo and in Syria. He is also said, with less certainty, to have been on the Newfoundland coast in command of a ship with Aubert of Dieppe in A. D. 1508. It may well be surmised that upon the outbreak of the war with Charles V. an enterprising sailor in a seaport like Dieppe, dominated by such men as Jean Ango, should have taken up the career of corsair, or as we now say, *privateer*, and in that way he may have recommended himself to the King; but however that may have been, we meet with him first in a letter preserved by Ramusio, dated at Dieppe July 8, 1524, immediately after his return, and addressed to King Francis I. At that particular juncture the King was not in a position to entertain questions of cosmog-

VOYAGE OF VERRAZANO 91

raphy. The defection of the Constable of Bourbon had developed into an invasion of France, and on July 7, the day prior to the date of Verrazano's letter, Bourbon at the head of an army had entered Provence and was pressing on to the siege of Marseilles. Francis was assembling an army and hurrying to the south, in defence of his kingdom. It is not surprising if the original of Verrazano's letter is not now to be found in the public records, and the absence of it is very slight ground upon which to base a charge of fraud. It is surprising how ready in recent years authors have been to charge deliberate fraud against collectors and compilers like Ramusio and Hakluyt, who could have had no motive but a simple desire for truth. Credulous they may have been, in believing reports of mariners, and ignorant they were, of necessity, about much that we have learned; but there is no reason to impugn their good faith. Nothing but a real love for their subject could have stimulated them to such literary labour.

Verrazano's letter appears first in Ramusio's collection of voyages, published at Venice in 1556. From thence it was translated by Hakluyt and published in his "Divers Voyages" in 1582. Another copy of the letter, known in 1767 to be in existence, was found and first printed in 1841. These two copies agree in substance, but in phraseology they differ so much that they could not have been copied one from the other. The two versions are like the evidence of two witnesses who have never met and who testify to the same facts in different language. They are translations into Italian made separately from a French original. That there was a French original Dr. Da Costa proves by many arguments, and especially by an extract from Pinello, a Spanish writer in 1627; and the late Abbé Verreau of Montreal, when searching the French archives for the Canadian Government, reports an incidental statement found in a manuscript in the Bibliothèque Nationale at Paris "that the Memoir of Verrazano was in the possession of Chatillon." The person intended was doubtless the Maréchal de Chatillon, a most important nobleman of that day, a favourite of the King and of the Queen Louise (sometime Regent), and father of the celebrated Admiral Coligny of after fame.

The debt that European literature and science owe to Italy is nowhere more apparent than in the early history of America. Columbus, Vespucci, Cabot, and Verrazano gave to Spain, England, and France their primary claims upon the western continent, and the Italian letter-writers, Soncino, the two Pasqualigos, Cantino, and others have preserved memories of deeds forgotten in the countries which reaped the benefit of the services of their countrymen. The second version of Verrazano's report is found in a letter from one Fernando Carli, at Lyons, addressed to his father in Florence, bearing on its face evidence of its genuineness in its omissions as well as its allusions—a most unaffected and natural letter.

Although the major part of Verrazano's voyage lay along the shores of the present United States, it included also the coasts of Acadia and southern Newfoundland, and is furthermore within the scope of the present volume because upon it the French kings based a primary claim to New France in all its extent. The expedition had been some time in preparation, for we learn, by a letter of the Portuguese ambassador to France to his master King John III., that on the 25th of April, 1523, Verrazano was "going on the discovery of Cathay but had not then left for want of opportunity and because of differences with his men." The ships were watched in the interests of Portuguese merchants, who feared that they were going to Brazil, and we may therefore be sure that the matter was not done in a corner. From Verrazano's letter we learn that four ships sailed and that they were scattered by bad weather. Two—the *Normandie* and the *Dauphine*—were driven back to Brittany in distress. These he refitted and started, first on a cruise along the coast of Spain, which lay right in his track. He went on to Madeira, and, changing his original plan, he continued his voyage with one, the *Dauphine,* alone.

VOYAGE OF VERRAZANO 93

What became of the other ships he nowhere says. He took his final departure on January 17, 1524, from the Desertas—two desolate rocky islands near Madeira, occupied, even now, by only a few hundred fishermen. This locality, he says, is on the extreme verge of the West. It is in fact almost exactly on the prime meridian of these days, and in lat. 32° N. From thence, after the custom of the early sailors, he struck due west on the same parallel across the ocean. He sailed west for twenty-five days, when he encountered a hurricane; then inclining to the north he sailed on for twenty-four days until he found land in lat. 34°, which is close to Cape Fear in North Carolina.

The description which Verrazano gives of the coast and the incidents of his coasting do not fall within the plan of this volume. Of the two able writers who have denied the reality of this voyage one finds it incredible because the description is so inaccurate and the other because it is so accurate; both circumstances being equally held to prove that the writer of the letter appropriated the results of Stephen Gomez' voyage of the following year. After a short excursion to the south, Verrazano sailed northward. Those who have followed his course trace it to Raleigh, N. C., New York, Block Island, Newport, and Portsmouth, N. H. He continued to the east without again landing, along the coast of Maine, Nova Scotia, Cape Breton, and the south and east coast of Newfoundland, to the latitude of 50° N. "Beyond that point," he says, "the Portuguese had already sailed as far as the Arctic Circle without coming to the termination of the land." He had touched the Spanish explorations on the south and the Portuguese on the north, without finding the opening to Cathay he was in search of. At 50° N. he was in the latitude of Dieppe, to which he directly sailed, and arrived there on July 8, 1524.

The copy of Verrazano's letter, sent by Carli to his father, had appended to it "a cosmographical exposition" in which Verrazano sets forth, in some detail, his distances, latitudes, and longitudes. These are of little value. The distances are too great, for they were calculated only by dead reckoning, and must have included the deviations necessary in a voyage close along shore. Again his longitudes are hopelessly out of the way, among other reasons, from the fact that he used Ptolemy's datum of 62½ Italian miles, instead of seventy-five (sixty nautical miles), to a degree, as is really the case. With these data he concludes that he sailed 90 degrees westward to his landfall; whereas, taking the Desertas as 0°, the distance to Cape Fear is only (in round numbers), sixty-one degrees. Scepticism concerning this voyage is singularly unjustifiable, seeing that there could be no motive for forgery. The only country to be benefited was France, and it is not upon French, but upon Italian records that the narrative rests. The only city which might gain some credit is Florence, and the first printed account is by the Venetian Ramusio, and he not only prints the letter, but supports it by his own opinion, and the testimony of "the Gran' Capitaine of Dieppe," that Verrazano was the discoverer of Norumbegue, in his work, only fifteen years after the event. The letter is inserted in his "Decades," by Herrera, a Spaniard, and by Hakluyt, an Englishman, in his "Divers Voyages," "Principall Navigations," and "Western Planting." It is accepted by Ribaut (1562), Laudonnière (1564-65), Belleforest (1570), and, generally, by all writers until 1864, when Mr. Buckingham Smith raised objections.

The voyage of Verrazano is recorded also upon some authentic and important maps; notably upon a large world map in the Collegio de Propaganda Fide at Rome, made by "Hieronimus de Verrazano" (a brother of the navigator), in 1529. In it all the region from the Carolinas to Cape Breton, inclusive, is inscribed "Nova Gallia sive Iucatanet," and marked with French flags; the region about what is now known as Cabot Strait, in Nova Scotia, is marked by the shield and ermines of the duchy of Bretagne. There is also a legend in Italian that

VOYAGE OF VERRAZANO 95

"Verrazana or New France, was discovered by Giovanni de Verrazano, the Florentine, by order of the most Christian King of France." In a map, by Vesconte di Maggiolo, dated 1527, the same region is inscribed "Francesca," and on the Ulpius globe, dated 1542, also is the inscription "Verrazana or New France discovered by Verrazano, the Florentine, in 15—." In Hakluyt's "Divers Voyages" is what is known as Lok's map, upon which are shown the geographical features of the preceding maps, including what is called the Sea of Verrazano. It is made, Hakluyt says, after the "plat of Verrazano," and he refers to a "mighty large olde map in the custody of Mr. Richard Locke," and to "an olde excellent globe in the Queen's private gallery at Westminster," both by Verrazano. These two last have disappeared. They, and all maps influenced by Verrazano's voyage, show a little neck of land at about lat. 40° N., separating the Atlantic Ocean and the Great South Sea like another isthmus of Darien. This "Sea of Verrazano" came close to the Atlantic coast, and dwelt long in the imaginations of the French geographers. Cartier, Champlain, and the voyageur explorers of Canada, in after years, wondered over each great river they came upon whether it discharged into the Gulf of Mexico or into the Great South Sea.

There was slight leisure for cosmography in France when Verrazano returned. Francis was off to the Italian wars, and in the following February (1525), he was defeated at Pavia, and carried captive to Spain. He did not regain his liberty until March, 1526. How Verrazano was occupied in the meantime does not appear, but we next find him in an enterprise, jointly with Philippe Chabot de Brion, Admiral of France, Guillaume Preudhomme, "General" of Normandy, Jean Ango of Dieppe, and several others, to fit out an expedition, under the command of Verrazano, to the East Indies, for spices. The shares, both of the profits of trade, and of any prizes from the enemies of the Faith, and of the King, were fully specified. Some have written as if Verrazano was a pirate, but this was legitimate warfare at sea in those days. All property of enemies of the King was fair prize, and modern distinctions of contraband of war were unknown. He sailed after May 11, 1526, for on that date Verrazano gave a power of attorney to his brother Jerome (the maker of the map), to act for him in his absence. That is the last record—he thenceforth disappears; but the imagination of subsequent writers has not been content, save with a tragical ending. Ramusio states that he went on another voyage to America, and was killed and eaten by Indians. Biddle combines this with Rut's voyage in 1527, and identifies him with the Piedmontese pilot who was killed in Norumbega, but there was an Italian, Albert de Prato, known to have been with Rut, and, therefore, there is no need of drawing upon Verrazano, who would, moreover, not be likely to have gone as subordinate in such an expedition. In 1723 Barcia ("Ensayo Chronologico") identified him with Juan Florin or Florentin, the corsair, who had captured the treasure ships of Cortez. This Juan Florin was certainly hanged as a pirate, in October, 1527, at Colmenar de Arenas in Spain, for that we have the evidence of the judge who condemned him, but who had no suspicion that he was hanging Juan Verrazano for deeds done when a captain in the service of France.

Charlevoix thinks he made another voyage, attempted to found a colony, and was killed in 1525, while building a fort. With such a variety of tragedies to choose from no reader can be at a loss. None of them have any real foundation, though the majority of writers, since Barcia, state that he was hanged by the Spaniards. It is, however, certain that the hanging of Florin was done in October, 1527. The following extract shows that Verrazano was alive in Paris on December 24, 1527. It is from a letter to João III., King of Portugal, written by his ambassador at Paris: "As it may happen that the letters I am sending to Your Majesty, by this bearer, may not reach their destination, he takes with him this one in a more secret manner, so that Your Majesty be

VOYAGE OF VERRAZANO 97

acquainted with their substance; *id est,* that Master Giovanni Verrazano is to leave from here with five battle ships, which he had been ordered by the Admiral to take to a large river on the coast of Brazil, which river is said to have been discovered by a Castilian. I have made many inquiries about this matter, and asked full particulars in writing, but so far the answer has been verbal only, that the Admiral, and the said Verrazano, are to leave in February or March. I think the river, above referred to, is the same as discovered by Christovão Jacques. It would seem to me they will establish a basis of operation, and then proceed further up the river," etc., etc., etc.

This letter was discovered in the archives of the Torre do Tombo, and has been published in the *Memorie della Società Geografica,* Roma, 1897. It is evident, therefore, that Verrazano and Florin were different persons. From Hakluyt we learn that Verrazano had some communication with Henry VIII. of England, probably after his return from the voyage of 1524, while Francis was a prisoner and France was in consternation. As to his ultimate fate the statement of Ramusio is most likely to be right, that he went on another expedition to America, and was killed. It is not necessary, however, to defend the Indians of North America from the charge of eating him, because the circumstance, whatever it was, occurred on the coast of South America.

CHAPTER VIII

THE VOYAGE OF STEPHEN GOMEZ

THE voyage of Stephen Gomez is of great interest because it was one of serious, leisurely exploration, and, while that part of the coast first, in the strictest sense, discovered by him was a region of the United States coast, yet it is certain that he visited and examined the Atlantic coast of British America, with more diligence than Verrazano, and reported upon it more fully than any explorer until Champlain. His original report has not come down to us, but the results of the voyage are embodied in later documents. Hitherto these have not yielded as much information as might have been expected; perhaps because the learned and careful scholars who have studied them had not that familiarity with the coast and localities described, which is of so great value in doubtful questions. Every sea and every coast has its particular physical characteristics, and statements which appear reasonable to a student of books and charts in a distant country are often felt by a native of the locality in question to be incredible or impossible. To one familiar with the region under debate, the whole scene rises vividly before the mind, associated with attendant circumstances of pleasure or adventure, and to any such a person it will become certain that Stephen Gomez really sailed along the coast of British America, and saw the places he described.

Much unnecessary discussion has been caused by the loose use of the word "discover" by early writers. At the present day the phrase "first discover" seems tautological; not so, however, with the old writers. Thus Hakluyt writes, "this coast from Cape Breton, &c., was *again* discovered," and elsewhere he narrates the "dis-

VOYAGE OF STEPHEN GOMEZ 99

covery" of the Isle of Ramea by James in 1591, and, on turning the page, we find that Cartier "discovered the said Isle of Ramea in the year 1534, as you may reade in page 250 of this present volume"; and again "John Verasanus and Stephen Gomez bothe which in one year 1524 discovered the said countries." A similar latitude obtained with the corresponding words in other languages at that time. It is proper to notice this usage here, for we have now to consider the voyage of Stephen Gomez, in so far as it was made along the same coast "discovered," as Hakluyt might say, by Cabot in 1498, and Verrazano in 1524.

Stephen Gomez was a Portuguese by birth—born at Oporto—who, in the same year as did his more distinguished fellow-countryman Magellan, transferred his services to Spain. Such a transfer was an ordinary occurrence at that time and elicited no comment; but, by a strange anachronism in the case of Sebastian Cabot, it has been exaggerated into treason. Gomez was a navigator of great ability, and urged upon Charles V. the despatch of an expedition to the southwest to find a passage to the Indies. The expedition sailed in 1519, but the chief command was given to Magellan, and Gomez was sent as pilot. Actuated by jealousy he deserted in the strait now named after Magellan, and, seizing one of the ships, returned to Spain, where he prophesied evil of the expedition. Certainly an envious and treacherous man; yet there is no word of reproach for him in all the modern books so eloquent in condemnation of Sebastian Cabot. In A. D. 1522 Sebastian del Cano returned to Spain with one of Magellan's ships. That great sailor had been killed; but his enterprise had succeeded, and Del Cano, first of all men, had in the little vessel, well named the *Victory,* circumnavigated the world—a feat, which, as Herrera well says, is worthy of eternal memory.

The return of Del Cano made the Emperor more anxious to discover the strait at the North, which the cosmographers, with the *a priori* reasoning of their day, believed must exist, and lead to the South Sea by a more direct route. Among them Stephen Gomez was the most confident and insistent; for, if such a direct passage were found at the North, the longer and more perilous voyage by the strait, named after his rival Magellan, would be superseded. Orders were given by the Emperor, in 1523, to fit out an expedition, and preparations were going forward when Gomez was summoned to Badajoz, to attend, as an expert, the sittings of the commission to settle the line of demarcation of the treaty of Tordesillas. As soon as he was able to get away he resumed his preparations. There were others concerned besides the Emperor (Charles V.), because it was stipulated that if any prizes were captured, one-third was to belong to Gomez and the crew, and the other two-thirds to the King, and to those who had supplied the equipment. In this economical method the advancement of science was combined with a little trading and a little cruising, at the expense of the enemies of the faith and of the Emperor.

Gomez sailed from Corunna very late in 1524, or early in 1525 (November, 1524, to February, 1525). He had only one ship. She was of fifty tons burden, provisioned for a year, and thoroughly well fitted out. No direct narrative or journal, and no maps from his hand have survived. It has been much discussed whether his course along the American coast was from north to south, or the reverse. The Royal instructions have been discovered and published by a writer in Santiago de Chili quoted by Harrisse. They were, " to examine all the coast from Florida to Bacallaos," and D'Avezac is clear that the course was from south to north—from Florida to Cape Race, but it must be observed that the opposite direction is implied by many authorities, and Kohl is very positive on that point. On the other hand, however, Galvano distinctly gives his course as from south to north, from Corunna direct to Cuba, and thence to Florida and northward until he struck homewards to Corunna again. Galvano wrote about 1555, and his

VOYAGE OF STEPHEN GOMEZ

book was printed in 1563, a few years after his death. He was a man of the rarest ability, as a soldier and administrator for Portugal in the Moluccas for many years, and he was as competent as a captain at sea. His book was written at Lisbon, where all information on such matters was available. That Gomez was absent for about ten months is well established, and it is also known that he sailed in the mid-winter of 1524-25. That being the case it is far more probable that he commenced at the south; for no sailor of experience would have sailed to the north in mid-winter, with the intention of working his way to the south. It would have been to fight against the succession of the seasons, and to run deliberately into the most unfavourable conditions of navigation on the northeast coast of America. He would have run counter to the trade winds and equatorial current, and to the Gulf Stream—influences by that time well recognised. Galvano's work is a concise abstract, and Herrera, forty years later, gives a fuller account. He says (Dec. III, Bk. 8, Cap. 8), that "Gomez sailed with the intention of going to the north, and he ran along the whole coast as far as Florida, covering a great stretch of land beyond that which had been sailed along by any Spanish ship up to that time; although Sebastian Cabot, Jean Verrazano, and others had navigated there." Unable to reach Cathay, he kidnapped, against the King's orders, as many Indians as he could get into his ship, and carried them to Spain. He crossed from Florida to Cuba, to the port of Santiago, where he refreshed his crew. He arrived at Corunna after ten months' absence, bringing back with him, not spices from the distant East, but a cargo of slaves. He had special instructions not to trespass upon territory assigned by treaty to Portugal, and did not go north of Cape Race.

Gomez had the strongest motives for effort—hatred of Magellan's reputation, and the desire to surpass it. Galvano describes, in a few words, his painstaking search, "sailing by day because the land was unknown to him, and so that he could see into every bay, creek, river, and inlet, whether it extended over to the other side [of the land]."

The report of Gomez was made to the King, and it passed, as such papers always did, to the official board of cosmographers and pilots, who had permanent charge of the Spanish marine, and of the *Padron Real,* or standard official map, upon which all discoveries were recorded. We know that it went there, for we find its traces on the official maps, and in 1536 Alonzo de Chaves, a distinguished Royal pilot and cosmographer, was instructed by the King to revise the official map, and bring it down to date. This revised map has not come down to us either, but Oviedo wrote his " Historia General y Natural de las Indias " at the command of Charles V., with Chaves' revision before him. The first nineteen books were printed at Seville in 1535, and reprinted at Salamanca in 1547. The remaining part lay in manuscript until 1852, when it was printed by the Spanish Academy of History. In the second part is a detailed description of the coast based upon Chaves' map up to 51° 30′ N., and continued to the north upon Ribeiro's map, the official map previous in date.

Alonzo de Santa Cruz held the office of Chief Royal Cosmographer under Charles V. and Philip II., at Seville. He wrote, in 1560, an " Islario General," which has not been printed. Several manuscript copies are, however, extant, and Mr. Harrisse has published some interesting extracts from them. The information Santa Cruz used was De Chaves' map and Gomez' report. They were among the documents in his office, and besides he was associated with De Chaves in the revision of 1536. He also gives a description of the northeast coast of America; but he makes his description follow the map from north to south, while Oviedo's account was from south to north, but the basis of both is the report of Gomez. The narrative of Oviedo is more diffuse, but is obscure, in parts, while the account of the sailor cosmographer is clearer, though shorter. Alonzo de Santa Cruz made a world map in 1542, which has survived,

VOYAGE OF STEPHEN GOMEZ 103

and is at Stockholm, where it has been reproduced in *fac-simile*. There is, also, a sketch map in his manuscript "Islario," which Mr. Harrisse has reproduced. These are the materials available to form a judgment.

There is often a semblance of precision in these old documents which is disappointing on close examination. The distances are given in leagues; but are stated in round numbers, such as twenty, forty, sixty, one hundred. Natural objects of interest do not lie at such even distances, and it is not, therefore, surprising to find these figures seriously astray. They are always in excess of the direct distances measured on a modern map; for they were, of necessity, the distances actually sailed, and in following a coast line the courses could not have been direct, as the explorers groped their way along without a guide, and with winds from all quarters. The latitudes are, with one exception, from one degree to a degree and a half too far north. Thus Cape Breton is given at 47° 30', instead of 46°, and Cape Race at 47° 30', also, instead of 46° 40', so that Cape Breton and Cape Race are made to be exactly east and west. That is usually the case, on the earlier maps, because they are drawn to a magnetic meridian. In comparing them with maps of the present day, drawn invariably to the true meridian, the bearings will always appear discrepant, in the ratio of the local variation. The leagues must also be reduced to nautical miles, sixty to a degree. The Spanish league in general use at that time measured four Italian miles, and there were seventeen and a half of them to a degree; or seventy miles to a degree of the world's circumference as then known. The exacter measurements of modern science have resulted in a degree five Italian miles longer. Therefore it requires seventy-five Italian miles to be the equivalent of the sixty nautical miles of our maps.

With all these drawbacks, however, we may arrive at some certain results, and from them we may proceed to sound conclusions upon other points. The natural features of the coast are unchanged, and they afford sure ground. Passing over the coast of the United States we find, at the Penobscot, close to the Canadian border, a sure point of departure. It is known on the Spanish maps as the *Rio de las Gamas*—Deer River. Santa Cruz says it is a large and deep river, with many islands, and Gomez sailed up confidently thinking he had found the passage to the west. He found the climate temperate. There were oak, birch, and *olive* trees (he was not a botanist), and wild vines with grapes. We may feel sure, then, that Gomez was not there in January, February, or March, which would have been the case if he had commenced his exploration at the North. He reported having found a mineral, which he took for gold, and he must, therefore, have landed, which will account for the near accuracy, in this instance, of the latitude recorded. The estuary is very wide. Oviedo gives it at 20 leagues (64 nautical miles)—an excessive measurement, for it is only forty miles. The name has survived all the vicissitudes of centuries, for the largest island at the mouth of the Penobscot is still called Deer Island.

At the eastern end of the course is another firm datum for a judgment—the Bay of the Bretons. This is not the Gulf of St. Lawrence. It is the expanse enclosed between Cape Canso, in Nova Scotia, and the south coast of Newfoundland. Santa Cruz leaves no doubt as to that. He tells us that every year the Bretons come to fish in that bay, and that in it are the islands of the eleven thousand virgins, which are shown on many maps on the south coast of Newfoundland; and he makes it certain, by adding that passing the bay to the west we come to a point of land called Cape Breton.

Another solidly established locality is the island of St. John. This is not Prince Edward Island. Santa Cruz says it is an island which extends to the east and the west, *close to the point of Cape Breton*. It is 56 leagues long by 20 leagues wide. Oviedo says it is 70 leagues long on the north, 55 leagues on the south, 20 leagues on the east, and that it runs to a point on the west, and is

145 leagues, more or less, in circumference. The measurement is excessive, but it is a large triangular island close to the land, and on the west of the Bay of the Bretons. Furthermore, Santa Cruz says it is of good appearance, with many trees, and rivers, which empty into the sea, and that it extends from 46° to 48° N. lat. It really extends from 45° 30' to 47° N. The most interesting point of Santa Cruz' statement is that Gomez changed the position of the island on the map. Before his time the island of St. John was in the Bay of the Bretons; but Gomez, he says, reported that it is adjacent to the land. He adds that no one had said anything about this island before. Evidently then Gomez discovered Cape Breton to be an island, and transferred to it the name of an island called St. John, which was shown by other cartographers to be in the bay.

Another firm geographical fact demonstrated by Gomez is the existence and location of the Gut of Canso. This is by no means the passage into the Gulf of St. Lawrence between Cape North and Cape Ray, recently named Cabot Strait. Santa Cruz informs us that between the island of St. John and the mainland is a channel (Sp. *canal*), and Oviedo gives the latitude of the point of it as 46° 40' N. The latitude of the north point is really 45° 30' but, as stated before, all the latitudes are 1° to 1° 30' too much to the north. Santa Cruz calls the passage the "canal" of St. Julian, but whether St. Julian or St. John (*Sanct Julian* or *Sanct Johan*) it cannot possibly be other than the Gut of Canso. Thus we have a firm *terminus a quo* on the west—the Penobscot —and a firm *terminus ad quem* on the east—the Gut of Canso; all between is of necessity on the coast of the mainland of Acadia. It is scarcely possible that Gomez could have overlooked the Bay of Fundy in so close an examination as he evidently made. Sailing from the south as the season indicates that he did, it would not be possible, and, sailing from the north, it would be highly improbable, to pass it over; for sailing south, there was nothing to lead him to strike one hundred miles across from Cape Sable to the Penobscot; and sailing north, he would, of necessity, have followed the coast in his search until he got involved in the bay and saw land on the other side. It has always been a cause of wonder that so remarkable a feature as the Bay of Fundy should have passed unmarked on the maps until Homem's in 1558. It was not necessary to sail to the head of it to know that there was no passage through. The phenomenally high tides and muddy water would soon reveal that; but one seeking for a passage through would get a long way up, and would see high land on the right, before being sure that this wide stretch was only a bay.

Having thus established firm ground at these two points the task of filling up the interval will be narrowed. Commencing then at the Penobscot, the next name to the east is *Costa de Medaños*, which is translated by Kohl "sandbanks." The word *medaños* is an old Portuguese word, and is defined as "large heaps of sand covered by shallow water near the seashore." It is the augmentative of *meda*, a rick or stack of anything, as hay, corn, sand (low Latin *meta*, a heap, *acervus*). The coast from the Penobscot to the St. Croix is described by Champlain, who examined it closely in 1604. "Nous passâmes par grande quantité d'isles, bancs, battures et rochers qui jettent plus de quatre lieux à la mer par endroicts." The main shore is low, and consists of hard Cambrian rocks, and it is fringed with numerous detached rocks and rocky islets. The tides rise from twenty to twenty-six feet, and at ebb, or half tide, the rocks show up clad with kelp and seaweeds, as far as the swash of the sea reaches. It is a very monotonous coast, and anyone passing along it near the shore at ebb tide will recognise the feature which Gomez meant to describe.

The next name is simply *Golfo*—a gulf—Oviedo calls it "another bay"; after that follows *Rio de Montañas*, the River of Mountains—a physical indication which identifies the locality. It is fifty leagues, or 160 nautical miles from the Penobscot, and in lat. 44° 15′ N., but, in

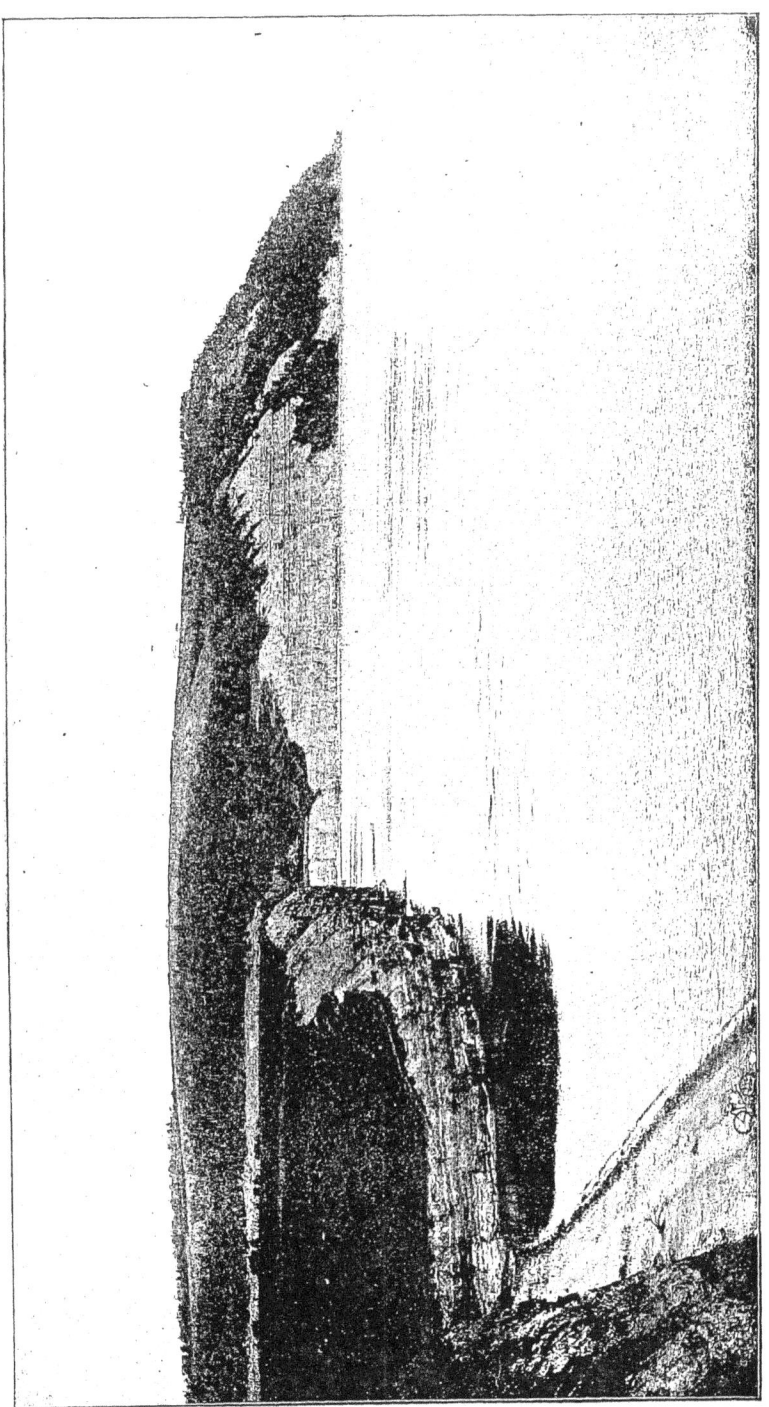

A. L. Hardy Photo

Cape Blomidon, at the entrance of the Basin of Minas

the map to the *Islario*, is at 45°. There is no locality on the New Brunswick coast answering to the description, but a course of 180 miles would bring Gomez as far up the bay as the opening of the Basin of Minas, where the Cobequid Mountains on the north terminate in Capes Chignecto and Cape d'Or, and, on the opposite side of the opening the two ranges which border the Annapolis valley terminate in Cape Split and Cape Blomidon—four headlands which might well suggest the name *Rio de Montañas*. Whether he went further up the bay there is no basis for a guess; but the Chignecto channel would be the *Golfo* of the maps and the descriptions, and, on later maps, we see this *Golfo* fork into the two arms of Chepody Bay and Cumberland Basin on either side of Cape Merangouin fifty miles farther up.

Oviedo gives twenty leagues (sixty-four miles), as the distance to the next point, *Rio de Castañas*. There is no river on the coast until the Annapolis River breaks through the long mountain ridge at Digby Gut. It is seventy miles direct from *Rio de Montañas*. The name, River of Chestnut Trees, indicates that the place was on the sheltered west side of Nova Scotia, and certainly not along the Atlantic coast. Gomez was not strong as a botanist, seeing that he found olive trees on the Penobscot.

The chestnut is not found on the coast of Acadia, but the beech is very abundant on the western shores of Nova Scotia, and, on Lescarbot's map of 1607, he inscribes C. des Noyers—Cape of nut-trees—at the west point of Digby Gut. In the memory of the oldest inhabitant that locality has been forested with beech trees, and, after long years, the name would still be appropriate, for the beech trees have reproduced themselves. The American beech (*F. ferruginea*) differs from the European beech (*F. sylvatica*), but in the autumn when the nuts are ripe the flavour is pleasant. The nuts grow in large quantities, and would attract the attention of an explorer.

The next point noted is the *Bahia de la Ensenada*—the

Bay of the Bay. This, says Oviedo, is at 45°. Bearing in mind that all his latitudes are 1° to 1° 30′ too high, we shall find that St. Mary's Bay, the mouth of which is at 44° 10′, will well answer to this name. It is a very remarkable, long and narrow bay. Oviedo calls it in another place *Ensenada o bahia,* and he says " from the Bay of the *Ensenada* to the mouth of which it is ten leagues " (thirty-two miles). The phrase is vague, but he does not count the ten leagues in with the distance along the coast, and it apparently indicates the length of the inlet or bay, and St. Mary's Bay is really twenty-eight miles long. Then from the mouth of this bay the distance commences to be measured anew along the coast, for exactly at this point terminates the first half of the entire distance between the two known and fixed points.

The next point named is *Rio de la Vuelta*—we meet this frequently on later maps as *Rio* or *Cabo de Buelta.* This has been translated the "river of return," where somebody is supposed to have returned, or turned back; but Harrisse happily translates it into French *rivière du détour*—the river of the turning or changing direction. This point is twenty leagues (sixty-four miles), from *Ensenada,* and at sixty-five miles we find Cape Sable at Barrington harbour on the S. E. point of Nova Scotia, where the coast does indeed turn; as, in the Portuguese map of Viegas, C. de Volta is Cape Ray, where the Newfoundland coast turns to the north.

We are now upon the Atlantic coast, and the next point named is *Rio Grande* (Great River), at a distance of forty leagues (128 miles), marked by three islets at its mouth, and in lat. 45° 45′ N. The islands do not assist; for many other harbours on the coast have islands, but Halifax harbour at a distance of 130 miles, and in lat. 44° 40′ would correspond to the indications, and, as a matter of fact, three islets are there.

Lastly, we come to our *terminus ad quem*—the fixed point at the east—sixty leagues (192 miles) from Rio Grande, is in Oviedo's words: " The channel made by

VOYAGE OF STEPHEN GOMEZ

the island of St. John between it and the mainland." The total distance is recapitulated by Oviedo as 240 leagues, divided into two exact halves—from *Rio de las Gamas* to *Bahia de la Ensenada* 120 leagues, and from *Bahia de la Ensenada* to the *Canal de San Julian* 120 leagues. We may well believe that no coast will divide up into such even portions, and that Gomez' distances are lengthened by the sinuosities of the coast. The following table will, however, indicate to what extent the explanation given accords with them. The difference between the two totals may be accounted for by the nature of Gomez' coasting, as described by Galvano:

TABLE COMPILED FROM OVIEDO'S DATA

DISTANCES GIVEN	LEAGUES	MILES
Rio de las Gamas to		
Rio de Montañas	50	160
Rio de Castañas	20	64
Rio de la Ensenada	50	160
	120	384
Rio de la Ensenada to		
Rio de la Vuelta	20	64
Rio Grande	40	128
Canal St. Julian	60	192
	120	384

DISTANCES ON A MODERN MAP	MILES
Penobscot to	
Basin of Minas	220
Digby Gut	70
St. Mary's Bay	50
	340
St. Mary's Bay to	
Cape Sable	65
Halifax	130
Canso	130
	325

Total course of two equal portions reported by Oviedo 768 miles
Total course, measured on a chart.................. 665 miles

The most interesting part of Gomez' narrative, and that which conclusively demonstrates his capacity as an explorer and observer, is the information he brought back of the northeast coast of Cape Breton. That he was there is certain, and also that his coasting was along Nova Scotia, Cape Breton, and the southern coast of Newfoundland to Cape Race. He was the first to explore the whole coast in a thorough and connected manner. The most interesting part of his report is that relating to the Island of St. John, known to us as the Island of Cape Breton. It is misleading to suppose that anyone sailing round that island would know how profoundly the Bras d'Or eats into the heart of the land. A stranger might visit the island now, and if he had no books or map, and was not told of it, he would know nothing of the Bras d'Or unless he went into the island, and sailed through the inland waters. No one seeing the two narrow openings (Rio de dos Bocas), or even landing on the narrow isthmus, at St. Peter's, could dream of the sylvan loveliness of those far-reaching stretches of bright water searching among the hills. It does not help us in this difficult inquiry to divide Cape Breton into two islands. It was one solid island to Stephen Gomez, as it is to every stranger; beautiful enough, even when its inmost landscape treasures are unrevealed. Gomez reported its peculiar exterior characteristics with the precision of an actual observer. It is an island to the west of the Bay of the Bretons, and adjacent to the mainland, from which it is separated by the " Canal de St. Julian " (the word is *canal*, and is not used elsewhere). The width of the canal is given as five to ten leagues, and there are islands in it which, being small, have no names (this is the eastern approach by Chedabucto Bay with Isle Madame and other islands), but it is narrowest at its western end (the Gut of Canso). On the Island of St. John " is the point of Cape Breton." The island is pleasant to the sight, and clad with trees; there are rivers which fall into the sea, and there are abundant fisheries close to it. Thirty-five leagues north

W. Notman Photo

View on the Gut of Canso

of the point of Cape Breton is Cabo Grueso (large cape, Cape North), and halfway between the two capes is the *Rio de dos Bocas* (two mouths, the two narrow openings through the hills of the Bras d'Or), and, as if to leave us no room for doubt, Santa Cruz adds: " Stephen Gomez relates that in sailing along that coast he saw a great deal of smoke on it, and signs of its being inhabited." Stephen Gomez saw what the tourist will see from any steamer's deck to-day. Within a few miles of halfway to Cape North (from Cape Breton), on turning Point Aconi, he will see on his left the two mouths of the Bras d'Or; and before him will be Cape Smoky (Cape Enfumé of the French maps). He will be in the *Baia dos Fumos* of the old Portuguese charts; before his eyes the smoke-like mists—the unique feature of the place— will still climb the steep cliffs, and on the north, to the right, will rise the lofty bulk of Cape North, the C. Grueso of the old Spanish sailor. There can be no doubt about the place. There is nothing like it along the whole coast of North America. Its singularity justifies the characteristic name it bears in all the languages of western Europe.

We may now proceed to follow the reports of Gomez, as represented by De Chaves, Oviedo, and Santa Cruz, concerning Cabot Strait, the Gulf of St. Lawrence, and the south coast of Newfoundland, for in following his course we have arrived at a definitely ascertained point. We know that Gomez found no western passage, and, though he firmly believed one to exist close to Bacallaos and Labrador, he believed it would be of no use because of the cold. To the northeast of Cape Grueso forty leagues " is a river without a name," excepting that of Rio de Muchas Islas, and " this coast is full of islands." Then follow the islands of St. Elmo, the Eleven Thousand Virgins, Cape St. Mary, and at last Cape Race. These four names show that he is dealing with the south coast of Newfoundland. The description reverts to Cape Grueso as follows: " Before the said [nameless] river there is a bay farther on from the same Cape

Grueso, which bay is twenty leagues across." This can be no other than Cabot Strait taken as a bay; for from Cape North across to Cape Ray is actually fifty-six miles, and Gomez reports it as twenty leagues, or sixty-four miles. So far it is plain, but then follows a confused and contradictory passage; which is yet important, because of its very obscurity, for it proves that at that time nothing was known of the Gulf of St. Lawrence, and that Cabot Strait was taken to be a bay: "And it [the bay] is called by the cosmographer Alonzo de Chaves up to the said cape, which is more to the east, River de Muchas Islas. But the bay between these two capes is 130 leagues or more across; which I neither deny nor approve, because in this land little knowledge is had of the details of the northern bays, and I think that in regard to what he drew upon the map he was perhaps less accurately informed than he might have been. And thus there are many differences on this northern coast on the navigators' charts and among cosmographers, and as it is a very cold and savage land, few care to navigate there." There is thus a bay twenty leagues across— Cabot Strait; a distance of forty leagues northeast to the *Rio de Muchas Islas*—on the Newfoundland coast; and a bay of 130 leagues across, between two capes not indicated, which can be no other than the Bay of the Bretons; for it is abundantly clear that all these distances are east of Cape North and of the Island of St. John (Cape Breton), and are measured outwards to Cape Race.

It must not be supposed that too much attention has been given to the voyage of Gomez, and the accounts of the above cited authorities, for upon the view taken of it depends our estimate of the extent of the discoveries of Jacques Cartier. We shall see later on that Cartier did not pass through Cabot Strait until his return from his second voyage. To him also, until then, it was a bay, and as a bay it was laid down on all the maps until the results of Cartier's discoveries were made known throughout Europe, and on the great map of Santa

Cruz (1542) it is still a bay. As for the Bay of Fundy, Champlain relates that in 1607, when Poutrincourt first visited the Basin of Minas he found there a very old cross covered with moss and nearly all rotted away. Champlain thought it conclusive evidence that Christians had been there a long time before him, and from the tenor of the preceding chapter it will appear probable that the cross was a vestige of the voyage of Gomez.

CHAPTER IX

RESULTS OF EXPLORATION UP TO JACQUES CARTIER'S FIRST
VOYAGE

BY 1534, when Jacques Cartier first appeared in the history of discovery, the whole Atlantic seaboard of the Dominion of Canada had been explored. Cabot had touched it in 1497, and, in his second voyage, in 1498, had sailed along its full extent from Labrador far beyond its southern border. Verrazano, as we have seen, sailed along it from south to north as far as lat. 50° N., when he turned off towards France, but there is no record of his having landed north of the present New Hampshire. Stephen Gomez, in 1525, made a real exploration of the whole Acadian coast, and John Rut sailed in 1527 from Belle-Isle to the West Indies and seems to have landed at several places in Acadia.

The Portuguese and Bretons had been fishing on the coast with increasing activity since 1504. The Portuguese had resorts on the Acadian coasts, and the islands off the south shore of Newfoundland had been included in the grant of 1521 to Fagundez, as well as that ocean terror now known as Sable Island. They had pushed up the east coast to Newfoundland, and yet, so far as the contour of the Labrador coast is concerned, the map of Salvat de Pilestrina (1503) is nearer the truth than the maps made fifty years later.

There are a number of Portuguese maps, dated in 1534 or a little before, which show graphically the results of discovery up to the time of Cartier, and of these the most characteristic is one of Gaspar Viegas, 1534. (See page 115.) Here appears in rudimentary form the Gulf of St. Lawrence. It is shown, as Gomez sup-

RESULTS OF EXPLORATION 115

posed it to be, as a bay. Cabot Strait is there leading into it, but the west coast of Newfoundland is brought round to enclose the bay by connecting with the coast of Acadia. The island of Cape Breton is shown separated by a narrow channel from the mainland. A map of the same year in the Riccardiana Library (No. xxxiii. of

Fig. 8. Gaspar Viegas' Map, A. D. 1534

Kretschmer) shows the same features in the main. In both maps rudimentary and conjectural rivers are indicated opening into the round basin, the nucleus from which the Gulf of St. Lawrence was soon to be developed and in the Riccardiana map the Island of Cape Breton is named the Island of St. John. In all these maps it is necessary first to find Cape Race if we would not go astray. It is the key to all maps, for its name never changes. It is shown in these maps at the east end of the south coast of Newfoundland, and at the west end is C. de Volta (Cape Ray), where the coast turns sharply to the north. The same rudimentary gulf is seen on the Wolfenbuttel map (1534), and the contour given delineates the Bay of the Bretons, as described by Oviedo and Santa Cruz, marked out by Cape Race and Cape Canso with the Island of St. John (beyond question Cape Breton Island), on its western side.

As shown in the previous chapter, the Bay of Fundy was not passed over by Gomez. On the Weimar map (1527), sometimes ascribed to Fernan Columbus, the name Golfo marks its place; and upon the map of Santa Cruz the same name also appears, where we expect to find it, between the Costa de Medaños and Cabo de Montañas. But these maps, and many others, show plainly why the distances are so frequently excessive. Even profound indentations, like the Bay of Fundy, are not laid down in their proportions, but are, as in this case, marked by small conventional river-mouths, which do not count in the measurement along the shore, though the bay or gulf was actually sailed round. In that way, until advancing knowledge checked the distances by actual observations of latitudes, made on land with care and precision, the coast of America was straightened and stretched out abnormally. In the case of Oviedo's description of the coast in the preceding chapter all the latitudes are shown to be too high; and, as he goes on, following northwards up the coast, the excess increases to 10° until it reaches at last a total latitude of 70° N., while Cape Chidley is really only at 60°. What is more suggestive is that the point of 70°, up to which the American coast is followed, is said to be "on the west-east line with Ireland and with Scotland." The American coast, compared with that of Europe, is thus stretched by fifteen degrees of latitude.

Before the year 1534, therefore, Cabot Strait was

known only as the entrance to a bay of unknown extent. In like manner, to the north of Newfoundland, the Strait of Belle-Isle was known as the entrance to a bay, also of unknown extent. These openings had been laid down as early as 1505 in Pedro Reinel's map (page 57); but there are no indications that they had been followed up. There is no reason to suppose they were. The coast was resorted to every summer by fishermen for the sole object of commerce, and there was no inducement to exploration, since the eastern shores of Newfoundland and Acadia swarmed with fish and abounded in safe and commodious harbours. It is, of course, possible that some sailor, more curious than the rest, may have penetrated farther; but, if so, not a vestige of his enterprise has come down to our day. The vessels frequenting the coasts were owned by merchants in the ports of western Europe. The merchants of St. Malo may be taken as a type of the rest. They did not care for discoveries, and they set themselves obstinately against Cartier's enterprise, and hid away their sailors and pilots to prevent them joining his expedition, until the King's authority was appealed to in court. In that very appeal, however, it is clear that the Strait of Belle-Isle was well known, for Cartier's intention is avowed "*passer le destroict de la baye des Chasteaux*," to go beyond the Strait off Chateau Bay—for that was the name by which the Strait of Belle-Isle was then known. Cartier's complaint was that these merchants, for their own private profit, were opposing the public interest as well as the express command of the King.

In the following chapters it will be seen that Cartier went to the east coast of Newfoundland with previous knowledge of its chief harbours. We shall find that his knowledge did not give out until he had reached what is now known on the charts as Esquimaux Bay; well to the westward of Blanc Sablon, the present boundary of the Province of Quebec. The name Brest, already at his visit attached to that locality, proves that Breton sailors had been there before him, and the name clung there for one hundred and fifty years. It is, therefore, incorrect to say that Cartier discovered the Strait of Belle-Isle; and it is also incorrect to say that in the Gulf of St. Lawrence he was antedated by morse or whale hunters of any nation. His own plain, straightforward narrative shows where his discoveries begin. We have now to follow him into the Gulf of St. Lawrence, and up the flood of its great river to the site of the present city of Montreal, the centre and heart of the commercial life of the Dominion of Canada. All attempts to detract from the merit of this achievement in favour of imaginary Basques or other problematical people will be found to be futile. As soon as the distracted state of France permitted it, the attention of the King and Court once more turned to the world beyond the sea, and Cartier was commissioned to demonstrate what had previously only been suspected.

Verrazano had returned from his voyage at a very unfortunate time; for the six months of his absence had been fraught with danger to France. It is doubtful whether Verrazano's letters reached the King, for he was then assembling a force to repel invasion, and was entering upon the fatal campaign which resulted in the overwhelming disaster at Pavia. Francis did not regain his liberty until March, 1526, and a period of exhaustion followed, during which France recovered from the losses and confusion of the Italian war.

The Duchy of Bretagne was becoming an integral part of France, although it was nominally, in 1534, a separate principality. Anne of Bretagne, the last Duchess, had successively married Charles VIII. and Louis XII. of France, but reigned all her life with her own Parliament in her own duchy. She had bequeathed the succession to her daughter Claude, who married Francis I.; and, although the estates had sworn allegiance to the joint sovereigns, they did not thereby annex the duchy to France, and Queen Claude at her death, in 1524, left the inheritance to her son—the Dauphin—and the revenues only to her husband during his life. Even that disposition was re-

RESULTS OF EXPLORATION

sisted by the Bretons as illegal, and the Parliament of Bretagne, while admitting the right of the King to govern them as Duke, subject to their own laws, claimed the right of separating the duchy from the Crown and settling it upon any of the younger princes, or even of continuing the succession in the female line. This danger to the monarchy was overcome in August, 1532, when the estates were won over by adroit management; and, although the Dauphin was proclaimed as Duke, the annexation of Bretagne to the crown of France was declared irrevocable, and the antagonism between Bretons and Frenchmen disappeared. In Hakluyt and the older writers, however, the distinction was for a long time maintained; and it has, sometimes, led to misunderstandings of the texts; for the word " Breton " was very often spelled " Briton," and was read as if it were equivalent to English. The period of Cartier's voyage, therefore, was an epoch in the history of France, for the Breton sailors, who had pursued their vocation undisturbed by the Italian wars, found themselves Frenchmen, with an undivided allegiance. Between 1529 and 1540 the French marine made great strides; for, disappointed abroad, France turned back upon herself, and there found that recuperative strength which has so often astonished her enemies.

The renewal of efforts towards discovery in the New World was due to Philippe de Chabot, seigneur de Brion, Admiral of France, a favourite courtier of King Francis and companion of his youthful years. He brought the subject before the King, and, this time, with a view to ultimate occupation and perhaps colonisation. The leader he selected to receive the Royal Commission was a Breton of St. Malo—Jacques Cartier—the revealer of the highway to the centre of the continent, the St. Lawrence valley.

Cartier was born at St. Malo in 1491, and, at the time of his first recorded voyage, was forty-three years old. From incidental remarks upon some new objects which he saw in Canada it is most probable that he had made a voyage in a Portuguese vessel to Brazil. He was acquainted with the Portuguese language, for on one occasion he acted as interpreter in court, and on another occasion was called upon to testify to the sufficiency of an interpreter in a trial at St. Malo for the adjudication of a Portuguese prize taken by some Breton privateers. His portrait hangs up in the town hall of St. Malo. It is, says Parkman, a painting of modern date, and of doubtful authenticity. Another portrait has been found in the print collection of the Bibliothèque Impériale; it is not idealised like the St. Malo portrait, and has not the same self-conscious look, but the one in the town hall has been received so long as an authentic portrait of the Breton sailor, and has been so generally accepted throughout Canada, that we give it here once more.

Lescarbot relates that Cartier himself made the first move and brought the enterprise under Admiral Chabot's notice, and, indeed, it may well have happened that Cartier on a previous voyage to the Strait of Belle-Isle had seen the shores widening to the west, and suspected that there lay the avenue to Cathay. To that spot he went confidently, as to a place he knew. Others also knew of the country; the " gran capitano Francese " of Ramusio told of Jean Denys and the pilot Gamart, who sailed from Honfleur in 1506, and of Thomas Aubert, of Dieppe, in 1508, and recent Norman writers have discovered and published the names of a number of vessels which sailed in those early times for Newfoundland from Norman ports. There were other ports in France famed for maritime enterprise besides those of Normandy and Brittany, and it was a ship of La Rochelle which Cartier met with, on his first voyage, inside the Strait of Belle-Isle, and within the present limits of the Province of Quebec.

Jacques Cartier
From Charlevoix History of New France, by permission of Mr. Francis P. Harper

CHAPTER X

CARTIER'S FIRST VOYAGE, A. D. 1534

AGAIN we must turn to Italy, even from the France of Francis I., if we wish to read the earliest printed accounts of Jacques Cartier's first voyage. Yet it was a time of great literary activity in France. Robert Estienne had been chosen by Francis as Royal Printer and was at the height of his fame. The presses teemed with books, but Cartier's first voyage was not of sufficient interest to be printed; so difficult has it been in every age to estimate the relative importance of contemporary events and of contemporary men. The narrative appeared first in the third volume of the great collection of Ramusio, printed at Venice in 1556, and from it John Florio made an English translation, published in 1580, which Hakluyt adopted and included in his collection a few years later. This is the version which has continually been reprinted and referred to. The first French version was published at Rouen, in 1598, by a book-seller—Raphael du Petit-Val. Only one copy has survived, and, strange as it may seem, it purports to be a translation from a version in some foreign language. This is the version used by Lescarbot for his "History of New France," in 1612. It was reprinted in 1843 by the Literary and Historical Society of Quebec, and by Tross (Paris) in 1865. It was not until 1867 that M. Michelant printed an original manuscript account which he had discovered in the Imperial Library at Paris. This version is distinguished as the "Relation Originale."

Those who have endeavoured to trace Cartier's course on his first voyage have complained of the obscurity of the records, and of its many contradictions. Even Lescarbot made that complaint, and Charlevoix remarks that the disappearance of Cartier's names from the coast has imparted much obscurity to his narrative. But the difficulty was really due to the fact that students had not Cartier's own narrative until 1867, and were endeavouring to understand narratives which were translations of translations. The translator from French into Italian had misunderstood many of the nautical terms used by Cartier; and Hakluyt, who, though a clergyman, was well informed in nautical matters, and might have understood them if he had seen the original, simply followed Florio's translation from Ramusio. What version Petit-Val's edition was translated from is not certain. It differs from Ramusio and from Hakluyt in minor ways, although there is a general correspondence among them all.

As might reasonably be expected, Jacques Cartier has found his best expositors in the country he discovered, since they could best know the localities he described. Very many writers in Canada have published expositions of his voyages, and the names of some of them will be found in the list of authorities at the end of this volume. The learned and careful Abbé Ferland had, among others, identified many of the places mentioned, but difficulties still remained. These were almost all solved in original studies by Dr. W. F. Ganong and Bishop Howley, so that the course of Cartier on his first voyage is now as clear from end to end as a voyage made nearly four hundred years ago can be expected to be. Mr. Ganong succeeded by subordinating all versions to the "Relation Originale," and Bishop Howley frankly ignored every other. Owing to that, and to the fact that he was familiar with many of the localities, because they were in his diocese, he cleared up some points on the coast of Newfoundland which had remained in doubt.

The "Relation Originale" is evidently from the hand of Jacques Cartier; for, although with singular modesty he has suppressed all direct mention of himself, there

CARTIER'S FIRST VOYAGE   123

shows out from time to time in his inexperienced effort an indication that the commander of the expedition is the narrator. The style is that of a man unaccustomed to write, excepting in the technical and abrupt manner of a sailor's log. It is a sailor's style, abounding in nautical expressions. The language is Breton French, with technical locutions, and the grammar and spelling are very incorrect. Spelling was unsettled at that period, both in England and France, but the spelling of the " Relation Originale " far exceeds the then current average of eccentricity. Nevertheless the narrative is clear, and intelligible compared with all the versions, and very rarely do these translations at second hand contribute anything to the elucidation of a difficulty; on the contrary, by their explanatory glosses, and their efforts to improve the mariner's style, they rendered it more obscure. Other difficulties arose from the fact that Cartier sailed in a region of great magnetic variation. Not only was that great in degree, but it varied abruptly, as it does at the present day. While the direction is affected by that cause, the distances are measured, not in the leagues of Columbus and the southern sailors, but in a league of three Roman miles. If then we would measure Cartier's courses on an Admiralty chart we must allow only two and a half nautical miles for each league, for that is the equivalent value to a small fraction. This old French league, as may be seen in Chabert's " Voyage," lingered even as late as 1753, and maps were made some of twenty and some of twenty-five leagues to a degree. His distances, moreover, tend to err by excess, for his course was not always in the most direct line.

The expedition consisted of two vessels, each of about sixty tons' burthen, and carrying in all sixty-one men, who took the oath of obedience before the Vice-Admiral of France in person. It sailed from St. Malo on the 20th of April, 1534. They had favourable weather, and arrived on the coast of Newfoundland on May 10, after a voyage of twenty days. The distance is about 2052 nautical miles, and from the voyage we may assume that ships in those days, when sailed by competent captains, and under the most favourable circumstances, could make one hundred miles a day, or a fraction over four admiralty knots an hour. Pedro de Medina in his "Arte de navegar" (1545) rates the utmost speed of a ship at four Italian miles an hour, so that the first voyage to Canada was exceptionally prosperous.

Cartier's landfall was at Cape Bonavista, on the east coast of Newfoundland—Cap de Bonneviste, as he calls it. He gives the latitude at 48° 30′ N.—not far astray, for it is really 48° 42′ N. He found the coast blocked with field ice. The conditions of navigation have not since changed. The easterly winds which sped Cartier on his way had blocked the east coast of Newfoundland with the Arctic ice. It was actually only May 1 of our present style, for the calendar had not been revised, and the dates had got ahead of the seasons by nine days. He was therefore obliged to go into a harbour five leagues S. S. W., called Ste. Catherine, and now known by the Spanish equivalent Catalina. There, sheltered from the northeast, he remained for ten days, waiting for the ice to clear away, and employing the time in fitting up his boats.

On May 21 the wind changed to the west, and he sailed N. N. E. from Cape Bonavista to the Isle aux Oiseaux; on some Portuguese maps *ysla de los aves*, but now known as Funk Island. He found it packed around with field ice, but managed to reach the island in his boats. It was a league in circumference, and so full of sea fowl that "it would be incredible to any one who had not seen it for himself." There has been so much difference of opinion concerning the birds mentioned by Cartier that the question is treated in a separate note. Cartier was much impressed by their number, and described them at unusual length. His crew were not the only creatures on the coast who enjoyed such food. The bears swam out to regale themselves, although the island was fourteen leagues from the mainland. They saw one jump into the water as they approached. It

CARTIER'S FIRST VOYAGE

was "as large as a cow, and as white as a swan." They missed it then, but the next day (which was Whitsunday) they found it halfway to shore, swimming as fast as they could sail, so they gave chase in their boats and killed it. They found the flesh as good "as that of a two-year-old heifer."

On Wednesday, May 27, they arrived at the entrance to the *Baye des Chasteaulx,* now known as the Strait of Belle-Isle. This must not be confounded with our Chateau Bay, for Cartier distinguishes that as *Hable des Chasteaulx.* He knew the place, but did not go there. The sheet of water opening thence in rear of Newfoundland was afterwards long known as *la grande baye.* The wind was contrary, and there was a great deal of ice in the strait, so they decided to enter a harbour near, called Rapont, in 51° 30′ N. lat., where they remained until June 9, without being able to get out. This harbour is down on the maps as Carpont, and is the Kirpon harbour of to-day. Its real latitude is 51° 35′.

While Cartier was waiting, as he says "to pass on further by God's help," he must have examined the adjacent coast, for he inserted in his narrative a description of the coasts of Newfoundland and Labrador, from Cape Rouge, on the east coast of Newfoundland, round to Brest Harbour, beyond the Strait of Belle-Isle. He had not spoken of Cape Rouge before. The locality still bears the same name, and is found on our charts. He tells us that the coast from Cape Rouge to Cape Degrat lies N. N. E. and S. S. W., and that it is the tongue of land which forms the entrance to "the bay"; that is, to the great bay in the rear of Newfoundland. He says that all that region consists of islands closely adjacent one to the other, and that they are separated by small channels, through which boats may pass. Here is the beginning of the error which, for a hundred years, cut up, upon the maps, Newfoundland into small islands. Kirpon Island, at the extreme northern point, is indeed a small island, and, in the channel between it and the main island, Cartier had taken refuge, but there are no other channels there, although the inlets cut in deeply from both sides. The extreme point of Kirpon Island is Cape Bauld. Cartier speaks of Cape Degrat, a name now restricted to the eastern point of the same island. He does not notice Cape Bauld, but took Cape Degrat for the characteristic point, which, indeed, it is, for it is the highest point on that part of the coast. Cartier evidently examined the place closely, for he tells us that from Cape Degrat two islands opposite Cape Rouge may be clearly seen. These are Groix Island and Bell Island, forty miles away to the south, in the Atlantic, and the distance is over-estimated, at twenty-five leagues. Standing on Cape Degrat and seeing the deep inlets which eat into the land, it is not surprising that Cartier supposed them to be connected through by narrow channels to the bay in the rear. Continuing, Cartier describes Kirpon harbour with much accuracy, giving the soundings and noticing the dangers of both entrances.

Passing on to the Strait of Belle-Isle from Cape Degrat on a W. N. W. course, Cartier noticed two islands on the port side. One was three leagues from the cape and the other seven leagues further on. This last was flat, and it closed in with the land. Bishop Howley rightly observes that there is no question here of Belle-Isle Island, which lay out of Cartier's course, far away to the starboard side, and, moreover, is detached in the ocean, and consists of high land. The first of Cartier's islands must be Sacred Island, and the second Schooner Island in Pistolet Bay. Here, for a moment, Cartier forgets his modest reserve, and says plainly, " I named this island Saint Catherine." It was the first land he named in the New World, and he named it for his wife, Catherine des Granches; for Cartier was attached to his wife after the simple Breton fashion, without any admixture of Renaissance manners. His Most Christian Majesty Francis I. might, with vast advantage to himself and his kingdom, have taken pattern in this respect from the plain mariner of St. Malo. The island is further identified by Cartier's statement that it lies N. N. E. with

CARTIER'S FIRST VOYAGE 127

Chateau harbour, which is precisely correct, though the distance (fifteen leagues) is over-estimated.

The description then passes to the Labrador coast, and taking the well-known *Hable des Chasteaulx* (our Chateau Bay) as a well-known point of departure (for he did not go there), Cartier refers to some points on that coast which, as he correctly says, lie W. S. W. Distant twelve and a half leagues is the harbour of Buttes (*Hable des Buttes*)—that is, of hills or hillocks. This beyond doubt is Red Bay; for that is nearly the distance given, and it is described in the " St. Lawrence Pilot " plainly enough: "The eastern side of the harbour is surmounted by a series of hillocks from 62 to 205 feet high connected by marshes with ponds in them." This harbour has sometimes been supposed to be Greenish Harbour; but the name *Buttes* implies a physical peculiarity which exists only at Red Bay. Stearns, sailing along the coast in 1881, describes its remarkable appearance incidentally, without any reference to Cartier's voyage—" a harbour at the foot of high, receding, unevenly sloped and gorged hillocks that look like a vast amphitheatre." Two leagues further on Cartier places *Hable de la Baleine* (Whale Harbour), which may be Carroll's Cove, five miles distant. There are several other harbours in the next indentation of the coast, shown as Black Bay on the maps, but Carroll's Cove is at the given distance, and the name Whale Harbour is not descriptive.

Some defect or obscurity must have existed in the first copy at this point, for two blanks occur here in the " Relation Originale." The distance between the *Hable de la Balcine* and Blanc Sablon is left out. Hakluyt gives fifteen, and Petit-Val twenty-five leagues, but the locality of Blanc Sablon is, fortunately, well known. The three or four lines which have puzzled so many have been explained in a satisfactory way. Cartier did not stay at any of these places along the coast, and when sailing abreast of *Hable de la Baleine* at a distance from land of one-third of the main strait he sounded and, at

38 fathoms, found bottom "taygnay," meaning a bottom of rocks covered with sea-weed. The word is used several times by Cartier in giving the results of his soundings. It is a sailor's word, and is not found in the ordinary dictionaries, but may be referred to *teigne*—strangle weed. Hakluyt skips it, and Petit-Val changes it to *fond a plomb,* which does not help. As a matter of fact the soundings in the strait in that locality are from 30 to 40 fathoms and the bottom is stony or rocky. Continuing west-south-west along the coast is Blanc Sablon (White Sands); a place well known then, and one which has retained its name. It is the boundary between the province of Quebec and that part of the Labrador coast which belongs to the Government of Newfoundland. The Canadian custom house is there, and it has been from the earliest times, and still is, an important fishing station.

Cartier was an observant navigator, and records all the dangers to ships in making the port of Blanc Sablon. He notices the two islands which form the harbour. One of them, *Isle de Bouays* (Wood Island) retains its name. The other is now called Greenly Island. It was, to Cartier, another *Isle des Ouaiseaulx,* the home of innumerable "godez," and of "richars," with red beaks and feet, which burrowed like rabbits. Doubling a cape (Long Point, also called Grand Point) a league from Blanc Sablon he entered a harbour which, in his time, was called *Les Islettes* (Bradore Bay)—a better harbour than the last, and one where, he says, a great deal of fishing is carried on. Ten leagues further on was a harbour called *Brest;* the latitude is given at 51° 40' (or 55', the MS. is uncertain; it is really 51° 25'), and there are islands all the way to it. Brest itself is an island, and for three leagues out all the coast is ranged for more than twelve leagues with low islands over which the high mainland appears. Cartier entered the harbour of Brest on June 10, to take in wood and water, and to prepare for the exploration of the new region he was entering upon. There the digressive description of the coast ends, and he resumes his diary or log. All his distances and directions are in the main correct and his descriptions are clear and accurate.

This harbour of Brest was the terminus of the previously discovered and named coast—named doubtless by the Breton fishermen who resorted thither in summer. As the business grew and the place became better known temporary structures may have been erected; but none such were there in Cartier's time, nor were there any residents for 150 years later. Nevertheless a story has crept into the books, of a town founded there 100 years before Quebec, with 200 houses, 1000 permanent inhabitants and a resident governor. The whole story is a myth, with less foundation than the mythical city of Norumbegue. In Brest harbour Cartier left his vessels at anchor and, on June 11, commenced an exploration westwards in his boats. They passed for ten leagues along a coast studded with innumerable islands, and camped for the night on one of the islands, where they found a great quantity of eggs of ducks and other birds. This range of coast was called *Toutes Isles.*

On the 12th of June, having got through most of the islands, they reached a harbour which was named St. Anthony. The 13th was the feast of St. Anthony of Padua, and, though he does not say so in express terms, Cartier must have given the name. It is now known as Rocky Bay. A league or two further he entered a harbour very deep—that is, running far into the land. There can be no mistake about this locality, for the physical characteristics recorded by Cartier identify it with Lobster Bay. The "St. Lawrence Pilot" describes it as a narrow inlet between steep shores, extending four and a half miles to the northeast. Cartier notices a small island about a league to the southwest, as round as an oven. This is now known as the *Boulet,* and the "St. Lawrence Pilot" describes it as a smooth, round islet in the position indicated by Cartier. He named the place *St. Servan,* after an important suburb of St. Malo, and there he erected a cross. Here occurs one of the very few instances where the translations are of assistance in correcting the error of a copyist. They concur in giving the distance at two leagues (instead of ten leagues, as in the "Relation Originale") to the next harbour—a large harbour which Cartier called the River St. Jacques, without doubt Shecatica Bay; and here occurred an incident which proves that Cartier was not the discoverer of the Strait of Belle-Isle, and that before 1534 it was a resort of French fishing vessels. He met there a large vessel from La Rochelle, which had come out to fish, and had been looking for Brest (evidently a harbour known to the crew), but having passed it in the night they did not know where they were. Cartier boarded the vessel and took her into another harbour now called Cumberland harbour, one league further to the west: which, adds Cartier, "I consider to be one of the good harbours of the world, and it was called the harbour Jacques Cartier." In this the Breton sailor anticipates the judgment of the Admiralty Pilot, which pronounces it to be "the best and easiest of access on the coast." It is *apropos* of this harbour that Cartier pronounces the unqualified condemnation of the Labrador coast which has been quoted at page 24. The practical eye of the explorer was not content with atmospheric effects of craggy hills and rocky shores sharply defined in the clear northern air or clothed with tender purple by the setting sun. What impressed itself upon his mind, and what, in his terse and vigorous style, he reported was that "while harbours were plenty there was not one cartload of earth on the whole stretch of coast." This was inside the Strait of Belle-Isle, for Cartier did not go north; he turned abruptly west round the head of Newfoundland, into the strait, without even going near Belle-Isle Island. What would have been his report of the grim rampart north of the strait battered for long ages by the surges of two thousand miles of the stormiest ocean on the globe?

This was the terminus of Cartier's exploration on the

Labrador coast. The boats returned to Brest harbour, where in the meantime his ships had been making preparations for entering upon the unknown regions beyond. He gives a short description of the natives he met; from which it clearly appears that they were not Esquimaux, and had come from a more southern country for seal fishing. They were doubtless of some Montagnais tribe of Algonquin stock. On Monday, 15th, they set sail and steered southward across the bay to examine a country which had caught their attention, and when first seen from across the bay had the appearance of two islands.

The west coast of Newfoundland, towards which Cartier now sailed, is bordered by a range of mountains from 1900 to 2000 feet high, running from Cape Anguille on the south to beyond Cape Riche, where they commence to lower as they stretch northwards. As they drew near the middle of the bay they saw that what they had taken for two islands was a double cape on the mainland—one point rising above the other. Their course had been south and the distance was about twenty leagues, which brought them to Cape Riche. The Highlands of St. John rise in rear of the cape to two points, respectively 1500 and 1600 feet. They named the spot *Cap Double*. The trend of the coast Cartier gives as N. N. E. and S. S. W., and he observed the belt of low land between the mountains and the sea, all which characteristics appear on the admiralty charts to-day. All the next day they sailed along the coast for about thirty-five leagues. The mountains were high and formidable, with cloven and craggy outlines—among them was one which had the appearance of a *granche* (old French for grange or farm building)—for which reason they called the whole range the Granches Mountains, all the more willingly, perhaps, because Cartier's wife's family name was des Granches. As night drew in they saw obscurely through the gathering mists an opening in the hills, as if of a river mouth, and a cape three leagues away, which they called *Cap Pointu*. It is now known as Cow

Head, and is identified by the low, flat island (Stearing Island) three-quarters of a mile to the north of it. Cartier wished to examine the land more closely by daylight and the ships shortened sail for the night.

And now the Gulf began to show another of its phases. A northeast storm broke upon them and they took in all but the mainsail and lay to the wind, but were driven to the southwest for thirty-seven leagues until Thursday morning (18th), when they found themselves abreast of a bay full of islands (Bay of Islands)—they called the islands *les Coulonbiers* because of their shape and the bay St. Julian. There can be no mistake about the locality; the high and steep islands occur nowhere else on the coast. Seven leagues further Cartier notes another cape, which he called *Cap Royal*. It is a very conspicuous headland 1200 feet high, now called Bear Head. Without giving the distance he next mentions a cape W. S. W. of Cape Royal, which he called *Cap Delatte,* about which there has been doubt. The name in Petit-Val's version is *Cap de Laict;* Hakluyt has it *Cape of Milk,* but it is *Delatte* in the " Relation Originale." There is a *Pointe de la Latte* in the English Channel near Brest. The name has nothing to do with milk; it is a marine term for a particular kind of thin, narrow beam. The word exists in England as *lath:* Italian, *latta,* and is of Teutonic origin. Some peculiarity of shape suggested the name. The description, when followed closely, will identify it with Cape Cormorant, a perpendicular limestone cliff rising 700 feet, and then sloping up to a conical top 268 feet higher. Red Island is a mile northwest of it and marks the locality. It is 290 feet above the sea, and would not be called low, excepting relatively to the lofty cape in juxtaposition to it. Cartier describes it as a headland eaten away at the base and round at the summit, with a low island to the north. He describes the land between these two capes as low, with high lands behind it and an appearance as if there were rivers within, all perfectly in accordance with the present charts. What he saw was the long spit which

CARTIER'S FIRST VOYAGE 133

makes the sea face of Port au Port. He describes it as a wonderful place for cod fishing, which is still the case, and while waiting for their consort they took more than one hundred large codfish in less than an hour.

The Gulf did not cease to show its teeth; for on the following day (18th) the wind was contrary, and it blew very heavily, so that Cartier turned back to Cape Royal seeking a shelter harbour. He searched with the boats, and, between Cape Royal and Cape Delatte they found what is now called Port au Port, which Cartier describes in his usual accurate manner. It is, he says, a great deep bay with islands enclosed towards the south by low lands, with flats which extend beyond them and shut in the bay on one side while Cape Royal closes in on the other. There is an island in the middle of the entrance to the bay (Fox Island), and the anchorage is bad. The "Admiralty Pilot" confirms Cartier's quick judgment: "Port au Port cannot be considered to afford secure anchorage round any of its shores, although the bottom is generally mud." So Cartier, rather than trust his ships there, put to sea for the night, and from that time until the 24th there was a continued heavy storm, with contrary wind, and the weather so thick that he did not once get a sight of land. On St. John the Baptist's day (24th) they saw a cape to the southeast which they judged to be thirty-five leagues from Cape Royal. They were very nearly right. It was Cape Anguille—a bold headland 1700 feet high, the projecting spur of a range of mountains in rear. They called it Cape St. John, but the weather was too rough to permit approach.

The weather the next day, 25th, was equally bad, with high wind and fog. For a part of the day they ran W. N. W. and toward night they hove to until the second watch, when they again set sail. They judged that they were seventeen leagues and a half northwest by west of Cape St. John. When they set sail the wind was from the northwest, and they ran southwest for fifteen leagues, when they discovered three islands. These were the Bird Rocks, for Cartier counted in a little rock which he saw between the two. This has now disappeared, but a patch of breakers still shows its position. The two islands were as steep as walls, and it was not possible to climb them. They were "as full of birds as a meadow is of grass." The larger one was full of margaux. It is now called the Great Bird; it is to the southeast and is 105 feet high. The other—the North Bird—was full of "godez" and "apponats." The disputed question of the species of birds found is treated in a separate note, only remarking here that the sailors managed to get on the lower ledge of the North Bird, for there is no proper shore, and killed in a short time more than a thousand of "godez" and "apponats." They filled their boats with them, and in an hour's time they might have filled thirty such boats. Cartier named the group *Isles de Margaulx*, and that name, or a syn-

Fig. 9. The Great Bird Rock, from an Admiralty Chart

onym of it, it has ever since retained. Five leagues to the westward was another island, which he named Brion Island, after his patron, Philippe de Chabot, Sieur de Brion, and Admiral of France. The name still survives, though some English maps absurdly call it Byron Island. Cartier lay there all night to procure wood and water. There is a good roadstead east of the island, which he found without the aid of sailing directions. He notes with his usual correctness that the soundings round the island are six or seven fathoms. He was pleased with it after his experiences on the Labrador coast, and records in his terse way his opinion that one arpent of it was worth the whole of the Terre

CARTIER'S FIRST VOYAGE 135

Neuve. He pauses to describe it, and almost waxes eloquent. There was a sandy beach all round it, it was full of fine trees, prairies, fields of wild corn, and of peas in flower as thick and as fine as any he ever saw in Bretagne, and in appearance as if they had been sown. There were in abundance gooseberries, strawberries, and Provence roses; parsley and other plants pleasant to smell. Brion Island does not seem such a paradise in the present day, but to Cartier, who had been coasting along Labrador and northern Newfoundland, it was delightful by contrast. Here also he had a new experience, for there was around the island a number of "beasts like large oxen, which had two tusks in their mouths like elephants." The Gulf abounded in those days with walruses, and Cartier met them first here, in their favourite haunt, the Magdalen Islands. They were hunted to extermination in after years, not only there, but all over the Gulf. A few were seen on the Magdalens and Anticosti as late as 1775. Cartier's sailors found one asleep on the shore and tried to take it, but it jumped into the sea. Then follows a remark which shows that the Gulf was unknown previous to his voyage. Cartier recognised that he had got in between Newfoundland and the continent; but was it a peninsula or an island? He says: "I think more than I did before from what I have seen that there may be some passage between the Terre Neuve (Newfoundland) and la Terre des Bretons (Cape Breton). If so it would shorten, not only in length, but in time, the accomplishment of this voyage." The passage is now called Cabot Strait, but not until on his return from his second voyage did Cartier pass through it.

Cartier lingered for a day at Brion Island, and on the 26th of June he passed on to a cape four leagues distant, which he named after the Dauphin—a name of special honour "because it was the beginning of good land." It was North Cape of the Great Magdalen Island, and all the 27th he sailed along the west coast outside the island, for the wind, which was evidently westerly, threw

136 THE ST. LAWRENCE BASIN

a heavy surf on the shore and he could not land. But he could see the island in the clear weather, and he described it as low and sandy, with hills of sand. Without a careful study of this group of islands on a large

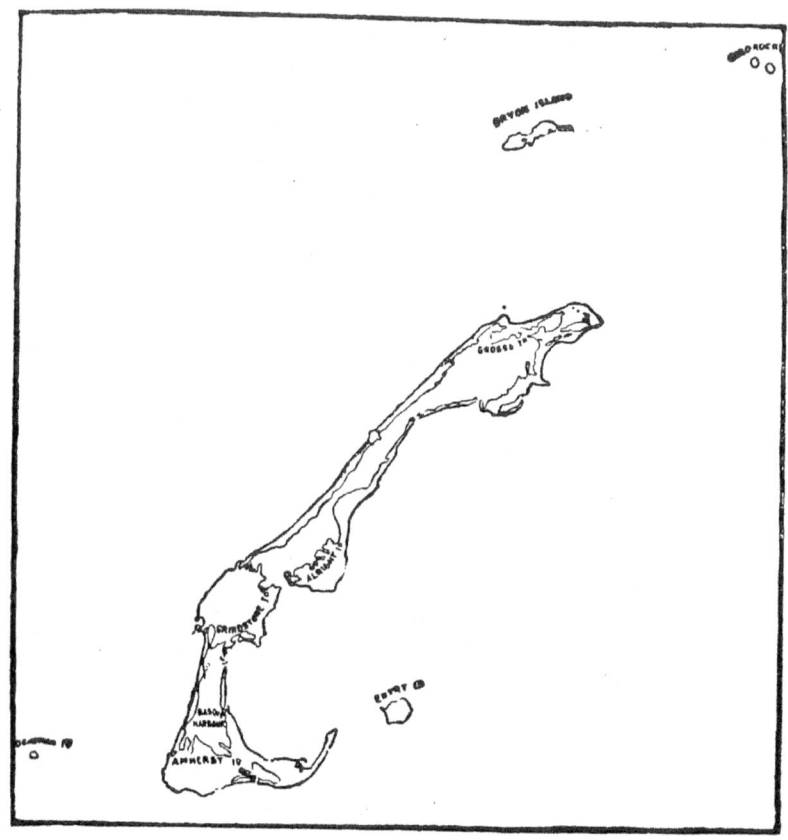

Fig. 10. The Magdalen Group—The Key to the Gulf
True shape, from an Admiralty Chart

scale map it will be impossible to understand, not only Cartier's voyages, but all the voyages during the next hundred years. The Great Magdalen is the key of the Gulf, and every ship bound to the St. Lawrence passes in sight of one of the group around it. The main Magdalen, although at a distance it appears to be several

CARTIER'S FIRST VOYAGE 137

hilly islands, is really one long island, lying, as Cartier says, E. N. E., for the hills are connected by a double line of low sand bars enclosing large lagoons opening at high tide by narrow channels to the sea. It lies in a curved, or rather bracket-like, shape, hollow towards the southeast. In the mouth of the bracket is a detached island (Entry Island), and west of the southwest elbow of the bracket is another (Deadman's Island). These peculiar characteristics stand out on the most archaic maps, and the three little islands adjacent to the north add to the certainty of identification. The names also point them out. That of the large island may always be translated "isle of sand," for it is in French maps *isle d'arènes,* and in Portuguese maps *y de Sabloen* or *Sabloes,* or sometimes *dorean,* a corruption of *d'arènes.* This point being fixed, the early geography of the Gulf is clear. From this point the expositors of Cartier's route differ radically, and until Ganong's study (in the Transactions of the Royal Society of Canada for 1887) the subject was hopelessly confused. All day Cartier sailed along the west side of the Great Magdalen, and the next day (28th) he sailed for ten leagues along the south coast until he came to a wave-eaten cape of red land, and inside of it was a bay (Pleasant Bay) looking northward to low land. The cape is easily identified as Entry Island. Opposite to this cape at a distance of *about* four leagues there was another cape—the hill (550 feet) of Grindstone Island, and between these two points the land was ranged round in a semicircle of sandy beach enclosing, as far as he could see, a sort of marsh or lake (*étang*). This view is supposed to be from Entry Island, the first cape. Opposite was Grindstone Island, the second cape, and from it, five leagues, or twelve and a half miles, to the southwest was a very high pointed island, which he named Alezay. Entry Island he called St. Pierre, for the 29th was St. Peter and St. Paul's day. Alezay is identified by its shape (see cut). It was Deadman's Island, described in the "Admiralty Pilot" as "170 feet high, with steeply sloping sides meeting at the summit like a prism." The maps all show it in its place with its name, as, for instance, the Dauphin map (see cut), where Entry Island is given, looking inward over the bay, and Alezay named to the southwest, as described. Cartier hove to and examined the place closely, and gives the soundings and the kind of bottom.

The wind changed to S. S. W. on the 29th and they left the Magdalens, sailing westward, and until midday of the 30th they saw no land. After the sun turned, however, they saw to the W. S. W., about nine or ten leagues off, what seemed to be two islands. They were coming upon the north shore of Prince Edward Island, which is very low, and they had caught sight of two com-

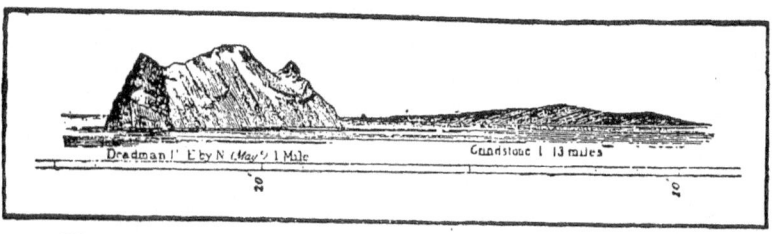

Fig. 11. Deadman's Island, from an Admiralty Chart

paratively high points, Cape Tryon and Cape Turner. The capes are not over 120 feet high, but are the highest land on the coast, and rise first out of the water. As they sailed along they saw that the country was a continuous mainland to a cape which they saw in the distance, and named *Cap d'Orleans*—Cape Kildare of our maps. They continued coasting until the morning of the following day, July 1, when a fog set in and they lowered their sails, for Cartier was anxious to examine the land. At 10 a. m. the fog lifted and they saw *Cap d'Orleans* close, and, further on, another cape (North Cape), which they called *Cap des Sauvages*. Their boats were got out and landings were made in several places. Cartier describes the country as a low, level land as beautiful as

CARTIER'S FIRST VOYAGE 139

could be seen, with fine trees and meadows, but not a harbour, and the coast ranged along with sandbars. The description of the north coast of the garden province of the Dominion could not be more accurate.

Among the places he saw, Cartier specially mentions one which he named the River of Boats (*Ripuiere de Barcques*). He said it was a fine river, but shallow,

Fig. 12. Representations of the Magdalen Group on early maps. 1. Correct outline for comparison. 2. Dauphin or Henry II. Map, 1546. 3. Homem's Map, 1558. 4. Mercator's Map, 1569. 5. Sebastian Cabot's Map, 1544. 6. Vallard Map, 1543. 7. Rotz Globe, 1543. 8. Hakluyt's Map, 1600.

and in several places he saw the natives in boats. He did not communicate with them, for the wind rose from the sea and he had to hurry back to the ship. The place is now known as Richmond or Malpeque Bay, and has always been frequented by the Indians, for there is a portage on its southern shore, barely two miles across, by which they pass from Northumberland Strait to the Gulf. It is the narrowest spot of the whole island.

Cap des Sauvages is described in a few words. The Breton sailor noted that off it there are a reef and a dangerous bank of stones. The Admiralty Pilot gives the same report. Here an Indian came running along shore making signs, but he had not courage enough to wait until they went ashore, so they left him a knife and a piece of cloth tied to a stick and went on. They examined the west coast very carefully, but found no harbour. Cartier is enthusiastic in praise of the country. The trees were marvellously beautiful and pleasant in odour—cedars, pines, yews, white elms, ash trees, willows, and others unknown. Where the land was clear of trees it was good, and abounded in red and white gooseberries, peas, strawberries, raspberries, and wild corn, like rye, having almost the appearance of cultivation. The climate was most pleasant and warm. There were doves and pigeons and many other birds. In short, Cartier thought that if the country only possessed a few harbours it would be perfect. He had touched Prince Edward Island at a bad spot, for there is not a harbour for thirty-three miles from North Point round to Egmont Bay.

Cartier had no idea that he had to do with an island, and as he sailed round North Cape and passed the west shore he saw before him the land to the east closing in to form a great bay. It was the projecting point of Nova Scotia, on the south, interlocking with the capes on the north. This part of the voyage was a stumbling block to all commentators, and, although the appearance which deceived Cartier may be seen by any tourist who crosses from Shediac in New Brunswick to Summerside, Ganong was the first to apply it to elucidate the question. This apparent bay Cartier named the Bay of St. Lunario, from Leonarius, a Breton saint of early times. It continued upon the maps for a hundred years longer, until what is now Prince Edward Island was recognised as an island, and called the Island of St. John. Seeing, as he supposed, the land thus closed before him, to the east, Cartier turned, on July 2, to a

CARTIER'S FIRST VOYAGE

land he saw at the north, which appeared to him to be continuous with the other and went, in his boats, to examine it. His description is accurate—a cape (Escuminac) of low land with shallow water in the offing; at the northeast another cape, and between the two a triangular bay running far into the land; a level country with sandy shores, and, as far out as ten leagues only twenty fathoms of water. What he saw was the coast of New Brunswick, and the remarkable triangular bay was Miramichi Bay, with its two low headlands.

The land stretched away to the north, one cape after another. The wind rose and the weather grew bad toward night, so that they had to lie to until the morning of July 3, when the wind came from the west and they made sail to the north; for they saw over the low headland (Miscou) high lands to the N. N. W., and they found between the low cape to the south and the mountains to the north a great bay, fifteen leagues across, with fifty-five fathoms of water. The whole passage is as correct as if it had been an abstract from a modern book of sailing directions. The low cape at the south was Miscou, the high lands were the Gaspé Mountains, and between, stretching westward to an unknown distance, were the bright waters of Chaleur Bay, blue under the clear, sunny sky, and the hope rose within them that here was the long looked for passage. The warm sun and the balmy weather quickened their anticipations almost to certainty, therefore they called the southern point Cape d'Esperance—Hope Cape. It was a golden dream, but the sequence was leaden, for the name was, in the lapse of years, unconsciously transferred to the north shore, just opposite, where it still mocks Cartier's hopes as Cape Despair, the English corruption of *Cap d'Espoir*.

Cartier describes the bay with his usual accuracy. His grammar may be faulty and his vocabularly nautical, but those who know the localities can see them again in his terse descriptions. He named it *la Baye de Chaleur*, because he found it as warm there as in Spain. He describes the New Brunswick side as a beautiful open country with arable land and meadows as fine as he had ever seen, and level as a lake. The Gaspé side was lofty, with mountains densely clothed with forests, among them cedars and firs of great size, fit for masts of ships of more than three hundred tons. Only in one or two places was the land clear of trees, and there it was low, with fine ponds (*étangs*). The latitude of the middle of the bay he fixes at 47° 30′ N., about twenty miles too far south, and the longitude at 73° W., which, taking Ferro as the prime meridian, is 25° 40′ too far west. It is impossible to guess how he arrived at that longitude, but it was probably worked out after his return, perhaps by someone else, for in other places the longitude is left blank. This instance shows how little dependence is to be placed on the longitudes of early explorers.

The 4th of July, Cartier says, was St. Martin's day, and although in the Roman Breviary that saint is commemorated at Martinmas, November 11, there still survives in the Anglican calendar a festival of the " translation of Martin," on July 4, indicating some peculiarity in the devotion to St. Martin in those days common to Britain and Bretagne. Cartier sailed along the Gaspé coast westward, looking for a harbour, and he found on that day *la couche St. Martin,* now Port Daniel. There the vessels lay from the 4th to the 12th of July, while the boats went further up the bay to explore. They went to the extreme end of the bay, and found that it ended in low lands with high mountains in rear, and, to their great disappointment, that there was no passage through.

While examining the coast from Port Daniel they came into contact with the natives. Chaleur Bay was the debatable region between the Indians of Canada and the Micmac tribes of Acadia. One of the boats met some canoes, and saw a large number of savages on the shores, who made signs to them to land, but being few in

CARTIER'S FIRST VOYAGE 143

number the French turned away. The savages quickly got out seven canoes and tried to surround the boat, and did not desist until the French had fired two or three shots. The next morning the savages came in their canoes to where the vessels were anchored, and after a little while confidence was established and the Indians gave the strangers a hearty welcome, with much dancing and singing. Cartier formed an opinion that they would be easy to convert to the Christian religion, but his reasons are not on record.

Disappointed in their search, they made sail July 12, and followed about eighteen leagues along the Gaspé shore and came to a point (White Head), which Cartier called Cape Pratto. The weather began to threaten, and they got shelter between the land and an island (Bonaventure Island) one league to the east of it. There they anchored safely for the night, but they found strong currents and a heavy sea. The next morning they made sail again, but had to return to the same shelter for the night. Starting again the following day they pushed along the coast, five or six leagues, when they came abreast of a river (Gaspé Bay), where they anchored until the 16th. Then the wind rose so high that one of the ships lost her anchor, and they were forced to go further up into a good and safe harbour, which their boats had discovered. There, in Gaspé basin, the finest shelter on the coast, they remained until July 25, and, strange to say, Cartier did not give it a name. At the entrance of the basin he erected a cross, with an escutcheon, on which were three fleur-de-lis, and, in large letters, " Vive le Roy de France."

At Gaspé Cartier met a great number of Indians, who had come down the River St. Lawrence from about Quebec for the mackerel fishery. He recognised that they differed both in nature and in language from the Indians he had previously seen. They were the first he met of the Huron-Iroquois stock. They came freely and frankly to visit the ships—men, women, and children, and welcomed the French with singing and dancing;

but they objected to the cross and explained by signs that the land was theirs. The French got possession of two of the sons of one of the chiefs, and managed to reconcile them and their friends by presents, telling the Indians by signs that they would bring them back with many more presents. The names of the youths were Taignoagny and Domagaya. They gave their old rags to their companions, and accepted the French dress. They were not altogether averse to being carried away, Cartier took them to France, and they were useful as interpreters on his next voyage.

At this point occurred the most unaccountable thing in all Cartier's narrative. He set sail on the 25th, and when he got out of Gaspé Bay he went in a direction to east-north-east, because the land swept round from the mouth of the bay making, as he saw it from his ship, a bay like a semicircle; and, in fact, there is such a bay from Cape Gaspé to N. N. E. (magnetic) as far as Cape Rosier. But Cartier, in sailing out, caught sight of Anticosti, about twenty leagues away, and he appears to have concluded that it formed part of the same bay, and that there was no opening through. If he had passed Cape Rosier he would have seen the land turning to the west, and, as he crossed the estuary, he must have seen open water to the west. He does not say plainly that he thought the land closed round; he merely says that he went to examine the new land which he had caught sight of. It has been supposed that a fog shut off the opening to the west, but the same fog would have hidden the low coast of Anticosti. The disappointment at finding no passage at Chaleur Bay may have influenced his judgment, but the fact is indisputable that he did cross over the main entrance to the river, and when he struck Anticosti followed its coast to the east, and not westward.

This apparent slip of Cartier does not stand alone. In 1818 John Ross was deceived by a fogbank, and not only imagined he saw a mountain range closing Lancaster Sound, but named the range after an Under Sec-

CARTIER'S FIRST VOYAGE 145

retary of Admiralty. In 1778 the celebrated Captain Cook sailed along the west coast of Vancouver Island, and thought it was the main continent. In Cartier's case, however, there was no fog, for Anticosti was visible. Could it have been that he intended to go no further west that year? He could not have been deceived. He was not prepared to winter in the country, and it might well be that he had gone as far as he thought safe that year. If so, his judgment must be approved; only, it would have been more satisfactory to his commentators if he had said so.

Cartier coasted eastward along the south coast of Anticosti until he reached a point (South Point) where the land began to turn to the east. Fifteen leagues further was a point he called Cape St. Louis, because it was the festival of that saint, when the land turned again (Heath Point). He describes the country at that place as level prairie and more clear of forest than the other part of the coast. He estimated the latitude at 49° 15' (it is 49° 05'), and he gives the longitude at 63° 30', nearly 20° too far west. It is characteristic of the wild longitude estimations, not only of Cartier, but of all the old mariners, that he makes a difference of 10° between Chaleur Bay and the east point of Anticosti, whereas the difference is only three degrees; but these figures may have been filled into the blanks in Cartier's manuscript in France by another hand; for there are many blanks for longitude still remaining, and, seeing that these also are blank in both Hakluyt's and Petit-Val's versions, that would be the most probable supposition. Here also occurs one of the few instances in which these translations assist to clear the meaning. The " Relation Originale " says that the coast from Cape St. Louis to the next turn in the coast, Cape Montmorency (Fox Point), trends to the northeast, but northwest is given in the versions, and that is really the only possible turn there could be.

At sunrise on Saturday, August 1, having followed round the channel north of Anticosti, they caught sight of other land (the Quebec Labrador), lying to the north and northeast, appearing to consist of highlands, with mountains in rear of low wooded lands with rivers. They continued coasting, examining both sides until August 5, looking for a passage on the north side. The distance between the two shores is given as about fifteen leagues, and the latitude of the centre of the channel as 50° 20′ N. It is really nearly 50°. They were able to make only twenty-five leagues in all that time, for they had to struggle against strong head-winds and opposing currents, and just when they reached the narrowest place, where the land was easily visible on both sides, and began to widen out, they had to continue the exploration in their boats, for the ships kept constantly falling off their course before the heavy head-wind. They started for a cape five leagues to the west, which projected furthest from the south shore, hoping to get a view from thence, and they found it consisted of rocks, and the soundings showed a rocky bottom. The spot indicated is High Cliff Point, the only point on that coast where the foot of the cliff has a talus of fragments of rock. The tide carried them westward against the wind, and one of the boats touched a rock, but they still rowed westward for two hours, when the tide turned, and the ebb was so strong that, with thirteen oars, they could not advance more than a stone's throw. Then they landed, and sent ten or twelve men on to the cape ahead, where the land began to trend to the southwest. Having seen and satisfied themselves of that, they all returned to the ships, which, though under sail, had dropped down more than four leagues. They had made their farthest west on this voyage, and had reached what is now called the north point of Anticosti. The 1st of August was the feast of St. Peter in chains,—the day they saw land to the north,—so they named it the Strait of St. Peter.

Cartier had now definitely ascertained that there was a great sea opening to the westward, but he was not prepared to undertake a discovery so extensive as the appearances indicated; and, besides, although his skilful seamanship had carried him round these unknown coasts with only a loss of one anchor, he had experienced an unusual amount of bad weather. When he got back to his ship he called together all the captains, pilots, masters, and companions of the expedition to consult upon the best course to take, for the engagement made with them was for a voyage, and did not include a residence over the winter, nor, in fact, was the expedition fitted out or provisioned for so long an absence. They decided to return to France for the reasons that the season of strong westerly winds was beginning; that they could not make head against the strong tides; that they could not explore any further during that season; that the stormy season on the coast of Newfoundland was approaching; that they were far from home and exposed to unknown dangers. In short, it seemed that they should either decide to winter where they were, or return at once; because if the north winds set in they could not get away. In all that company not one knew of the route south of Newfoundland, through Cabot Strait.

Now that their ships were heading homewards the wind was fair, and they had plenty of it. They coasted along the north shore, and on the projecting point of Natashquan they saw the smoke of the camp-fires of the natives; but the wind was on shore, and they could not approach. Seeing that the ships were passing on, about twelve of the savages came out in their canoes and came on board, without any more hesitation than if they had been Frenchmen. They informed Cartier that they had been on the coast in the Grand Bay, and were now on their way, laden with fish, to their own country, whence he had last come. The chief of the band was waiting on the cape, and Cartier called it Cape Thiennot after him. The ships were headed first for the coast of Newfoundland, which they reached at Cape Double (Cape Riche), and from there they went to Blanc Sablon, which they reached on August 9. On August 15 they started homewards through the Strait of Belle-Isle, and after experiencing some very heavy weather they arrived at St. Malo on September 5. The Gulf Coast of the Dominion had been thoroughly explored.

NOTE A

BIRDS MENTIONED BY JACQUES CARTIER

Much conflict of opinion exists concerning the sea-birds of Cartier's first voyage; for the names he called them have disappeared from the dictionaries, and one of the species—the most remarkable in many respects—has become extinct. Cartier was much impressed with the prodigious numbers of these birds, and devoted, comparatively, a great deal of space to describing them.

The first locality mentioned is Funk Island, the *Isle des Ouaiseaulx* of Cartier. This is a flat island, forty-six feet high, off the northeast coast of Newfoundland, thirty-three miles north of Cape Freels, and the same distance east of Fogo Island. He describes the number of birds as incredible, and, although the island is a league in circumference, it was so full of birds that they seemed as if they were stowed there as close as if in ship's hold; and, besides those on the island, there were a hundred times as many more hovering in the air and swimming in the water. They were of three kinds—"apponatz," "godez," and "margaulx."

The apponatz were as large as geese, black and white in colour, and with beaks like a crow. They could not fly, but were always in the water; for their wings were very small, and they used them only for swimming, as other birds use their wings for flying. Two boats were filled with these birds in less than half an hour. The sailors loaded them on as quickly as if they were stones. They were wondrously fat, and four or five hogsheads were salted down for food.

The bird so graphically described by Cartier was the great auk, *Alca impennis,* now and for eighty years back as extinct as the dodo; but then as abundant on the coasts of America as the buffalo was on its prairies. "These birds," wrote Anthony Parkhurst in 1578, "are also called penguins, and cannot flie; there is more meate in one of these than in a goose: the Frenchmen that fish neere the grande baie, doe bring small store of flesh with them but victuall themselves always with these birdes." Richard Whitbourne, writing a few years later, says: "These penguins are as big as geese and fly not, for

CARTIER'S FIRST VOYAGE 149

they have but a little short wing, and they multiply so infinitely upon a certain flat island, that men drive them from thence upon a board into their boats by hundreds at a time." The work of extermination was so thorough and ended so suddenly, that most of the museums of natural history found themselves without specimens. The last bird was shot in 1844, and is in the museum at Copenhagen. Several expeditions have been made to Funk Island to obtain skeletons; notably one in 1887, when a vessel belonging to the United States Government went there, and Mr. Frederick A. Lucas made a collection for the Smithsonian Institution. These auks were harmless creatures, helpless on land. Their legs were so short and placed so far behind that they seemed to squat with their bodies upright. As late as 1796, Cartwright tells us, the sailors would lay a gangway from the shore to the gunwales of the boats and drive those poor creatures on board. The memory of the great auk still persists on the coast in the repetition of such names as "the Penguin Islands."

Besides the apponatz (or apponath of Lescarbot), Cartier continues, there are incredible numbers of a smaller bird he calls *godez*. They pack themselves away among and under the large birds. These not only swim in the water, but fly in the air. They are now called guillemots—sometimes murres, and are yet numerous on the coast. There are several species; the one which Cartier saw was the "common or foolish guillemot," a confiding sort of a creature that does not know enough to get out of the way of a destructive animal like a white man. Still, as it can fly, it has survived. Sailors call them *guds* to the present day.

The birds Cartier calls margaulx are larger than geese, and are white in colour. They do not associate with the other two kinds, but live by themselves in a separate part of the island. "They bite like dogs," he adds, "when attacked."

On the coast of Labrador, off Blanc Sablon, Cartier found another Isle des Ouaiseaulx, in what is now called Greenly Island. There he found innumerable godetz and birds he calls richars. These last have red feet and beaks, and make their nests in holes in the earth like rabbits. They were puffins; and Greenly Island is still, from June to October, the resort of myriads of puffins. Farther down, on the coast he explored in his boats from Brest and called Toutes Isles, Cartier found, among others, great quantities of eggs of ducks. He calls them *cannes*, and the French people of the lower St. Lawrence brought the word over in early colony days, and use it yet.

The islets near the Magdalens known as the Bird Rocks were called by Cartier Isles de Margaulx. These islands are still white with birds, for their summits are almost inaccessible, and the lighthouse keeper is the only human inhabitant. The southern one is called the Great Bird; Audubon calls it the

Great Gannet Rock. With characteristic accuracy Cartier records the fact that the gannets (margaulx) occupy the larger island. The other island, he says, was full of godetz and apponatz, and there again his men secured for food a large number of birds. The auks being on the lowest ledges were the chief victims; the godetz were higher up.

The birds of the Gulf are much the same now, save that there are fewer of them, and the great auk is gone. The razor-billed auk still frequents the coasts in immense numbers, and breeds in company with the guillemots, as in Cartier's time. This species of the auk can fly well. It is sometimes called *tinker*, and sometimes *turre*. The *puffins* are called *sea parrots* and Perroquet Island is named from them. The island is tunnelled with their burrows. They bite viciously, as a confiding stranger quickly discovers when he is persuaded to put his hand into one of the holes. Some idea of the impression made upon Cartier may be gathered from Audubon's description of his visit, in 1833, to the Bird Rocks. There was no lighthouse for fifty years after, and the birds had been practically undisturbed. He was approaching the "Great Gannet Rock." "At length we discovered at a distance a white speck which our pilot assured us was the celebrated rock of our wishes. We thought it was still covered with snow several feet deep. As we approached it I imagined that the atmosphere around us was filled with flakes; but on my turning to the pilot, who smiled at my simplicity, I was assured that nothing was in sight but the gannets and their island home. I rubbed my eyes, took out my glass, and saw that the strange dimness of the air before us was caused by the innumerable birds, whose white bodies and black-tipped pinions produced a blended tint of light grey. When we advanced to half a mile the magnificent veil of floating gannets was easily seen, now shooting upwards as if intent on reaching the sky, then descending as if to join the feathered masses below, and again diverging towards either side, and sweeping over the surface of the ocean."

Who will dispute with Audubon as to the species of these birds? Then, as if confirming Cartier's account, he tells us: "The whole surface of the upper platform is closely covered with nests, placed about two feet asunder and in such regular order that a person may see between the lines which run north and south, as if looking along the furrows of a deeply ploughed field." Cartier observed this at Funk Island, and he expressed it by one word. It seemed as if they had been "arimez"—a word used by sailors for stowing away cargo.

Cartier makes no reference to gulls, no doubt because they were, and are, common birds upon the Atlantic Ocean and its coasts in both hemispheres.

CHAPTER XI

CARTIER'S SECOND VOYAGE, 1535-36

THE view which opened up before Cartier's eyes when he stood upon the north point of Anticosti decided his action. It is the narrowest part of the Mingan Channel. On both sides the land receded, but upon the south more than the north. The point itself is not high, but the turn in the trend of the coast is very decided, and Cartier could see the inner basin of the Gulf spreading out as far as his eye could reach. Here, then, opened up at last the passage to the South Sea, and on returning to his ships he straightway called his captains and pilots together and they decided to return home. The decision was wise. This voyage was only a reconnaissance, and they were not fitted out to remain over the season. Now the path was found, the sooner he could get home the better, for he could the quicker begin his preparations for a greater enterprise.

He lost very little time. He arrived at St. Malo on September 5, and October 30 is the date of the new commission from the Admiral of France for a second voyage "to complete the navigation in the lands which he had *commenced to discover.*" No one thought then, or suspected, that French Basques, or any other Basques, had sailed up into that bright basin whose waves rippled before Cartier's gaze under the clear blue August sky. Philippe de Chabot, the Admiral of France, knew, and the King of France knew, and so should we all know, that the Breton sailor was the first European to enter what they fondly believed to be the gateway of the sunset. To follow up the enterprise Cartier's commission empowered him to engage three ships, for the succeeding season, and to victual them for fifteen months.

The merchants of St. Malo met the preparations of

Cartier for his second voyage with the same covert opposition as they presented to the first. He had to appear before the municipal assembly and to invoke the authority of the admiral, and have his commission read and recorded. Under it he had the first choice of the vessels of the port, and until his had been manned and equipped no vessels could sail to the fisheries of the west. It was Chabot's influence which carried Cartier through; for he was then one of the most powerful nobles of the court. Enterprising and high-spirited, he had been one of the best of the youthful comrades of the monarch, and retained his favour for many years. During the preparations we find Cartier's name in the records of St. Malo, taking part in the deliberations of the municipality. He was genial in his disposition and sociable in his habits, but not a man to be moved from his purpose by the opposition of a few interested traders.

The original narrative of this voyage, generally cited as the "Bref Recit," exists in French. It was published at Paris in 1545, and is one of the scarcest books in the world, for only one copy has survived, and it is in the British Museum. Three manuscript narratives, similar in handwriting and differing very slightly from each other, and from the printed version, have been found in the Bibliothèque Impériale at Paris. Ramusio has a version in his great collection, translated from the French edition of 1545, and the version of Hakluyt has evidently been translated from Ramusio. While we may be assured from internal evidence that the version of 1545 was written by one who took part in the expedition, we are, on the same evidence, convinced that it was not, like the "Relation Originale" of the first voyage, written by Cartier himself. The vocabulary is not that of a sailor and the style is more correct and less like that of a ship's log. It is prefaced by a letter to the king written in high-flown style, and full of far-fetched allusions. Most certainly Cartier did not write that. It is usually attributed to Belleforest. In the literature of the sixteenth century we will find nothing to gratify our

CARTIER'S SECOND VOYAGE 153

curiosity concerning Cartier's life, while the annals are full of the doings of Madame de Chateaubriand, Madame d'Etampes, Diane de Poitiers, and such like persons. Cartier's discovery had a very wide influence upon the destiny of France, and for a period it was possible that his voyage might secure to France the whole interior of the continent from Quebec to New Orleans. But, as D'Avezac mournfully remarks, the French have taken very little interest in the distant discoveries of their sailors, and, even now, in one of the most important histories of France Cartier is mentioned in a few words as *Jean* Cartier, and the same error is repeated in a learned German work recently published on Norse discoveries in America.

At last everything was ready, and on Whitsunday, May 16, 1535, Cartier with his whole command received the sacrament at the Cathedral of St. Malo, and were afterwards all presented to the bishop in the choir and received his blessing. The expedition consisted of three ships, the *Grande Hermine,* of 120 tons, Thomas Frosmond, master, in which Cartier sailed; the *Petite Hermine,* of 60 tons, Mace Jalobert, captain, and *l'Emerillon,* of 40 tons, under Captain Guillaume le Breton. There were a few gentlemen, volunteer companions, with Cartier on the *Grande Hermine.* The names of 74 of the crew are preserved in the official records of the port, and 10 more, not on that list, are mentioned in the narrative. The two Indians whom Cartier took to France on his return from his first voyage were taken back as interpreters, and, together with a number whose names are not recorded, the total amounted to 112 souls. Two names on the official list have been the occasion of keen controversy in Canada,—Dom Guillaume le Breton and Dom Anthoine; some writers insisting that they were priests, "aumoniers," attached to the expedition, and others being equally certain that there were no clergymen present on either voyage. The matter is discussed later, for a good deal may be said on both sides; though fortunately it is not important from a geographical point of view. It is important, however, to observe that no basis exists for the statement that any portion of Cartier's crew, on this voyage, consisted of "impressed criminals," and therefore it is ungracious and uncharitable to characterise as "a motley crew" the party which Cartier led to church on that memorable Whitsunday to partake of the Holy Sacrament and receive the episcopal benediction under all the safeguards which the Roman Church has prescribed.

On Wednesday, May 19, 1535, the wind turned fair, and the expedition sailed, but Cartier did not have the good fortune of the previous year. He had five weeks of the worst weather the North Atlantic could produce: contrary wind, thick fog, and heavy storms, so that the ships parted company and did not see each other until they arrived at the rendezvous at Blanc Sablon. Cartier arrived on July 15, but it was the 26th before the other two ships joined him. At Blanc Sablon he refitted the ships and took in wood and water, and he sailed westward on July 29. They did not cross to Newfoundland, as before, but followed along the Labrador coast, which he describes as peaked and rocky and thickly ranged with islands. At twenty leagues from Brest, at sundown, he came to Great Meccatina Island, and named the group the *Isles de St. Guillaume*. Cartier was upon a very dangerous coast, and he struck sail every night and lay to until daylight. There is nothing remarkable upon it—it is uniformly rocky and dangerous. He noticed a roadstead full of islands (Watagheistic Sound), and named the group *Isles Ste. Marthe*—they are now called St. Mary Islands. Slowly feeling his way along he notices what he called the *Isles de St. Germain*. It is difficult to identify these among the multitude of islands. The ragged coast is monotonous with dangers, and the water is so deep that the lead gives no warning. At last, on July 31, the coast changed its character. It became flat and sandy, and shoals took the place of reefs—a wooded shore with no sign of harbours. He recognised Cape Thiennot of his former voyage, now Natashquan Point. On some modern maps there is a mountain there marked Mont Joli; but Cartier saw no such mountain, and describes the coast as it is, flat and sandy, and turning away to the northwest. He had reached familiar waters, and was able again to sail at night.

The wind turned contrary and Cartier took refuge in a harbour he called Havre St. Nicholas. He gives the distance from Cape Thiennot as seven leagues and a half. Charlevoix says this is the only name of Cartier's which persists upon the coast, and, indeed, the name is found in Sanson's atlas of 1676, but in a manner which gives no clew to its identification. Here Cartier lay from August 1 to August 7, and he planted a cross as a beacon on one of the four islands which he says form the harbour. It was probably Pashasheeboo Bay.

From Havre St. Nicholas Cartier sailed to cross over to the Anticosti shore towards Cape Rabast, that is, to the north point of the island, his extreme west point on the previous voyage, where the land began to fall away (*rabattre*) or widen out; but the wind changed and there were no harbours on that shore, so he turned back to the Labrador coast. He entered "a very fine and large bay, full of islands, and with channels of entrance and exit in all winds. It was marked by a large island at its mouth" (St. Genevieve Island). This bay is now called Pillage Bay. Cartier named it *Baye Sainct Laurens,* because he entered it on August 10, the feast of St. Lawrence. Gradually and insensibly the name spread until it finally extended over the whole St. Lawrence Gulf and River. There cannot be any doubt about the locality, for its physical features are described by Cartier with his usual accuracy. "I have seen," writes a missionary priest on the coast, "the mountain shaped like a stack of wheat, and I have seen the large island like a headland which projects beyond the others."

On August 12 Cartier resumed his westward course and steered for a cape upon the land to the south (Anticosti), and now the two Indians began to recognize the coast familiar to them. They told Cartier that the land on the south was an island, and south of it again was Honguedo (Gaspé), from whence he had taken them the previous year. Two days' sail from there commenced the kingdom of Saguenay, beyond which was Canada. These names occur here for the first time, and, as Cartier could not have heard them, save from his Indian companions, they must have been the names then current in the speech of the nation to which Taignoagny and Domagaya belonged. The words are Huron-Iroquois, and settle the question as to the race then occupying Canada. This has been the subject of so much controversy that it has been reserved for separate discussion. Doubtless much had been said by the captured Indians during their winter in France about their native country, for the names come in without explanation, as if well known. Cartier sailed across the estuary of the river to the Gaspé shore, and his incidental remark that the number of whales they saw during the traverse passed all experience throws much light upon the conditions of the Gulf at that time. He named the island (Anticosti) L'Assumption, for on that festival he passed out of the Mingan Channel and saw the west point of Anticosti. On that day and the next he followed along the lofty Gaspé coast, remarking upon the high mountains: for the whole peninsula of Gaspé is a high tableland, and the Shickshock and Notre Dame mountains rise from three thousand to four thousand feet above the sea and come down bluff to the shore.

The two Indians were now thoroughly at home, and they told Cartier that he was about to enter upon the great river of Hochelaga, and that it was the highway to Canada, and would grow narrower all the way to Canada, evidently meaning Quebec, and that there he would find the water fresh. They said that they had never heard of any man who had been to the end of it, and that he would have to use his boats—all of which was true, for at Cape Rouge, nine miles above Quebec, is the narrowest point on the river, and thirty miles below Quebec the

CARTIER'S SECOND VOYAGE 157

water becomes fresh. This information was disappointing, for it appeared to close the avenue to the west, and Cartier was in search of a passage to the great South Sea, and seeing to the north, on the opposite side in the distance, a range of high mountains in rear of the shore, he turned back on his course and surveyed the coast eastwards lest by any chance he might miss the through passage of which he was in search.

It was Wednesday, August 18, when he put about. He had reached Point de Monts, for he observed the great arc which sweeps from it round to the northeast. At that point is, properly, the commencement of the estuary of the river, and it narrows there to twenty-five miles. The Indians said it was the beginning of Saguenay, where red copper was found. Cartier's quick eye could not miss the magnificent harbour of Seven Islands Bay—the best on the whole coast. The islands are, as he describes them, very high, and a few miles in rear of the shore the tableland of Labrador rises from 1300 to 1700 feet. He named the place *Isles Rondes,* and there he left his ships and explored in his boats every mile of the coast he had omitted, back to the point where he crossed to the south—stopping on his way to examine the river Moisic. He had now seen the whole Labrador coast—not at a distance, but close to, and, without one accident, he had run in and out among islands and reefs and shoals in places where only the most experienced skippers now venture with the aid of the charts of modern surveys. Those old sailors seemed to sail by instinct. At the Moisic Cartier saw some strange fishes, shaped like horses, and his Indians told him that they went on land at night, but remained in the sea by day. He saw plenty of them in the river, but none on land, nor has anyone seen such fishes since. Lescarbot tries to explain them in a chapter heading by calling them *hippopotames.* Unless they were walruses, it is impossible to guess what they were. Disappointed in his search, Cartier returned to his ships in Seven Islands harbour. There was clearly no passage on that shore.

Contrary winds and fog detained the ships until August 24. The south shore of the Gulf had been examined on his first voyage, and the only course open was to follow up the great river before him—a magnificent avenue leading to the southwest. Who could guess what possibilities it might reveal? On August 24, then, Cartier set sail from Seven Islands, and on the 29th he arrived at Bic. Nothing had escaped his notice by the way. He observed the Outarde and Manicouagan rivers. They seemed to him one large stream opening out upon the low lands with high lands in rear, and he observed the extensive Manicouagan shoal a long distance from shore. He took soundings at several points, and records his opinion that it is a very dangerous locality; in which everyone will concur who has seen the line of white foam curling along its outer reef. The river widens out to nearly thirty miles, and he kept up a sharp lookout on both sides. Bic and the adjacent roadstead of Rimouski are the first secure roadsteads in the river; and vessels passing inwards now take on pilots there. As the 29th was the anniversary of the beheading of St. John the Baptist, he called the islands the *Islots de Saint Jean*.

"On the first day of September," writes Cartier, "we set sail from the said harbour for Canada." Canada was to him a town—the chief town of a territory. The name is in the vocabulary at the end of his narrative. It is a Huron-Iroquois word, and is a generic name for any town or village. He soon arrived at three islands in the middle of the river (Green Island, Red Island, and Basque Island), and abreast of them on the north shore was the mouth of a profoundly deep river between high mountains of bare rock, and, notwithstanding the scarcity of earth, they were clothed with forest. Many trees large enough to make masts for a thirty-ton vessel seemed to grow straight out of the rock. It struck Cartier as being very strange—these precipitous mountains green with forest, yet without earth. His Indians told him that this great river was the main avenue to the

CARTIER'S SECOND VOYAGE 159

kingdom of Saguenay. Four canoes of savages were fishing there, and two of them approached, and at the call of an Indian tongue the people came confidently on board. Taignoagny and Domagaya were at last among acquaintances.

On the following day Cartier pushed on " for Canada," and here it should be noted that, for him, the whole region was divided into three kingdoms—Saguenay, where he then was; Canada, which he was then entering; and Hochelaga, which he was to visit later. Kingdoms they are called in the old books, and their chiefs were kings; but these kings we know to have been sachems, and their kingdoms the tribal hunting grounds. At this point occur some difficulties of navigation in the river. In the present day, when the river has been surveyed and charted minutely, and when the channel is lighted like a city street, it is easy to pass up or down; but Cartier's seamanship was here strained to the utmost, for the ebb and flow of the tides are swift and eddies are formed by the nature of the bottom and the character of the reefs and islands. The galleon would have touched if they had not got out the boats; for there were two islands (the Pilgrims) on the south shore, with shoals all around them strewed with great boulders. He tried to anchor abreast of a high island on the north side (Hare Island) to wait over the ebb tide, but he could not find an anchorage, and had to run back to the islands at the Saguenay.

At the mouth of the Saguenay Cartier was surprised to find large numbers of white whales: " a kind of fish," he says, " which no man had ever before seen or heard of." They were " as large as porpoises, and had no sword," like swordfishes. They were shaped like greyhounds as to the head and body, and they were as " white as snow, and without a spot." The Indians called them adhothuys, and told Cartier that they frequented only places between fresh and salt water. These creatures still exist in the same locality, but in largely reduced numbers, and in Canada are now called white porpoises (beluga). There can be no doubt as to what fish was meant, though the head is not pointed like a greyhound's.

The following day (September 6) a fair wind arose, and Cartier pushed on to the west as far as an island on the north shore, which made, with the land, a good roadstead. He called it Isle aux Coudres, because of the wild hazel trees found there (Hakluyt translates the word, *filbert*), loaded with nuts; but he was chiefly struck with the rush of the flowing and ebbing tides, reminding him of the Garonne at Bordeaux. The next day, Cartier says, was the 7th, and the day of the Nativity of Our Lady, and before they started they heard mass. His voyages have been very thoroughly discussed in Canada, and it has been supposed that Cartier was wrong, for the festival is on the 8th. Hakluyt, following Ramusio, says it was the *eve* of Our Lady's Day, but Lescarbot and all the MSS. concur with the " Bref Recit " of 1545. It is not likely that the vigils of the Church were observed on an expedition like this, but as the question is not geographical it does not require discussion here. On that day he arrived at the Traverse at the lower point of the Isle of Orleans. The fourteen islands he reports are the islands now known as Crane Island, Goose Island, Grosse Island, and others smaller. Here, the Indians said, was the division between the territories of Saguenay and Canada. The ships were anchored in the channel between the Island of Orleans and the north shore, and Cartier landed, taking his two Indian passengers as interpreters.

It will be remembered that Taignoagny and Domagaya were taken by Cartier on his first voyage, when he knew nothing of Canada or the great river, and they were taken from the Gaspé coast. Nevertheless this locality (the present Quebec) was their real home, and there were their friends and relatives. There were people fishing on the island, who began to run away until the two Indians called after them and told them their names, and that they had come back. Whereupon they crowded around and there was much dancing and rejoicing, and the people came from all sides as the news spread,—men, women and children,—and food was brought and presents made. The event was as startling and sensational as would be, in our day, the return of two missing friends telling us that they had come from the moon. We may, therefore, conclude with safety that the Huron-Iroquois race were spread far more widely to the east than when Champlain arrived sixty years later.

The following day "the lord of Canada" came down the river with twelve canoes and many people. His name was Donnacona, and his title was Agouhanna, which we shall translate by the more appropriate word *chief*. The consequent ceremonies became familiar in after years, but they were new to Cartier. The long harangues, with "surprising movements of body and limbs" and the dancing astonished him. Then Donnacona came on board the captain's ship, and Taignoagny and Domagaya told him of the wonders they had seen in France and of the kind treatment they had received; at which the chief's welcome became more demonstrative. The interview closed by Cartier getting into Donnacona's canoe and ordering bread and wine to be brought for him and his party, which pleased them all. As soon as the Indians left Cartier got out his boats and started up the river to find a secure harbour. He followed the north channel, and at the end of the island he came upon a very beautiful and pleasant bay (the basin of Quebec harbour), and they found a small river falling into it, with a bar with two or three fathoms upon it at high water. This Cartier settled upon as a suitable place in which to lay up his vessels in safety. He did not move them there until Holy Cross Day, September 14, and for that reason he named the place Sainte Croix. The little river is now called the Saint Charles.

In September the environs of Quebec are at the height of that beauty which is equalled by very few of the most favoured localities in the world. The great river contracts to the narrowest point in its whole course. The

Island of Orleans divides the channel below, and, above, the river sweeps round in a curve from the southwest. In front of the city is a deep basin, forming a harbour, where the largest ships afloat may swing at anchor with the flowing or ebbing tide. The blue hills close the horizon with the rounded outlines characteristic of the Laurentides, and curve round in a vast amphitheatre clothed with forest and sloping down to the border of level land on the margin. Just as the river begins to expand the northern bank rises to the lofty promontory of Cape Diamond, and at that point the little river St. Charles falls in at an acute angle. A populous suburb of the city has extended across and obscured its beauty, but the memory of the older men of the present generation vividly reproduces the lovely stream winding in long curves through the meadow lands interspersed with groves of elms and maples. Few who have seen Quebec can ever forget its charm, and Cartier's narrative rises out of its log-book style as he tells of the rich and fruitful land, the beautiful trees, as fine as any in France, the oaks, the elms, the ash trees, the chestnuts, the cedars, the hawthorns. The Island of Orleans particularly excited his admiration for its beauty and fertility, and, from the quantity of vines upon it, he named it the Isle of Bacchus. Donnacona and his people assiduously assisted at his exploration of the vicinity, but it is evident that if the old chief had not possessed so remarkable a gift of oratory Cartier would have been better pleased. These preachments (*preschements*), although enlivened by dancing and gesticulation, must have been tedious in the Huron language, or in any other; but all who in future years came in contact with the Huron-Iroquios race had to learn to endure them without wincing.

The place which Cartier had selected for his winter settlement was a point less than two miles up the St. Croix (St. Charles) River, where a small stream, now called the Lairet, falls in. At the point of junction he ordered a fort to be built, and the Quebec people have

CARTIER'S SECOND VOYAGE 163

marked the site by a monument, inaugurated at a national fête with orations which would have delighted the old Huron chief could he have heard them. The Indian town of Stadacona was situated on the opposite side of the valley of the St. Charles, on the Coteau Ste. Genevieve, sloping down to the bank of the little river on the reverse side of Cape Diamond; for these Huron-Iroquois were sedentary tribes, with fixed habitations, and cultivated, to some extent and in a rude manner, the adjacent land.

The two larger vessels were warped into their winter dock in the St. Charles River on the 14th, and Cartier had marks (balises) placed in the stream to indicate the channel; but his mind was set upon going further up the river to the chief city of the next kingdom westwards, for he had heard from his Indian interpreters of its importance. He, therefore, left the *Emerillon* out in the stream, and called upon Taignoagny and Domagaya to fulfil their promise and go with him to Hochelaga. At first they assented, but a sudden change came over them and they showed by their conduct distrust and ill-will towards the French. They would no longer enter the ships at the captain's invitation, and would stay apart with a band of their people on a neighbouring point of land. Taignoagny, who in fickleness was a typical Huron, came forward and told Cartier that Donnacona was grieved because the French always wore their arms while the Indians went unarmed. Cartier replied that the French always wore their arms when at home, as he and Domagaya well knew. Taignoagny turned out to be a treacherous rascal. He could not be blamed for taking part with his own people and putting them up to the slight value of the presents the strangers were scattering around, but later on Cartier learned that he was stirring up mischief, and that the proposal for the French to lay aside their arms originated with him.

That cloud passed away and the Indians crowded around the ships again; but the two interpreters told

Cartier that they would not go to Hochelaga, and that Donnacona was sorry that Cartier wanted to go, and that he had forbidden all his people to take part in the proposed expedition. Every possible effort was put forth to dissuade Cartier from his purpose, and the ill-will and malice of Taignoagny was evident through it all. As a last resource the Indians concocted a piece of theatrical devilry. The Indians assembled in large numbers in the woods near the ships and, suddenly at the set time, a canoe came swiftly down the river containing three men dressed in dogskins with faces blackened and with long horns. They passed the French without turning their heads and went on towards the shore. The middle devil made a speech, and, as soon as the canoe touched land, all three fell down, as if dead. The Indians carried them all into the woods and made the whole place resound with their howlings. At last Taignoagny and Domagaya came out with gestures of consternation, and with many exclamations told Cartier that their god Cudragny had sent them word from Hochelaga that there was so much ice and snow that it would be death for anyone to go there. Much palavering followed, with yells and dancing, as the Indians swarmed out of the woods on hearing Cartier's contemptuous reply to this jugglery, and then the interpreters told him that Donnacona would not consent to let them go unless they left hostages to stay with him until the expedition returned.

Unmoved by the representations and jugglery of the Indians and by the defection of his promised guides, Cartier started, at the turn of the tide, on the following morning (September 19), with the *Emerillon* and two boats. It was a bold undertaking in view of the opposition of the Indians and the evident malice of Taignoagny. He took with him fifty sailors and all the gentlemen companions on the expedition. He soon passed the narrowest point, and the great river spread out to a width of from two to three miles. Its course is approximately directly from the southwest, and it flows through the alluvial plain with few windings, looking more like an arm of the sea than a river. On both sides the rich plain spreads out level to the far distance. The voyagers were delighted. Better land, reports Cartier, could not be found anywhere. The beauty of the trees pleased him, and the profusion with which the native vines grew surprised him. They almost seemed, as he thought, to have been planted. The grapes were not so large and sweet as in France, but that he ascribes to want of pruning and cultivation. He found huts along the banks, for many of the people were fishing, and they came out without fear to greet the strangers and to bring them fish. At a distance of twenty-five leagues from "Canada" (Stadacona) he came to a place called Ochelay (variously spelled in the MSS. and versions, Achelay, Hochelay, Achelacy), where the currents are very swift and dangerous and the channel is obstructed with large stones. The place is called the Richelieu (from an island there so named by Champlain, who built a fort upon it), and ocean steamships time their departure from Montreal or Quebec so as to pass it at high tide. It appears on all the old maps, and there was a village near, probably at what is now called Point Platon, a conspicuous point at a bend of the river. The chief of the place came on board the vessel with demonstrations of welcome. He presented Cartier with two of his children, but the captain would accept only one, a little girl of seven or eight years. This little girl survived all the other Indians whom Cartier carried to France the following spring. The distance as given, 25 leagues, is far too great. It is really only 35 statute miles. The total distance from Quebec to Montreal is really 160 statute miles, but Lescarbot puts it down as 200 leagues. The name Richelieu, given later to this place by Champlain, has led to much misconception among writers who do not know the locality, and even an accurate scholar like D'Avezac takes the name of the chief to be Ochelay, and supposes a river to exist there, which he calls the Richelieu. The River Richelieu is seventy-five miles further up, and is at the western end of Lake St. Peter. It is very surprising also that Charlevoix, Lescarbot and Père Le Tac should suppose that Cartier wintered at this very dangerous point; in fact, more misconceptions have gathered round this locality than round any other spot on the river.

On the 28th they arrived at the expanse now called Lake St. Peter. It is not recorded that Cartier named it, but on the maps made in his time it is put down as Lac d'Angoulesme, after the title of Francis before his accession. At the western end of the lake he found no inlet, and the water which had been two fathoms all over the lake fell to one fathom and a half; so he anchored the *Emerillon* and searched for the channel in his boats. Three important rivers fall in close together from the south, the Richelieu, the Yamaska, and the St. Francis, and from the north another, the Maskinongé, and at their junction with the St. Lawrence they form an archipelago of low islands, in which it is very easy to miss the channel. Cartier observed by the banks that it was the season of lowest water, and that there had been three fathoms more upon the bars at high water. He decided to leave the *Emerillon* there and make the rest of his journey in his two boats. There he met five Indians, who came on board without the least hesitation, and when the boats touched the bank one of the Indians lifted Cartier in his arms and carried him to shore as easily as if he had been a child. From them he learned, by signs, that he was still on the right way to Hochelaga.

It was the 2d of October when the boats arrived at Hochelaga. More than a thousand people came down to the bank, manifesting their welcome by dancing—men, women, and children in separate bands, and they loaded the boats with fish and bread made into cakes from their corn. Cartier made them presents as they clustered round him when he landed. They brought their children in arms to touch the strangers. No welcome could be warmer, and when evening came and the Frenchmen went to their boats for supper and sleep

CARTIER'S SECOND VOYAGE 167

the Indians made fires and danced all night on the shore adjacent. Early the following morning Cartier and his people put on their best accoutrements and prepared to visit the town. He had with him his gentlemen companions and twenty-eight sailors. The boats were left in charge of eight men at a place now called Hochelaga, below the current St. Mary. It is the eastern suburb of the present city of Montreal, and the river runs there with a current of eight miles an hour. The Indian town was about two leagues away, and, from the description in the narrative, was upon the first rise or terrace on which the present city stands, somewhere near the site of the present Windsor Hotel, or of St. James Cathedral on Dorchester Street. Cartier took three Indians as guides, and, well armed and in regular order, marched up along a thoroughly well beaten road to the town. After a league and a half they came to a large fire, where a chief, surrounded by many attendants, made signs that they were to rest. The bonfire of welcome still persists among the remains of the Iroquois tribes on the Grand River in Ontario. Then followed the usual preachment and giving of presents. A half a league further the cultivated fields of Indian corn commenced, and in the midst was Hochelaga, near to the mountain.

Ramusio has handed down to us a plan of this town, upon what authority based is not known. The following illustration fairly represents the written description of the narrative, and will give an approximate idea of the construction of the towns of the Huron-Iroquois race. It was circular in outline, and surrounded by a stockade of three rows of upright timbers. The centre row was perpendicular, and the inner and outer rows leaned towards each other inward and touched, so that, in section, the rampart was pyramidal. The wall was about the height of two lances, and on the outside the framework was tied together and made solid by timbers, laid lengthwise all around. Inside, at a convenient height, a platform ran round the rampart with a store of stones ready to repel assailants. One door only pierced the rampart, and inside there were about fifty houses surrounding a public square where the inhabitants could make fires. The houses were about fifty paces long by twelve or fifteen wide. They were covered with bark and above they had storerooms for food. The people of each house ate in common, cooking their food by the same fire made upon a spot of earth left in the centre of every house, and each family had its own room.

Cartier then goes on to describe their method of making bread. Maize he saw for the first time, and he called up his Brazilian experience to describe it. "It is as large or larger than peas, and like the millet of Brazil." He describes the wampum which answered for money, and gives a far-fetched account of how it is obtained. We must not, however, suppose, with Hakluyt, that the melons he saw were muskmelons, and wander with others into far-fetched theories of unknown Europeans having brought the seed at unknown times. They were the pumpkins and squashes indigenous to America and cultivated everywhere by the Indians. They are called by later writers *citrouilles du pays,* or *citrouilles Iroquoises.*

Cartier and his companions entered the town and met with the warmest possible welcome. Men, women, and children crowded around seeking only to touch them, and bringing their babies to have them touched by the strangers, whom they took for superhuman beings. Then mats were laid, and when he and his company were seated they brought their sick and lame and blind to be healed; and among them their great chief or agouhanna, and signed to Cartier to stroke his palsied limbs. At this part of the narrative we should expect the priest to come forward, if there was one in the party. Evidently there was none, for Cartier, touched with pity for the groundless confidence of these poor people, repeated the " In principio "—the first part of the first chapter of St. John's Gospel—and signed them with the sign of the cross, praying that God might give them knowledge of the faith and grace to receive Christianity and baptism.

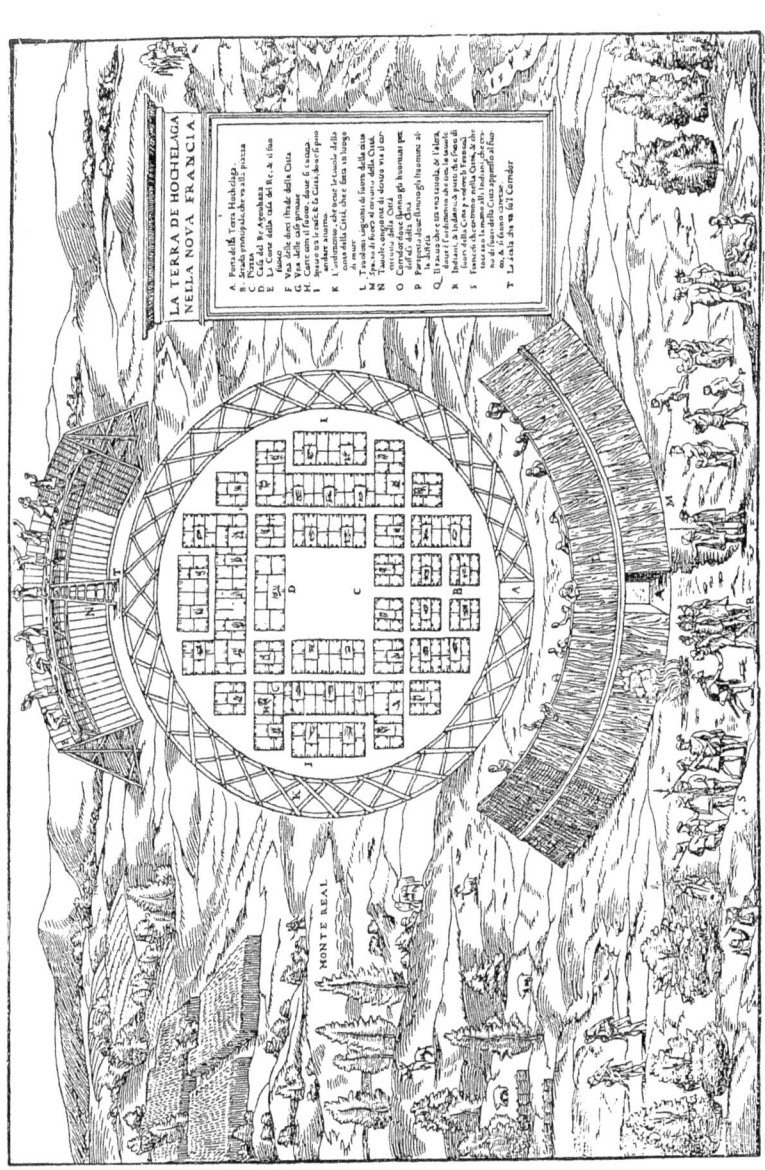

Plan of Hochelaga
From Ramusio's *Navigationi et Viaggi*

Then he took his "Book of Hours," or Prayer Book, and slowly read the story of Our Lord's Passion, word by word, pointing to heaven and making other gestures of devotion, the Indians all the while listening with great attention. When we compare the conduct of this brave and simple sailor with that of the reckless swashbucklers who in the southern parts of America for the most part abused the confidence of the natives, we cannot but feel touched with the childlike faith of the Breton captain, who relates it so simply, and impressed with the true instinct which suggested his selection for reading. It was a happy augury for the fair city of future years that the opening words of St. John's Gospel and the recital of the Passion of Our Lord inaugurated its appearance on the field of history. Might it perchance be that some charm lingered on the leafy slopes of Mount Royal and spread up the diverging streams of the great valley?—for in all that land persecution has never reared its hateful head, and there are no arrears of religious violence and bloodshed in its history to be atoned for.

Cartier and his people ascended the mountain, and his narrative witnesses to the deep impression the view from its summit made upon his mind. Looking in the direction of all his efforts—the mysterious west—he saw the Ottawa River opened out into the Lake of the Two Mountains—to the southwest was the main flood of the St. Lawrence broadened in its far distance into Lake St. Louis. Nearer, and of a still evening within hearing, were the rapids where the great river rushes down forty-five feet in seven miles. On his right, on the north, was the Laurentian range in the dim distance fringing the fertile valley, and on the south were the Adirondack Mountains of New York and the Green Mountains of Vermont, looking far nearer in the clear October air than they really were. Three detached hills sprang up through the forest-clad plain on the south. All these Cartier noted, and on turning he saw the Indian town just below, and his boats five miles away lying at the foot of the current. He again grew enthusiastic over the beautiful level valley, and he called the place Mont Royal. It still bears that name, and has communicated it to the busy city of Montreal, which lies below, and is fast encircling it.

Cartier's guides tried to understand and answer his questions, but with little success. He gathered from them that the river he saw flowing from the west surrounded the Saguenay country, and that from the same country came metal like some red copper he showed them. From the narrative it is clear that the Saguenay of the Hochelagans was the far west of the upper lakes. At last the day of novel incidents drew to a close, and the Frenchmen turned back towards their boats. Such of them as seemed tired the Indians took up and carried on their backs. The Indians parted with their strange guests with sorrow, and followed the boats along the river bank until night closed in. The day was Sunday. Many churches now adorn the city, and near where Cartier stood when he read to the wondering Indians of the Passion of Our Lord stands a stately cathedral, but that first day in Montreal with its service of intercession and the simple appealing prayer of the devout sailor captain still touches the religious imagination through the mists of three hundred and fifty years.

It did not take long to reach the *Emerillon* at the head of Lake St. Peter. They stopped at the present Three Rivers on the way down and searched the lower reach of the St. Maurice. Cartier called it the *Rivière du Fouez,* a name which has puzzled many; but Cartier was not strong in orthography, and, to borrow the words of Lescarbot, " I think he meant Foix." On Monday, October 11, he arrived at the " Province of Canada " and the " Harbour of St. Croix." He found that his crew had worked faithfully during his absence and had constructed a fort with heavy timber close to the ships, and mounted cannon and made the place defensible against any force the natives could bring against it.

The extreme western point of exploration for sixty

CARTIER'S SECOND VOYAGE 171

years to come had now been reached, and it is unnecessary to dwell at length upon the relations between Cartier's people and the Indians of Stadacona. They were glad to welcome him back, and he went in formal state to visit Donnacona and the town. He found the houses well stocked with food for the winter, and the chief showed him five scalps stretched on wood. They had been taken from a hostile tribe called Toudamans, dwelling to the south, with whom his people were constantly at war. These we shall meet with in Champlain's time as Mohawks. Cartier again betrays the extent of his voyaging by remarking that the Indians lived in a community of goods "as is the custom in Brazil." He saw tobacco for the first time, and his description of the way the men filled themselves up with smoke until it poured out of their mouths and nostrils as out of a chimney stack is very quaint. The town was a league distant from the ships, and the natives came down, at first, in crowds to visit them, but Taignoagny and Domagaya sowed distrust between them and the French, so that the chief of Hagonchenda, a neighbouring town, as well as some of the people of Canada (Stadacona) warned Cartier to be on his guard. Nor is it necessary to repeat his favourable descriptions of the country, the birds, the beasts, the fishes, and the trees. Vague accounts reached him of the Saguenay, by which name he indicates a region west of Hochelaga, for he thought the Ottawa beyond Montreal joined the Saguenay. He heard also of two or three great lakes, evidently the expansions of the St. Lawrence, west of Montreal, and of a great lake of fresh water, of which no one had seen the end. The Indians had not been there, but had heard of it from the people of Saguenay. He heard also of a river (the Richelieu) leading to the southwest, where, after a month's travel, one would reach a region where there is no ice or snow, and oranges, apples, nuts, and almonds and other fruits grow in abundance. The people there are constantly at war. Cartier thought by their signs and marks that this country was near Florida.

Thus early was the wonderful river system of Canada indicated by the rough diagrams of the natives.

Cartier strengthened his fort as the distrust grew deeper, and prepared for the coming winter as well as one might who had never known what a winter in Canada could be. Still, in all his trouble, he does not complain of the cold, unusual as he found it to be; nor did any of his people suffer from frost. As December came in he discovered that the Indians were suffering from some disease, and he stopped communication for fear of contagion; but in vain. It was scurvy,—land scurvy,—and the same conditions and the same food brought it among the Frenchmen. Day by day they grew weaker and weaker, and the disease, with all its loathsome symptoms, attacked man after man, until there were barely ten men of the whole crew in good health. It speaks well for Cartier and his men that no sign of insubordination showed itself. This was no "motley crew," as injuriously represented by a learned writer in a moment of negligence, and they had not, in a body, partaken of the sacrament at the cathedral of St. Malo unworthily. Patiently they bore the infliction of an unknown and dreadful malady in all obedience and without a murmur; but as they tried to bury their dead comrades and had to leave the bodies in the deep snow because they had not strength to dig the frozen ground, they lost all hope of seeing France again. The surroundings were strange and threatened new and mysterious dangers. Shut up in the heart of an unknown continent, wasted by an unknown disease, the ships fast in ice-bound waters, the ground covered with snow, such as they had never seen before in depth, surrounded by strange tribes whose good will they had reason to mistrust, it is no wonder their hearts sank and increasing discouragement increased their predisposition to disease. In this very darkness and shadow of death they fell back for help and comfort upon the teachings of their Church. About a bowshot from the ships they erected a statue of the Virgin Mary, and Cartier ordered mass to be said

CARTIER'S SECOND VOYAGE 173

there on the following Sunday. On that day all who could walk went in procession, singing the Seven Penitential Psalms and the Litany, and mass was celebrated and prayer offered for the intercession of Our Lady in their behalf. They were, in truth, in sore distress. That same day Philippe Rougemont died, a youth of twenty-two years, and an autopsy was held to see if, perchance, the cause of the malady might be found. The appearances now so well known gave no clew to the origin of the disease, and it raged unchecked until only three sound men remained in the whole crew. Cartier himself kept well, and used every means to conceal from the Indians the weakness of his party. They were kept away and led to suppose work was being done in the fort and ships. His ingenuity and resource as captain were exercised to the utmost, and with success, for the Indians did not discover the helplessness of the strangers.

At last the tide turned. Donnacona, Taignoagny, and many of their people were away on their winter's hunt, but Domagaya had remained, and Cartier met him well and strong, although he had seen him, only ten days before, grievously afflicted by disease. In answer to his inquiries Domagaya told him of the healing virtues of a tree called ameda. On Cartier's explaining that one of his servants was sick, Domagaya got two women to bring branches and show how to make an extract for drinking from the leaves and bark, and how to apply the residue to the inflamed limbs. One or two at first doubtfully drank of the extract, but its beneficial power was immediately felt, and so eager were the others for the remedy that they quickly used up a tree as large as an oak in preparing it. The effect was miraculous, for in six days all the crew were sound and well. They would never have seen France again, writes Cartier, "unless God in His infinite goodness and mercy had not looked upon them in pity and given them knowledge of a remedy against all diseases, the most excellent that was ever seen or known in all the earth." Twenty-five persons, among the best and most companionable of the crew, died of the disease. Cartier, with his usual good judgment, limits the miracle to the apparent accident of the way he obtained knowledge of the remedy by his meeting with Domagaya; but some late writers go further, and, forgetting that the pagan Indians partook of the benefit to an equal extent as the Frenchmen, imagine that the virtues of the tree were specially conferred and did not avail on subsequent occasions. The tree has been the subject of much discussion. It is now known as balsam fir, *Abies balsamea,* and will be found among medicinal trees in the United States pharmacopœia.

From the middle of November, 1535, to April 15, 1536, the ships were shut in. The ice was two fathoms thick, so Cartier reports, and doubtless it seemed very thick to his unaccustomed eye; but the snow was only four feet deep, so probably the measurements should be interchanged, and then largely abated. Naturally all the drinkable liquids were frozen, and the ice was four inches thick on the sides of the vessel. What is remarkable is the courage and continued subordination of the men. We need not dwell upon the other incidents of the winter. Monotonous and weary as it was, spring came at last, and the vessels were got out into the main river, but there were not men enough left to navigate all three, and *La Petite Hermine* was abandoned and the hull given to some Indians of a neighbouring village for the sake of the iron, so precious to savages. Donnacona had returned from his hunt, but a very large number of Indians had come with him—a gathering quite unaccountable, Cartier thought, unless in contemplation of mischief, though it might well have resulted from a natural curiosity to see the strangers. Taignoagny was back and scheming in his characteristic manner. The huts in Stadacona were full of men, and Donnacona feigned illness, so as to avoid seeing Cartier's messengers or allowing them to enter the house. Taignoagny was a characteristic type of Huron, and tried to engage Cartier to carry off one of the chiefs who apparently stood in his way. But Cartier was meditating a plan

CARTIER'S SECOND VOYAGE

to carry off Donnacona, Taignoagny, and five or six of the chief men besides.

Donnacona was a man past middle age, who had seen a great deal of the country, and he was addicted to telling very astonishing tales of things seen on his extensive excursions in the west, in the fabulous Saguenay region. Infinite gold and silver might be found there, with rubies and other riches. Another country he had visited where the natives never ate, and had no occasion to digest, and still another where the people have only one leg. Such facts as these related to the King of France by a potentate as important and as widely travelled as the "lord of Canada" would carry conviction and lead to future voyages. Donnacona was a victim to his own imagination, for Cartier felt that he needed him in France.

On May 3 the ships were ready to sail, and by a sudden manœuvre Cartier seized Donnacona and the other men he wanted. The Indians howled and lamented all night, and next day Donnacona was set up to speak to them, and told them that Cartier had promised to treat him well, and would certainly bring him back the following year, and that the King would give him great presents. This partly reconciled the people, and Cartier allowed the leading men to come on board and talk to their chief, and the same communication was permitted until the ships finally got away. It was not a proceeding to be proud of, for it savoured strongly of the very treachery they had suspected in the Indians. Compared, however, with the conduct of other nations toward these wild people, that of the French was very humane. They did not take these poor Indians as slaves; but with the intention of treating them kindly, teaching them the Christian religion, and bringing them back to their homes. This aspect of Christianity does not accord with present notions of righteousness, but Cartier must be judged by the practice and belief current in his time. Of all the European nations who came in contact with the Indians the French have ever been the most kind and considerate.

The ships got away on May 6, but had to wait at Isle aux Coudres for a fair wind until the 16th, and Donnacona's people visited him and brought presents to the last moment. Among them was a great knife of red copper, which came from the Saguenay region, showing that there was communication among the eastern tribes and those on Lake Superior, where native copper was found and worked. Cartier returned to France by the channel between Gaspé and Anticosti, which, he says expressly, had not before been discovered. The wind being fair, he sailed day and night, and the following day he made Brion Island. This was the point he sailed for, and that he should have struck it at the centre shows how carefully he had recorded his previous courses. The "Bref Recit" must be corrected by the three manuscripts and Lescarbot, for Cartier's intention, as clearly expressed in the same sentence, was to shorten the passage home by that route. He gives the latitude of Brion Island as 47° 30'. It is really 47° 48'.

From Brion Island he sailed to Magdalen Island. On his first voyage he had struck it at the North Cape and coasted along its western shore. Now he touched at East Cape and followed down the eastern coast. He had not given it any name on his first voyage, but now he called the island *Les Araynes,*—the sands,—and so we shall find it in various languages on succeeding maps, under some orthographic modification of *sablon* or *arène*. The wind changed, and Cartier could not make any outward progress, so he went back to Brion Island.

There follows now the most obscure passage in the narrative. In several places the "Bref Recit" is clearly wrong and must be corrected by the three manuscripts. On June 1 Cartier set sail again on a southeast course from Brion Island, and he went to examine a high land which appeared to be an island. He ranged along the coast of that land for $22\frac{1}{2}$ leagues, according to all three manuscripts and Lescarbot. The "Bref Recit" says $2\frac{1}{2}$ leagues, but that is too short a distance to be called "ranging" a coast, and while so coasting he saw three high islands, which were towards the Araynes. Here we must supply from the three manuscripts and Lescarbot an omitted sentence, "and we likewise perceived that the Araynes was an island and that the aforesaid land was certainly a high and continuous mainland, inclining to the northwest." Cartier had been coasting some distance down the western shore of Cape Breton, and the three high islands were three lofty capes on that coast looking toward Les Araynes. The passage is obscure, but the only real difficulty is the direction "northwest," for the whole western coast of these lands—that which faces inwards upon the Gulf—runs to the east of north. We must suspect an error in copying.

The narrative continues: "After we perceived these things we returned to the cape of the aforesaid land," that is, to the headland of the coast he had been ranging, now called Cape St. Lawrence. There he found two or three capes wonderfully lofty, with a great depth of water and a strong current, thus describing accurately the north point of Cape Breton Island with its two bold headlands, Cape St. Lawrence and Cape North. There is a bay sweeping round between them, the land is high and steep all around, the water is deep and the main outflow of the River St. Lawrence is on that side of the strait. On the same day they arrived at Cape Lorraine—a name given by Cartier. The place is identified as the present Cape Ray by his description; for the land is low at the shore and three miles inland Table Mountain rises abruptly 1700 feet, and there are "barachois," suggesting a river mouth, although, as Cartier remarks, there is no harbour there worth anything. The latitude is given by an evident error at 46° 30' instead of 47° 30', as it is in Hakluyt; it is really 47° 37'. This is made clear by the remark that they saw another cape to the south in latitude 47° 15', which they named Cape St. Paul. The place is now known as St. Paul's Island, and is really in 47° 12'.

The dates are now clear. On June 4, Whitsunday, Cartier recognised that he was on the coast of Newfoundland, running east-south-east. It was true east, but the remark showed that the variation experienced was two points west, not quite so much as it is now. The wind turning foul, the vessel took shelter for two days at a harbour they named *de Saint Esprit*, probably the present Port aux Basques. Then they sailed to the well-known island of St. Pierre, where they found French and Breton fishing vessels, and from whence they went to Cape Race. They stopped at Rougnoze, the present Renews, for wood and water,—the place had been known by that name since 1506,—and from thence Cartier took his final departure for St. Malo, where he arrived on July 6, after a prosperous voyage of seventeen days.

CHAPTER XII

SOME DISPUTED POINTS OF CARTIER'S VOYAGES

WHEN Cartier returned to France in 1536 Canada had been discovered to its very heart. Four of its seven provinces had been revealed, and at Montreal the central point of its diverging waterways had been touched. There are, however, some questions, apart from the discovery of the country, which demand notice from everyone who may write upon the subject. These voyages are a never-failing source of interest in Canada, and Canadians have unceasingly discussed them; for the most part with learning and diligence, and always with earnestness. In the United States also, and in France, they have occupied the attention of many scholars, and some questions concerning them have been the subject of warm controversy.

It is therefore within the scope of this volume to inquire what were the tribes or races of Indians with whom Cartier came in contact. To this it may be answered first negatively—they were not Esquimaux. Cartier met the natives first on the Labrador coast near Blanc Sablon. He describes their hair as twisted on the top of their heads and tied like a handful of hay; something of the nature of a pin was passed through it and for ornament they used birds' feathers. They were clothed in the skins of beasts and they painted themselves with dark reddish colours. But the characteristic mark is that their boats were made of birch bark. If the men had been Esquimaux their canoes would have been made of skins. Cartier, however, disposes of the question by adding—" Since I saw them I have learned that they come from warmer countries to kill seals and other things for their sustenance." Later on, when returning, he met some of these same Indians at Cape Thiennot (Natashquan

Point). They came freely on board and told him that they had come from "the Grand Bay" (Strait of Belle-Isle), and that they were on their way home in the direction whence Cartier was returning, and they informed him that the ships (the fishing fleet) had sailed from the bay laden with fish. It will not then be necessary to discuss the migrations of the Esquimaux; these savages were not Esquimaux, they were Montagnais.

Cartier on his first voyage saw Indians on the coast of Prince Edward Island. He could not get speech with them, but during the time he was exploring Chaleur Bay and waiting for fair weather in Gaspé Basin he had much communication with the natives. Those he met in Chaleur Bay at first attempted to surround one of his boats, and he fired some shots to frighten them, but afterwards he found them very friendly. He describes those he met at Gaspé as very poor, going almost naked, and their whole possessions, excepting their canoes and nets, not being worth five sous. They were not of the same race or speech as the Indians he met in Chaleur Bay. Their heads were shaven, excepting one long lock, which they wound upon the top of their heads and tied with thongs. He afterwards learned that Gaspé was not their home and that they came there in summer to fish. Their nets were made of hemp grown in their own country, and they used for bread maize grown there also. It is clear that these people seemed poor because they were far from their homes and, in fact, two of the sons of their chief, Taignoagny and Domagaya, who acted as interpreters on Cartier's second voyage, were found to have their homes at Stadacona (Quebec.) We conclude, therefore, that the Indians on Chaleur Bay were a tribe of Algonquins, probably Micmacs, and those who were making their summer fishery at Gaspé were of the same race and tongue as the Quebec and Hochelaga Indians. In short they were Hurons and not Algonquins. A comparison of the few words embodied in Cartier's vocabulary will put this beyond doubt.

It should be observed that, although Cartier carried off these two Indians, it was to prepare them to act as interpreters, and that they and their relatives, though alarmed at first, were reconciled and content with his promises. The two youths were provided with good clothes and their people received presents and came off in numbers to take leave of them and bring them food, and they promised that the cross Cartier had erected should not be interfered with. It is not accurate, therefore, to say that "he bore away to France, carrying thither as a sample of the natural products of the New World two young Indians, lured into their clutches by an act of villainous treachery."

There is no reason to believe, with some, that these Gaspésians were a separate race or tribe of Indians, or in the myth that they had been, from old times, worshippers of the cross. Whether the stories of the worship of the cross by the natives of Central America are or are not true is irrelevant; they are certainly untrue here. The *Porte-Croix* Indians, as some enthusiasts have called them, were Micmacs, or Souriquois, among whom neither the Jesuits nor Poutrincourt, Lescarbot nor Champlain ever found a trace of such devotion. The *Porte-Croix* tribe may be classed among the other mythical Indians who spoke Basque or Irish or Welsh.

The discoverers and early settlers of Canada came in contact with two races of Indians only—the Algonquins and the Huron-Iroquois. These were radically distinct in language, as the most cursory consideration of the surviving Indian names of localities will show. In the Maritime Provinces, formerly Acadia, names such as Musquodoboit, Kouchibouguac, Kennebecasis, Buctouche, Chebucto indicate that the primitive occupants of these provinces were of Algonquin race; while such names as Ottáwa, Torónto, Hochelága, Stadacóna, Caughnawága, Cataráqui testify to the presence of a people of the Huron-Iroquois stock, and that their ears and tongues were formed to a different class of sounds. It is better to use the compound word Huron-

Iroquois, because they were originally the same people; although, when the Europeans arrived, a war had commenced which ended in the practical extermination of the Hurons. The Algonquins were hunters, and had no settled abode. The Huron-Iroquois lived in palisaded towns, in wood and bark houses, and supported themselves chiefly by agriculture. Although the cultivation of their crops of maize and pumpkins was left to the women, while the men hunted or made war, the Huron-Iroquois were sedentary tribes and developed a political system superior to anything which existed among the nomadic tribes around them.

On his second voyage Cartier came in contact solely with Huron-Iroquois tribes, for they were the occupants of the valley of the St. Lawrence from the sea to the upper lakes. To the south the tribes of New England and New York were Algonquins, and to the north the scattered tribes extending, inclusively from the Montagnais on the northeast to the Ojibways on the northwest, were all Algonquin, so that the Huron-Iroquois people were encircled by alien tribes inferior in organisation and skill in politics and war. A great revolution was impending at the period of the Cartier voyages. Tragedies of unknown horror would be enacted before many years, but the St. Lawrence valley seemed peaceful then, though there were indications of gathering storm on the south and west.

There is much diversity of opinion as to the race of the Indians who gave Cartier so warm a welcome at Montreal; but of late years it has been generally conceded that they were of Huron-Iroquois stock, and the doubt is, mainly, whether they were Hurons or Hurons and Iroquois side by side. The fact that all Cartier's vocabularies are Huron should put the question beyond dispute, for there were differences of dialect between tribes of the same race, and the Mohawk (the oldest dialect of Iroquois) is the nearest to Huron. That being the case, it follows from the facts recorded that the people of Stadacona were of the same stock, because their speech was the same, their god Cudragny was the same, the name of their town Stadacona was Huron, and the manners and customs of both people were the same. It also follows that Taignoagny and Domagaya, whom Cartier took to France on his first voyage, were Hurons, and the Indians who were at Gaspé Basin were Hurons, for the relatives of the two interpreters were met by Cartier at Stadacona, and that most certainly was their home. The first act of a long tragedy had been played. The Iroquois had been expelled from their homes beside the Hurons in the St. Lawrence valley, and in their retreats on the south and west were gathering strength for their great revenge.

It is, moreover, evident that the town of Hochelaga was then in some real sense the chief place on the river. Cartier says "that notwithstanding the Indians of that town are sedentary and do not move about, like the people of Canada and Saguenay, these people [the Canadians] are subject to them, as also are eight or nine other nations who live upon the river." Cartier had heard of Hochelaga from his two interpreters before his second voyage, probably in France, for on arrival he claimed from them the redemption of a promise to go there with him, and when they tried to dissuade him he said that he had orders from the King to go there. We find, then, the Hurons in possession of the river from Gaspé to the Saults above Hochelaga and an indefinite distance beyond.

The country was, however, by no means populous. In the whole stretch of the river from Stadacona to Hochelaga one town only is mentioned by Cartier—Achelay, at the Richelieu rapids. Below Stadacona he mentions Araste, Starnatau, Tailla (which he says is on a mountain), and Scitadin. Apparently not far from Stadacona was the town of Tequenondahi, also situated on a mountain. These are the only places mentioned in the narrative as having inhabitants, although frequent mention is made of houses—fishing huts—both above and below Stadacona, and in a general way of several tribes living in open towns. These places had their own chiefs, over whom Donnacona seems to have had no authority, but the people and the chiefs are met at Stadacona as visitors. The people of Scitadin were very friendly, and the chief of a town Cartier calls Hagonchenda warned him of the treachery of Donnacona and the two interpreters.

From Donnacona Cartier heard of a hostile people to the south—the Trudemans. These were the Mohawks who had been expelled from the St. Lawrence valley. Donnacona exhibited five scalps taken from them, and told a story which is corroborated by Mohawk tradition. Only two years before a party of his people, on their way to Gaspé, were encamped on an island opposite the Saguenay. The Trudemans attacked them at night, set fire to their fort, and killed the whole party, men, women, and children, save five who escaped. This incident confirms the presence of people from Stadacona at Gaspé Basin, and explains their apparent poverty. They were there for their summer fishing only. The island is at the entrance of Bic harbour and is still known as *Isle au Massacre,* and in recent years a cave strewed with human bones was discovered there. At Hochelaga Cartier was told of another evil nation called Agouionda, dwelling up the river and waging continual war among themselves, and who wore defensive armour made of strips of wood laced with cord. These were other tribes of Iroquois in league with the Mohawks and constantly at war with the Hurons and Algonquins.

Much interest has been taken, not only in Canada, but in the United States, in the tree called in the "Bref Recit" ameda, in the Paris MSS. amedda, and by Lescarbot annedda, whose healing power saved Cartier's whole party from death by scurvy. Justin Winsor and J. G. Shea attribute the cure to the bark of the white pine. Parkman thinks the wonderful tree was a spruce, or more probably an arbor vitæ. The Abbés Ferland and Faillon suppose it to have been the white spruce, and that is

DISPUTED POINTS

apparently the opinion of Charlevoix; but he identifies the tree he means. He was a skilled botanist, but botanical nomenclature, especially that of the large and complicated family of pines and spruces, was then not settled, and the white spruce, *abies alba* of our books, was not the tree he meant. It was, as he says, the tree from which Canada balsam and oil of terebinthine is derived. This tree is found in our books as *abies balsamea*, or balsam fir (Gray). It is sometimes called the balm of Gilead, and sometimes the American silver fir, and will readily be found in the pharmacopœias. The oil of terebinthine is the active healing constituent of the balsam. It is a volatile oil, and possesses strong antiseptic properties, besides being a stimulant. It has not lost its healing virtues, although other anti-scorbutics may have displaced it. All the spruces yield an extract of value in medicine; but in old colony days, and still in the old-fashioned towns on the seaboard, spruce beer is made in the spring with an extract from the young branches of the black spruce, *abies nigra,* and this used to be taken to sea as an anti-scorbutic by the sailors of the American colonies. It is a pleasant and healthful drink at any time.

Another unfailing subject of interest in Canada presents a problem absolutely insoluble, fortunately not an important one. In the narrative of the first voyage three expressions, "after hearing mass," "we caused mass to be sung," and "after having heard mass," lead the reader to suppose a priest was with the expedition, although one would expect to have seen him come forward on such an occasion as the elevation of the cross at Gaspé. On the second voyage a list of the crew, almost complete, has been preserved, and among them are Dom Guilliaume Le Breton and Dom Anthoine. No other mention is made of these two men, and the most diligent research has discovered no single fact concerning them. Ordinarily their clerical status would not be doubted, for even in old English writers the word "Dom," for "Dominus," was recognised as an aca-

186 THE ST. LAWRENCE BASIN

demical title, and translated by "Sir"; so a curate or parson was called Sir, as we find in Shakespeare,—"Sir Hugh Evans, a Welsh parson," and "Sir Oliver Martext, a vicar." It was likewise the custom in Bretagne to use the word "Dom" for an unbeneficed priest or chaplain, quite independently of its application to certain religious orders. Naturally one expects to hear of these persons, if they were clergymen, for in certain junctures of the second voyage their offices were needed, if ever the ministrations of the Church were needed; but they never appear exercising their functions of baptising, comforting, exhorting, or burying. On one occasion, at Isle aux Coudres, the vessels are said to sail "after hearing mass," but at Hochelaga, Cartier himself read the Gospel of St. John and the Story of the Passion out of his Book of Hours. He stroked the limbs of the paralytic chief and prayed for the conversion of the savages. He may have left the priests behind on that occasion, but a little later on, at Stadacona, we find him explaining the Christian faith to the Indians with some apparent result, for a number of the people, and among them Donnacona and the two interpreters, asked several times for baptism, but he refused, as he says, "because he did not know their minds and their resolution, and there was no one then who could teach them the faith." He told Taignoagny and Domagaya (the interpreters) to say that he would return on another voyage "and would bring priests and chrism and that he could not baptise without chrism." No priest could have been there when he said that, for the excuse was not valid. Afterwards, when the scurvy was at its height, and he had an image of the Virgin Mary erected, "he ordered that mass should be said there the following Sunday," and "mass was said and celebrated before the said image." These two passages cannot be taken in their obvious meaning and be consistent with the other statements, for mass in any proper sense cannot be celebrated without a priest. While the clergymen in Canada who have treated the subject are for the most part certain

DISPUTED POINTS 187

that priests were present, other writers of authority are certain of the contrary, and others are content to remain in doubt. This last is in fact the most philosophical course, because the narrative is self-contradictory, and everyone must decide according to his own sense of the probabilities. Hakluyt, who was a Protestant clergyman and well knew the meaning of the word " mass," translates it " service," recognising the difficulty, and knowing the usage on English ships in his day— as in ours, where the captain leads service in the absence of a clergyman. One thing only is certain, that if there were clergymen on the expedition they were of a milder and more self-effacing type than any met with elsewhere in the history of the continent of America. Cartier could not talk Huron any better than the other Frenchmen. All communication was through interpreters, and if there were priests with him one expects to read that he was told to attend to his ships and leave theology alone.

It might have been supposed that the origin and meaning of the word " Canada " would have rested undisturbed where Cartier placed it. At the end of his account of the second voyage is a vocabulary of the language of the country and kingdoms of " Hochelaga and Canada," where it is expressly stated that the natives " call a town *Canada.*" Stadacona was only the specific name of the town he found, and this is abundantly evident in the narrative, as, in one instance out of many, where Donnacona asks Cartier to go the following day to see Canada—that is, Stadacona—just as one man might ask another to come to town. Nevertheless, some suppose that, at some unspecified time—any time will do so long as it is prior to Cartier—the Portuguese went up the river, and, in their disappointment at finding it a river, said *Cà nada* (nothing here). The natives, by theory, caught up that phrase and repeated it to Cartier, as the only Portuguese they knew. Still another Portuguese theory is that *Canada* is an old Portuguese word, still in use in the Atlantic islands, meaning a strait, and that the pre-Cartier discoverers, when they arrived at Quebec, thought the river was a channel by which they might pass to the East Indies. Charlevoix reports another theory—that the pre-Cartier sailors were Spaniards who, finding no gold mines, exclaimed *Aca nada* (nothing here). Thevet, Belleforest, and Lescarbot have each a theory; but the most far-fetched is the derivation from the Sanscrit " *Kanada*—one who eats little." All this learned labour, and there is a good deal more of it, might have been saved by permitting the Huron-Iroquois to know their own language. We have Cartier's testimony that Canada signified in Donnacona's mouth a town, and the missionaries in after years —many of whom, like the late Father Cuoq, spent their lives preaching and teaching in the Indian languages of Canada,—testify that *Kanata*, which Charlevoix says was pronounced Canada, signified, in Iroquois, town, village, or collection of huts; and from Quebec it was extended over the whole country.

Like many other points of Cartier's voyages, the place where he laid up his ships for the winter has been disputed. Twenty-nine miles up the river from Quebec is a place called Ste. Croix, and on the north shore opposite is a river now bearing the name Jacques Cartier. Some writers have supposed that to be the site of Cartier's winter quarters. Lescarbot led the way into the error; but, as he was never in Canada proper, he is not to be credited when in Canadian questions he contradicts Champlain. Wherever the Ste. Croix was, Cartier most clearly asserts that he left two of his ships there, and then went twenty-five leagues up the river in the galleon and two boats to a place he calls Achelay, where the river was swift, full of rocks, and dangerous. Lescarbot betrays his ignorance of the localities in the note No. 74 to his map, for he there says that Champlain's Quebec is Cartier's Achelay, while he identifies the former place by the narrows and the high (Montmorenci) fall close to it. This is to confuse Quebec with the Richelieu rapids and to ignore Cartier's plain

DISPUTED POINTS 189

statement that when he was at Achelay his two largest ships were safe in winter quarters in the Ste. Croix, twenty-five leagues down the river. Père Le Tac follows Lescarbot, and tries to reconcile the difference by introducing a new error in supposing that Cartier wintered at the St. Charles only on his third voyage, instead of at Cap Rouge; and again in stating that the river narrows across from Ste. Croix to the Jacques Cartier River. Even across from Pointe Platon it is not nearly so narrow as at Quebec. The channel is narrow because of obstructions, but the river there is wide. Père Le Tac says, moreover, that the Recollet convent was on the far side of the St. Charles, close to the little river de la Raye (Lairet), at a place commonly called " Jacques Cartier's Fort," just in fact where the monument has been erected. The site of the convent is clearly identified by Père Sagard. Charlevoix has varied the error by confusing the Ste. Croix and Jacques Cartier; the Ste. Croix opposite the Jacques Cartier was not a river, but a point of land.

The question should be set at rest by the testimony of Champlain and his conclusive reasoning. He says of the St. Charles:

" I am of the opinion that this river, which is north-north-west from our settlement, is the place where Jacques Cartier wintered, since there are still, a league up the river, remains of what seems to have been a chimney, the foundation of which has been found, and indications of there having been ditches surrounding their dwellings, which were small. We found also large pieces of hewn worm-eaten timber, and some three or four cannon balls. All these things show clearly that there was a settlement there, founded by Christians; and what leads me to say and believe that it was that of Jacques Cartier is the fact that there is no evidence whatever that anyone wintered and built a house in these places except Jacques Cartier, at the time of his discoveries. This place, as I think, must have been called Ste. Croix, as he named it, which name has since been transferred to another place fifteen leagues west of our settlement. But there is no evidence of his having wintered in the place now called Ste. Croix, nor in any other there, since in this direction there is no river or any other place large enough for vessels, except the main river or that of which I spoke above."

He then goes on to demonstrate that it was not possible to lay up vessels for the winter in a place such as Ste. Croix, exposed to strong currents and ice, and that the place so claimed for Cartier's winter quarters was then called Achelacy, where the river is swift and dangerous, and can only be passed at flood tide. He points out that there are no narrows on the river excepting those near Quebec, and adds that he was astonished, when he was told that Cartier wintered at Pointe Ste. Croix, to find there no trace of a river for vessels. That led him to make a careful examination of the question, which no one had previously done. The astonishment of Champlain will be shared by anyone familiar with the narrative and the localities.

Another theory has been stated—that Cartier lost a vessel in the St. Lawrence, near the Jacques Cartier River; but there is no record of any such loss having occurred. According to J. G. Shea this report originated with La Potherie. Cartier's vessels are all accounted for. Cartier did, indeed, abandon to the Indians one of his vessels, the *Petite Hermine,* which he could not man for the return voyage in consequence of the ravages of the scurvy. He presented the dismantled hull for the sake of the bolts and nails to some Indians who had been very friendly to him. In 1843 the remains of a vessel were found a little higher up the St. Charles, at the junction of the rivulet St. Michel. These remains were assumed to be the hull of the *Petite Hermine,* and were presented to the town of St. Malo, where they are preserved as relics of Cartier's vessel, and are supposed to identify the site of Cartier's fort. But it was not shown that the iron had been removed; in fact, the spikes and bolts were still in good preservation. Moreover, the site at the junction of the Lairet is identified by the location of the Recollets' and Jesuits' houses, as recorded in the annals of those orders, and after much controversy it has been accepted by the people of Quebec and marked by the monument they have erected.

CHAPTER XIII

CARTIER'S THIRD VOYAGE; ROBERVAL, 1541-43

FRANCE was again in confusion when Cartier arrived home in the summer of 1536. The sudden death (attributed to poison) of the Dauphin and the impending invasion of Provence by the Emperor Charles V. absorbed the attention of the King and his court, and effectually threw Cartier and his ten abducted Indian notables into the shade. We may well imagine that in the midst of private calamity and public danger Francis had neither time nor inclination to listen to Donnacona's marvellous stories about Saguenay, or about men with one leg, and suchlike prodigies. Cartier was, therefore, unable to keep his promise to the Indians of Canada. He could not return in a year, nor in several years; but the poor savage exiles in France were in the meantime well treated and cared for bodily and spiritually. They were instructed in the Christian religion and baptised. Thevet reports that he had often talked with Donnacona, and that the chief had become a good Christian. That was possibly the case; but Thevet was as great a romancer as Donnacona, and had more opportunities to display his natural gifts, so he must not be taken too seriously. Cartier did, however, make a report to the King, both verbally and in writing, and the savages were presented at court and the King talked with them; but time passed in delays, and the poor wild people all died, excepting the one little girl from Pointe au Platon, whom the chief of Achelay had given to Cartier on his way down from Hochelaga. One would gladly know more of the fate of this little savage lady from Lotbinière, for she was the daughter of a chief (un grand seigneur), but the records are silent, and she, no

CARTIER'S THIRD VOYAGE 193

doubt, died like Pocahontas, a victim to the diseases of civilised life.

In 1538 a truce for ten years was signed. It did not last long, but the turmoil of war quieted down for a while, and in the following year Francis, with a generosity wasted upon Charles V., permitted the Emperor to pass from Spain through France in order to reach more quickly his turbulent provinces in the north. At last, in 1540, Francis resumed his Canadian plans; and on October 17, 1540, his commission to Cartier for a new voyage was issued. This document is worthy of close attention, for it places beyond doubt Cartier's claim to be the "discoverer of the countries of Canada and Hochelaga," without the least deduction for Spaniards, Portuguese, or Basques. It sets forth the intention of pressing the discovery of the country of Saguenay. This region was, as has been observed, not the region of the Saguenay River, but the upper regions from whence the great river came which Cartier saw from the top of Mount Royal—the region where copper was found, and where there was a real fresh water sea of which no man had seen the end. These lands, the commission sets forth, are "a portion of Asia on its western side," and the object of the expedition was, not only to discover them, but, if need be, to settle there. Cartier was commissioned in the amplest manner as captain-general and master pilot, with corresponding honours and privileges, and all upon the expedition were to be obedient to him. This commission was sent by the Dauphin, as Duke, to the estates of Bretagne on October 20; and on December 12, 1540, the King sent a mandement to the Seneschal of Rennes, ordering him to prevent the people of the seaport towns of Bretagne from obstructing Cartier in collecting his crew.

Suddenly there came a change in the councils of the King; and this, as pointed out by the late Abbé Verreau (one of the most painstaking and learned scholars of Canada), could only have been caused by the disgrace of Cartier's patron, the Admiral Chabot de Brion.

Never was disgrace more unmerited, but it reacted upon Cartier; and on January 15, 1541, the King issued a commission to Jean François de La Roque, Sieur de Roberval, giving him the chief command. This change of counsel has been obscured by many writers from want of attention to the fact that at that time in France the year commenced at Easter, and therefore while Cartier's commission is really October 17, 1540, Roberval's is subsequent, and its true date in our reckoning of time is January 15, 1541, although the date it bore in the French calendar was 1540. The commission will be found at length in Harrisse's " Notes sur la Nouvelle France."

Roberval's commission was wider than that to Cartier. It created him lieutenant-general, and chief leader and captain of the expedition, over each and every ship, and over all persons, sailors as well as soldiers; with power to appoint, remove, or change captains and pilots from ship to ship, and to replace them at his pleasure. He had the power to appoint lieutenants and to invest them with authority as he saw fit. He was authorised to enter upon these distant lands, peaceably or by force, and to build forts and castles, and to grant lands in fiefs and seigniories to worthy followers; but without touching territories occupied by the Emperor or the King of Portugal. All these, and such like powers, were granted in the most absolute and unreserved way; but what is chiefly important is that Cartier's commission was revoked, for the document plainly stated " that if we have previously granted any letters or power to any person contrary to the tenor of these letters we from the present time have revoked, and do revoke, cancel, and annul them, excepting so far and so long as our said lieutenant may allow and permit."

Here, then, was created a totally new condition of things. The experienced and successful sailor who had conducted two expeditions with success was rudely deposed and put under the command of a courtier, a landsman, a soldier, a person of no experience, nor even of

CARTIER'S THIRD VOYAGE

especial note in the history of the time. In all this long document Cartier is not mentioned, nor are his discoveries recognised. Cartier had been given power to select fifty criminals from the gaols, such as might seem to him suitable for the expedition; but to Roberval all the prisons of France were thrown open. It was the scheme of a foolish courtier, and success was impossible. Cartier was already involved in preparations, and could not retreat. The plain mariner of St. Malo had no friends at court powerful enough to protest against this injustice. He did not expect any good result from an expedition so organised, and, before leaving France, made his will.

The expedition was to consist of five ships. The King advanced 30,000 livres to Cartier, and 15,000 to Roberval. Early in May Cartier had the five ships ready, the *Grande Hermine* and *Emerillon* among them, and they had dropped down to the outer harbour of St. Malo victualled for two years, waiting only for the arrival of Roberval. The King's command was urgent, for he had written to Cartier charging him to sail immediately after receipt of his letter, upon pain of incurring the royal displeasure and of being held responsible for all the delay. When Roberval came down he found that the powder and artillery and provisions he had ordered in Champagne and Normandy had not arrived. His convicts also were only beginning to arrive, in chained gangs, and it was decided that Cartier should sail with his five ships and Roberval should follow forthwith with two others, bringing the belated supplies and the rest of the expedition. A few days before Cartier sailed Roberval left St. Malo for Honfleur with all his people. The haughty and inexperienced lieutenant of the King having departed, difficulties ceased, and Cartier sailed on May 20, 1541, but as representing Roberval, not the King of France.

While the two previous expeditions had attracted no attention outside of a small circle in France, and were, as the maps show, unknown in the rest of Europe, the fuss and stir made in getting up this expedition excited the jealousy of Charles V., and the Council of the Indies sent spies to France to watch and report on all that was done. It was admitted that the Bacallaos was outside the demarcation of Spain; but according to the Treaty of Tordesillas it was within the line of Portuguese authority, and pressure was put upon the King of Portugal to induce him to despatch an armed force to crush this attempt of the French to interfere with the ownership of the New World. The King of Portugal would not move, and the Council of the Indies apprehended no evil results. They seem to have had a fairly clear idea of the American coast. The Cardinal of Seville expressed it plainly: "The motives of the French are that they suppose these lands are rich in gold and silver. In my opinion they are wrong, because the whole coast as far as Florida contains no other wealth than that dependent on the fisheries." Both were sure the French would fail, but it is believed by some excellent writers that the Emperor did send Ares de Sea, one of his chief captains, to Terrenéuve to see what Cartier was doing. If he sailed on that errand in July, 1541, Cartier was safe up the river before he could have arrived.

We are indebted to the indefatigable Richard Hakluyt for all we know about the actual occurrences upon this voyage, and that of Roberval the following year. Neither Lescarbot, nor Ramusio, nor Champlain appears to have known of them. The untiring research of Ramé, Joüon des Longrais, Harrisse, and a few others has unearthed a number of documents from which much may be gathered concerning transactions in France; but it is to the enthusiastic efforts of the Anglican parson that we are indebted for information as to the voyages themselves. This has not been as cordially recognised as it ought to have been. The voyage was tedious. Roberval's delays had postponed the time of sailing until May 23, after the easterly winds were over; and, what with the delays caused by bad weather and fighting against the westerly winds, and the delays taking in wood and water

CARTIER'S THIRD VOYAGE 197

and waiting at Newfoundland for the arrival of Roberval, which they expected from day to day, it was August 23 before the five ships, reunited after having been separated by storms, reached Stadacona. No sooner had they arrived than the Indians pressed on board to inquire after their countrymen. They were told that Donnacona was dead, and the others had become great lords in France, and were married, and did not wish to return. The Indians concealed their real feelings and manifested great joy at seeing the Frenchmen again, but Cartier now felt the recoil of his error in abducting their chief men; for, he adds, " it was all dissimulation, as afterwards appeared." He decided that the former harbour was not sufficiently secure from attack, and he selected a spot now known as Cap Rouge, also on the north shore, four leagues above the other, where a small stream falls into the main St. Lawrence. There he landed his stores, and in the little river he put up three of his ships. The other two anchored in mid-stream, and on September 2 they sailed for St. Malo, one under the charge of his brother-in-law, Mace Jalobert, and the other under charge of his nephew, Stephen Noel,—both skilful pilots,—with letters to the King, informing him of the non-arrival of Roberval, and their fears for his safety. The ships arrived in France a few days previous to October 19.

The little river chosen for a harbour was not more than fifty paces wide, and while at low water there was nothing but a channel a foot deep, there were three fathoms at high tide. The country around was very beautiful, as it still is, and the trees—oaks, maples, beeches, and others—were finer than in France. Among them, to his great content, Cartier recognised the ameda, and he gratefully says " that it hath the most excellent virtue of all the trees in the world." What it did for him on this occasion he promises to narrate. At the mouth of the little stream is a steep cliff. He built a fort on the top of it, to protect a lower fort at the level of the water. He found there some things which, unlike the fine trees and beautiful landscape, have since disappeared —an iron mine and leaves of fine gold. Near by there was "slate, stone with mineral veins looking like gold and silver, and stones like diamonds, the most fair-polished and excellent cut that it is possible for a man to see. When the sun shineth upon them they glisten as it were sparkles of fire." From the crystals of quartz supposed by Cartier to be diamonds the cape on which Quebec now stands still retains the name Cape Diamond.

While the main body of the sailors was engaged in erecting the forts and landing the stores, under the supervision of the Viscount de Beaupré, Cartier started up the river with two boats to revisit Hochelaga. His main object, however, was to examine what he called the three Saults (the Lachine rapids). These he had partially seen from Mount Royal on his previous visit, and he gathered from the Indians that they were the only obstacle to navigation on the route to the country of Saguenay—the country whose wealth loomed so large in the imagination of the French, from Donnacona's mystifying romancing. His intention was to get ready during the winter and to push westwards in the early spring. He could not, however, think of passing Achelay without calling on the chief who had given him the little girl, still living in France, and who had so often put him on his guard against the schemes of Taignoagny and Domagaya. He was received with much gladness, in appearance, and he bestowed gifts of more than usual importance upon the "lord" of the land, and such was his confidence in the said "lord" that he left two young boys there to learn the language. But the glamour of the former voyage had worn off, and the poor savages, though they dissembled their distrust, remembered their abducted leaders. As soon as Cartier passed up, the potentate of Pointe au Platon went down to Stadacona to concert with his fellow tribesmen hostile schemes against the people who had carried away their friends to an unknown fate.

On September 11 Cartier arrived at the place where,

CARTIER'S THIRD VOYAGE

six years before, was the town of Hochelaga. Perhaps it was there still, only he does not make the least allusion to it; but he speaks of a town of Tutonagay, or rather Hakluyt so reports the name, and we have no other authority by which to check him. On the Desceliers map C, however, Ochelaga has become a district, and Tutonagay occupies the position at the junction of the two rivers where the Hochelaga of the second voyage stood. This is a real difficulty not to be cleared up until a "relation originale" of this voyage also turns up in some neglected corner. From Hakluyt's narrative we learn that the two boats were moored at the foot of the current St. Mary, and that Cartier double-manned one of them and rowed past the site of the present city of Montreal. When he arrived at the foot of what are now known as the Lachine Rapids he could go no further; for, not only was the current too swift, but there were great rocks and "bad ground," as there are still in the same place. He therefore landed and found close by the waterside a beaten track, now replaced by the "lower Lachine road," which he followed for some distance, and on the road he found another town of friendly people, who gave him a warm welcome and by means of short sticks showed that there was one more sault not much further up. We may gather from the record that Cartier did not go as far as the quiet water of Lake St. Louis, probably not further than the sharp turn of the river, but accepted the statement of the Indians that the river was not navigable to Saguenay. The total distance, as Cartier estimated, from the foot of the current St. Mary to the head of the last of the three saults was six leagues, or fifteen miles by land. The day was far spent, and his people had neither eaten nor drunk, so they were glad to get back to their boats. The natives seemed friendly and manifested signs of joy and welcome. Cartier made them presents, but he felt that the former confidence and good-will were gone, and, he adds, " a man must not trust them for all their fair ceremonies and signs of joy, for if they had thought they had been too strong for us, then would they have done their best to have killed us, as we understood afterwards." So Cartier did not delay, but having ascertained that the country of Saguenay could not be reached by boat he dropped down the river to his fort near Stadacona, which he had named Charlesbourg Royal. There he found that the savages seemed unfriendly and kept away from the fort, nor would they bring in provisions as before. Some of the crew who had been at Stadacona reported that Indians from the country around were assembled in great numbers; Cartier therefore strengthened his forts and prepared for an effective defence.

Here the narrative preserved by the diligent care of the most worthy Richard Hakluyt ceases, and there is no other source of information now extant. We may surmise from scattered indications that Cartier passed a miserable winter at Charlesbourg Royal. There does not seem to have been any actual fighting with the Indians, but suspicion and distrust on both sides isolated the garrison. Nothing has survived about any attack of scurvy, and Cartier's ameda, or "hanneda, the most excellent tree in the world," as Hakluyt has it, was there in plenty. His promise to tell more of its virtues may have been carried out, but as the narrative is cut abruptly off we are only able to gather that it stood him in good stead once more.

Roberval had, as we have seen, left St. Malo and gone to Honfleur a week before Cartier sailed. It had been arranged that he should sail in a few days, and Cartier lost much time waiting for him on the coast of Newfoundland. But he delayed all through the summer, being apparently unable to bring his preparations to a completion. He did hire two vessels at Honfleur; but not until June 19. In July the King complained of his procrastination. The records show that he was in France, still preparing to sail, on August 15. And, again, that one of his vessels was at Honfleur at Christmas, 1541; from which it is evident that he did not sail during that year. During the winter he did some free-

CARTIER'S THIRD VOYAGE

booting work in the Channel, for we find a private letter to the King, from the French Ambassador at London, complaining of his operations. He had established his headquarters at Camaret, on the coast of Bretagne, a few miles south of Brest, from whence under various pretexts he plundered not only friendly foreigners, but even subjects of France. This work was more congenial to his nature than colonisation. The special feat which provoked the letter referred to was the plunder of an English ship, from which he took six hundred quintals of iron and four hundred skins of morocco, which he sold for his own profit. These facts are established by documents, and it follows that the theories of his having made a voyage to Cape Breton and built a fort there are unfounded. There is a great deal of obscurity about the doings of Roberval, and it is mainly caused by a disregard of the calendar then in use in France. To this fertile source of error must be added the contradictory statements of Charlevoix, Lescarbot, and many others who, although nearer to the time, had not the records before them which the diligent research of recent writers has brought to light. Without dwelling upon these errors, one fact must be noted, that Paul d'Auxillon, Seigneur de Saineterre, was captain of one of Roberval's ships, the *Ste. Anne,* lying, at Christmas, 1541, in the harbour of Audemer close to Honfleur; and, a tumult having arisen, he killed a sailor called Barbot. Noting this for the present, we may pass on to the established fact that Roberval really did sail for America on April 16, 1542, and from La Rochelle, not from Honfleur.

We are dependent upon Hakluyt for the only account of this voyage which exists, and his narrative of this also, unfortunately, breaks off abruptly in the middle; but we learn that Roberval's fleet consisted of three ships, with two hundred persons, men and women, for his object was to found a colony. His lieutenant was M. de Saineterre, above mentioned, and his pilot the well-known Jean Alphonse of Saintonge. There were some gentlemen of quality upon the expedition, but on the other hand many of the crew were convicts from the prisons. The weather was so bad that the fleet had to seek refuge for a time at Belle-Isle in Bretagne. It was not until June 7 that they reached Newfoundland, and on June 8 the ships entered the harbour of St. John's. He had not been long there when, to his great surprise, three ships arrived bearing Cartier and all the survivors of the party which had left St. Malo the preceding spring. They had abandoned Charlesbourg Royal and were on the way to France. Cartier at once paid his respects to Roberval, but we may gather from Hakluyt that the interview was stormy. Cartier gave a good account of the country, and showed what he supposed to be diamonds and gold ore. He reported that the Indians had been incessantly hostile, and that, his party not being strong enough to resist them longer, he had decided to return to France. Roberval ordered Cartier to put back and join the expedition, but in the night Cartier weighed anchor and sailed for St. Malo, where he arrived in safety. Cartier and his companions had suffered enough from Roberval, and would not risk a winter in Canada under his inexperienced command. Roberval's haughty and imperious character would have led him to exercise force to compel obedience, and Cartier settled the matter very simply without bloodshed. He had fulfilled the orders of the King in conducting the expedition to Canada. He had not engaged for an indefinite time dependent upon the will of Roberval. His vessels had been fitted out in great part before his commission had been superseded by that of Roberval. No reproach was made to Cartier upon his return, for, although he may have fallen into disfavour with the court, his conduct was not contrary to the usage of the period, or some attempt would have been made to blame him in the after suit at law with Roberval.

Roberval remained at St. John's all the month of June, His voyage had been long, and he had to take in wood and water; but his time was chiefly wasted in deciding quarrels between the French and Portuguese, for there were seventeen sail of fishing vessels in the harbour when he arrived. His commission did not cover Newfoundland, and a delay of three weeks might easily have been prejudicial to his main enterprise, but the opportunity to exercise a little additional authority could not be lost. He sailed at the end of June, and by the end of July he was landing his stores and erecting forts and buildings at Charlesbourg Royal. The fact that Roberval reached Canada from St. John's by way of the Strait of Belle-Isle shows how little was known of the passage through Cabot Strait.

The narrative we have been following is Hakluyt's. It may be checked occasionally by contemporary documents, but there is no other narrative extant, and nothing has been found to shake its authority. Roberval settled upon the site of the Charlesbourg of Cartier, and there erected forts and buildings on a large scale. He named the place "the fort of Françoys Roy," and it was situated, says Hakluyt, upon "the great river of Canada, commonly called France prime by Monsieur Roberval." The names were not happily chosen. They appear in various other forms, as " France roy," " Franci Roy," " Françoys prime," in the books and documents. The great viceroy could hardly be expected to have rested content with names given in his domain by a mere sailor like Cartier. All through the months of August and September the men worked at these buildings. There is no trace of them now, but as they were all of wood, and it was three hundred and sixty years ago, that is not surprising.

On September 15 Roberval sent back two ships to France. One of them was under the command of his lieutenant, Monsieur de Saineterre, the same who, on or about Christmas of the preceding year (1541), had killed one of the crew of the *Ste. Anne* in the harbour of Audemer. He had been found guilty of manslaughter at the time. Roberval issued a formal pardon (the first official document issued in Canada), under his great seal in lofty vice-regal style addressed "to all royal judges, seneschals, and other officers," setting forth the circumstances of the homicide, and that the people who convicted Saineterre did not understand the matter. These ships carried intelligence of the expedition, and were to return in the following spring with such supplies as the King might grant.

After the ships had left an inquiry was made as to the stores and provisions for the winter, when it was found that they were short, and the company had forthwith to go upon a stinted allowance. The Breton pilot had taken the great nobleman at his true value. The viceroy, upon whom all depended, had not been able to foresee the requirements of his own party for a year. He was able, however, to maintain discipline. Hakluyt's narrative gives a good idea of it: "One was hanged for theft; John of Nantes was laid in irons and kept a prisoner for his offence, and others also were put in irons and divers were whipped, as well men as women; by which means they lived in quiet." Parkman quotes from a MS. by Thevet, showing that the arbitrary viceroy made a little *inferno* at Cap Rouge: "Forced to unceasing labour and chafed by arbitrary rules, some of the soldiers fell under Roberval's displeasure, and six of them, formerly his favourites, were hanged in one day. Others were banished to an island and there kept in fetters; while for various offences several, both men and women, were shot. Even the Indians were moved to pity and wept at the sight of their woes." With all allowance for Thevet's powers of exaggeration they were an unhappy lot, and the day when they all went back to France was a fortunate day for Canada. To crown their miseries, the scurvy broke out among them and about fifty of the party died.

The ice broke up in April, and on June 5, 1543, Roberval started with eight boats up the river "for the said provinces of Saguenay," by which phrasing we may be sure that the "said province" had no relation to the river of that name east of Quebec, excepting that the river was supposed to rise somewhere there. He left thirty men as a garrison, with orders that if he did not return by

CARTIER'S THIRD VOYAGE

July 1 they were to sail for France. Some of his party returned to the fort on June 14, and some more on June 19, with letters postponing the time of departure to July 22, and bringing news that one boat had been lost and eight men drowned. Here the narrative of Hakluyt abruptly ends, and we have nothing but scattered incidental notices to guide us. No reports exist of discoveries or adventures on his western journey. He was not a man to succeed in any serious enterprise, and is not likely to have discovered anything. He did, however, get back to France that summer with all the survivors of the expedition. How he got back is a question much disputed.

It has been shown above, by the evidence of a document given at length by Harrisse, that Paul d'Auxillon, Seigneur de Saineterre, was captain of the *Ste. Anne* on or about Christmas, 1541, while Cartier was wintering in Canada. It has also been shown by Hakluyt's narrative that he sailed with Roberval from La Rochelle, and that he acted as Roberval's lieutenant. Moreover, that Roberval, having on September 9, 1542, issued a formal pardon for the homicide committed by him near Honfleur, Saineterre was sent back to France from Canada on September 14, 1542. Harrisse has given in his "Notes" two documents which, taken with these facts, conclusively settle the question as to how Roberval got back. The first is dated January 26, 1542; that is really January 26, 1543, when translated into our reckoning, because by the calendar in use in France the new year 1543 did not commence until Easter, which fell that year on March 25. Saineterre then being in France and appealing to the King for aid to Roberval in Canada, Francis issued the document (dated St. Laurent, January 26), ordering two ships to be got ready and despatched to the relief of Roberval. It then sets forth that M. de Saineterre, having been the lieutenant of Roberval, and having already made the voyage, he, Saineterre, is competent to carry out the King's intention in that respect "as well and better than any other person." How far these last words are a reflection on Cartier it is not necessary to inquire; but they completely exclude the idea that Cartier was sent to relieve Roberval, and they establish the fact that the relief expedition was to sail under Saineterre's command. The second document confirms this. It is a power of attorney, executed by Roberval, then in France, dated September 11, 1543, to Saineterre, empowering him to proceed to La Rochelle and to sell or charter his ship, the *Ste. Anne,* and dispose of the stores and artillery to the best advantage. He was also to dispose of the other vessel, "the gallion," which was a King's ship, and to pay off all the soldiers and mariners. The evidence is thus complete. Saineterre sailed in the spring of 1543, and brought Roberval and all his people back to France, where they arrived at some date not long prior to September 11.

The idea of Jacques Cartier having made a fourth voyage to Canada is thus effectually disposed of; and the documents printed by Joüon des Longrais confirm this conclusion. We find that Cartier was present at a baptism on March 25, 1543, and is witness in a lawsuit on July 3, 1543, in both cases at St. Malo. M. Joüon, who otherwise would incline to a fourth voyage, in view of this last date, leaves the question in doubt; but Cartier, if absent, would hardly be summoned as a witness, and he could not have testified by attorney. The question has been much debated in Canada, and opinion is divided as to whether the supposed fourth voyage was in the summer of 1543 or extended from the autumn of 1543 to the summer of 1544, thus giving Cartier another winter in Canada, and making Roberval stay over two winters. The basis upon which the theory of a fourth voyage has been built up is a sentence in the award of the Commissioner of Inquiry into the accounts of Cartier and Roberval, which Lescarbot took to refer to Cartier; but the Abbé Verreau has justly pointed out that the point is one solely of the hire of a vessel for a second voyage, and does not involve any statement that Cartier had sailed in the vessel.

Roberval, having returned in the autumn of 1543, soon

CARTIER'S THIRD VOYAGE 207

got into a dispute with Cartier about the accounts for the expedition, and the King, on April 3, 1544, appointed a commission to inquire into the whole matter. After minute inquiry it reported that Cartier had paid out more than he had received, and there was due to him the sum of 8638 livres, 4 sols, 6 deniers. This sum was never repaid him. Roberval was ruined. He had dissipated his great patrimony in extravagant living, and had procured the vice-royalty of Canada in hope of restoring his fortune by mines of gold and precious stones to be found there. He is met with, later in the documents, as holding a royal commission to rebuild the fortifications of Senlis; then, in 1553, as commissioner and controller of all the mines in France, and again as commissioner on the fortifications of Paris. He disappears about the year 1560, and Thevet records that he was assassinated at night near the Church of the Innocents at Paris—which, like all of Thevet's statements, requires collateral confirmation. Another story is that he again made an effort to take possession of his Canadian vice-royalty and perished in the attempt. It was not by men such as he that Canada was to be explored or colonised.

It is impossible to close this episode of Canadian discovery without reference to the romantic story of Marguerite, the niece of Roberval. Passed through the alembic of Thevet's imagination, an island on the coast of Labrador became the theatre of a struggle for a human soul between the powers of the celestial world and the demons of the pit. As a piece of constructive mendacity it has been successful in inspiring the graceful prose of Parkman and in becoming the theme of a Canadian poem of much merit. Like all good story-tellers, Thevet personally knew the parties. Marguerite, a high-born damsel, niece of Roberval, with her duenna had sailed with her harsh uncle for his Canadian domain. Her secret lover sailed also upon the expedition, and on the voyage her passion became known. Roberval dissembled his anger until they were off the Isle of Demons, when he ordered the sailors to put his niece and her old nurse ashore and leave them to their fate. Four guns were given them and a small supply of provisions. Her lover, thereupon scorning concealment, threw himself into the surf and got safely ashore; Thevet says with two more guns and a supply of ammunition and other necessary things. Let no sceptic doubt, however, the existence of the Demon's Isle, for it is in the maps of the period, and is especially prominent in the map "of that most excellent cosmographer, Jacomo di Gastaldi," in Ramusio's Collection of Voyages. There may be seen the devils, with wings, tails, and claws, eagerly alert for poor human souls. Abandoned in this savage wilderness the lovers made out to live upon the wild creatures on the island; but the youth died, and the child which came to them died, and at last the old nurse died, and the poor lady was left alone with the wild beasts. The bears, " white as an egg," and creatures still more hideous and repulsive thronged round; but worse than them all were

> "The shrieks and howls
> Of fiends malignant high o'er roar of waves
> Torturing the souls of men."

But Heaven was on the side of the repentant Marguerite, and Our Lady of Pity barred her round with invisible safeguards. The story lends itself readily to the most touching embellishments, but we cannot follow them farther. For nineteen months Marguerite struggled with beasts and demons, until at last a passing fishing vessel, seeing smoke, as of a fire kindled by human hands, and the despairing gestures of a wild human being dressed in skins, ventured upon these shores of evil omen and carried away the poor lady to her home in France. The story, says Parkman, has no doubt a nucleus of truth; and the ever-judicious Abbé Ferland says it contains very much less truth than falsehood. This nucleus of truth may surely be found in the "Heptameron" of the "pearl of Marguerites," the sister of Francis, Queen Margaret of Navarre. It is the sixty-seventh tale, and re-

CARTIER'S THIRD VOYAGE 209

lates how a poor woman, to save the life of her husband, risked her own, and never left him until his death. Here everything falls into rational order, and as it was published in 1559, only fifteen years after the occurrence, we may reasonably accept it. She relates that Roberval, when by the King's orders he went to "the island of Canada," took with him all sorts of artisans to build his projected cities and castles, and among them was a man whom Roberval pronounced guilty of treason, and condemned to death. His wife, with tears and supplications, and pleading his former services, endeavoured in vain to soften the viceroy's anger. She was only able to modify his sentence to abandonment upon a small island inhabited solely by wild beasts. She would not leave her husband, but willingly shared his fate. There they built a little hut and lived upon herbs and the animals they killed. The man died, and the poor woman buried him as best she could, and fought off the wild beasts which came to devour his body. She supported herself by her arquebus, killing the game so abundant in those early days, until at last she was taken off by some passing sailors and carried to Rochelle. There, says the Queen, when her story became known, she was received in great honour among ladies, because of her great confidence in God, and as an example of his great mercy. Jean Allefonse was Roberval's pilot, and must have witnessed the incident, whatever it was. In his "Routier" he partially confirms the story by giving the name "Isle de la damoiselle" to what are now called the Meccatina Islands on the coast of the Quebec Labrador. It will add some interest to Grand Meccatina Island to know that it is the scene of this touching story.

The character and voyages of Cartier are an unfailing subject of interest, not only to the people of the Canada he discovered, but to the scholars of the United States who have done so much for Canadian history. The national pride of Canadians of French origin has, with the aid of a few kindred scholars in France, followed with pious diligence every trace of his career. The Literary and Historical Society of Quebec published in 1843 an edition of his voyages, in which, following Lescarbot, his name is spelled Quartier; but as he himself spelled it Cartier, we may be content therewith. He was the prime mover in the first expedition to follow up the avenue opening to the west by the Grand Bay—Belle-Isle Strait. He made the proposals to the Admiral Chabot de Brion, and the latter carried them before the King. The King contributed the chief part of the expense, but Cartier in the sequel lost heavily out of his own private means.

It has been said that Cartier was ennobled, but there is no proof of it, and the evidence inclines the other way. It has also been said that the King gave him the manor of Limoileu, but Cartier bought and paid for that out of his private means. It was his home in summer, looking over the open sea, as a sailor's house should do. In winter he lived in the town of St. Malo near by. If he is occasionally styled Sieur de Limoileu, it by no means implies the existence of a patent of nobility, for it was not uncommon for proprietors, even small proprietors, to be called sieurs or seigneurs of any estate they might own, no matter how acquired. The discoverer of Canada owes nothing to the King. When he had opened up the St. Lawrence valley leading to unknown possibilities of wealth and power, Francis gave the lordship and the command to an unworthy court favourite who had squandered his own patrimony and whose only qualifications were arrogance and harshness. The King used his royal power to compel Cartier to put his abilities at the service of a man without knowledge, capacity, or foresight, and it was owing solely to his practical assistance that the first part of Roberval's expedition was got off. Roberval was fitted to dissipate, not to administer, to intimidate his followers by whipping, hanging, and shooting, or to abandon them to perish for imagined crimes. Cartier conducted three expeditions, and his men gave him the willing obedience which only a competent master can obtain. There were no mutinies, no treasons, no punishments in Cartier's crews.

CARTIER'S THIRD VOYAGE

When Cartier took out the first portion of Roberval's expedition he obeyed the command of the King and performed his task. He was not bound to serve permanently under Roberval in Canada, the more especially since Roberval had failed to follow and support the first detachment. The incompetence of Roberval is evident from the one fact that instead of having provisions for two years he had to put his party on short allowance within a month of their arrival in Canada. Cartier could have done nothing under Roberval, for he would have been subordinate even to the viceroy's favourites. He was no courtier to keep his ground by fawning and intrigue, and his career would have ended by being shot or marooned on some desert island by order of the truculent viceroy, who was all the more jealous of his dignity and suspicious of his followers because of his own unfitness to command.

In previous chapters we have seen great sailors coasting along the northeastern shores of the continent, but Cartier penetrated to its heart. To borrow the words of the King's commission, it was he "who discovered the great country of the lands belonging to Canada and Hochelaga"—who discovered the regions of Quebec and Montreal and the adjacent lands, and opened up the great river to the impassable rapids of Lachine. We shall come to another Frenchman of the same stamp, who took up Cartier's task and revealed the upper valley as Cartier did the lower. Not to Cabot, to Verrazano, to Corte-Real, to Gomez, or to Fagundez,—not to English, to Spaniards, to Portuguese, or to mythical Basques was it given to discover the valley of the majestic river of the north,—but to the brave, good-hearted, practical, competent sailor of St. Malo.

In his profession Cartier may be easily counted in the front rank. He never lost a vessel, although when on the shores of Labrador he sailed close in examining the most dangerous coast in the gulf; and elsewhere in the gulf and river he followed along the shores, noting the rocks and other dangers and recording them with wonderful accuracy. His powers of observation were quick and strong, and his curiosity led him to note and describe with accuracy the strange objects which presented themselves in the New World. He was a religious man in the fullest and best sense of the word. That he was a good Catholic would naturally follow from his Breton birth; but Cartier's religion led him to perform all the ordinary duties of life faithfully and in a kindly spirit, whether in his family or among his fellow-townsmen. His social qualities enabled him to enjoy the life of his native town. Everywhere his name is found in its records. Sometimes he is found acting as an expert in trials about captures at sea, about the price of ships' stores, about the number of vessels available in the ports of Bretagne, about the currents in the waters near St. Malo. We find him acting as Portuguese interpreter in a case before the court and taking part in family councils and settlements. He had no children, but it was his delight to assist at baptisms, often as sponsor, and the dates of his career are traced by his presence at more than seventy. In these days, in the simple customs of the province, a baptism was a great social event and celebrated with rejoicing and a generous feast. One of them, in 1552, throws a sidelight on the natural gaiety of his character, for it is gravely recorded that the entry was made in the presence of Captain Jacques Cartier " et aultres bons biberons." This little touch of humour in the formality of the register reveals the discoverer of Canada off duty, mixing as a joyous companion in the social affairs of his fellow-citizens—equal not only to watch over his comrades in the wilds of the New World, but to join heartily in the gaieties of their social life at home. Five years later, on September 1, 1557, Cartier died at the age of sixty-six years, probably of the plague then prevalent at St. Malo.

Compared with Columbus, the Breton captain was inferior in education, learning, and intellectual power. Bretagne was far removed from the influence of the Renaissance, then at its height. The duchy had kept aloof

CARTIER'S THIRD VOYAGE

from the national life of France, and French influences were not always welcome. The narrow life of a town in a remote province was far different from the brilliant activity of cities like Rome, Venice, Genoa, Seville, or Lisbon, where the life of Columbus was passed. But he was as brave, and possessed greater ability as a commander of men. The morbid vanity of Columbus and his overweening estimate of his own merits unfitted him to secure the willing obedience of his men. He was envious of the merits of others and insatiable in exacting recognition of his own. The achievement of Cartier was infinitely less, for Columbus showed the way to the New World; but on the moral and religious side of character Cartier is a fitter subject for canonisation than Columbus. Cartier carried away ten natives, intending to bring them back baptised Christians as interpreters to their people; but Columbus inaugurated the system of deceit and cruelty, of forced labour and slavery, which exterminated the Carib race in one generation and ran up a score of bloodshed and oppression which long years of despotism, confusion, and anarchy have not yet worked out.

CARTOGRAPHICAL RESULTS OF THE CARTIER VOYAGES

Students of the history of exploration in the New World are much indebted to the Earl of Crawford for the reproduction of the three world-maps, A, B, and C, in the "Bibliotheca Lindesiana." The Harleyan map (lettered A) was described by Harrisse, in 1882, at p. 197 of his "Jean et Sebastien Cabot." A tracing of the northern part of the American coast had been communicated by Jomard to Kohl. It was a mere outline, and is No. 157 in the Kohl Collection at Washington. Winsor reproduced the same outline ("Narr. & Crit. Hist.," Vol. IV., pp. 88-89), in 1889, having received it from Kohl, and, from the fact that the tracing had been originally received from Jomard, it was called in America the Jomard Map. Winsor did not recognise its importance nor identify it with the Harleyan Map of Harrisse in the British Museum.

Map B of Lord Crawford's collection has long been known to scholars from the fac-simile reproduction in Jomard's "Monuments de la Géographie," 1862. Extracts from it have frequently been published in the United States and Canada. It was usually referred to as the "Henry II.," or sometimes the "Dauphin," map. It has become discoloured by age, and on that account is difficult to reproduce. It is of great historical value.

Map C was fully described by Harrisse, at p. 229 of his "Jean et Sebastien Cabot," in 1882, and is mentioned by Winsor; but its value was not recognised and no extract from it has appeared. The extracts from Maps A and C now given reproduce in effect Cartier's lost maps, for the information upon which they are based must have been communicated by him, and hence arises their great importance in the history of the St. Lawrence valley.

CHAPTER XIV

CARTIER TO CHAMPLAIN

ALTHOUGH, as we shall see, the Gulf of St. Lawrence continued to be visited, it was by private traders, and no advance was made in the cartography of that part of North America for fifty years after the result of Cartier's last voyage became known. This will not be surprising if we reflect that those who frequented the gulf had every reason to keep their information secret, lest when one had discovered a good place for trade and had established relations with the natives some rival merchant should intervene and destroy his profits. Newfoundland had, indeed, been demonstrated by Cartier to be separated from the main continent, but for many years the cartographers broke it up into an archipelago of fragments corresponding to the deep indentations of its coast line. These islands gradually coalesced as knowledge increased. Mr. Harrisse, in his "Découverte et Evolution Cartographique de Terre-neuve," has set forth the process of disintegration and reintegration so thoroughly that to go over it again would be lost time. In the St. Lawrence river valley there was no progress in geography. As Cartier left it Champlain found it, and we may pause for a moment to consider the results recorded on the maps.

The motive of Cartier's voyage is shown by a map of Agnese, dated 1536. In it the routes to Cathay are given. To the south is Magellan's Strait; in the centre is the route by Panama; and further north a dotted line shows the direct route from France to Quinsay, by that ocean which Verrazano thought he saw when he looked into Cheasapeake Bay, or into one of the sounds on the Carolina coast, across the isthmus reported to be only six miles wide. Another map, bearing the same date, 1536, bears evidence of Cartier's influence, for a dotted line indicating the route to Cathay passes through an opening between Newfoundland and Cape Breton, showing that some report of the promise of Cartier's first voyage had reached the cartographer.

The results of Cartier's efforts began to appear clearly in a world map, dated 1541, by Nicholas Desliens of Dieppe. This map embodies the discoveries of the second voyage as far up the St. Lawrence as Quebec, but not beyond. It is in the Harleyan world map, given to scholars among the reproductions of the "Bibliotheca Lindesiana," that we find the complete discoveries of the Cartier voyages for the first time. An extract from the American portion of this important map is given at page 216. All the names given by Cartier in his first and second voyages are laid down in it. Hochelaga is represented as a territory, not as a town, and the junction of the Ottawa with the St. Lawrence is shown there as Cartier saw it from Mount Royal. No one but he could have given information so detailed and so nearly accurate. The river is recognisable at a glance, and compared with the delineations of the Penobscot and the La Plata, repeated for so long a period in distorted and exaggerated forms, this map of the great river of Canada marks the careful accuracy of Cartier's reports. The map is anonymous, but is supposed to have been drawn at Arques, near Dieppe, by Desceliers, upon the information, as regards Canada, of Cartier's own maps. One point of special interest appears on the map, though not in the narrative—the name of his native town and point of departure, St. Malo, marks the farthest point west reached by Cartier. The date assigned on the reproduction, "Circa 1536," must be liberally interpreted, for Cartier did not return from his second voyage until July, 1536, and this is a world-map requiring considerable time to compile after the information had reached Dieppe. The delusion of a central route to China goes in this map to

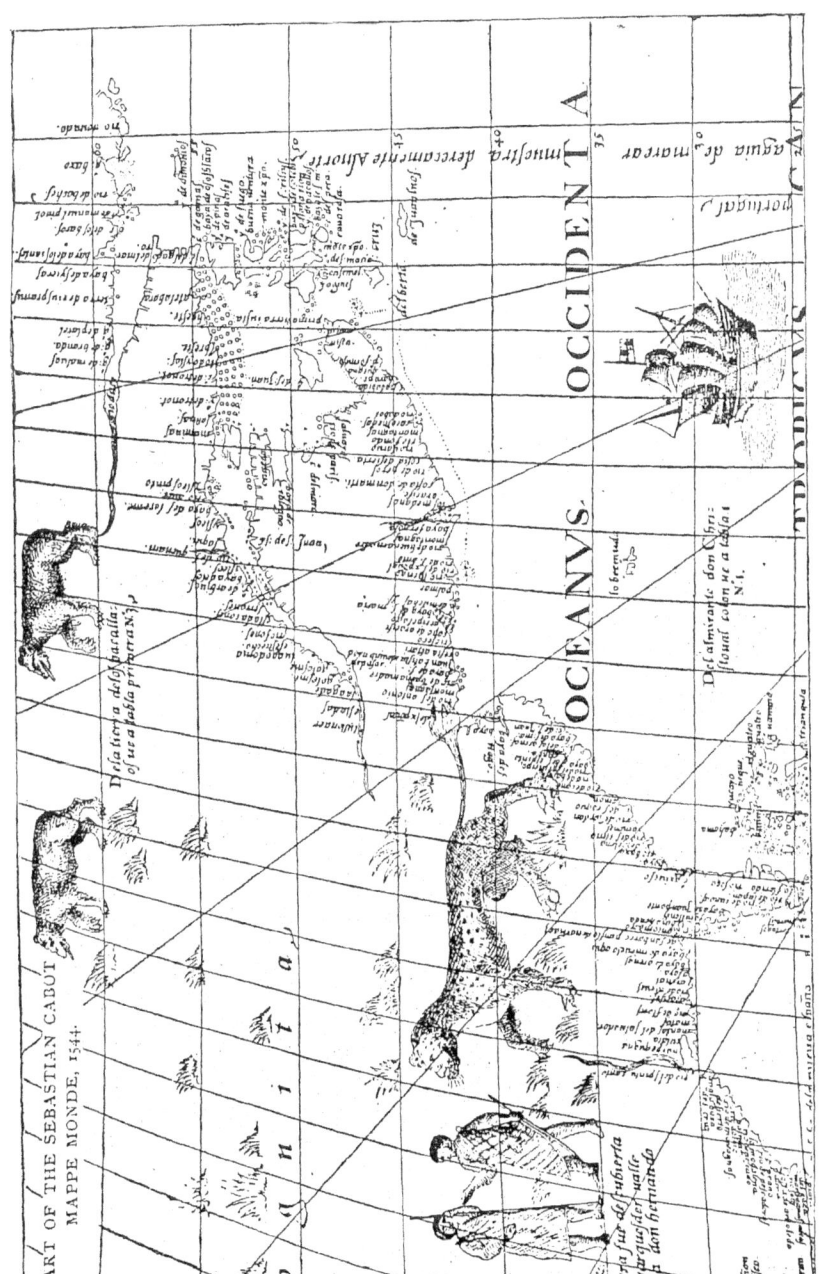

North American portion of the Cabot Map of 1544

CARTIER TO CHAMPLAIN 217

its farthest limit, for the "Great South Sea" of Verrazano not only sweeps through the continent to within a few miles of the Atlantic coast at North Carolina, but a channel, the River de Ste. Helene, connects the two oceans across the imagined isthmus.

Another map has been reproduced in the "Bibliotheca Lindesiana," very important in this connection, for it contains the results of the third expedition under Cartier, in 1541-42, and Roberval, in 1542-43. It also was made by Desceliers at Arques, and is dated 1546. Jomard published an excellent fac-simile in his Atlas, but the map is known in the American books as the Henry II. or Dauphin map. The geography of the St. Lawrence and the names are a repetition of the Harleyan map, but the additional name, Franciroy, and the drawing of Roberval and his men mark the later date. From this we may see that Roberval went no farther west than Cartier.

The third of this invaluable series of reproductions is another by Desceliers, dated 1550; a beautiful specimen of cartographic art, profusely adorned with pictures of the quaint notions then current about Canada—among them a battle between the pygmies and the cranes in the region around the present city of Ottawa. These annual battles in Homer's time were in Africa, but succeeding authors changed their habitat northwards, and one ancient commentator places them in England. In the Middle Ages Tartary was the field of these perennial conflicts, and Jean Allefonce, Roberval's pilot, expressed the opinion, then and for many years later current in France, when he wrote of the regions west of Hochelaga, that "these countries form part of Tartary." In Cartier's commission Canada is said to be the "end of Asia in the west," and the Dieppe cartographer saw nothing irrational in portraying so usual an occurrence in Tartary. The map, although at least six years later than the Harleyan map, is as regards Canada hardly as correct geographically. The location of "Totunagay" and the remark, at the junction of the St. Lawrence and Ottawa, that "Monsieur Roberval went as far as here," shows that the latest reports of Cartier and Roberval are embodied.

At this point also comes in the map of Sebastian Cabot, dated 1544, the subject of much misconception and controversy. This map, though published in the Netherlands, was based upon the information of Cabot, who was then at Seville. Its conclusive testimony in favour of Cape Breton as the landfall of John Cabot's first voyage has been already pointed out. A sketch of the Cape Breton portion has been given, see page 32. It will be seen at once that the American portion, at least, is little more than a copy of Desliens' map of 1541, with additional information from Cartier's reports or maps, and the name *tuttonaer* at the most western point on the St. Lawrence shows that the information was brought down closely to date, for it is the Tutonagay of Cartier's third voyage. The Ottawa River is not shown, but in their strangely distorted Spanish translation the French names of Cartier will be recognised.

The maps drawn by Cartier have perished, and while those above mentioned embody, so far as the scale of world maps would allow, most of his discoveries, we learn from a letter from Jacques Noel, a nephew of Cartier, written in 1587, and preserved by Hakluyt, that there was laid down on Cartier's own charts a great lake west of Hochelaga. Cartier learned of it from the Indians at the saults (Lachine Rapids), and that it was ten days' journey distance from thence. This is the first indication we meet with of Lake Ontario, and Noel says, in another letter, that upon a sea chart at St. Malo, the only map of Cartier's he could find, he saw in his uncle's own writing at the place beyond the junction of the two rivers (St. Lawrence and Ottawa) the words, " By the people of Canada and Hochelaga it was said; that here is the land of Saguenay, which is rich and wealthy in precious stones." This map also has disappeared, but the chief results of Cartier's expeditions are recorded on the maps cited above, and the geography of what is now known as Canada remained unchanged for sixty years.

CARTIER TO CHAMPLAIN 219

Although the name of Jean Allefonsce, or Alphonse, occurs frequently in the records of early voyages, he does not seem to have added anything to existing knowledge. He was celebrated in those days for his skill and experience, and after Cartier left France in 1541 he was engaged by Roberval and sailed with him in 1542. His *Routier* in Hakluyt's voyages goes only as far as France Roy, giving the compass bearings and latitudes of the different places with much detail. He supposed the Saguenay River to connect with the Sea of Cathay, and in one of the sketch maps of his manuscript *Cosmography* a sea called the Sea of Saguenay is laid down. Some report of the Indians concerning Lake St. John, at the head of the river, must have misled him. He has left, also, a description of the coast from Cape Breton southward, which, while interesting as bearing upon the fabled Norumbege, does not contain any original discoveries. He was convinced that what we now know as the Penobscot connected with the St. Lawrence near Hochelaga, an opinion held also by Cartier. This notion accounts for some of the distortions of Gastaldi's map in Ramusio's collection.

It is unnecessary to dwell in detail upon the succeeding records of voyages to Canada, or to New France, as Jean Allefonsce informs us the country " for just and proper reasons " was commencing to be called. The people of Bretagne, and particularly of St. Malo, not only continued their voyages for fishing on the coasts of Newfoundland and Acadia, but gradually extended their operations into the Gulf and up the River St. Lawrence, not so much for fishing as for trading with the Indians and buying furs. The long confusion of the wars of religion of Charles IX. and St. Bartholomew, of the League and Henry III., interfered very little with the steady conduct of this business. It was free to all—a period of untrammelled free trade—in which, by degrees, the cities of Normandy, Rouen, Dieppe, Havre, and Honfleur took part; with more or less jealousy on the part of the citizens of St. Malo (Malouins, as they were called), who claimed a prior right from their townsman, Jacques Cartier. For a long time the trade was in private hands. The energies of people of influence at court were absorbed in politics or war. The records comprehend all the northeast coast under the general name *Terreneuve,* and the sailors or owners did not care for geographical discoveries. They made no settlements, but traded everywhere along the coast, and their relations with the Indians were most amicable. The French were trusted and liked by the natives, and in the records of St. Malo we meet with baptisms of Indians, and of Indians brought over to be taught French and act as interpreters. As for the fisheries on the coast, they were well established before Cartier's voyages and rapidly grew in importance. The letters from Jacques Noel, preserved by Hakluyt, throw light on this period. He, too, had been up the " great river of Canada " to Hochelaga, and had stood on the top of Mount Royal. He had gone even a little further, and had passed the saults and seen the river widening into the Lake St. Louis beyond, and had also heard from the natives of the great lake ten days' journey to the west. In the meantime the nomenclature was becoming settled as the name St. Lawrence gradually extended itself over the whole gulf and river. The Spaniards knew the former as the *Golfo Quadrado* (the Square Gulf), from its shape. *La Grande Baye* was the French name from Cartier's time for the upper part near the Strait of Belle-Isle. Gomara, in 1555, wrote of a great river named San Lorenço, which fell into a square gulf, and in 1565 Ramusio reports the " Gran' Capitano Francese " as speaking fifteen or twenty years before of a great river called San Lorenzo. But Cartier's nephew, in 1587, has no name for it but the " River of Canada," and even Champlain, in 1603, calls it by that name. In 1609, on Lescarbot's map, is Golfe du Canada; but on Whytfliet's, in 1597, is Sinus St. Laurentii, so that the present names, St. Lawrence River and Gulf, seem to have been imposed from without.

In 1588 we meet with the first attempt at monopoly.

Cartier, as has been shown, was a loser by his voyages in the King's service to the extent of 8630 livres. Henry III. granted to his nephew, Jacques Noel, and to one Chaton, Sieur de la Jaunaye, who had performed some service as captain of marine, a monopoly of trade with Canada for twelve years, including the fur trade and general traffic in merchandise of all kinds, but excluding fisheries. They obtained, also, a monopoly of all mines and the right of settlement, of building forts, and of taking over a certain number of convicts. All this was under the pretext of continuing the memory of the discoverer of Canada and recompensing him vicariously, through his heirs, for his loss. The grant struck at the interests of too many citizens of St. Malo to pass unchallenged, and in consequence of urgent remonstrances made by the Parliament of Bretagne it was revoked the same year. Canada again escaped a colony of convicts, and the times of monopoly were postponed for a few years.

Normandy was more involved in the wars of religion than Bretagne, and was the theatre of severe struggles; but, whether Catholic or Huguenot, the people required food, and private ship-owners and merchants of Dieppe, Honfleur, and Havre shared the fisheries and the trade of Terreneuve with the Bretons in continually increasing proportion as the times became more settled. It was in Normandy that the first successful settlements in Canada were planned, and the French Canadians are not of Breton, but of Norman origin.

Lescarbot in his "History of New France" records his meeting at Canso, in 1607, with a Basque from St. Jean de Luz, Captain Savalet, who had made forty-two annual voyages to that place. This old "Terre-neuvier," as those who sailed to these regions were called, employed sixteen men fishing and drying cod. He was a type of many in those days who frequented the northeast coasts of America. His first voyage must have been in 1562, but, as pointed out elsewhere, the Basques began to frequent these waters shortly after the voyage of Gomez in 1525, and for many years both French and

Spanish Basques in great numbers followed the cod fisheries. The Spanish Basques declined in number at the time of the war between Spain and England, and later, when the French became firmly established, they prohibited the Spaniards from cod fishing on the coasts. The Basques have left their traces along the south and west shores of Newfoundland. Trepassy, Placentia, Santa Maria, Portochova, Miquelon, among many other places, are mentioned in the records of Basque towns in northern Spain. On Vallard's map (1547) and on Desceliers' map (1550) we meet with the name Placentia, called after the town of that name on the Rio Deva in Guipuzcoa. Tombstones with Basque inscriptions have recently been deciphered at Placentia bearing date of 1676 and later. These apparently mark the graves of French Basques; but they were Spanish Basques who named the place. Port au Basque still retains the name telling of its former days. It is near Cape Ray, and is the terminus of the Newfoundland railway where passengers cross to Sydney, Cape Breton. Rogneuse, where Cartier called on his return from Canada in 1536, still retains its name in the English corruption, Renews; but the word is claimed for the Basques as derived from Orrougne or Urugne, the last post station in France on the Spanish frontier.

In the years immediately succeeding their discovery by Cartier, the Gulf of St. Lawrence and the adjoining waters, as well as the estuary of the river, became known to the Basque whalers, both French and Spanish, for the abundance of whales, walruses, and seals to be found there. From the central station of the Magdalen Islands, then called the Ramea Islands, the Basques followed up the river at least as far as the Saguenay, for their presence is still witnessed by the names Echafaud aux Basques and Basque roads a little west of its mouth. From walrus and whale hunters the Basques developed into traders, and De Monts and Champlain found them far up the river trafficking with the Indians for furs—very successfully, it would seem, since thence arose the mythical story that the natives would not trade in any other language than Basque. When Champlain appeared in these waters the activity of the Basques was at its height. We find them in 1608 resisting Pont-Gravé at Tadoussac and firing on his ship, and in 1623 we hear of a Basque establishment at Miscou. The men who conspired against Champlain at Quebec in 1608 intended to take refuge with Spaniards (Basques) then at Tadoussac. The paralysing hand of Philip II. killed the marine enterprise of the Spanish Basques, and the grants of monopoly to trading companies of merchants interfered with the trading of the French Basques, so that the memory of that interesting people survives only in names here and there persisting on the coast. When in more recent times the Basques commenced to emigrate they went to South America.

The history of the Portuguese is the saddest story, for their claims to these waters were antecedent to all, and in their annals the captaincy of Terra Nova was continued in the family of the Corte-Reals down to 1567. In 1580 Philip II. seized the brilliant little kingdom, and for sixty years it remained in bondage. It recovered its independence, but not its maritime importance. The memory of the Portuguese has faded off the coasts of America, and only in old maps and records, studied by a few scholars, may we learn of their skill and daring as sailors and their enterprise as fishermen on the northeast coast of America.

We have seen how England neglected—almost forgot—her transatlantic discoveries; how she was content with a very small part of all she might have claimed as her own; how she imperilled by non-user her presumptive right of prior discovery; and we will leave to the general historian the narrative of its revindication in later years. We have seen English merchants who permitted the Cabots to fall into obscurity willing to send their vessels to Newfoundland under Portuguese pilots, and entering into partnership with sailors of the Azores to follow in a hesitating way the road the Cabots had pointed out. The first notice of the "new-lands" on the English statute book is an Act, 1541-42 (33 Henry VIII. c. 11), and it brings out into strong light the remissness of the English sailors who, instead of going themselves to fish, waylaid off the coasts the returning fleets of foreign fishing vessels and bought fish to supply the English markets. A penalty of ten pounds was later enacted for buying fish at sea or in foreign ports. The Tudors had many faults, but they were real monarchs, and under their strong rule the English marine was formed. Doubtless some English vessels made the voyage, but the King was determined that all should do so, or give up the profit of selling fish in English ports. In 1548-49 an Act was passed under Edward VI. to protect fishermen from certain exactions of the Admiralty, and the provisions of both Acts were re-enacted in 1580-81 under Elizabeth with injunctions " touching certain politick constitutions for the maintenance of the Navy," that fish should be eaten on Wednesdays and Saturdays throughout the year—solely, however, as a matter of national policy, for Her Majesty also enjoins that any man who teaches that eating fish has the least connection with the service of God shall be severely punished.

This view is confirmed by Hakluyt. He states that the fisheries were common and frequented by the English about the beginning of the reign of Edward VI., A. D. 1548; but the Bretons and Portuguese were there in great numbers before that. Parkhurst, in a letter to Hakluyt (1578), tells him that he had made four voyages to Newfoundland, and that the English ships had increased in that short time from 30 to 50; but he gives also the number of vessels of other nations. There were 100 sail of Spaniards, 30 sail of Basque whalers, 50 sail of Portuguese, and 150 sail of French and Bretons. Parkhurst accounts for the comparatively small number of English by the trade carried on with Iceland. This is even more strongly set forth by Edward Hayes, in 1583, for, writing of these coasts, he speaks of "the little we do yet actually possess therein and by our ignorance of the riches and secrets within those lands which unto this day we know chiefly by the travel and report of other nations and most of the French who albeit they cannot challenge such right and interest into the said countries as we, neither these many years have had opportunities nor means so great to discover and plant (being vexed with the calamities of intestine wars) as we have had by the inestimable benefit of our long and happy peace; yet have they both ways performed more."

It was in 1578, while Newfoundland and Acadia were a common ground of enterprise for the nations of western Europe, that Queen Elizabeth issued letters patent to Sir Humphrey Gilbert for taking formal possession of and colonising the new lands across the ocean. Cartier and Roberval had taken possession of Canada, but their attempts at settlement had failed, and there was not a single settled post of Europeans on the coast north of Florida. Gilbert was the first Englishman to make an attempt at colonisation, after Cabot's unfortunate voyage of 1498. He sailed in 1583 and touched at Newfoundland on his way, intending to go further south. On arriving at St. John's he found many vessels, Portuguese, Spanish, and French as well as English. He took possession in the Queen's name, and set up the arms of England with the usual ceremonies. No objection was made by any of the foreigners, but all assisted at the ceremony and they contributed of their stores such provisions as were required for Sir Humphrey's fleet. The enterprise failed; for, of the five ships, one deserted and returned home after being out only a few days, another was sent home from St. John's, a third was cast away on Sable Island. Gilbert's own vessel foundered at sea on the return voyage, and the fifth reached England with the broken and discouraged remnant.

Although the English were in smaller number upon the coast, their ships were larger, and it is recorded by Hakluyt that the admirals in the harbours of the southern ports of Newfoundland were usually English. These wild regions were like the far west mining camps in the years of early discovery. Law was improvised on the spot, and in these harbours of the west a usage grew up of choosing a "fishing admiral" in each, who kept a rough order over all the vessels of whatever nation. Usually the first captain to arrive was "admiral" for the season, but the Portuguese custom was that the office should be held for a week only and by the captains in orderly succession. While the English increased in number constantly on the coast of Newfoundland, it was not until the last years of the century that they began to enter the Gulf of St. Lawrence. Thus we find Thomas James writing to Lord Burleigh in 1591 to tell him of an island (Magdalen) he had heard of from two smaller vessels of St. Malo which he had captured. Hakluyt knew of the island and of the immense number of the walruses there, but the Bristol merchants evidently had heard of it for the first time. In 1593 the knowledge was utilised, for two ships sailed from Falmouth for the "Island of Ramea" (Magdalen) to kill "the huge and mighty sea oxen with great teeth," whereof fifteen hundred "were killed by one small bark in the year 1591." To this Hakluyt appends a note of information received from Mr. George Drake, who made the same voyage that year, and adds "that these are the first for aught that hitherto has come to my knowledge of our own nation, that have conducted English ships so farre within this Gulf of St. Lawrence and have brought us true relation of the manifold gaine which the French, Bretaynes, Baskes and Biskaines do yerely returne from the sayd partes; while wee this long time have stood still and have bene idle lookers on."

The following year the English got as far as Anticosti in the *Grace* of Bristol. Everywhere they met or found traces of the Basques of St. Jean de Luz whale hunting in the Gulf. Returning they called at Placentia Bay, and found over sixty Basque vessels there, of which eight were Spanish. In 1597 we read of the *Hopewell* and *Chancewel* of London sailing for "the river of Canada," and touching at the places discovered by Cartier sixty

years before. There they had many adventures with
" Britaines, Baskes and Biskaines," showing that the
Basque cities were then at the height of their activity in
the transatlantic fisheries.

When Sir Humphrey Gilbert sailed for Sable Island he
was acting upon information received at St. John's from
a Portuguese sailor who had been present when, thirty
years previously, the Portuguese had placed upon it neat
cattle and swine to breed. He thought it would be a
good place from whence to procure a supply of food for
the settlement he intended to make near by in Nova
Scotia or New England. To us, who know the place as
the "graveyard of the North Atlantic," the idea seems
absurd, but the sailors of these early days seem to have
had no dread of it. The island is on the earliest maps,
under the name of Santa Cruz, and finds place often in
grants and commissions, as in that to Fagundez, in 1521.
It is now not over twenty miles long, some three or four
miles having been washed into the ocean during the last
fifty years. It must have been much larger in early days,
for as it is now a bar of seventeen miles projects at each
end, and in heavy weather the ocean rages with a roar
like thunder against the island and its banks in a continuous line of breakers extending for fifty miles.

The century closed with a tragedy on this island. In
1577 and 1578 Henry III. had granted commissions to
the Marquis de La Roche, a Catholic nobleman of Bretagne, as viceroy of the new region across the ocean,
couched in the extravagant terms of the commission
formerly given to Roberval. These powers, in the confusion of the wars of religion, lay dormant. The wars
ceased in 1596, when the leaders of the League submitted
to Henry IV. In 1598, on January 12, Henry IV. renewed this commission. The date of the voyage has
been disputed, but there can be no reasonable doubt
about it, for the document may be found in Lescarbot.
The commission has also been published in Volume II.
of the "Edits et Ordonnances" in Canada. La Roche
raked the prisons to make up a crew, and with sixty con-

victs for prospective settlers he sailed across the Atlantic. He stopped at Sable Island under some such notion as influenced Sir Humphrey Gilbert, for, in fact, he did not know where he would finally place his colony. In the meantime he landed fifty of his convicts and his stores on the island, and sailed in a small vessel to reconnoitre the coast, intending to return for them when he had decided on a suitable place. But a very heavy storm set in and blew his little ship back to France. The convicts thus abandoned did not lack for food, for they had the cattle left there by the Portuguese; marine animals, such as seals and walruses, frequented the shores, and fish were abundant, as were also ducks and other sea fowl; but the evil passions of such a crew made a pandemonium of hatred and murder. For five years it lasted, until in 1603 the matter came to the ears of the King, and he gave order to send a skilful Norman pilot, Chefd'otel, to rescue them. Eleven shaggy men, clothed in sealskins, and with long, untrimmed beards, were presented to the King—the sole surviviors of the fifty who had been left. Human cupidity could steal even from these wretches, for the pilot robbed them of the furs they had collected and had to be forced by law to make restitution. Canada and Acadia again escaped being made convict settlements, and the close of the sixteenth century left the northeast coast of the American continent clear of European settlers of every kind. From St. Augustine, in Florida, to the arctic circle every attempt had happily failed. A remark of Lescarbot has set many writers astray. He states that when La Roche landed in France, on his return, he was thrown into prison by the Duke de Mercœur. That could not have been the case, for the leader of the League had then submitted, and France was at last united and tranquil under the Edict of Nantes. That La Roche should have left these men so long was probably due to want of means, for his losses ruined him, and he died of grief not long after. The interpolation of the Duke de Mercœur has led to much controversy. It is, however, recorded that the Marquis de La Roche made an abortive attempt previously, for Hakluyt, in his "Western Planting," twice speaks of an expedition under him in 1584, with three hundred men, which "was luckily overthrown, in respect of us, by reason that his great ship was thrown away on the Travers of Burwage (Brouage)." An imprisonment by the Duke de Mercœur, or some other political occurrence of that stormy period (for La Roche was an active partisan of Catharine de Medici), may then have intervened to prevent a renewal of that attempt; but the expedition now in question was in 1598. There is no room for doubt, since the charters of two vessels which sailed in it survive. They were dated on the 15th and 16th of March of that year, and were signed by La Roche at Honfleur. With the ruin of La Roche and the collapse of his attempt at colonisation the sixteenth century closes. The springs of the history of Acadia and Canada were freed from the suspicion even of moral contamination when the eleven convicts of Sable Island were carried back to France.

A legend has grown up to brighten the gloom of this island of terror. The fishermen tell of a Franciscan monk who shared the horrors of exile with the convicts, whom he incessantly, but vainly, strove to influence for good. When the ship came to carry away the survivors he refused to leave the island. He was sick unto death, and in a few hours his heart-break would be over and the wind would bury him in the ever-shifting sand. So they left him. But the story goes on to relate that he recovered and lived for many years, passing the time not occupied in tending his little garden, in prayer and meditation, or in collecting shell fish for his daily food. The ocean threw upon the island shipwrecked sailors to whose spiritual needs he ministered, and fishermen from the neighbouring coasts often visited him. These last brought him presents of the elements necessary for celebration of the mass, and he requited them with advice and consolation. The spirit of the holy monk yet hovers round the scene of his trial and victory; for the fishermen sometimes see him still in fair weather pacing the shore or outlined aloft against the blue sky. At other times they see his figure bright against the black wall of storm cloud, his arms stretched out as at the foot of the altar, in supplication for the sailors in peril of impending wreck, or extended in blessing or absolution as some vessel on the crest of the breaking surf is dashed against the shore.

CHAPTER XV

CHAMPLAIN

WITH the opening years of the seventeenth century came a turning point in the history of New France. The idea began to impress itself strongly upon the minds of far-seeing and enterprising Frenchmen that the new regions exploited only by fishermen and traders might be useful as colonies, and that it might be advantageous to establish real extensions of France there; not penal settlements or dumping grounds for criminals, but settlements of honest, sturdy Frenchmen who would loyally serve France in the New World and permanently occupy the road to Cathay and the East. Practical statesmen were against it. The Duke de Sully has left it on record " that to make plantation in Canada was absolutely contrary to his opinion," and he opposed every attempt in that direction, laying down with confidence the maxim that no advantages were to be derived from America north of 40° lat. That is to say, in the language of our day, there was nothing of value north of Philadelphia. Practical statesmanship must look for its reward in its own generation. It was the policy of practical statesmen which blocked the development of Newfoundland and forbade in England's oldest colony, until after A. D. 1820, the inclosure and cultivation of land and the building or repairing of houses without the license of the royal governor.

For many years Tadoussac had been a rendezvous for the fur trade on the St. Lawrence. No settlement or permanent post had been founded, but there the Indians in spring and early summer used to meet the vessels of the traders. François Gravé, Sieur du Pont (whose name continually recurs in Canadian history as Pont-Gravé, Pontgravé or Dupont-Gravé), an adventurous sailor merchant originally of St. Malo, seeing that the competition of private traders rendered a promising business unprofitable, sought the co-operation of someone with influence at court sufficient to obtain a monopoly of the trade with Canada. He applied to Pierre de Chauvin, a shipowner of Honfleur who had been a distinguished captain in the service of Henry IV. in the wars of the League, and Chauvin procured a commission as Lieutenant of the King in Canada, with exclusive privilege of trade under the stipulation that he would take out people to settle and defend the country. Chauvin was not a courtier, but a man of abundant energy and capacity. In the year 1600 he himself sailed for Tadoussac, with Pont-Gravé as his lieutenant in charge of another vessel. It was a memorable voyage, for the Sieur de Monts went as passenger to see the country. It was the first voyage in what M. Sulte has happily called "the Canadian movement," and it was taken by three men, of whom two were Huguenots, for the Edict of Nantes had opened to all Frenchmen, without distinction of religion, a career in the service of their common country. Pont-Gravé advised settlement at Three Rivers, for he had made several voyages to Canada and knew the place, but Chauvin would go no further than Tadoussac, and there, on a site overlooking the roadstead, he built a house. The voyage was really a fur-trading venture, but sixteen men were left to winter at Tadoussac, so that it was a colourable commencement of settlement. But it did not succeed, for Tadoussac is a bleak, exposed place, and insufficient precaution had been taken against the winter. The men were not under control, and the provisions were wasted. Some of the men died, and the rest took refuge with the Indians and anxiously awaited the spring and the return of the ships. Chauvin made a second voyage in 1602, and in 1603, while preparing for a third, he died.

Pont-Gravé was a good man of business and did not

Tadoussac

The Saguenay River is over the neck of land. The old Jesuit church is in front of the Hotel

allow his project to drop. Aymar de Chastes, governor of Dieppe, a Catholic nobleman who had done notable service for Henry IV. in the recent wars, obtained a similar commission and became the head of the enterprise. Pont-Gravé was the ruling spirit, but leading merchants of St. Malo, Rouen, and Rochelle had an interest in the profits. De Chastes intended to go out to Canada in person, but in the meantime an expedition was sent out in 1603. Pont-Gravé had charge of the business of trading, and Champlain—the real founder and father of Canada—made his first appearance in the country in charge of the projected explorations and discoveries. The influence of Pont-Gravé upon the history of Canada was slight, but he and his family were interested for generations in the trade of the country, and long afterwards he brought out his little grandchild, at the age of twelve years, to see the Indians in their own homes and early learn to bear privation and face danger.

Samuel de Champlain was born about the year 1567 at Brouage, now a small town on the Bay of Biscay seven miles south of Rochefort, but then a port of considerable trade, held as a fortified city during the wars of the League. He came of bourgeois stock, but the offices and positions he held would of themselves raise him to the class of nobles. Those who dispute his right to the particle *de* are more fastidious than King Louis XIII., who addressed his commission, dated April 27, 1628, to "*nostre cher et bien amé le sieur de Champlain*," and signed it with his own hand. Champlain's father was a sailor by profession and his uncle held the position of pilot-major in the service of Spain. From boyhood he had a passion for the sea, and during all his life he held navigation to be the most useful and excellent of the arts. His first service, was, however, as a soldier for Henry IV., and at the close of the war he held the rank of quartermaster. Brouage was in the centre of a Protestant district, but there is no reason to believe that the family of Champlain was Huguenot. He himself was an unwavering Catholic, and in fighting for Henry IV. he did as very many other Catholics were doing—he fought for France against a conspiracy hatched in Spain to supplant the legitimate line of monarchs by the offspring of a foreign adventurer, and to graft Spanish narrowness and bigotry upon the broader and more tolerant character of the French people. At the close of the war the town of Blavet, in Bretagne, where Champlain was serving, was occupied by a Spanish garrison, and Champlain's uncle was commissioned by the King of Spain to carry back the soldiers to Spain. Young Champlain went with his relative, and when in Spain managed so well that he was permitted to visit the West Indies as captain of a ship chartered for the service of the King. It was a rare chance, as foreigners were jealously excluded from the Spanish colonies. Champlain availed himself of it to the fullest extent. He was absent over two years and visited not only the chief islands, but the city and territory of Mexico. It is characteristic of his quick eye and farsighted intelligence that he pointed out the possibility of a canal at Panama, and that, by making use of a small river falling in near Porto Bello, there would be only four leagues of canal to cut. On his return he presented to Henry IV. a full report upon these regions, illustrated by many plans and drawings which, though not very artistic, are sufficient. Henry IV. was pleased with the work, and gave the author a pension and the title of Geographer to the King. While disengaged he happened to visit M. de Chastes at Dieppe, who was then preparing an expedition to Canada under the command of Pont-Gravé and meditated an exploration of the country to find a better site for a settlement than Tadoussac. For such a task Champlain was of all men most fitted, and, the King's assent to his absence being obtained, Champlain sailed from Honfleur on March 15, 1603, in a ship happily named *La Bonne-Renommée*. This voyage was the commencement of a life-long companionship and sincere friendship between him and Pont-Gravé. The men were very different. Pont-Gravé was a merchant, a loyal friend, and a loyal Frenchman, but

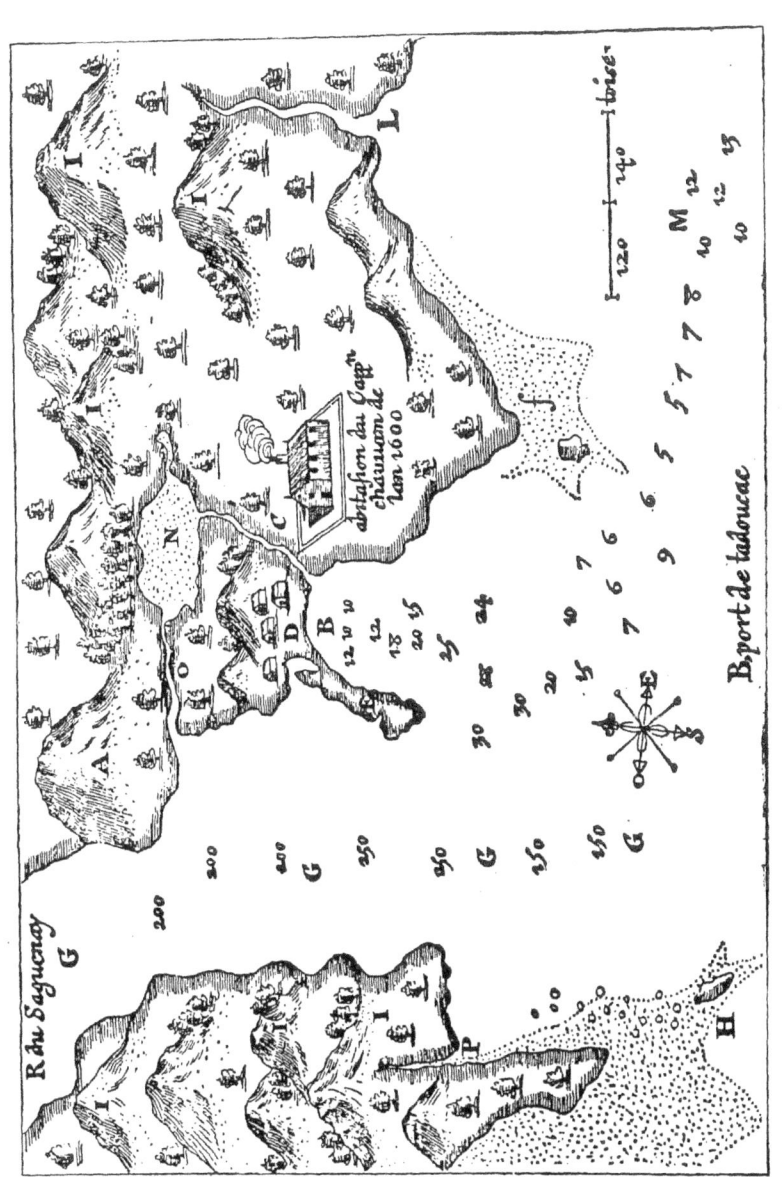

Champlain's Chart of Tadousac
From Laverdière's *Œuvres de Champlain*

busied with trade and cognate matters; and Champlain, while practical and efficient in his daily duties, aimed at establishing a settled industrial colony which should hold for France the gateway of the golden East. With unflagging perseverance and imperturbable patience he devoted his whole life to this patriotic task—the most single-hearted and single-eyed servant France ever possessed.

The vessel arrived at Tadoussac on May 24. They had brought with them two Indians, who had been taken to France the preceding year by Pont-Gravé to make a report to their countrymen concerning the wonders of the world across the sea. A number of Indians were encamped on the western point of the mouth of the Saguenay, including bands from the Etchemins of New Brunswick, the Algonquins from the Ottawa, and the Montagnais of the Saguenay. They had been on an expedition against the Iroquois, and had brought back a hundred scalps, over which they were making great rejoicings. A formal assembly was held, at which the two Indians made an address, and told of the power and greatness of the French people; and, it should be especially noted, they told their people of the good reception accorded them by the King, and that he had promised to be their ally, and either to make peace, or to send men to assist them against their enemies, the Iroquois. Here, therefore, before Champlain had set foot in the country, a definite policy had been decided upon and announced, which he has been blamed by some for carrying out. With one voice the assembled savages cried out, *Ho! Ho! Ho!* in their satisfaction that they were to have the support of so great an ally.

Champlain, after the formal assemblies and festivities of the Indians were got through, lost no time in commencing his explorations. He ascended the Saguenay about sixty-three miles, to a point a little beyond Chicoutimi, where the river becomes impassable from rapids and rocks. He questioned the Indians very closely, and gathered from them a very fair idea of the upper country. They told him of the lower rapids, of the stretch of quiet water on the upper river, of the rapids of the Décharge, of Lake St. John, of the three large rivers which fall into it, of the height of land and the savages from the north who lived in sight of a sea which was salt. Champlain concluded correctly that it was a gulf of the ocean stretching in from the north, and seven years later it was discovered so to be by Henry Hudson.

On June 18 Champlain, accompanied by Pont-Gravé, started for the Sault. Cartier's name, "Hochelega," had passed away, and until the city of Montreal was founded the place was known from the rapids which blocked navigation, as "The Sault." He noted on the way the falls of Montmorenci, and named them after the Seigneur de Montmorenci, admiral of France, to whom he dedicated the narrative of his voyage. There was no settlement of any kind at Quebec. The name Stadacona had disappeared with the Huron-Iroquois people who were there in Cartier's time, and now for the first time the name appears as Quebec,—the strait or narrows,— because the river is narrower there than anywhere else in its whole course. As Detroit in the west is the French word for the narrows on the upper river, so Quebec is the Algonquin word for the narrows on the lower river. Detroit and Quebec are synonyms, and it is trifling with history to drag the Portuguese or their discoveries in Africa into an etymology so obvious.

Champlain left Quebec on the 23d, and went as far as Ste. Croix—the Ochelay of Cartier—"a low point rising from both sides." This cannot have been other than "the Platon," or Pointe au Platon. The place now called Ste. Croix is a village six miles lower down, and both are on the south shore. On the north shore, opposite the village of Ste. Croix, the Jacques Cartier River falls in. The St. Lawrence is very nearly three miles wide at that point. Here Champlain, no doubt taking his information from Pont-Gravé, observes that it was the limit of Cartier's explorations. It was his first visit to Canada, and he had not read Cartier's narrative.

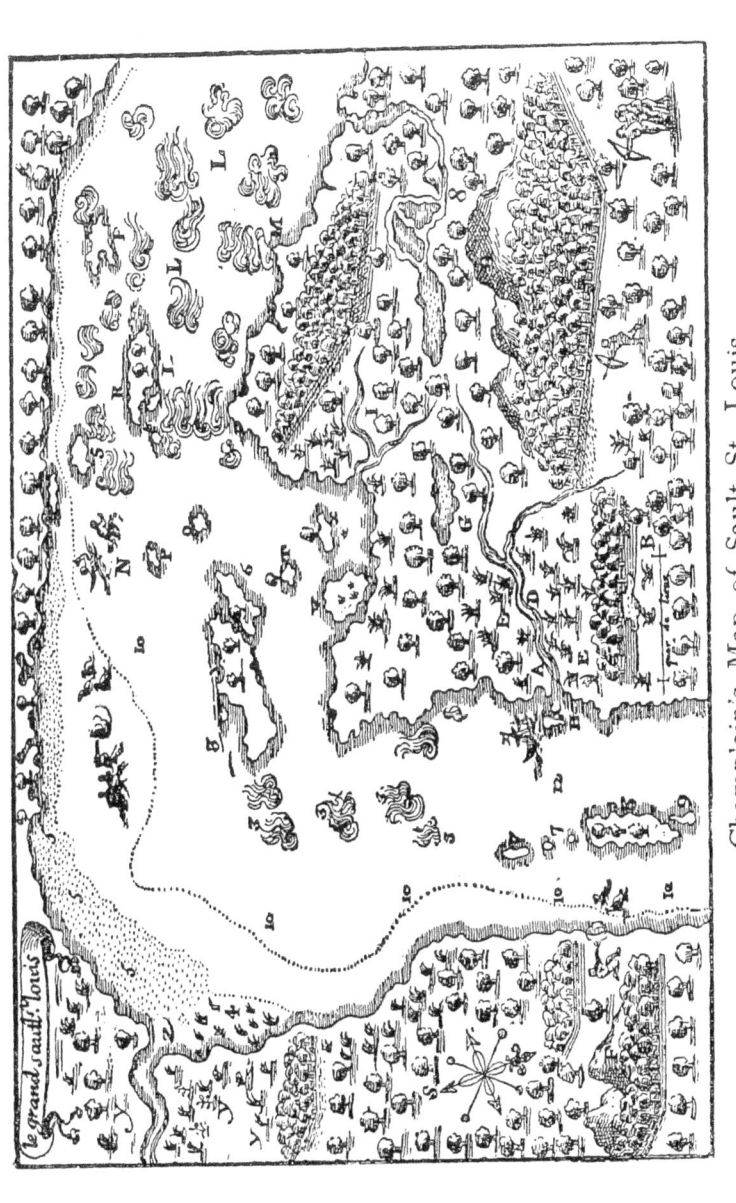

Champlain's Map of Sault St. Louis
From Laverdière's *Œuvres de Champlain*

A Place cleared by Champlain where the Custom House now stands
C Island. Now covered by a wharf also marked H
8 St. Helen's Island
N Isle aux Herons in the rapids where Champlain's man Louis was drowned

CHAMPLAIN 237

Later, in 1608, when he founded Quebec and began to explore the upper country, he examined the question at length, and recorded his conviction that Cartier's Ste. Croix was the St. Charles River, at Quebec. That is the received opinion now, but this passage has led many writers astray, and it is a warning against what is called "immemorial tradition," for the erroneous notion must have existed as early as 1600. Champlain observed the advantages of Three Rivers as a site for a trading post, and learned from the Indians that the head-waters of the rivers St. Maurice and Saguenay were close together. These wild people are of necessity good geographers, and Champlain, all his life, drew incessantly from their information. After passing Lake St. Peter, which he named, he attempted to ascend the Rivière des Iroquois (the Richelieu), but finding the current too strong returned after reaching St. Ours, and passed on to the Sault (Montreal).

The localities around the present city of Montreal are described with much detail in his first volume. He was evidently struck by the natural advantages of the place, and, the rapids being impassable, he went on foot to the lake (St. Louis) above. The Indians told him of the upper river and its rapids and expansions, and of the great lake (Ontario), and then of a fall "somewhat high, and with but little water." We must suspect here a misunderstanding in interpretation, for that was the notion Champlain got of Niagara. After that came another great lake, and then a strait (Detroit), which led into a very large lake (Huron), so large that the Indians would not venture upon it. Reflecting upon what he had seen, and what he had gathered from the Indians, Champlain thought that this distant water was the "South Sea," but with the good judgment natural to his character he observes that, before forming a conclusion, more evidence is necessary. He sought it from other Indians on his way back, but although he got more information as to the rivers falling into the lakes, and concerning the lakes (Champlain and George) to the south, and the river

(Hudson) flowing to "Florida," he could not learn with any certainty that any of the water flowed westward or that anywhere it was salt.

Immediately after his return to Tadoussac Champlain sailed to explore the lower river, and visited Gaspé and Percé. At Percé he met the Sieur Prevert of St. Malo, who had gone in another vessel, which stopped at Gaspé, to discover a mine in Acadia. The locality he was in search of was Cape d'Or, at the mouth of the Basin of Mines on the Bay of Fundy, and could only be reached overland. How he had heard of it does not appear, but all were confident about it, and, indeed, the cape derives its name from small quantities of native copper found there. This Sieur Prevert was a romancer, for he said that he had been to the mine, whereas he had only persuaded some Indians to go there, as Champlain found out later. He reported concerning a formidable tribe of savages—the Armouchiquois—of strange form, for their heads and bodies were small and their arms and thighs as thin as skeletons. Their legs were of the same size all the way down, but so long that when they squatted on their heels their knees were half a foot above their heads. Very agile savages they were, and the Sieur Prevert did not trust himself among them. He reported a supernatural danger, even more serious, the Gougou—a female monster dwelling at Miscou head, where Chaleur Bay turns on the New Brunswick side. The masts of a large ship did not reach to the waist of this creature, and it caught and devoured many savages, putting into its enormous pocket any surplus of human beings it had no immediate need for. Some savages who had managed to escape said that the pocket was large enough to hold a ship. The Sieur Prevert naturally did not trust his person near enough to the Gougou to run any risk of being pocketed, but he went so near that he and all his crew heard the horrible noises and strange hissings made by the monster. Evidence so unanimous, confirmed as it was by the testimony of the Indians, led Champlain to believe that the Gougou was some devil which tormented the poor pagan Indians. Miscou Island was a good position, for a creature of that size could reach a long way over the bay. This, concludes Champlain, "is what I have learned about the Gougou."

On August 24 they set sail from Gaspé for France, the Sieur Prevert's vessel in company. The Montagnais sent a son of one of their chiefs with Pont-Gravé, and they, kindly acceding to his request, also threw in an Iroquois woman whom they had intended to eat. The Sieur Prevert took home in his ship four savages, and as one was from the coast of "La Cadie" the citizens of St. Malo doubtless heard from the mouths of numerous witnesses many other particulars concerning the Gougou and the long-legged Armouchiquois. Champlain describes the coast of the south and west shore of the Gulf, not from his own knowledge, but from hearsay. He heard of Tregate (Tracadie) and Misamichy (Miramichi), and of a strait (Gut of Canso) separating the island upon which is Cape Breton from the mainland. He calls the island the Island of St. Lawrence. He speaks of many rivers falling in on the New Brunswick shore, and of the Island of St. John (Prince Edward Island), but the island had not then got into the maps. In the two maps with the voyage of 1611 this island is not shown, and in the map drawn in 1612 it is given only as a little round island. Along the shore of the adjoining mainland of Nova Scotia is a notice that the "author was not acquainted with the coast." In Lescarbot's map of 1608 there is no sign of Prince Edward Island, so that up to this time it was not distinguished from the mainland either in the mind of Champlain, who sailed into the gulf northward of it, or in the mind of Lescarbot, who was as near to it as Canso on the south. Whatever knowledge existed of it could not have been recorded on any map accessible to either up to that time.

During the absence of the expedition De Chastes died, and another head had to be found for the association. Champlain, who was always welcome at court, made his report to Henry IV., and presented his maps. He prepared an account of what he had seen and heard in Canada, which was published the same year. The King recognised the importance of settling a permanent colony in the New World, and of securing by actual occupation the prescriptive rights which France had obtained. But the royal exchequer was low, and, above all, the influence of the Superintendent of Finance, the Duke de Sully, was hostile. It was pointed out that there was no need to draw upon the treasury. The enterprise would be self-supporting if the King would grant to the company a monopoly of the trade with Canada frittered away in competition among a few merchants of St. Malo and Dieppe. The fisheries were not to be included, but would still be open to all. The trade in furs would pay for the expense of the projected and much desired colony.

The project was reasonable, Sully was not called upon for money, and there was no reason to consider the traders, who for many years had exploited these regions beyond sea without one thought for France, or for anything beyond their own profit. The place of De Chastes was taken by Pierre du Guast, Sieur de Monts, a native of Champlain's own province, Saintonge. He was a Huguenot who had done good service for the King in the late wars, and had strong influence at court. To him Henry gave the required privilege; he was commissioned as Lieutenant Governor for the King, and notices were forthwith posted in the maritime cities of France warning all against infringing on the rights of the company. Immediately an outcry arose from the little knots of merchants in St Malo, Dieppe, Honfleur, and Rouen who had not joined the association, but had been sending vessels out to the coast, and unhampered by any obligations had been exploiting the trade with a single eye to their own interest. The parliament of Normandy refused twice to register the letters patent, and it required a special letter of the King to overcome its resistance. The first reply of the King states that he had given orders that clergymen, of sound belief and good reputation, should be sent out, and he endeavoured in that way to remove the newborn anxiety of the merchants lest the eternal welfare of the Indians should be imperilled by the "pretended reformed religion of De Monts." Seeing that, in the fifty preceding years of "free trade," no sign of anxiety for the souls of the Indians had ever been manifested, it was transparent hypocrisy to put it forth then as the chief ground for opposition. Passing to the real reason, the King points out that the object of the enterprise is the public interest of France, of which the royal council is the best judge; that the association of De Monts is, and was, open to all who might desire to enter it, and it was inadvisable to allow an irresponsible and irregular trade to thwart so laudable an undertaking. This reply of the King is the key to all the early obstacles to the settlement of Canada.

De Monts was a man of singular energy and enterprise, and the fact of his having made as a pleasure trip a visit to Canada with Pont-Gravé in 1603 shows the breadth of his views, and the interest he had taken in the country. What he had seen at Tadoussac had prejudiced him against Canada as being too far north, and, indeed, as the object aimed at was to found a self-supporting agricultural colony, Tadoussac was utterly unsuitable. He decided upon settling somewhere in Acadia or in the mythical region of Norumbegue, corresponding vaguely to the present New England.

On April 7, 1604, De Monts sailed from Havre, taking with him some gentlemen, including Champlain, and one hundred and twenty artisans. It was a colony he was leading out in good faith. Pont-Gravé followed on the 10th with supplies, and the rendezvous was fixed at Canso. On the voyage De Monts changed his mind and steered for Port au Mouton, still called Port Mouton in the maps of Nova Scotia. After narrowly escaping shipwreck on Sable Island, they sighted Cap de la Héve, still known by the same name, and they touched at Port Rossignol (Liverpool). At Port Mouton they landed and encamped. A small pinnace was sent to Canso to meet Pont-Gravé, and Champlain was sent in the opposite direction to explore for good harbours for the ships. He examined the southwest coast of Nova Scotia round as far as the head of St. Mary's Bay. Many of his names still survive on the maps,—as Cape Negro, Cape Sable, Cape Fourchu, St. Mary's Bay, Long Island,—while others, such as Shag Island (Isle au Cormorans), are translated.

Champlain returned safely to Port Mouton, much to De Monts' relief. Pont-Gravé had joined in the meantime, and, as Lescarbot puts it in his bright style, " all of New France being assembled in two vessels," they weighed anchor and sailed round Cape Sable into the great bay, named by De Monts la Baye Française (French Bay), but which the Portuguese knew long before as Baia Fundo (the Deep Bay), and is now called the Bay of Fundy. After examining St. Mary's Bay they sailed out into the main bay by what is still known as the Petite Passage, and followed along the coast until, to quote Champlain, they found " one of the finest harbours I had seen along the coasts, in which two thousand vessels might lie in safety." It was Annapolis basin, and Champlain's enthusiasm for the place was well founded. It was in his opinion the most favourable and agreeable place for a settlement they had seen, but they sailed on in search of the copper mine reported by the Sieur Prevert. They reached Advocate's Harbour at Cape d'Or, but did not find the place as described. They then knew that Prevert had not been there, and that his story of the mine was as mythical as that of the Gougou. Nevertheless the expanse of water inclosed by Cape d'Or is called the Basin of Mines to this day. Still searching, they coasted to Cape Chignecto, crossed the Bay to Quaco, and followed westward to a river called by the savages Ouygoudy, and as it was June 24, St. John the Baptist's Day, they named it after him. The river is still called the St. John, and

CHAMPLAIN 243

gave its name in after years to the city at its mouth. Champlain gives a chart of the harbour. He describes the place

> "Where Ouygoudy's wondrous stream
> Flows in and outward with a double fall,"

but, writing some years afterwards, he has made full tide, instead of half tide, the proper time to pass through it in a vessel. There was an Indian village at the mouth of the river—a large enclosure on a hillock—where a sagamo called Chkoudun lived. Lescarbot afterwards met many savages from Gaspé there, for the St. John was the highway to the waters of the St. Lawrence and of the rivers falling into Chaleur Bay. Still sailing along the coast they came to Passamaquoddy Bay, studded with islands, and noted the Schoodic or Ste. Croix (river of the Etchemins) falling into it. De Monts selected an island at the mouth of that river to be the site of his settlement, and called it Ste. Croix.

The descriptive details given in Champlain's narrative are very accurate and exceedingly interesting. With the unwearying patience of an enthusiast in geography he noted the peculiarities of each locality along the coast; supplementing his observations by questioning the Indians. He learned from them of the portage from the upper St. John to the rivers falling into the St. Lawrence at Tadoussac, as well as many other interesting facts about the country. He fixed the latitude at $45°\ 20'$, twelve miles too far north, and he noted the variation of the compass to be $17°\ 32'$ west.

The other vessel, waiting in St. Mary's Bay, was sent for and "all New France" being assembled on Ste. Croix Island (now Dochet Island), De Monts set all to work clearing and building and planting. Champlain designed the plans, and so far-reaching has the influence of this single man been in Canadian history, that the foundations of the buildings he erected, when discovered in 1797 during a boundary dispute with the United States, fixed the starting point of the boundary and saved to Canada a threatened mutilation of her eastern territory.

Among the gentlemen who accompanied De Monts was Jean de Biencourt, Sieur de Poutrincourt, Baron de St. Just, a name highly honoured in Canadian history. He fell in love with Port Royal (Annapolis Basin), and determined to bring out his wife and family and dwell there for the rest of his life. He readily obtained a concession of the locality from De Monts, whose grant covered from 40° to 46° north latitude. He had come out only for pleasure, but he went back with the returning ships on August 31, 1604, to arrange for removal to the land of his adoption. The King confirmed his grant, and he spent the winter of 1604-5 in preparation. Poutrincourt was a strong Catholic, and had fought in the armies of the League against the King. His personal worth had won for him the King's favour, he had filled important positions in the public service, and won high consideration as a brave and capable soldier. After the ships sailed Champlain was sent westwards along the coast, and he examined it as far as the Kennebec. It was the region known since Verrazano's time as Norumbegue, and fabulous tales were told of its wealth and of a great and rich city on the Penobscot which was often called the river of Norumbegue. Champlain reported that none of the marvellous things ascribed to that region had any existence, and Lescarbot, who had a very low opinion of the " Voyages Advantureaux" ascribed to Jean Allefonsce, asks "who pulled down this beautiful city, if it ever existed? for now only a few bark wigwams can be found there."

The Island of Ste. Croix was badly chosen for a settlement. During the winter thirty-nine died of scurvy, out of a total of seventy-nine. The party suffered much from the cold of an unusually early winter as well as from lack of proper food, so that when in June, 1605, Pont-Gravé arrived from St. Malo with supplies everyone was eager to leave. Champlain went with De Monts to examine again the coast to the west for a better site, and this time he went as for as Mallebarre (Nauset), beyond Cape Cod. Some of the names he gave still survive, as Monts Deserts, Isle Haute, but most have been overlaid by English names. He visited, among other places, Menane (Grand Manan, in New Brunswick); the River Quinibequy (Kennebec); Chouacouet (Saco), a bay unnamed, now known as Boston Bay; the Rivière du Gas (St. Charles) and Port St. Louis (Plymouth). Champlain gives a chart of this harbour, where fifteen years later the Pilgrims were to land on their storied rock; Cape Cod he called Cap Blanc, because of its sand dunes. On this voyage he became acquainted with the Armouchiquois—the people whose knees, when they squatted on their heels, reached, according to the veracious Sieur Prevert, a half a foot above their heads. The patient Champlain makes no comment. He confirms the statement that they were "agile," but found them well formed.

As a result of this reconnaissance De Monts resolved to remove his colony to Port Royal. He established himself, not at Annapolis, as is often supposed, but on the north shore of the Basin at Lower Granville and opposite Goat Island. There, with renewed hope, they cleared the ground and erected buildings, partly with the lumber brought from the dismantled settlement at Ste. Croix. De Monts had to return to France, and Pont-Gravé was left in charge for the winter. Champlain remained also, in the hope of making further explorations towards Florida. The winter was passed more successfully than the previous one, although they lost twelve out of forty-five men by scurvy. On leaving for France De Monts had instructed Pont-Gravé to return home in case no communication should arrive from him by July 16. When that time arrived, no intelligence having been received, all the party set out to return, except two men who volunteered to remain with the stores. Membertou, the grand chief of the Micmacs, promised to take care of them as if they were his own children. One cannot resist expressing admiration for the French who led in the settlement of Canada, because of the way they won the confidence of the savage tribes around them. Champlain, De Monts, Poutrincourt, Lescarbot, were a galaxy of men of lofty character, wide charity, and exceptional capacity.

The two brave Frenchmen who remained under Membertou's protection now stood alone for New France. The rest of the colony sailed in two little vessels for Canso, to find some fishing craft to take them back to France. After a narrow escape, through the loss of their rudder in a storm, they were rejoiced at meeting a small shallop off Cape Sable under charge of Ralleau, the secretary of De Monts, from whom they learned that De Monts had sent out another vessel with Poutrincourt in command as Lieutenant General. He himself had to remain in France, but Poutrincourt came out to stay, and had brought out a number of people to settle. The ship had touched at Canso, and the shallop had been sent inshore to meet any of the garrison of Port Royal who might happen to be on their way back, as ordered. All returned in high spirits, and at Port Royal they found Poutrincourt. The little colony once more resumed its building and clearing and planting. The site of the present town of Annapolis was cleared as a farm, and a mill was erected on a little stream near by. Then Pont-Gravé returned with some of the men who had wintered over, and Poutrincourt and Champlain started once more to explore along the New England coast, for De Monts was still desirous of having his settlement in a warmer climate farther south than Mallebarre.

Among those who came with Poutrincourt was Marc Lescarbot, Seigneur de St. Audebert, a bright, witty advocate of Parliament of good family. The enthusiasm of his friend for Port Royal had fired the imagination of the genial lawyer, and he enlivened the winter of 1606-07 with his gaiety. He was not only witty, but industrious, and his information was wide and accurate. His "History of New France" is highly esteemed, not only for its matter, but for its style, and in its pages the doings of the early French explorers are recorded in vivid as well as

Digby Gut—the Entrance to Annapolis (Port Royal) Basin

truthful colours. Lescarbot was not an explorer or a trader, and not much of a sailor. He went no farther than the St. John and the Ste. Croix rivers. Champlain and Poutrincourt searched the Bay of Fundy to its farthest depths. They went, of course, to the Sieur Prevert's mine, and with difficulty got a few specimens of native copper. There was as little then as now. Lescarbot worked busily at his garden, and long before Boston was founded he cultivated the Muses on the forest-clad shores of the Annapolis basin. It was a bright group which assembled that winter at Port Royal. Champlain, with the experience of two winters in the New World, knew the importance of cheerfulness and good food. He instituted the *Ordre de Bon-Temps,* an association of practical good-fellowship, by which each one who sat at Poutrincourt's table was charged, in turn, with providing the food for the day. At dinner time the brethren of the order marched in procession into the dining hall headed by the purveyor of the day with his napkin on his shoulder and the badge of the order around his neck. The members followed, bearing the dishes he had provided, largely from the surrounding woods and waters; for game was plenty around Annapolis in those days.

The winter passed pleasantly enough, but with the spring ship came evil tidings. De Monts' privilege had been revoked, and with it fell the fund necessary to support the colony. Orders came for all to return, and Lescarbot went, with most of the settlers, to Canso to take a fishing vessel for France. Poutrincourt waited to get in his harvest so as to demonstrate to the King the fertility of the soil. Champlain waited to finish his map, and, without a touch of impatience at the wreck of the colony, calmly describes those points along the coast which he had not noted before. Among them was an island called Sesambre (from a small island near St. Malo), now corrupted into Sambro, and an adjacent bay very clear of all obstruction, now Halifax harbour. They all sailed together from Canso on September 3, 1607. That same year the English made at Jamestown in Virginia their first permanent settlement in the Western World.

During the term of De Monts' privilege his officers had seized some vessels trading on the coast of Acadia, and when he arrived in France he found an outcry from the maritime cities against his privilege of exclusive trading. He had sent out a number of men, erected buildings, engaged and built vessels, and supported a colony during three consecutive years. Nothing had been drawn from the public treasury and yet the enterprise was supremely in the public interest. Cartier had been a heavy loser, Roberval had been ruined, La Roche had died broken down by his losses, and De Monts, no trader, but a high-spirited soldier who had left his easy position in France to encounter the hardships and perils of the New World and attempt the almost desperate effort of founding a colony for France, was now sacrificed to the selfish clamour of a few traders who had no thought beyond their individual profit. De Monts' privilege was for ten years, and in that time he might have established his colony and built up a permanent trade open to all and for the benefit of all. Not content with the cry of "free trade for all," these traders, who during all the years they had been on the coast had never thought of it before, mourned that no Indians were being baptised and that souls were being lost because De Monts was a Protestant. This latter cry waked up a number of people who really believed it, and under their united attack the exclusive privilege was revoked. De Monts got only 6000 livres to recompense him for all his outlay, and that had to be recovered from the traders, so that the cost of suits to collect the amount in small sums would swallow up the total amount.

The chapter of discovery in Acadia now closes. What follows is history—history touched with passion and incident so romantic that it is difficult to pass it over. The French did not forsake Acadia. Poutrincourt and his family kept up a small colony at Port Royal,—not a colony of fur traders, but an agricultural colony,—and titles of concession were granted as early at 1610. In the following year Madame de Poutrincourt came out, and, although she returned in 1612, her son, a young man of enterprise, kept up the colony in spite of determined opposition in France. It was untrue that no attempt was made to convert the Indians. The Abbé Aubry went out with Poutrincourt, and Lescarbot, an unquestioned Catholic, taught the Indians during the winter of 1606-07. His address to France breathes a sincere spirit of love of country and zeal for the spread of the gospel, with hatred of Spanish and Portuguese cruelty. Poutrincourt had been a prominent soldier of the League, and his orthodoxy could not be questioned. Champlain was a sincere Catholic all his life. The influences which prevented the success of the colony were incongruous and insincere, but to set them forth further is beyond the scope of the present volume. Champlain, De Monts, Poutrincourt, and Lescarbot were far-seeing and patriotic men. They were Frenchmen of the highest type of their race. They founded the first permanent settlement of Europeans on the continent north of the Spaniards. They won the hearts of the Indians of Acadia, and if those who controlled the destiny of France could have risen to the height of Henry IV., or Richelieu, or could have seen beyond frivolous gallantries and ephemeral court intrigues, North America would now be a French continent.

NOTES TO CHAPTER XV

ACADIA

The origin and meaning of the word Acadia has been much discussed; but the opinion generally held in America is that it is derived from the Micmac word, akade, signifying a place or locality. This word was not used alone, but in conjunction with some other word to express the distinguishing peculiarity of the place. Thus in Nova Scotia *Shubenacadie,* the place of ground nuts. In New Brunswick, by the change of dialect of a kindred tribe, it becomes *quoddy* as in *Passamaquoddy,* the place where pollock are abundant. There is no question that the word exists as a locative suffix in all the aboriginal dialects of the maritime provinces of Canada, and therefore it would of necessity be constantly in the mouths of the Indians. Dr. Rand, the most learned of scholars in these languages, gives a long list of Micmac place names ending in *akade,* and many still survive upon the maps. The word Acadia therefore, in this view, has a rational origin and significance. It first occurs in the books in De Monts' petition for a commission in 1603 as *la Cadie.* Champlain in his first voyage spells the word *Arcadie* and afterwards *Accadie* or *Cadie.*

It has, however, been argued recently that it is a European word of doubtful origin and meaning. This theory is based on the fact that in Gastaldi's map (1548) and Zaltieri's (1566), as well as on some others, it appears as Larcadia, and it is pointed out that the letter *r* does not occur in the Micmac language. But the *a* is long and the sound is similar. Moreover, the spelling on these old maps is too erratic to permit of any argument being based upon a letter. The argument from Ribeiro's "larçales" falls to the ground, because both Kohl and Harrisse read the word "sarçales"; Kohl translates it "brambles." It is the name of a bay on the coast of Nova Scotia, apparently near the present Halifax. *Larcadia* as a European word has no significance, and is more likely to be a misspelling, suggested by the classic word "Arcadia" common on the maps of Greece.

The name Acadia is now used to denote the three Atlantic provinces of the Dominion when taken collectively.

ANNAPOLIS BASIN

Annapolis Basin, the old Port Royal of the French, has an enduring charm even for those most familiar with it. The Baron de Poutrincourt was willing to abandon his position and lands in Old France to dwell there, and the vivid Lescarbot becomes idyllic in his description. He quotes Moses in Deut. viii. 7: "For the Lord thy God bringeth thee into a good land, a land of brooks of water, of fountains and depths that spring out of valleys and hills; ... a land whose stones are iron, and out of whose hills thou mayest dig brass." And again in Deut. xi. 10, to the same effect. Then he goes on to apply the texts, and points out the wooded hills round the still basin and the brooks falling in cascades of white foam against the green background. A little further westward, on the basin of Mines, are the hills "whose stones are iron," and the copper at Cape d'Or represents the hills whence one may "dig brass." Then he goes on to describe the meadows on the river where Annapolis now stands. The charm this part of Nova Scotia always had for the French is most remarkable in view of the way they now cling to the cities of France and their preference for an asphalt pavement over a carpet of greensward. In the sorrowful days of the dispersion the hearts of the exiles yearned for their home in Acadia with the yearning of the captives by the waters of Babylon, and many returned in the face of incredible hardships. Pont-Gravé did not like Port Royal, on account of the narrowness of the entrance from the sea, and Charlevoix thought that Canso was the most suitable place for the capital of Acadia.

ST. SAUVEUR

It is foreign to the object of this volume to enter into the reasons which led to the weakening of the colony at Port Royal by the foundation of another, in 1613, on the Island of Mont Desert at the mouth of the Penobscot. This last was founded under the patronage and at the cost of Madame de Guercheville; and De Saussure, whom she sent out with some colonists, erected her escutcheon instead of the arms of France. The two Jesuit missionaries who in 1611 had come to Port Royal left for St. Sauveur, for so they called it, and at a place now called Frenchman's Bay on the desolate rocky island of Mont Desert they made their landing. The English under Argall destroyed it the same year and carried all the people off to Virginia, for settlers they could scarcely be called, who had chosen so savage a wilderness.

ENGLISH VOYAGES

The conflicting claims of the English and French to the northeastern regions of America are manifest in the grants, commissions, and patents issued by the two governments. They overlap each other and ignore all opposing pretensions. As has been shown in the earlier chapters, Spain claimed the whole continent up to Nova Scotia, and Portugal claimed the rest. England claimed everything north and east of the Carolinas, on the strength of the Cabot voyages, and France claimed nearly the same region, partly because of the voyage of Verrazano, and also because of the early fishing enterprises of the Bretons. The discussion of the charters granted to Roberval and De Monts by France, and to Gilbert, Raleigh, the Virginia and New England companies, and Sir William Alexander are beyond the scope of this volume, for they are documents of policy, not facts of discovery. The fact is plain that the French under De Monts made the first permanent settlement, and that although the settlement on the Ste. Croix in 1604 was removed to the opposite shore at Port Royal (Annapolis) in 1605, the colony through all its vicissitudes was continuous, and the French never dropped their hold from the Penobscot northwards and eastwards. That river was the true boundary between the two nations.

Before and at the time of Champlain's surveys English sailors had examined the coast of New England under the vague name of Norumbega; but until the Pilgrims landed at Plymouth in 1620 there was no permanent, continuous settlement. Simon Ferdinando, a Portuguese living in England, made a voyage to Norumbega in 1579, and John Walker, under the authority of Sir Humphrey Gilbert, in 1578 made a voyage preliminary to Gilbert's own expedition, which got no farther than Newfoundland. In 1602 an attempt at colonisation was made by Captain Bartholomew Gosnold. He made a landfall about Casco in Maine, and coasted New England westwards as far as Massachusetts. He landed his colonists and built a house for them, but they would not stay, and he had to carry them all back. In the following year (1603) two vessels under Pring went to the Massachusetts coast for a cargo of sassafras. In 1605, while De Monts and Champlain were examining the coast west of the Ste. Croix, they heard of an English vessel having been there. This was the *Archangel* from Dartmouth, commanded by Captain George Waymouth. He anchored at Monhegan Island off the Penobscot on May 18. He explored the Kennebec River and planted a cross some distance up the stream. Then kidnapping five Indians, he sailed home without making any attempt to settle. Then followed the attempt of Sir Ferdinando Gorges and Sir John Popham under English patents. Their first ship was captured by the Spaniards in 1606, but in 1607 an expedition sent out by them coasted Nova Scotia, visited the Bay of Fundy, and settled at Sagadanoc at the mouth of the Kennebec. The settlers built a fort and remained there during the winter of 1607-08, when they returned to England.

Samuel de Champlain
After a painting by Hamel from an engraving by Moncornet.
Reproduced from Dr. Shea's translation of Charlevoix History,
by permission of Mr. F. P. Harper, New York

CHAPTER XVI

CHAMPLAIN IN QUEBEC

HITHERTO we have seen Champlain as explorer and cartographer, sailor and soldier, builder and planter, writer and amateur artist; but not in chief command. Now, in 1608, he enters upon his lifework as chief. What had passed was exploration, but now his career commences as discoverer and coloniser, as the real father of Canada—the far-sighted leader who, with a prophet's instinct, if not with clear vision, recognised the real pathway to the west and sought to seize for France the continent at its very heart. If in the sequel France failed to reap the harvest he had sown, the fault lay with those in after generations who squandered her resources by peculation and wasted in the pursuit of trifling aims the energies which might have built an empire.

After an absence of three years and four months in Acadia Champlain landed at St. Malo. He went at once to De Monts, with his maps and plans, and related all he had learned of the country from Cape Cod along the coast of Acadia and up the Gulf and River of Canada as far as the rapids at Montreal. De Monts resolved to make another attempt, and having procured from the King an exclusive privilege of trade for one year only, sent out Champlain as his lieutenant, and in another vessel Pont-Gravé to attend to the fur trading out of which the expenses were to be recouped. The St. Lawrence River was chosen as the field of the enterprise. Champlain was to remain there over the winter and Pont-Gravé was to return with the furs in the autumn. The name of De Monts does indeed survive in Point de Monts, the point of land on the north shore which marks off the gulf from the river, but his initiative in the history of New France has not been sufficiently recognised. The vessel sailed from Honfleur, and Champlain arrived in Tadoussac on June 3, where he found Pont-Gravé wounded in an attempt to seize the ship of some irrepressible Basques whom he had found trading, instead of whaling, as they had been sent out to do. The matter having been settled, Champlain built a small vessel for use upon the river, and went up to the narrows, called Quebec, he expressly says, "*by the savages.*" This place he rightly judged to be the key of the river, and after searching around the basin he selected for the site of his settlement a level spot covered with nut trees between the cliff and the narrowest point of the river. He commenced to clear and build close to the place where the Champlain market now stands in the lower town of the present city, and partly on the site now occupied by the Church of Notre Dame des Victoires.

The "abitation," to use Champlain's name, consisted of several two-story buildings surrounded by ditches, outside of which were spurs (*tenailles*) with platforms for cannon. Two are shown on the plan—there was probably another in rear. The gate was approached by a drawbridge, a promenade ran round the lower story and a gallery round the upper one. A lookout tower (*colombier*) stood at the angle. Gardens were laid out and planted (for the soil was good), and in superintending all these works Champlain was occupied until autumn. On September 18 Pont-Gravé set sail for France and left Champlain to face his first winter in Canada.

The winter passed without any unusual occurrences. Eighteen of the party were attacked by the scurvy, and of these ten died. Nothing was heard of the ameda—Cartier's tree of health—either here or previously at Ste. Croix Island on the Acadian coast. Lescarbot says that Champlain made diligent inquiry about it without success, and he shrewdly conjectures that the savages at Quebec in Champlain's time were of a different race from those Cartier found there. This we now know

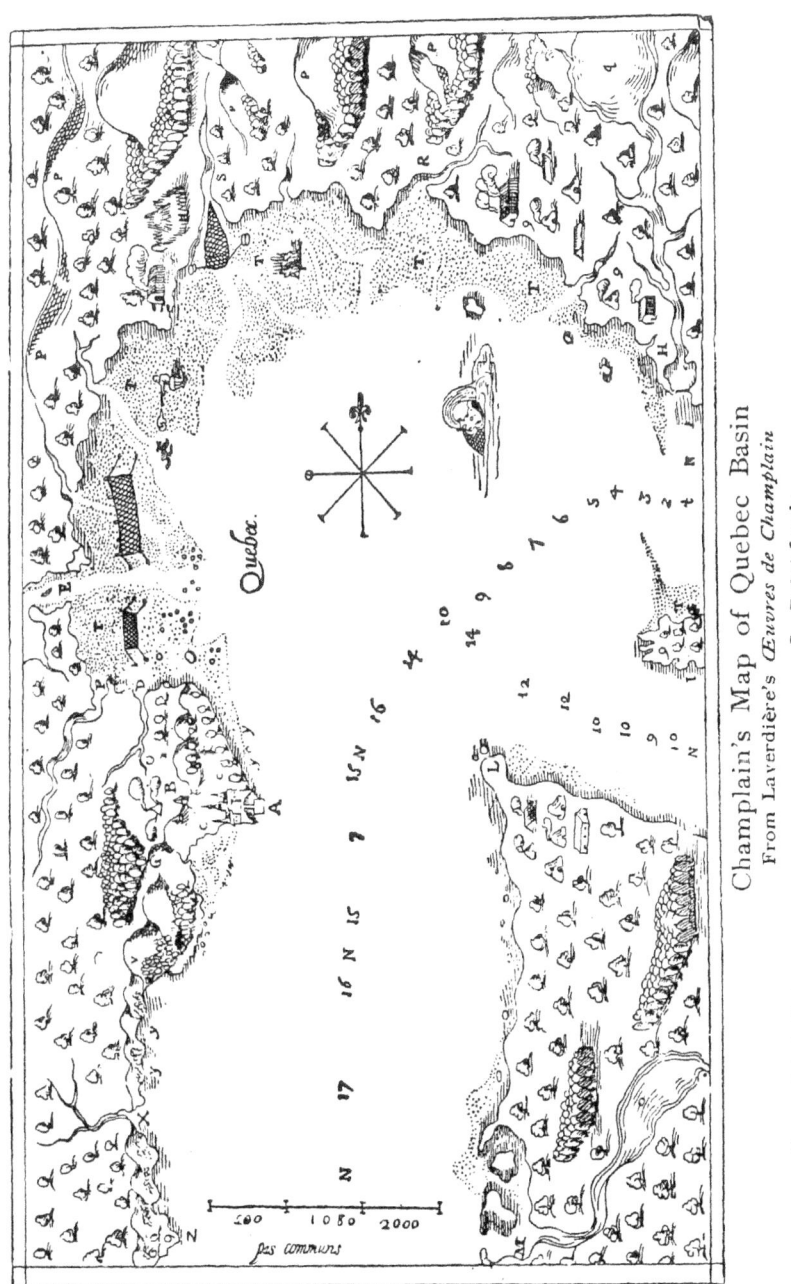

Champlain's Map of Quebec Basin
From Laverdière's *Œuvres de Champlain*

A Champlain's fort
F Place where Cartier wintered—the St. Croix now St. Charles
H Montmorency Falls
L Point Levis

A few of the most important references are given. The point of the Island of Orleans is shown in the centre at the bottom of the plan

CHAMPLAIN IN QUEBEC 255

to have been the case. The Huron-Iroquois race was farther advanced than the unsettled tribes with whom Champlain was now brought into close relation.

Pont-Gravé returned to Tadoussac on May 28, 1609, and on June 7 Champlain went down to meet him and talk over the exploration to the west, which formed part of the original plan. Exploration was a passion with Champlain, and in their representations to the King, while De Monts would dwell upon the fertility of the soil, the prospect of a new route to China was the theme of Champlain's discourse, as it was ever in his mind. So without loss of time he started on June 18, with twenty men in a shallop, to meet some Indians who had promised to be his guides. He found them encamped on an island near St. Mary's River (now the Ste. Anne). There were two or three hundred on their way to Quebec; they had planned a large war party to invade the country of the Iroquois, and they were counting upon Champlain's assistance.

It is necessary to dwell for a moment upon some points of Indian history and politics, since Champlain has been blamed by many because the course of action he now entered upon involved, in the sequel, many disasters to the colony. When Champlain first saw Canada in 1603, with no thought of any further relations with it, he found the war between the Algonquins and Iroquois in full force, and the French already committed to the policy of an alliance. Nor in fact even in the light of succeeding history would any other course have been possible, because the settled policy of the Iroquois confederacy was to force every nation they came into contact with either into their political system or into strict alliance. There was no neutrality possible, for the Iroquois, with the astuteness of the old Romans, concentrated their energies on one enemy at a time and temporised with the others. When a hostile tribe was conquered the work never had to be done over again. They used no half measures—they utterly rooted it up and renewed their own losses by the adoption into their tribes of the remnants. Then they turned their energies upon some other people and readily found ground for quarrel. The tribes—kindred to themselves—who occupied the peninsula of the present Province of Ontario were neutral in the war between the Iroquois and the Hurons, but that did not prevent the Iroquois, after they had destroyed the Hurons, from turning first upon the Tobacco nation and then upon the Neutral nation, whose very name testified to their policy, and utterly destroying them also. Even if the French had possessed less than the usual aggressiveness of Europeans, no other course was open than to take sides with the tribe in occupation of the valley of the St. Lawrence.

The French court, while exhausting the energies of the nation and squandering incalculable blood and treasure upon unnecessary wars for trivial causes in Europe, permitted a savage nation, not strong in numbers, but formidable by political intelligence and public spirit, to bring the French colony repeatedly to the brink of destruction and to destroy their Indian allies. Champlain saw the remedy clearly and in 1635, only four months before his death, writing from Quebec to Cardinal Richelieu, he tells of the beauty and richness of the land, of the avenue to commerce and the open door to the preaching of Christianity—a land stretching more than fifteen hundred leagues from east to west and watered by one of the world's noblest rivers. He asks for only 120 men, light armed against arrows, and with them and 2000 or 3000 Indian allies he asserts that a peace could speedily be conquered in one year. He pleads that 120 men are so little for France, and that the enterprise is so honourable. It would bring incalculable benefits to France, he urges, for the English and Dutch, who were commencing to settle, would be confined to the coasts, while the whole interior would be open to French trade. Champlain was not responsible for the initial policy nor for the succeeding neglect to carry it out. The hostility of the Iroquois diverted the course of exploration from the St. Lawrence, and was the reason that Lake Huron and even Lake Superior were discovered before Lake Erie.

CHAMPLAIN IN QUEBEC 257

Champlain at the urgent request of the Indians returned with them to Quebec, where five or six days were spent in festivities—feasting, and dancing, and speech-making. The war party consisted of Hurons from Georgian Bay and Algonquins from the Ottawa. The former had not yet received the nickname of Hurons (bristled heads). Champlain calls them Ochasteguins, after the name of their chief. Their real name was Wyandots, Wendots, or Yendats. He knew of their racial identity with the hostile tribes at the south, and in telling his adventures to the King he calls them "the good Iroquois." The other tribe which he already knew as Algonquemins (Algonquins) were under a chief called Iroquet. The use of "Algonquin" as a generic word, including a great family of tribes of cognate speech, was not then known.

On June 28 the war party started from Quebec. There were only twelve Frenchmen in all, for Pont-Gravé returned to Tadoussac with his people. Many new features of the country were observed by Champlain, and he drew from the Indians much information about the surrounding country. He gave names to places on the route, some of which have survived. Lake St. Peter (the Lac d'Angoulesme of Cartier's maps) had by this time received its present name. The mouth of the St. Maurice (the Rivière de Fouez or Foix of Cartier) was known as Three Rivers. Pont-Gravé had traded there and had advocated building a fort there; other localities have not retained their names. The Ste. Suzanne of Champlain is now the Rivière du Loup, his Rivière du Pont is the St. Francis, and the Rivière de Gennes is the present Yamaska. They stopped for two days to hunt and fish at the mouth of the Rivière des Iroquois (now the Richelieu). This is the most important tributary of the St. Lawrence from the south. It drains Lake George and Lake Champlain, and from the former by a short portage the head-waters of the Hudson River are reached, flowing directly south to the ocean at New York. This was the route leading to Florida which Cartier heard of from Donnacona. The Mohawk tribe of the Iroquois league occupied the water-parting, and the expedition was striking at the heart of their territory.

The river is navigable for large vessels for forty-five miles to Chambly, where there are rapids now overcome by a canal of seven locks. The Indians had told Champlain that the navigation was unobstructed, and that his shallop could pass up into the lake; but here he found an impassable obstruction, and, after landing, and searching in vain for some way of carrying his vessel round through the woods, he had to abandon the idea. But he would still keep his promise to the Indians at any hazard. Two Frenchmen volunteered to go with him, and he sent the shallop back with the rest of his men to Quebec. The canoes of the Indians were carried round the rapids, and the three intrepid Frenchmen, in the bark canoes of their savage allies, continued on their hazardous journey. The primæval forest clothed the banks in dense continuous masses, and the broad stream, shimmering in the summer sun, seemed an avenue of light opening upon unknown mysteries; but in these tangled woods might lurk bands of hostile Iroquois to cut off their return. If any thoughts of fear could disturb the calm of Champlain's mind, here would certainly have been justification for it, but duty was the dominant motive in his character. He had been sent to Canada to make explorations and to found a colony; this Indian war being part of the policy adopted, no other course was possible for him; besides, he had given his word, and although his wild allies had deceived him about the obstruction to navigation, he would not break his promise even to savages.

Some of the Indians, with characteristic inconstancy, had abandoned the expedition when at the mouth of the river, and after passing the rapids they had a review of their force, and found they had remaining sixty men with twenty-four canoes. They stopped at an island (Isle Ste. Thérèse), where they hunted and then proceeded to a place somewhere near the present town of St. Johns and encamped. The chiefs now indicated to each man his position in action, using for that purpose small sticks,

CHAMPLAIN IN QUEBEC

which they stuck into the ground for the men, and longer sticks for the chiefs. The Indians crowded round to study the plan and learn their places. Their canoes were drawn up on the river bank, and as they were in an enemy's country they erected at night a breastwork of trees to cover their camp—a task which, to Champlain's surprise, they completed in two hours. The next day they continued their course up the river and into the lake, to which he gave its present name, Lake Champlain. His eyes dwelt upon all points of interest, and he records his impressions with much detail. The trees, the game, the beauty of the country, the signs of former occupation before the ruinous war with the Iroquois, all caught his attention. Then as they went up the lake he noted the Green Mountains of Vermont in the distance on the left, and on the right the Adirondacks of New York State, closer to the shore. They were now in the Mohawk country, and they travelled only by night, resting during the day. At last near the point of Ticonderoga, the outlet of Lake George, where a short portage leads from one lake to the other, they met a party of Iroquois. The spot became historic in after years, for it was the key of French Canada on the south and the scene of many conflicts. There, a hundred and fifty years later, Abercrombie ordered a magnificent British army to slaughter, and was beaten by an inferior force with a loss of two thousand men. There fell the gallant and capable Lord Howe, and there Campbell of Inverawe struggled through the tangle of fallen trees to meet the doom seen in vision years before on the hills of Scotland. A fatal field of bloody memories. The ruined fortress still bears silent witness to the wrath of man, but nature has clothed the place with abounding beauty, and summer tourists linger long on the spot where lurking savages awaited their approaching victims, and where the French bugles rang defiance for so many years to the assailants of New France.

Champlain gives an account of the battle, and illustrated it by a drawing, which is interesting, for it shows that the Indians changed their tactics after the introduction of fire-arms. Here we see compact bodies of men advancing steadily under the lead of chiefs, and we see the stockade which the Iroquois quickly improvised when they discovered their enemies. For the first time they encountered fire-arms, and quickly realised as their two leading chiefs fell at the first discharge of Champlain's arquebuse that some deadly magical power was before them. The two Frenchmen had been sent to the flank and began to fire from the woods. This completed their discomfiture; they broke and fled before the strange and malignant power, and the allies had an easy victory. Many prisoners were taken, and for the first time Champlain saw a captive tortured at the stake, and in pity he ended the poor creature's sufferings by a shot. The cruel customs of the Indians shocked him as they have shocked all Europeans since. Yet torture at the stake was common then all over Europe, though not for the same reasons. The savages tortured their enemies only, and as a retaliation for their own losses and sufferings. Europeans burned their own countrymen.

The expedition then returned, and on the way Champlain learned much from the prisoners concerning the country to the south of the water-parting of the St. Lawrence and Hudson. The Indian allies separated at the "Falls of the Iroquois" (Chambly) for their respective homes. Champlain went to Tadoussac to confer with Pont-Gravé, and they decided to return to France and to leave Capt. Pierre de Chauvin, Sieur de la Pierre, of Dieppe, in charge of the settlement at Quebec. He was of the same family, probably nephew of Pierre de Chauvin, Sieur de Tontuit, who died in 1603, and who had first attempted settlement at Tadoussàc.

On his arrival in France Champlain hastened to court to meet De Monts. He narrated his adventures to King Henry, who took great delight in such matters, and presented him with two scarlet tanagers, a girdle of porcupine quills, and the head of a gar-pike caught in Lake Champlain. But opposing interests were too powerful.

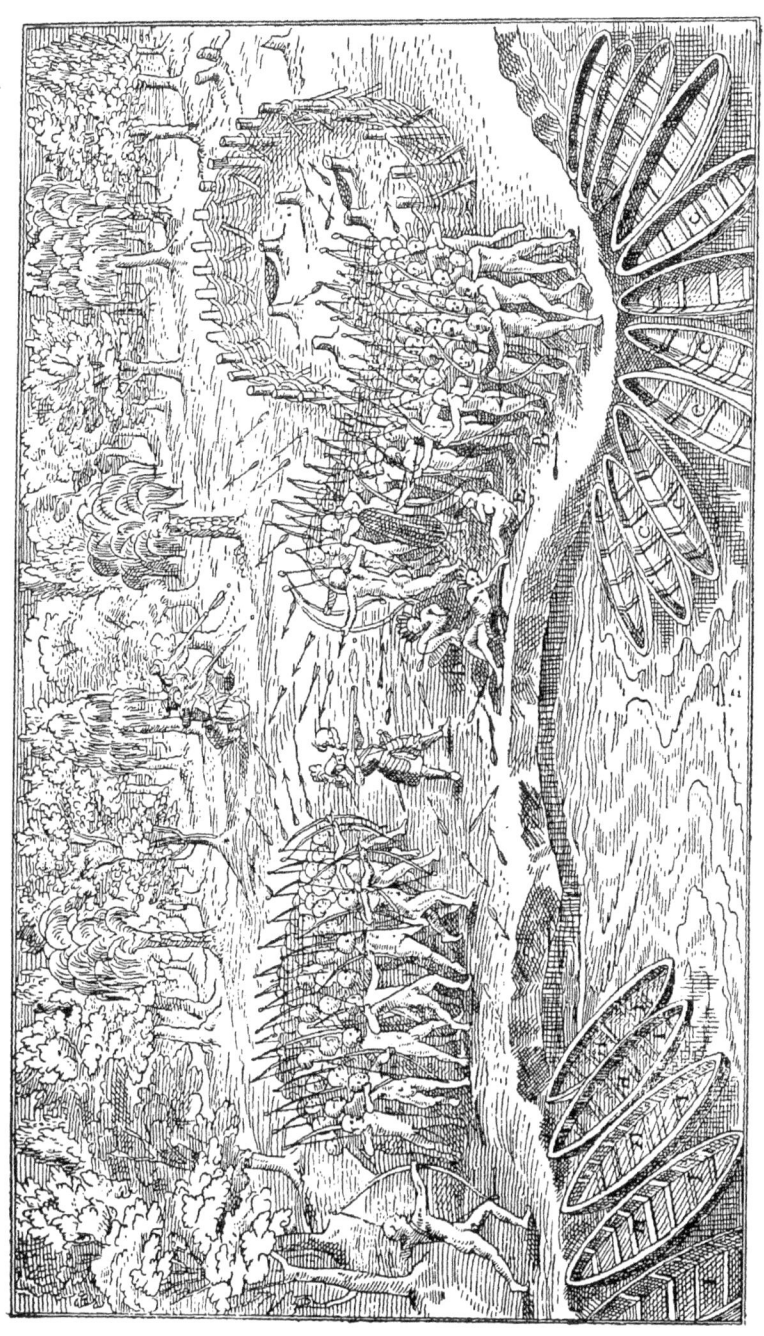

Defeat of the Iroquois on Lake Champlain
From Laverdière's *Œuvres de Champlain*

CHAMPLAIN IN QUEBEC

An extension of their privilege of exclusive trade could not be got, and De Monts and Champlain went down to Rouen to consult with their partners as to their future course. It was decided that Pont-Gravé should go to Tadoussac to cover expenses by trading, and Champlain was to continue exploration up the St. Lawrence with the aid of the Hurons, whom he was to assist in their wars. On arrival at Quebec the following spring he found that everything had gone on well; the winter had been unusually mild, they had had plenty of fresh meat, and consequently there had been no sickness. The Montagnais had been expecting him at Tadoussac, and, as had been arranged the year previous, went ahead of him up the river to the mouth of the Richelieu. The Hurons had engaged to meet Champlain there with two hundred men, and Iroquet, the Algonquin chief, was to bring two hundred more.

On June 19, 1610, when Champlain's people and the Montagnais were preparing to camp on an island (probably St. Ignace) opposite the mouth of the Richelieu, word came that the Algonquins were not far off, and were engaged with a war party of a hundred Iroquois who had built a fort and that assistance was urgently required. Getting through the woods and swamps with much difficulty, the Frenchmen arrived before the fort and found that their allies had been repulsed with loss and that the Iroquois were holding out successfully. The fort was circular, built of large trees piled one upon another, and afforded perfect shelter to the garrison. Champlain was wounded in the neck by an arrow as he was firing his first shot, but he continued in action and directed an assault upon the stockade. A few independent fur traders who had gone to the rendezvous on their own account joined in, and the fort was carried. The Iroquois tried to escape, but were all killed or captured.

After the battle trading commenced, and to Champlain's disgust the private traders carried off most of the peltries. "It was a great service to them," he writes, "to find out a strange people in order that others should, without risk or danger, carry off the profit." The next day the chief Iroquet arrived, and another band of Hurons. Three days were spent together on the island, when each tribe returned to its own country. Champlain took with him a Huron youth to be sent to France, and he left with the Algonquins a young French boy, of whom we shall hear later, to go to their country and learn the language. The year 1610 passed without any further enterprises, for while Pont-Gravé and Champlain were consulting upon their plans for the winter, news arrived of the assassination of their patron, Henry IV., and they both returned to France. A palisade had been erected during the summer to protect the buildings at Quebec, and Du Parc, who had spent the previous winter with Chauvin, was left in command of the settlement.

Champlain sailed again for New France from Honfleur on March 1, 1611, but gained nothing by so early a start, for he got into the ice and passed through many dangers, arriving at Tadoussac only on May 13. On the 17th he set out up the river to the Sault (Montreal) to meet the Indians from the Ottawa, as arranged the year before. He stopped at Quebec to repair his shallop, and found that there had been no sickness, and that during the winter everything had gone on well. He arrived at the Sault on May 28 with the Huron he had taken to France, but the Indians had not arrived. He examined the locality with great care, with the view of founding another settlement, and decided that the most suitable spot was what is now called Pointe à Callières, and there he ordered the trees to be cut down and a clearing made. It is the centre of the present city of Montreal. The Custom House now stands upon the site he chose, and the Montreal ocean steamships discharge their cargoes there. A little river, now covered in and utilised for drainage, fell in at that point, and on its banks were the clearings cultivated by the Hochelagans of Cartier before the great war drove them westwards. He found the deposit of blue clay on the upper levels of the present city, and tested it

CHAMPLAIN IN QUEBEC

by making bricks, with which he built a wall to see the effect of the ice and high water of winter The river broadened there to an expanse like a lake, and south of the rapids were beautiful prairies at the place still called La Prairie de la Madeleine. While the party waited for the Indians and explored the country around, they heard of an island in the rapids where there were so many herons that the air was darkened with them. A keen sportsman, servant to Champlain, called Louis, contrived to reach the spot in the middle of the rapids, but he overloaded his canoe with birds, and was drowned. The island is still called Isle aux Herons, and the Grand Sault commenced from that time to be called Sault St. Louis—a name it still bears.

On the 13th of June a large party of Indians arrived. They expected to meet Champlain only, but besides his boats they found a swarm of independent fur traders who came up for their own profit, without care or responsibility for anything beyond. Later on people such as these made a pandemonium on the river by selling the savages brandy and fire-arms, until wholesome restrictions of trade were again enforced. The Indians distrusted the traders, and moved their camp to the Lake of Two Mountains, where the shallops could not go, and they invited Champlain to a midnight council. They renewed their alliance with him and Pont-Gravé. The Frenchman who had wintered with the Hurons, and the Huron who had wintered in Paris, related their experiences and acted as interpreters. The Indians promised to show the wonders of the upper country to Champlain or anyone he would send with them. The result was that the chief Iroquet took with him as far as the Petite Nation a youth from one of the trading barques, and the Algonquins of Allumette Island, on the upper Ottawa, took a youth from Champlain's party who, like Ananias, is remembered in history for his effrontery as a liar. Champlain returned to France and arrived at La Rochelle on September 16, 1611.

New difficulties arose, which De Monts and Champlain

could not overcome, and the latter had to stay over the following year in France, to the great disappointment of the Indians, who came down to the Sault St. Louis to meet him. Champlain's men told them he would come the following year, but the free traders asserted loudly that he was dead. In France the shareholders in De Monts' company very naturally refused to go on with an enterprise when all the risk was theirs and the profits were gathered by others. De Monts bought out their shares and left the management to Champlain, who, seeing that the death of Henry IV. had changed the channels of court influence, arranged that the Count de Soissons should be head of the company. That nobleman, however, died shortly afterwards and the Prince de Condé took his place. He appointed Champlain as his lieutenant, and a commission of exclusive trade was granted for twelve years. The old free trade cry was raised again, and the Parliament of Rouen thrice refused to register the papers. At last it was compelled to do so, and in response to the clamour of the merchants they were told if they wanted profits to take shares in the company, which was open to all. "It is not reasonable," argued Champlain, "that one should capture the lamb and another go off with the fleece." The opposition from St. Malo was very strong, and the Breton merchants claimed the trade because of the discovery of the country by their countryman Cartier. From about this period the influence of the Bretons in Canada began to wane and the Norman ports took the lead in the trade. A movement towards colonisation commenced, and the colonists were nearly all from Normandy.

On March 6, 1613, Champlain sailed from Honfleur with Pont-Gravé, and after a short stay at Tadoussac he arrived at Quebec on May 7, where he found everything to his satisfaction. The winter had been mild. The river had remained open and everyone had kept in good health. On the 21st he arrived at the Sault St. Louis (Montreal). The results of the free trade clamoured for by the merchants were evident. There were no Indians

Notman Photo, Montreal. Running the Sault St. Louis in the present day.

CHAMPLAIN IN QUEBEC 265

there. They had been disgusted with the ill-treatment they had received from the traders, who had also told them falsehoods about Champlain, and said that he would never return. This decided Champlain to push his explorations further up the river of the Algonquins (Ottawa), and seek the Indians in their own homes. The young man, Vignau, whom he had sent with the Algonquins in 1611, had wintered with them at Allumette Island, and had returned to France in the fall of 1612. He there reported that he had seen the Northern Sea, that the river took its rise in a lake which also communicated with the sea, that he had seen the wreck of an English ship on the shore, that he had seen the scalps of eighty Englishmen whom the Indians had killed, and that there was a young English boy still a captive among them. All this was absolutely false, but he swore to it, and added such details that Champlain laid the matter before the leading men of the company in Paris, and they instructed him to follow up the clew and discover the great northern sea. The story seemed to be confirmed by the news of Hudson's discovery of the Bay,—brought to England in 1612 by the mutineers,—and the report of the expedition under Sir Thomas Button, sent to rescue him in the same year.

With four Frenchmen, one of whom was Vignau, and with one savage as guide, Champlain started from St. Helen's Island, opposite Montreal, on May 27, 1613, with two canoes. He carried them over the portage to Lake St. Louis, and from there commenced his memorable exploration of the Ottawa, then called the River of the Algonquins, and later the Grand River. Passing through Lake St. Louis he noticed three rivers falling into it—one from the Iroquois territory at the south (the Chateauguay), another from the Huron territory from the west (the St. Lawrence), and the third, which he followed to the north (Ottawa), from the country of the Algonquins and Nipissings (Nebicerini). He made a short portage (Ste. Anne's) the same day, and spent the night upon one of the small islands just above the rapids. The following day (May 31, 1613) was spent in passing through the tranquil reaches of the Lake of Two Mountains,—he called it Lac de Soissons,—but on June 1 he arrived at the Long Sault, a series of rapids now overcome by the Carillon and Grenville canals—twelve miles of very turbulent water. Here he narrowly escaped death, for the woods were so dense they could not carry their canoes by land, and they had to pull them up the stream with ropes. There was only one Indian in the party, and the Frenchmen were awkward at managing canoes in such difficult water. His canoe dragged him in, and if he had not fallen between two rocks, he would have been drowned. The rope was twisted round his wrist, and he was seriously hurt, but held on to his canoe. This experience at the Chute à Blondeau gave him a severe lesson in the art of canoeing. Two years before, shortly after his servant Louis was drowned, Champlain insisted upon the Indians taking him down the Sault St. Louis, but they made him strip to his shirt, and warned him to hang on to his canoe if it should upset. He ran the Lachine rapids in safety, but it was the Indians who managed the canoe. He had courage enough for anything, but to track a canoe up the Long Sault of the Ottawa required skill, and after they had got up they rested for the remainder of that day, "having done enough." The following day he met a party of Algonquins on their way down, and he changed off the most awkward Frenchman of his party for an Indian guide to manage the second canoe. Continuing on along the north bank the Petite Nation River attracted his notice by the islands and the beautiful woods near it. This part of the Ottawa country was the hunting ground of the "Little Algonquins," and the river is called the Little Nation River to this day (Petite Nation).

It was the 4th of June, 1613, when Champlain reached the site of the capital of the Dominion—Ottawa. He mentions a river with a countless number of falls (the Gatineau), from the north, and just opposite, falling in from the south, another at whose mouth is a marvellous

Topley Photo, Ottawa

Chaudiere Fall (The Big Kettle)

CHAMPLAIN IN QUEBEC

fall, making an arch under which the savages delight to go. The French called it, in after years, the Rideau (curtain)—a descriptive name; for the river flows smoothly over, and even now, disfigured as it is by sawmills, enough remains of its pristine beauty to suggest the features which attracted attention in those early years, when issuing out of a dense background of pine forest it fell in a curtain of white foam over the bank and into the main river. It must have been a very beautiful spot, for the fur trader Henry speaks of it when passing up in 1761: "The fall presented itself to my view with extraordinary beauty and magnificence and decorated with a variety of colours." A league farther up, "rowing against a strong current," they reached the (Chaudière) falls, where the main Ottawa drops forty feet between many little rocky islands covered with brushwood. In one place he observes that the falling water had hollowed out a large and deep basin, round which it forms swift eddies. The natives, he adds, call this Asticou—the kettle. The French translated the word, and the falls are called Chaudière (Kettle) Falls to this day. The chasm in the rock may still be seen, and the sound of falling water, which Champlain heard two leagues away, still soothes the ear on a calm evening. The islands are all bridged and built over, but even yet, cribbed and confined though it is with sawmills and paper mills and other factories, the great "Kettle" foams and steams before the eyes of every visitor to Parliament Hill, an object of admiration, though its wild forest setting has disappeared.

The carrying place (portage) at the fall was short; only a quarter of a league, says Champlain. According to Mackenzie it was 643 paces, and Henry says a quarter of a mile, over smooth rock, though to Champlain's unaccustomed efforts the rock seemed rough enough. The Recollet Sagard, in passing this portage a few years later, made the first palæontological observation on record in Canada, for he remarked the fucoids in the Trenton. Limestone, and took them to be slugs petrified by the cool spray. Champlain had to make a second portage, higher up, of about three hundred paces (the fur traders with heavily laden canoes used to make three), and then he entered a lake now called Lake des Chênes, from the oak trees at the third portage—a long stretch of quiet water until the Chats rapids were reached. Here the river falls over a long circular ridge of rock in a fall interrupted by islands, and forms a series of foaming falls looking like banks of white snow around a curve two miles long of forest. At that spot he lightened his burden by leaving the least necessary food and clothing, trusting to hunting and fishing for support. The falls and lake are now known as "Des Chats," from the number of raccoons (chats sauvages) which were found in the vicinity.

He continued up the river, noting everything out of the usual course. The mosquitoes troubled him more than the portages. He writes "their persistency is so marvellous that one cannot describe it," and no doubt, as he scrambled over the portages, although he was "laden only with three arquebuses, three paddles, his cloak, and some small articles," the flies availed themselves of the novel chance at a European skin. He passed a river (the Madawaska), where a people dwelt called Matou-ouescarini, and, having left the main river to avoid the heavy rapids, he found a number of savages settled at Muskrat Lake, who gave them a kind reception and sent some people to assist them and guide them to Allumette Island, where they regained the Ottawa.

Allumette Island, where Champlain now arrived, figured largely in the early history of Canada. It was the stronghold of the greater Algonquins as distinguished from *La Petite Nation,* who hunted near the site of the present capital. Their chief Tessouat (who had met Champlain at Tadoussac in 1603) was an important personage, and as the river all round the island was broken by rapids he availed himself of its unique position to levy toll on the western Indians on their way down the river to dispose of their furs. He received Champlain very cordially, and made a great feast (tabagie) in his honour, after which a formal council was held. Champlain told them that he had come with the intention of going to visit the Nebicerini (Nipissings), and that he wanted four canoes with eight savages as guides. Tessouat, as spokesman for his people, replied that while Champlain had always shown himself their friend, and had gone with them to war, he had not kept his promise and met them at the Sault (Montreal) the year before. Two thousand of their people had gone there, and were not only disappointed at not seeing him, but had been badly treated by the French traders, and had decided not to go there again. Moreover, that the Nipissings were sorcerers, and that they were cowardly, and were no help in war, but would kill them by charms and poisons, and also that the way was long and difficult. Champlain reproached them for unfriendliness, and brought forward Vignau, who had wintered with them in 1611, who insisted that he had visited the Nipissings; and then Champlain told them Vignau's story of the North Sea, and the wrecked English ships, and the eighty English scalps, and the English captive. This tissue of lies scandalised the Indians, and they were eager to put Vignau to death. At last, confronted with the indignant savages, Vignau broke down and confessed that he had never left Tessouat's Island, and that the whole story was false from end to end. Champlain was greatly disturbed, for this journey to the North Sea had been concerted at Paris with the leading men of the company on the strength of Vignau's reports. It is the only instance in Champlain's record when his even temper was ruffled, and although Vignau was eventually pardoned, his position for a short time was critical.

There was nothing to be done but to return, and he started for the Sault (Montreal), but with a retinue of forty canoes, increased on the way to sixty. Nothing occurred to be noted, excepting that they stopped at the Chaudière Falls (at Ottawa) to perform a ceremony, immemorial among them, of propitiating the presiding spirit of the place. All assembled in one spot and took up a collection on a wooden plate. Each savage put in a little piece of tobacco. They then put the plate in the middle of the group and danced around it, singing in their usual style; after which one of the chiefs made an address, and when that was over he emptied the plate into the Chaudière. Their religious instincts being satisfied they passed down to Montreal. There, besides some boats belonging to the company, they found the Sieur de Maisonneuve of St. Malo. He had procured a permit from the Prince de Condé to bring out three vessels. It is a name to be ever remembered in Montreal, for twenty-nine years later Paul de Chomedey, Sieur de Maisonneuve, founded the city. Until then it was only a fur trading centre for a few weeks in summer, where the Indians from the west and north congregated to meet the French trading boats. Here, before assembled white men and savages, Vignau made an open confession of his falsehoods, for the object of Champlain's voyage was known to all connected with the company. The Indians took back with them two young men at Champlain's request, but none of them would have anything to do with Vignau. Champlain then sailed for France.

There was much for him to do—much that only he could do, for in all the tangle of conflicting interests and court intrigues he was the only man with a single eye for the good of France, the advancement of exploration, and the social and spiritual welfare of the savages. He willingly left the trading to others—he wanted nothing for himself but his narrow salary. Pont-Gravé managed the commercial part of the enterprise; he assumed for his share the cares of the infant colony, the labours of exploration, and the risks of warfare. Upon his noble and unselfish devotion was built the colony of New France, and in years long after it fell by the greed, luxury, and corruption of men who embodied the negation of everything he held dear. His first care was to conciliate the jarring interests of the merchants by pointing out that no one could be benefited by the reckless competition which was their only wisdom. By personal efforts with the

CHAMPLAIN IN QUEBEC 271

court and the Prince of Condé, and by personal representations to the merchants of the maritime cities, he matured the plan of a company, with an exclusive charter for eleven years, but open to all to join—one-third of the stock to be held in Normandy, one-third in Bretagne, and one-third in La Rochelle. The Rochellois delayed until the time set had expired, when the Normans and Bretons divided their third between them. Champlain then turned his attention to the spiritual interests of the savages, and arranged with the Recollets (a branch of the Franciscan Order) to send out four brothers to make a commencement of a mission; he himself obtained contributions for the expense and procured the requisite ecclesiastical authority. At last everything was ready, and on April 24, 1615, he sailed with the friars in the *St. Etienne* from Honfleur under the command of Pont-Gravé.

With the arrival of these four Recollet fathers commences the era of Catholic missions in Canada. Up to that time the Huguenot influence had been very strong in the councils of the trading and colonising companies. Many of the merchants of Normandy were Huguenots, and if the wrong-headed burghers of La Rochelle had taken up the shares reserved for them, the Huguenot influence would have maintained its ground. The merchants had never taken any interest in the colonisation of the country, but looked upon it as a field for trade, and in that respect they were not in sympathy with Champlain, who, apart from his interest in the spiritual welfare of the savages, felt that the work of the missionaries would lead to the opening up of trade in the interior. The Huguenots lost their lead, and the religious orders of the Catholic Church took up at that juncture the work of missionary exploration, and by the natural sequence of events Canada became a Catholic country.

A large number of Indians had assembled at the Sault St. Louis, and when Champlain arrived they reminded him of his promise to assist in their wars. After consultation with Pont-Gravé he decided to join them in another expedition, and so obtain an opening for the exploration of the upper country. The Indians promised to gather 2500 men, and Champlain was to supply as many Frenchmen as he could. Leaving most of his people behind, he started for Quebec to make arrangements for an absence which would probably extend over three or four months. When he returned to the Sault the Indians had all gone home, taking with them the Recollet, Father Le Caron, and the twelve Frenchmen who were to assist on the expedition. They had grown impatient and supposed that Champlain would not return, or that he had been captured on the way by the Iroquois. Champlain at once started off with two Frenchmen and ten savages to follow into the region now known as the Province of Ontario.

Topley Photo, Ottawa

Entrance to French River, Lake Nipissing District
(Champlain's route to Lake Huron)

CHAPTER XVII

CHAMPLAIN IN ONTARIO

WE have followed Champlain in his explorations in the present provinces of Nova Scotia, New Brunswick, and Quebec. As stated in the preceding chapter, in the year 1615 he entered the Province of Ontario, and before he returned he had explored all the older part of the province except the Niagara peninsula. He followed up the Ottawa in the track of the returning Indians to Allumette Island, where he had been in 1613, and passed through what he called the Lake of Algonquins (Lac des Allumettes), and up the Deep River and the stream beyond until he reached the Mattawa. There he branched to the left and followed that river up to its head. Thence by a short portage he crossed over to Lake Nipissing, and followed down the French River, its outlet, into the Georgian Bay of Lake Huron. The route looks easier upon the map than it is in reality, for there are many falls and rapids to be overcome only by laborious portages; nevertheless, it continued to be the fur traders' highroad to the west until the days of steamboat navigation. In the early years of the colony it was beyond the usual reach of Iroquois war parties, and it is, in fact, the shortest and most direct course to Lake Superior, for from the Strait of Michilimackinac to the head of tide water, at Lake St. Peter, below Montreal, is an absolutely due east line—the parallel of 46° N. On the French River he met a party of the *Cheveux Relevés*—a people who went absolutely naked, but were very particular about their hair, which they dressed high up on their heads with great pains. They were afterwards known to the English as the Ottawas, and the river derived its name from them in after years. In fact, they claimed an especial right in the river, for they used it for trade more continuously than the other tribes.

The Huron nation, whose homes Champlain was now to visit, had been driven from their original seat at Montreal and Quebec by the incessant incursions of the Iroquois. They were the elder branch of the main stock of the Huron-Iroquois race, and their language more closely resembled the Mohawk dialect than the other dialects of the Iroquois league. The French afterwards, because they wore their hair in a ridge, called them Hurons, and the name clung to them and was applied to the lake on which they dwelt. If we are to believe the dim traditions of their tribe, the cause of all their "unnumbered woes" originated with a woman. The war which followed was internecine, demanding the absolute extinction of one or the other nation. Fortune was against the Hurons, and, making friends with the alien tribes of Algonquins on the Ottawa, they retired to a region in the west, beyond, as they hoped, the reach of Iroquois war parties. Like the Iroquois, they were sedentary tribes, living in villages and drawing much of their support from the cultivation of the soil. Rough and primitive as was their agriculture, it raised them above the level of the surrounding Algonquins, who were hunters, and for the most part had no settled abodes. The French found the Hurons dwelling in a fertile territory south of the River Severn, and between Lake Simcoe and Nottawassaga Bay, approximately corresponding to the present county of Simcoe. In that comparatively narrow territory there was a population variously estimated at from twelve to thirty thousand souls, living in towns and villages estimated to be thirty-two in number. These were connected by well-worn trails, and the density of the population may be gathered from the fact that in three days Champlain visited five villages. The towns on the southern margin of the territory were fortified after the manner of Hochelaga, as seen by Jacques Cartier. The drawing from Ramusio, given at page 167, shows a perfectly circular

CHAMPLAIN IN ONTARIO

rampart, and was doubtless made from the description in the text. The cut following, at page 278, is from a drawing by Champlain of the Onondaga town he assisted to attack. It is a type of all the fortified towns of the Huron-Iroquois tribes. At one of these towns, Carhagouha, there was a warm welcome, for Father Le Caron had settled there, and with him were the twelve Frenchmen of his party. These with Champlain and his two men made a good congregation, and the happy priest celebrated for the occasion the first mass in the Province of Ontario.

After issuing from French River upon Lake Huron, Champlain's course was south along the shores of the region now known as the counties of Parry Sound and Muskoka. He crossed Matchedash Bay and landed not far from the present town of Midland in Simcoe county. It was in the territory of the Attigouautan, a sub-tribe under the *totem* of the Bear, the chief of the four tribes constituting the Huron nation, and from them at first Champlain called the lake, but afterwards he named it the *Mer Douce* (Freshwater Sea). From thence he went from town to town, everywhere received with welcome and feasted with a greater joy inasmuch as they thought he had been taken by the Iroquois. They had given up all hope of seeing him again, and had postponed their intended war party; now they commenced anew to assemble their forces, and in the meantime he examined the country. He found great quantities of Indian corn (maize) and squashes growing. Sunflowers grew also in abundance, from the seed of which they extracted oil. He noted the soil, which he says is a little sandy, but good for Indian corn, and he comments on many other productions of the country around. He remained longer with the Arendaronons, or tribe of the Rock, than with the others. They dwelt at the outlet of Lake Couchiching, and were especially friendly with the French.

Meantime the warriors were gathering, and news kept coming in from all sides. Word came that a kindred people beyond the Iroquois, to the south, were preparing five hundred men to take part in the proposed attack. These were the Andastes (called also Conestogas and Susquehannocks), who dwelt on the head-waters of the Susquehanna River in Pennsylvania. They also, though kindred in race, were enemies of the Iroquois. They had come into contact with the Dutch, who had just made the beginning of a settlement in the Mohawk territory near Albany on the Hudson and were in close alliance with the Iroquois.

At last, early in September, everything was ready and the great war party started. They passed through Lake Simcoe, then carried their canoes over the portage trail to Balsam Lake, from thence down the Otonabee River, passing the site of Peterborough, to Rice Lake. From the extreme end of Rice Lake the River Trent flows southwards, and they followed it down to the Bay of Quinté, where, at the site of the present town of Trenton, they issued out upon the waters of Lake Ontario. The route is much broken by falls and rapids, but in recent years it has been improved by canals and other aids to navigation, under the general name of the Trent River Navigation System.

Two of the great lakes were now discovered. Father Le Caron had reached Lake Huron before him, but Champlain was the first white man, excepting, perhaps, Etienne Brulé, to dip a paddle into Lake Ontario. The war party followed along the north shore to the eastern end of the lake, where there "are many large and beautiful islands," but the point where they crossed is not precisely ascertained, nor is it absolutely certain where they landed upon the south shore. There they hid their canoes in the woods, and for four days marched by land until they crossed a river containing some fine islands, which discharges a large lake. The place is easily identified as Oneida River and Lake. They were striking at the very heart of the confederacy, at the country of the Onondagas, where burned the central council fire of the formidable league of the Five Nations.

CHAMPLAIN IN ONTARIO 277

The Iroquois confederacy at that time occupied the southern water-parting of the St. Lawrence River and Lake Ontario, from Lake Champlain on the east to the Genesee River on the west. They commanded the headwaters of the Hudson, Delaware, and Susquehanna rivers, and their war parties had depopulated an enormous extent of adjacent territory. The league was composed of five tribes, and was at first called the Five Nations by the English. In after years the Tuscaroras, a kindred tribe from North Carolina, took refuge with them, and thereafter they were known as the Six Nations. The idea of an offensive and defensive league in perpetuity originated in the mind of Hiawatha, not a mythical person, but a real historical character, around whose name many myths have gathered. One such myth is embodied in Longfellow's beautiful poem, for it is absolutely certain that Hiawatha was not an Ojibway of Algonquin stock, dwelling near Lake Superior, but an Onondaga of Huron-Iroquois stock, dwelling south of Lake Ontario. Some time about the middle of the fifteenth century he conceived the idea of putting an end to the incessant wars which raged among the Indians, by an offensive and defensive league. The idea was distasteful to the Onondagas, and, like Mahomet, he had his *hegira,* for he had to flee to the Mohawks. They received him and accepted his views, and from them the league extended westward. They were called the "elder brethren" from this fact, and they wielded great influence at the councils of the confederacy. Their home was at the head-waters of the Mohawk River, and from that point their war parties kept the whole region to the north and east in terror. Next, to the west, were the Oneidas, who dwelt near Oneida Creek and Lake. The Onondagas were the central tribe, and the fire of the grand council of the league was kept burning among them. Their headquarters were on the Onondaga River. Then succeeded to the west the Cayugas on Cayuga Lake, and the western gate of the "Long House," as they figuratively called their league, was kept by the Senecas, who reached to the Genesee valley. The turnpike roads from the head-waters of the Hudson River to Buffalo on Lake Erie are on the main trail which used to connect the chief towns of the Iroquois league. At the time of their greatest extension, about 1650, they had subdued the whole extent of territory now known as Ontario as far as the Sault Ste. Marie; they kept the French in constant alarm at Quebec, and their war parties struck even as far east as Chaleur Bay, and far north among the Montagnais. They held all the tribes in subjection as far south as the Tennessee River; on the west they reached the Mississippi, where they met the powerful tribes of the Sioux, and on the northwest they were held in check by the warlike nation of the Ojibways, with whom they had been for two hundred years at peace. They were never very numerous, for their total population is estimated by Parkman at 10,000 to 12,000 souls. Their fighting strength was from 2000 to 2300 warriors of all the tribes, but the Dutch first, and then the English, supplied them with fire-arms before the other savage tribes were able to procure them. They were the most politic nation of Indians on the continent, and for one hundred and fifty years preserved their independence by playing off the English on the south against the French on the north. In the main they clung to the English alliance, and their policy preserved the continent to the English, for if they had thrown their strength on the side of the French the English colonies would have been confined to the seaboard. They utterly destroyed the Huron and Tobacco nations in 1650, the Neuter nation in 1651, and the Eries in 1654; they subdued the Andastes in 1675; they terrorised the wandering Algonquins, and domineered over all the central tribes east of the Mississippi. Their numbers wasted in war were renewed by their custom of adopting into their nation the residue, and especially the youth, of the nations they conquered. They were not more cruel than other Indians, and Lescarbot says, with much truth, that when he recalls the troubles in Europe he thinks that neither

Onondaga Town

Attack by the Hurons and Algonquins and the French Auxiliaries
From Laverdière's *Œuvres de Champlain*

CHAMPLAIN IN ONTARIO 279

Spaniards, Flemings, nor French owe the Indians anything in respect of cruelty. This formidable nation of warriors—the Romans of the New World—Champlain now marched to attack in their strongholds.

It was the 9th of October when the scouts of the war party first met any of the Iroquois, and the next day they arrived at one of the fortified towns of the Onondagas. The site of the town has been much disputed, but has been ascertained with reasonable certainty to have been in Madison County, New York, at Nichol's Pond, a little southeast of Oneida Lake. It was a position well selected for defence, and was strongly fortified, as will be seen upon the plan given by Champlain, page 278. It was in the shape of a hexagon, one side rested on the pond, and streams making a sort of moat were made to flow along the bases of four other sides. The whole village was inclosed within a rampart made of palisades four deep, interlaced together and made of strong timbers thirty feet high and about six inches apart. Galleries ran around the inside for the defenders, with loopholes for discharging missiles. The insubordination of the Huron character soon manifested itself. It had been planned not to show their strength until all preparations were complete, but the Indians could not be restrained from a premature attack, and Champlain and his Frenchmen had to disclose themselves to cover the retreat of the attacking party. Although angry at their wilfulness, he devised a plan of assault which they agreed to carry out. A sort of tower of wood, called a *cavalier*, was prepared higher than the palisades, and on it some of the Frenchmen with arquebuses were placed so as to clear the rampart, mantelets were also made to cover the attacking parties in setting fire to the palisades. The Indians were discouraged at the non-arrival of the five hundred men promised by the Andastes, but as the Iroquois were availing themselves of every delay to strengthen their position, and the assailants were sufficiently strong to carry the fort, Champlain urged on an immediate attack. The *cavalier* was carried and placed by two hundred savages, and the arquebusiers cleared the rampart, but instead of bringing up the mantelets the Indians got excited and capered round, yelling and shooting their arrows without any result. They brought up wood, but it was insufficient in quantity, and in their excitement they placed it on the lee side, so that the flames were carried away from the palisades. Champlain's efforts to direct the savages were in vain; his orders and shouts were unheeded in the din of their whooping and capering. The result was that the attack failed. The Iroquois had abundance of water and extinguished the fire, and the Hurons, discouraged, returned to their camp. Two of the chiefs and fifteen other Indians were wounded, and Champlain received an arrow wound in his leg and one in the knee. With great difficulty he prevailed on the Indians to wait four days longer for the arrival of the Andastes. The time was spent in skirmishes, and the impetuosity of the Hurons repeatedly led them into difficulties, from which Champlain's arquebusiers had to extricate them; but they could not be induced to make another assault, and in spite of his councils resolved to retreat. The only thing Champlain found to commend in their tactics was the secure way they conducted their retreat, by covering their flanks and rear and carrying their wounded in baskets placed in the centre of the main body. Champlain was strapped up and carried on the back of a sturdy savage. After a long retreat, harassed for a while by the Iroquois, they arrived at the place where they had left their canoes, and found them safe. Then the party prepared to break up—some to fish, some to hunt, some to trap beaver, and some to return to their homes.

Champlain was anxious to return to Quebec, but the savages had other designs. They wanted him and his Frenchmen, partly for the protection of their fire-arms and partly for their aid, to arrange in winter council for another expedition. He could not get a canoe to carry him home, and was obliged to go back to the Huron country with his intractable allies. They crossed the end of the lake and went hunting for their winter supplies up the Cataraqui and among the lakes between Kingston and Ottawa. They spent a month in that locality. Three days and two nights of it were anxious ones for Champlain, for in his eagerness to shoot a strange-looking bird he lost his way in the woods. He was without his compass, and wandered round in the forest, for the weather was cloudy and rainy. It is good evidence of his resourcefulness that he supported himself by his gun, and could kindle a fire and cook the birds he shot. Coming upon a stream he followed the flowing water. He came out upon a fall and an opening in the forest leading to a far-reaching meadow, where there was a large number of wild animals, and then he saw a long stretch of broad river and recognised the portage track he had been over. That night he slept in better spirits, after making his supper of the rest of the birds. The next morning he considered carefully the lie of the country and the bearings of the mountains on the river bank, and concluded that the camp was four or five leagues further down. He could now walk with leisure along the stream until he perceived the smoke of the camp. After that the Indians never would allow him to go alone into the woods, and he was careful never again to leave his compass in camp.

December had come, and the lakes and streams were frozen. The Indians started for home, going across the country in a toilsome march, laden with the deer they had killed. The Indians each carried a load of a hundred pounds, but Champlain found twenty pounds very heavy in tramping through the woods. For passing over the ice they used "trainées de bois"—flat sledges, still used in Canada, and called *traineaux* and *toboggans*. They were sixteen days on the march, over a broken country, from somewhere northeast of Kingston, not far from Rideau Lake, to Lake Simcoe; and to add to their labours they had a few days' thaw. Soldiering on the open plains of France or sailing on the stormy North Atlantic did not try Champlain's courage and endurance so much as this march, but he was a many-sided man, strong in body as in mind. He was as much at home in the brilliant court of France as in a wigwam on a Canadian lake, as patient and politic with a wild band of savages on Lake Huron as with a crowd of grasping traders in St. Malo or Dieppe. Always calm, always unselfish, always depending on God, in whom he believed and trusted, and thinking of France, which he loved, this single-hearted man resolutely followed the path of his duty under all circumstances; never looking for ease or asking for profit, loved by the wild people of the forest, respected by the courtiers of the King, and trusted by the close-fisted merchants of the maritime cities of France.

It was close upon Christmas, 1615, when he arrived at the Huron town of Cahiagué, near the site of the present town of Orillia, at the outlet of Lake Simcoe. To the same town also came the chief Iroquet and his band of Algonquins from the Ottawa. Champlain did not rest long there, but in the first week of the new year set out to visit a neighbouring tribe to the west—the Tobacco nation. They were kindred to the Hurons, and spoke the same language. Their name was derived from the fact that they gave great attention to growing a kind of tobacco much valued by the Indians. They were a sedentary people, living in villages and growing maize for support, and occupied an extent of land to the southwest of the Hurons, corresponding to the present counties of Dufferin and Grey. From thence he went to the *Cheveux Relevés* (Ottawas), who dwelt on the shores of the lake in the present counties of Bruce and Huron. They were of Algonquin stock, and were friendly with the Hurons, though their language was different; but they were in deadly enmity with the Mascoutins, an Algonquin people dwelling to the west of Lake Huron. South of the Tobacco nation and the *Cheveux Relevés* dwelt the Neutral nation, whom Champlain was dissuaded from visiting—a powerful and fierce people, living in villages and occupying a wide extent of territory reaching down

Barrie on Lake Simcoe
(In the Huron country)

W. H. Butery Photo

CHAMPLAIN IN ONTARIO 283

to Lake Erie and across the Niagara River. They touched the Seneca tribe of Iroquois at the Genessee River on the east and the Erie nation on the west. All were of the kindred Huron-Iroquois stock. In the wars between the Iroquois and Hurons they preserved a careful neutrality, which, however, did not preserve them from extermination after the Iroquois had rooted up the Huron nation. The manners and customs of all these tribes are described by Champlain with many details, but all fall under one of the two great families—Algonquin or Huron-Iroquois. Their customs differed little within each of these families.

On returning from this journey it had been Champlain's intention to go northwards to the great northern sea of which he had heard, but in his absence a quarrel had broken out between the Hurons and visiting Algonquins, and he was appointed umpire by both parties. It was a difficult task, for there had been bloodshed, and the process of reconciliation was slow. The northern journey had to be abandoned, and on May 20, 1616, Champlain set out on his return to Quebec, in company with the Nipissings and Algonquins of the Ottawa. They took the route of French River, Lake Nipissing, the Mattawa and the Ottawa. After a journey of forty days he arrived safely at Montreal, where he found Pont-Gravé and the Recollet Fathers, who had despaired of seeing him again. On July 11, 1616, he reached Quebec, and after putting matters in order sailed for France with Pont-Gravé and arrived at Honfleur September 10.

Champlain's work as an explorer was now done. He had searched out every part of the Atlantic coast of Nova Scotia and New Brunswick. He had not seen Prince Edward Island because vessels bound for the St. Lawrence pass too far north and see only the Magdalen Islands, or the Bird Rocks, on their course. The Province of Quebec was well known to him. He had been up the Saguenay and up the St. Maurice to the head of navigation of each river, and knew, from Indian reports, the geography of the country farther to the north. He had penetrated to the southern edge of the St. Lawrence basin at the Strait of Ticonderoga and at Oneida Lake. He had followed to the west up the Ottawa, up the Mattawa, and down Lake Nipissing and French River to Georgian Bay. He knew the eastern shores of Lake Huron, and apprehended its vast extent; he had heard of Lake Superior, to the westward, and he had paddled across Lake Ontario, and knew its relation to the St. Lawrence water system. Not only was the present Province of Quebec well known to him, but he had penetrated to the heart of the Province of Ontario and had entered the northern regions of the State of New York. He had hunted in the country between Kingston and Ottawa; he had passed down the whole series of waters from Lake Simcoe to the Bay of Quinté; he had gone on foot through the northern portions of the counties of Frontenac, Addington, Hastings, Peterborough, and Victoria, in central Ontario. In the western peninsula he had visited the counties of Grey, Bruce, Huron, Wellington, Simcoe, and Dufferin, and had touched the headwaters of the Grand River. His " Voyages " are the record of magnificent achievements. Few Canadians, even in these days of railways and steamboats, have such an extensive personal knowledge of Canada as Champlain acquired in the years of his activity as an explorer. His powers of observation were great. He noticed the quality of the soil and the natural productions of all the country he passed through, and his descriptions of the different tribes of Indians he met are accurate and full.

We must not, however, take his map of 1632 as the result of his own personal experience, for there are indications of lakes west of Lake Huron which he never saw, and which were reported by men he trained, and by missionaries, after his own explorations were over. Even then Lake Erie was unknown. The restless activity of the hostile Iroquois sealed for many years the lower route, and that lake was not known until all the sister lakes to the west had been discovered. Lake Michigan is shown

CHAMPLAIN IN ONTARIO 285

as stretching north instead of south from the Sault, and upon it are placed the copper mines which belong to Lake Superior. The Sault Ste. Marie is laid down as the Sault de Gaston, and it broadens out into a great unnamed lake. Champlain's idea of Niagara Falls was very inadequate, for he supposed them to be merely rapids, like the Sault at Montreal. They are marked on his great map, in 1632, with more emphasis as "very high," but evidently with inadequate information.

The contradictory reports of the Indians, which had misled Champlain, were disposed of by his journey of 1615. He reached the great sea, and the water was not salt, and it did not flow to the west—but might there not be a double discharge from so great a basin? Lescarbot, while he knew that the St. Lawrence flowed from lakes, thought that there was also a western opening from them to the South Sea, and instanced the Nile as a parallel case, for it flows from a lake which discharged into the main ocean, in opposite directions, by several rivers. Champlain's merits as a cartographer are very great. His maps are entirely modern in their methods, and for New France and New England are original and based on survey. Every entry on his maps has some foundation. There are no long strings of purely fictitious names, nor drawings of fictitious monsters, nor revivals of oldworld myths, such as the battles of the pygmies and the cranes on the site of Ottawa, portrayed only fifty years before on Desceliers' maps. There is in his maps a strenuous effort to convey the exact truth to his readers, as when, in his map of 1612, he writes along the southwest coast of the Gulf, where Prince Edward Island was in a few years to detach itself from the mainland, "the author has not examined this coast." His knowledge of America was so extensive that he could use all preexisting materials critically, and if he misunderstood his Indian informants, as he did in the case of Lake Michigan, he was at least working upon something and not making the geography out of his own head.

The remainder of Champlain's life was spent in constant efforts to establish the colony at Quebec on a solid, self-supporting basis. In this he had to overcome the antagonism of the merchants who controlled the companies, and of their servants in the colony. His aim had a farther reach than theirs. He saw that the only way to open up the country to commerce was to win over the Indians by evangelising them. Every missionary established in a savage tribe was a pioneer of civilisation and of trade. His aim also was to win a peace for the western tribes, and to do that it was necessary to make the Iroquois feel the power of France. He asked for a hundred men only, and though they were not sent, his vigorous policy made him respected by the Iroquois, and in 1622 they sent emissaries to Quebec and concluded a peace with the French and their Indian allies. It lasted for nearly five years, and was broken by the reckless folly of the Algonquins in 1627. It was in the time of his successors that the allies of the French were crushed, and for years the scanty colonists did not dare to move away from the immediate neighbourhood of Quebec. The merchants were opposed to settlement, lest it might interfere with the fur trade and detract from the large dividends on their investments. The majority were Huguenots, and if their hostility was not open, it was persistent, and they favoured neither Recollet nor Jesuit. This selfish policy led to the destruction of the Huron nation, and in consequence the Iroquois held the upper country and for years cut off communication with the west. The successive viceroys—the Count de Soissons, the Prince de Condé, the Duke de Montmorenci, the Duke de Ventadour—all appointed Champlain as their lieutenant and representative, but the servants of the trading companies were subject to their own masters, and discouraged the colonists from extending the cultivation of the soil, while the company left them insufficiently provided with food and with the means of defence. Recollets and Jesuits were well, but a few soldiers would have opened up the country very much more quickly.

Without entering upon debatable ground, it is evident

CHAMPLAIN IN ONTARIO

that the colony was retarded by religious dissension. Champlain was above all narrowness, but he was a sincerely religious man, and a convinced Catholic, tolerant, not with the tolerance of scepticism, but with the tolerance of charity. The traders and settlers at Quebec formed too small a community to agitate religious controversies with safety. The Huguenot side of the story has not been recorded, but enough appears through the writings of the Recollet and Jesuit authors to indicate that there were faults on both sides. The Recollets were the first to petition for the exclusion of Protestants, and when at last the colony was formally declared to be a Catholic community, open only to settlement by Catholics, it is impossible to avoid the conclusion that it was the only possible course to secure the unity necessary to its continued existence. The United States historians unduly magnify this exclusion and exaggerate the freedom of the English colonies. There was no religious toleration in the English colonies in early times, and if Huguenots were not allowed to settle in New France Roman Catholics were not allowed to settle in New England.

For these reasons the growth of the colony was very slow. When the English took Quebec there were scarcely one hundred Frenchmen in all Canada. This handful was, however, the beginning of the Canadian people—no trace existed of any settlers previous to Champlain's settlement in 1608 at Quebec and De Monts' in Acadia in 1604. The company of merchants was at last superseded and the trading privileges transferred to the De Caens, uncle and nephew,—Huguenots of Normandy,—but no improvement followed. At last Cardinal Richelieu took up the matter and established, in 1627, the company called the One Hundred Associates, of which he became the head. The business was managed by a small committee of merchants of Rouen, Dieppe, and Paris. But in 1629, before the new system was fairly installed, the English took Quebec and sent Champlain to England as a prisoner of war. He did not even then lose heart, but encouraged the colonists to remain loyal to Canada and to France. He was rewarded for his constancy by finding, on arrival in England, that the capture of Quebec had been made after the declaration of peace, and that it would be restored to France. Faithful to the passion of his life, he returned to Canada in 1633, and on December 25, 1635, he died at Quebec, the city he founded and loved. The destruction caused by the bombardment under Wolfe and the changes of years have destroyed the marks which might indicate the exact resting place of his remains, but the somewhat tardy piety of recent years has erected a statue to his memory on the magnificent terrace which overlooks the great river where his lifework was spent.

CHAPTER XVIII

EXPLORATION OF THE WEST, FROM CHAMPLAIN TO THE DISPERSION OF THE HURONS

THE work of exploration passed on to a small band of men whom Champlain had, with characteristic foresight, selected and prepared by sending them to winter with the Indians to learn their languages and to become a ready means of communication and a bond of union between them and the French. There were indeed other interpreters, but they left no trace in history, and their influence, like that of the traders who employed them, was often hostile to Champlain and his aims. The men formed by Champlain, after living for years with the Indians, for the most part returned to the settlements, married and reared families, and their descendants are numerous in Canada to the present day. The others either left the country or disappeared into the woods, and, taking Indian wives, became the forerunners of the *coureurs de bois,* or wood rangers, who made the labours of the missionaries doubly difficult by their disorders and evil example.

Exploration in Canada was not as difficult as in other continental regions. The Acadian provinces are deeply indented by the sea, and no part is at any considerable distance from the shore. Old Canada is, in brief, the valley of the St. Lawrence, and myriads of tributaries pour into the lap of the great river. In the summer the streams are a network of water-roads, and the light canoes of birch bark may penetrate with ease into the farthest recesses, following up the rivers and the streams to their ultimate sources in morasses or lakes. Ofttimes these are on water-partings and issue forth in two streams flowing in different directions. More frequently the portages are short, and the voyageur, turning his canoe over and taking it upon his shoulders, carries it across the intervening distance and launches it upon a new system of waterways. In the English colonies these intervals were called "carries," but in Canada the French word "portage" has never been displaced. The French Canadians were ideal voyageurs, and such travelling became in them an instinct. Water is everywhere, and it stretches out by rivers, streams, and lakes into an immense system of anastomosis gravitating to the main arteries of the country. The streams open up gateways through the forests and tunnel through the overhanging foliage of the densest woods,—or in reedy places where no channel is visible to the untrained eye the guide, skilled in forest lore, parting the reeds with his paddle, leads the light skiff into sudden expanses of lake or into unexpected river turnings. The St. Lawrence River was thus the main highway of the continent, for its valley cuts transversely across and touches the head-waters of the rivers flowing north and south. Especially does it open up communication with the great river of the interior, the Mississippi, for at certain places, such as Chicago and the heads of the St. Joseph and Fox rivers, during times of spring freshet the water flowed indifferently in either direction. In the winter the country is still accessible, for the streams are frozen and land and water is covered with a mantle of snow. The hunter or traveller may go anywhere on snowshoes, and draw after him his necessary outfit as before explained (p. 281) on a toboggan. Only in spring, at the break-up of the ice, is travelling impossible. For these reasons the country was very rapidly explored as soon as the Indian wars ceased and voyageurs could move about without endangering their scalps.

The Recollet friars whom Champlain brought out in 1615 were the pioneer missionaries of the west, and led the way into those fastnesses of heathendom where the Jesuit fathers who followed them laboured with

Shadowy River—Muskoka
on the Northern border of the Huron Country

such heroic self-sacrifice; but, in truth, the fur-trader or interpreter preceded the missionary in most of the discoveries on the western waters, for the missionary was helpless until he could communicate with his savage hearers, and communication at its first stage was by the means of some interpreter, who of necessity had learned the language by a residence more or less extended. Some of these men were educated and very intelligent, and their adventurous explorations have only in recent years received adequate acknowledgment. That followed naturally from the fact that the books and other literature were written by ecclesiastics, and are chiefly concerned with matters of spiritual interest. Mention is no doubt made in the Jesuit Relations of some of these pioneers of commerce, but these Relations are, primarily, missionary reports published for the purpose of enlisting sympathy and obtaining support for the extension of missions and the salvation of souls. Bancroft's statement that "not a cape was turned nor a river entered but a Jesuit led the way" must be taken with a large deduction for rhetorical effect. The " Relations" themselves make no such claim. They are precious records of the experiences and trials of devoted men, and inasmuch as the missionaries were highly educated and trained in the science of that day, their letters contain most important observations and even treatises upon the ethnology, philology, and natural history of the regions they traversed; but these latter themes were accessory to the ground subject of their thoughts. It was nothing to them who first, from a geographical standpoint, had reached this river or that lake or had dwelt with some distant tribe; the question with them was, who had first brought the Gospel there. Consequently, while the reader may detect minimising or even suppression of due credit to Recollet, Jesuit, or Sulpician, according as the writer may lean to one or the other of these orders, any failure to dwell upon the mere priority of discovery is probably unintentional and due to a want of appreciation of its importance.

In the remnant of eight souls who survived the terrible winter of 1608-9 at Quebec was Etienne Brulé, a quick-witted, adventurous youth whom Champlain took with him when, in 1610, he went to the Indian rendezvous at the Richelieu. When the savages prepared to return to their homes Brulé asked to go with the Algonquins to learn their language, which was a veritable *lingua franca*, from the Micmacs on the Atlantic to the farthest tribes on the west and north. Champlain willingly consented and entrusted the lad to Iroquet, a chief of the Little Algonquins (Petite Nation), who hunted over the territory of the lower Ottawa, and this youth was the first white man to visit the site of the capital of the Dominion of Canada. For the other great family of Indian languages Champlain provided by taking with him to France a young Huron, whom he brought back the following year—a bright, intelligent youth who took kindly to French ways. They named him Savignon, and when the following year they all met at the appointed rendezvous at Montreal, Champlain could communicate with all the assembled tribes. He had them both with him to interpret at the great midnight council on the Lake of the Two Mountains, and in relating his descent of the Lachine Rapids he states that he was the first Christian to run them, excepting Brulé; but whether he meant that Brulé had run the rapids with his Indian hosts when descending to the rendezvous, or that Brulé was with him on that occasion, does not clearly appear.

In the summer of 1611 one of the private traders wished to send a youth to winter in the Indian country, and Champlain consented, with the stipulation that he should go with Iroquet where Brulé had been. He himself sent a youth up to the Huron country, and Brulé, who disappears for four years, probably went up also. These were the first white men to reach Lake Huron. Champlain sent the impostor Vignau to the Algonquins of Allumette Island at the same time.

In 1615, when Champlain started off to join the great war party, he found Brulé at Montreal and took him, together with another Frenchman, along with him. After the expedition had assembled there was a grand council at the outlet of Lake Simcoe, and it was decided to send a deputation to the Andastes to inform them of the departure of the war party and to hurry up the promised contingent. Twelve Indians were selected, and Brulé begged to go with them. The opportunity for discovery induced Champlain to consent, and the deputation departed on September 8. It was an enterprise of great peril, for the country of the Andastes lay far to the south, on the head-waters of the Susquehanna, and the direct route passed through the country of the Senecas—the western canton of the Iroquois. The only safe route was by a long circuitous trail through the country of the Neutrals and across the Niagara River. The route they followed is indicated by the fact that they took two canoes, and by the necessity of reaching their destination well before the arrival of the war party. It was by the portage from Lake Simcoe to the Humber River and down to the site of the present city of Toronto, thence directly across the head of the lake to that part of the Neutral territory east of Niagara. By that route they would avoid the main Iroquois trails and traverse the southwestern corner only of the Seneca country. By dint of great circumspection they accomplished their task safely, capturing on the way, or killing, a small party of Senecas. Brulé, then, was the first white man to stand on the site of Toronto and to paddle on Lake Ontario, but he heard nothing of Niagara Falls, and must have landed on the southern shore well to the east of the mouth of the Niagara River.

As we have seen, Brulé was not able to move the Andastes out of the conventional Indian routine of feasts and harangues, and the contingent arrived, therefore, two days too late. He spent the winter at Carantouan, the chief town of the Andastes, and from thence explored the surrounding region of central Pennsylvania. He went down the Susquehanna River to Chesapeake Bay, and his explorations thus touched those of the

English and the Dutch on the coast and the Hudson River. Chesapeake Bay had been thoroughly examined seven years before by the English under Captain John Smith.

In the spring of 1616 he set out, with guides from the Andastes, to return to the Huron country, but the party fell in with a stronger party of Senecas and was scattered. Brulé lost his way, and after much wandering chose to take his chances with the Senecas rather than starve. They were friendly at first, but soon discovered his real nationality and commenced to torture him. While he was being stripped for burning the Indians snatched away an *Agnus Dei* which he, though not in the least a pious person, wore next to his skin. He solemnly warned them that it was a medicine of great power and would certainly kill them. At that moment a storm of unexampled fury suddenly burst, and the superstitious Indians, terrified by lightning and thunder, quickly following a serene sky, realised that they had to do with a being of supernatural powers. They released him, bound up his wounds, and took him to their towns, where he became so popular that no feast or dance was held without him, and at last they gave him guides to return to the Huron country.

He disappeared for a while among the Indians, but in 1618 he came down with the Hurons to trade, and met Champlain at Three Rivers, to whom he related his adventures and described the country explored. Champlain encouraged him to go back with his Indian friends and continue his discoveries. We hear of him occasionally at the trading posts, and in fact he had a salary of one hundred pistoles a year to induce the Hurons to come down regularly to trade. In 1621 he was at Toanche, a town of the Hurons, and with a Frenchman named Grenolle he went on an expedition of discovery to the north and reached a place where there was a mine of native copper. Later he pushed farther to the west, and from the narrative of the Recollet Sagard it is certain that he was the discoverer of Sault Ste. Marie, and was

EXPLORATION OF THE WEST 295

the first white man on Lake Superior. He was also the first white man to visit the Neutral nation. Champlain had been upon their borders, but deterred by reports of his Huron guides he did not cross. Brulé went over the country and gave a glowing account of it to the Recollet father Le Caron. Still there is no hint anywhere of his having seen the Falls of Niagara.

Brulé seems to have been almost ubiquitous, and also to have absorbed from his Huron friends some of their fickleness, for we find him in 1629 at Quebec and Tadoussac, assisting the English commander Kirke, and with Marsolet, one of Champlain's interpreters in Montagnais, accepting service under the English. The influence of the "noble red man" of the novelists is not elevating, and the Hurons were not up to the level even of the Iroquois in questions of morality or fidelity and honour. Whoever edited the last volume of Champlain's voyages (1632) denounces Brulé, not only for accepting English pay, but for his licentious life among the savages. The passage is too rhetorical to have been written by Champlain, but Brulé's conduct nevertheless was more consonant with his Huron associations than with his French birth. He went back to the Huron country, and in 1632 he was murdered by his savage friends—who also boiled and ate him. Their superstitious fears led them to abandon Toanche, the village where the murder occurred, and in 1635 the missionary Brébeuf was surprised to find it burned. The Indians attributed to Brulé the pestilence which shortly after broke out, and one of the sorcerers saw the spirit of the murdered man's sister flying over the infected town, though most of the Indians said that it was the spirit of his uncle.

From 1615, when Champlain brought out the four friars, to 1629, when the English broke up the colony at Quebec, the Recollets, or reformed Franciscans, were the pioneers in Christian missions throughout Canada. While Le Caron went up to the Huron country, Father d'Olbeau undertook the mission from Tadoussac to the Montagnais, and the others, Father Jamay and the

Brother Pacifique Du Plessis, ministered to the French at Quebec and Three Rivers and to the Indians who gathered around these posts. Other Recollets soon came out and laboured among the Indians at Miscou and on the St. John River in New Brunswick, and at Ste. Anne's on Cape Breton Island. Putting aside the question as to whether Cartier had or had not priests with him, it is indisputable that the services of the Roman Catholic church at Tadoussac, Quebec, Three Rivers, Montreal, and on the shores of Lake Huron were celebrated first by the spiritual children of St. Francis of Assisi. Le Caron was with Champlain on his visit to the Tobacco nation and the *Cheveux Relevés*. In 1616 they both returned to Quebec, and the same season when Champlain went to France Jamay and Le Caron went with him, leaving Dolbeau and Du Plessis at Quebec. The fathers went and returned frequently, and their number was increased, but no new explorations in the west are recorded for a few years. In 1623 Father Le Caron brought out Fathers Nicholas Viel and Gabriel Sagard, and all three went up to the west with the Hurons or Ottawas returning from their annual trade. With them went eleven Frenchmen, who might be useful as protectors of the mission or as promoters of the fur trade. In the winter of that year the Recollet Father Bernardin perished of cold and hunger in attempting to go from Miscou, across New Brunswick, to the mouth of the St. John—the first missionary to perish in the work of evangelisation. We learn also from Champlain that the Recollet missionaries had obtained great influence over the Acadian savages, although their labours have not been as widely known as they deserved.

The Recollets, who returned to the Hurons in 1623, found there five or six Frenchmen living in the cabin built by Le Caron. Sagard and Le Caron came down the following spring (1624) and with them came Etienne Brulé, from whom Sagard obtained the information concerning Lake Superior recorded in his book. Brulé told him that beyond the Mer Douce (Lake Huron) was another very large lake discharging by a fall, and that the length of both lakes was four hundred leagues. Sagard, writing in 1632, adds that the fall had been called the *Sault de Gaston* and under that name it is laid down in the Champlain map of 1632. It cannot be shown, however, that Brulé went to the head of the lake. On the map the shores are portrayed widening out, but the outline is unfinished.

It was in 1624 that Champlain negotiated at Three Rivers a peace between the Iroquois on one side and the Hurons, Algonquins, and Montagnais on the other. The same year he took Madame de Champlain, who had been four years in Canada, back to France. The merchant company had left the colony without provisions and even without munitions for defence. Sagard went to France at the same time and with him went Father Irenæus Piet—the latter charged with a mission fraught with far-reaching consequences. The Recollets in Canada felt that the resources of their order were unequal to the task of evangelising the country. The company of merchants were indeed bound to support six Recollets, but it was against their will and they discouraged and starved the missions, as well as the colonists, as far as they dared. The Jesuits had powerful friends at court and, if they chose to use them, they had independent resources of their own. The Recollets resolved to invoke their assistance, but they concealed their design, for they knew that Champlain and everybody else in the colony would oppose it. They arrived in France at an opportune moment; for the Duke de Montmorenci, wearied by the incessant quarrels of merchants and colonists and the religious jealousies of Huguenot and Catholic, had turned over the Vice royalty to the Duke de Ventadour, a very strong Catholic whose zeal had led him so far as to take orders in the church. Father Irenæus succeeded; but, on going to take passage in the spring ships, the Recollets were astonished to find that, while it had been settled that two Jesuits were to go out, it had also been arranged that their sustenance was to be charged against the six missionaries the Company was bound to support; so that a substitution of two Jesuits for two Recollets on the Company's funds was all that had been effected.

A controversy has long existed concerning the transfer of the Canadian missions to the Jesuits, but the details are foreign to the object of this book. In 1625 three Jesuit Fathers embarked for Canada, Charles Lalemant, Ennemond Masse, and Jean de Brébeuf, with two lay brothers, and the Recollets sent Father Joseph de la Roche d'Aillon. On their arrival no one would receive the Jesuits. The employees of the Company pleaded that they had no orders to take them into the fort and it seemed, for a time, as if they would have to go back to France. The Recollets, however, offered them half of their convent, which was gratefully accepted and enjoyed for two years, until the Jesuits could build a house of their own. There is no reason for doubting the sincerity of these apostolic men; for, from whatever quarter came the influence which six years later excluded the Recollet missionaries, it most certainly was not from them or from any Canadian source whatever.

In the meantime Father Nicholas Viel had been left in charge of the Huron mission. The Recollet Father d'Aillon and the Jesuit Father Brébeuf went up to Three Rivers to meet him, for he was to come down with the Huron trading canoes. He reached as far as the rapids in rear of Montreal, and there the pagan Hurons, who were paddling, threw him and a young Huron Christian with him into the whirling waters. The place is known to this day as the Sault au Recollet, and the scene of the first Christian martyrdom in Canada is now a pleasure resort for the citizens of Montreal. The new missionaries had counted on Viel's aid, and as they were without knowledge of the language or of the needs of the mission, they returned to Quebec, where they spent the winter in preparation, and where Le Caron assisted them with the dictionary he had compiled on his mission of 1615-16. In the following year (1626) D'Aillon went up, and with him two Jesuits, Brébeuf and La Noüe. Then the Company of Jesus entered upon those western waters, doomed to become the scene of brilliant promise but of ultimate defeat—then commenced an attack on the stronghold of paganism, to which the storm of Pampeluna was child's play; and as, through long years, the devoted children of Loyola mounted to the assault and the long story of war and blood and fire and fiendish cruelty is unrolled, the reader is amazed at the indomitable courage, the unshrinking fortitude, and the boundless charity of these chosen soldiers of the cross.

Leaving La Noüe and Brébeuf in the Huron mission, Father d'Aillon went south into the territory of the Neutral nation. Brulé, the interpreter, had been the only white man to visit this region, and he had told such wonders of its fertility and beauty that Father Le Caron wrote to D'Aillon to make the attempt. It is a region often spoken of as the garden of the present Province of Ontario. A line drawn from Toronto, on Lake Ontario, to Goderich, on Lake Huron, would roughly indicate its northern boundary, and from thence it extended south to the north shore of Lake Erie. To the east it reached across the Niagara River to within a day's journey of the Genessee River—the western boundary of the Iroquois. D'Aillon describes the country as exceeding rich, abounding in game of all kinds and with a climate less severe than the other parts of Canada. It had twenty-eight towns and six or eight villages. The people were numerous and warlike and could turn out four thousand warriors. At first they received D'Aillon with politeness, but when he began to inquire about the entrance to the river where the lake discharged and to suggest a traffic directly down the lake and river to the French posts, the Hurons took the alarm lest the fur trade with the French should go direct instead of passing through their hands. They secretly whispered that D'Aillon was a sorcerer who cast evil spells bringing sickness and death. Black looks and hatred and blows followed, until the Recollet was forced to leave and postpone to a more auspicious time the evangelisation of this fierce people.

The war between the Iroquois and the northern Indians broke out with renewed fury in 1627. No further discoveries are recorded for some years, and the missionaries busied themselves in establishing their footing. D'Aillon, and Brébeuf, with most of the French in the Huron country, went down to Quebec in 1627, 1628, and 1629, and the three Recollets working in Acadia were also summoned there, so that, in 1629, when Quebec was surrendered to the English, all the ecclesiastics in New France were at Quebec and Tadoussac. They were all carried off to England, and the incipient churches of the Montagnais at Tadoussac, the Algonquins at Three Rivers and Lake Nipissing, and the Hurons on the Freshwater Sea were abandoned. The few converts who had been made were left without spiritual support. Le Caron, the Superior of the Recollets, was afterwards blamed because even the French who remained at Quebec were deserted. The English would have permitted the Recollets to stay, and they respected their convent, but they had many old scores to pay off with the Jesuit order in Europe, and their convent was pillaged and wrecked. Missions and discoveries alike ceased until the country was restored to France. The Recollet order disappeared from the annals of Canada until 1670, when the days of discovery in the St. Lawrence valley were almost over.

It was July, 1632, when Emery de Caen arrived at Quebec and again took over, for France, the sovereignty of the country. He had obtained a monopoly of the fur trade for a year to indemnify him for his losses in the war. With him came the Jesuits Le Jeune and La Noüe. Champlain arrived the following year and retained command for the "Company of One Hundred Associates," formed by Richelieu in 1627, and with him came Jean de Brébeuf, hastening to the post of danger, and to the cross he was to bear and the crown of martyrdom he was to win. There was a pause for a few years in discovery in order to gather up the threads of the work done previously, not only by themselves, but by the Rec-

EXPLORATION OF THE WEST 301

ollets, for the latter were not allowed to return. The first thought of Cardinal Richelieu was to replace both orders by the Capuchins; and in fact a few Capuchins were sent to Acadia; but, representations being made on behalf of the Jesuits even by the Capuchins themselves, he modified his commands in regard to the Jesuits only. That, after their reorganisation of the missions, the Jesuits may have objected to the introduction of other religious orders is probable enough, but it is not just to blame them for the original exclusion of the Recollets. Richelieu did not favour the Jesuit order and his action must have been taken with regard to the interest of the colony, which had suffered from dissensions.

In Champlain's commission, as late as 1625, he was empowered to follow up the river flowing past Quebec and to seek out a direct passage to the kingdom of China and the Eastern Indies. The thought never left him throughout all his troubles, and while the Jesuits were reorganising their mission-stations he turned, in 1634, only one year before his death, to Jean Nicollet and charged him with the discovery of the secret of the western sea—the great water of the west of which he had heard reports from Brulé and from the Indians. Nicollet had arrived in Canada in 1618. He was born in Normandy, almost certainly in Cherbourg. At Quebec his courage and spirit at once attracted notice and his natural capacity, excellent memory, and happy temperament marked him out as suited to become a skilful interpreter and manager of the fitful Indian allies of France. He was not more than eighteen or twenty years old when he was sent to the Algonquins of Allumette Island. He lived with them for two years as one of themselves, going with them on all their expeditions and living on the same food—feasting or starving as the fortune of Indian life might require. He had learned their language perfectly, and went with four hundred Algonquins to negotiate the peace of 1622 with the Iroquois, on which occasion he acquitted himself well. Afterwards he went to the Nipissings and settled down among them for eight or nine years. They adopted him as a member of their tribe and he took part in all their councils. His skill in swaying the Indians to his will was very remarkable, and when Champlain determined upon another attempt to reach the great western water there was no other man so well fitted as Nicollet for the task. He had returned to the settlement, after the restoration of the colony, and was acting as clerk and interpreter to the Company at Quebec.

On the same day of July, 1634, three expeditions started from Quebec: Brébeuf to restore the Huron mission, Nicollet on his western exploration, and a party of men sent to build a fort and make a permanent settlement at Three Rivers—then the centre of the western fur traffic. All joined in the ceremonies at Three Rivers and then the western voyageurs proceeded on their way up the Ottawa. Nicollet left Brébeuf at Allumette Island and went on to his old friends the Nipissings. But the task he had undertaken lay first among the Hurons; for he was to arrange a treaty of peace between them and a mysterious people further west, whose home was near the great western sea and who had lived upon its shores in former years. To the Huron country he therefore proceeded, and having made his preparations, he started in a bark canoe with seven Hurons on his adventurous journey. There is no reason to suppose that his object was to visit the Strait of Ste. Marie. That was already known and, as the Sault de Gaston, it had been laid down on Champlain's map, published in 1632, two years before. What was not known, however, was the Strait of Michilimackinac leading into Lake Michigan. And the utter confusion of the geography of that region is shown on the same map. Upon that map we may see some results of Brulé's explorations to the north, in the copper mine laid down on the north shore of Lake Huron and in the Sault de Gaston; but, with an extraordinary inversion of geographical fact, Fox River, falling into Green Bay, Lake Michigan, is made to flow from the north and to drain Lake Winne-

EXPLORATION OF THE WEST 303

bago into the north channel of Lake Huron close to the Sault. We may easily conclude then that Nicollet's course would be directed to clear up this confusion and that in passing out of Georgian Bay he would follow the north channel, inside of the Manitoulin islands, up to the Sault. This view is confirmed by the Jesuit Relation of 1640, in which the Superior, Vimont, writing from Quebec, gives a list of the Indian nations from the Hurons, on Georgian Bay, round to the Sault, evidently following the information of Nicollet, then permanently resident in Three Rivers. Returning from the Sault we may trace Nicollet's course backwards following the south channel through "a smaller lake" "from which one passes into the second Freshwater Sea." There are difficulties in the narrative, but, translated into the language of our present maps, it appears to be in effect that Nicollet's course from the Sault was along the southern passages, inside of St. Joseph's Island, which, though now called Hay Lake and Mud Lake, are plainly seen in passing through to be simple outlets. These open out into an expanse, Potaganissing Bay, which is so closed in by overlapping islands as to present the appearance of a lake—the "smaller lake" of the Relation. Then turning suddenly to the right, Nicollet passed by the Détour channel and the Strait of Michilimackinac into "the second Freshwater Sea"—Lake Michigan.

When Jean Nicollet guided his bark canoe through the Strait of Michilimackinac he turned the first leaf of the final chapter of the exploration of the St. Lawrence basin. It is the key-point of the western lakes, for there Lakes Superior, Huron, and Michigan touch each other and, near the west shore of Lake Michigan, the two enormous basins of the St. Lawrence and Mississippi come not only into close proximity, but their waters brim over so that at certain seasons a canoe might pass at certain points either down to the Gulf of St. Lawrence or down to the Gulf of Mexico without being lifted out of the water. Indian tribes ebbed and flowed through this strait in the ceaseless vicissitudes of savage warfare, and romantic legends clustered round every headland and haunted every island. In the very neck of the strait the forest-clad island of Michilimackinac seems to float on the water, rising towards the centre in sweeping curves—the delightful resort of pleasure-seekers now, as in far-off times it was the favourite abode of the great dancing spirits of Algonquin mythology. First among white men Nicollet passed through this fairy portal going to he knew not what of mystery; looking for and expecting to find the pathway to the golden East. He was prepared for any contingency of Eastern state, for among the scanty baggage in his birch canoe was his dress of ceremony of Chinese damask, embroidered with birds and flowers of all colours. The ripple which lapped against the bow of his canoe came over three hundred and fifty miles of water, but he did not know it. On his right was Point St. Ignace, soon to be sanctified by the presence of the saintly Jesuit, Marquette, and on his left was Mackinac Point, to be the scene in later years of Pontiac's perfidious massacre of a British garrison. It is a spot of unrivalled beauty. Where Nicollet's solitary canoe glided quietly on with no sound but the dip of the paddles, an enormous traffic from the western lakes now passes. Monstrous steamers glide up and down on inland voyages of perhaps a thousand miles; but the distances are so great that the effect of calm still dwells there; and whether the smoke on the distant horizon be from a steamer bound to Port Arthur, on Lake Superior, from Chicago, or Detroit, or even Montreal, there is space as of the ocean itself and no sense of hurry or thronging jars even yet the restful quiet of the scene.

Much history was to be enacted round this charmed region, and Nicollet was opening the book as he pressed on. His mission was, in the first instance, to the Winnebagoes—the men of the sea; how should he know yet of what sea? Champlain had heard of them from the Hurons, with whom they were at war, and now he was sending Nicollet to discover them and their sea, if it were possible; and to negotiate a peace also and open up

EXPLORATION OF THE WEST

trade—trade west of Chicago—and the Pilgrims only fourteen years landed at Plymouth! The clew to the secret of America lay along the St. Lawrence waters, and Champlain almost solved it while the sound of the wash of the Atlantic was still in the ears of the English settlers.

Hitherto the French had come into contact with only two families of Indian nations—the Huron-Iroquois and the Algonquins; and the Algonquin language had been a *lingua franca* intelligible, through many dialects, from the Atlantic to Lake Superior. But now Nicollet reached the eastern outlier of a race different from both, and neither the Huron nor the Algonquin tongue was of any service. The Winnebagoes were of Dakota stock—a powerful family of nations of which the Sioux confederation and the Assiniboines are the chief members. Their home is on the plains of the Mississippi and Missouri, but these Winnebagoes had drifted away eastward nearly to Lake Michigan. The French followed the more usual meaning of the Indian name and translated it *Puant;* so that the Winnebagoes are laid down on the French maps and figure in French works for a hundred years as the *Nation des Puants,* and Green Bay as *La Baie des Puants*—a malodorous and misleading name. This was recognised from the first, for Vimont, in the Jesuit Relation of 1640, writing almost from Nicollet's lips, thus explains the word: "Some Frenchmen call them the *Nation des Puants* (Nation of Stinkards) because the Algonquin word *Ouinipeg* means stinking water; but they call the water of the salt sea by the same name, so that these people are called Ouinipegu (Winnebago) because they come from the shores of a sea unknown to us, and consequently they ought not to be called the *Nation des Puants* but the *Nation de la mer* (Nation of the Sea)." The word is an Algonquin translation of the name of these people, who had formerly lived upon the "great water" (Mississippi), but the great water of the ocean is dirty water in the Algonquin languages. Bishop Barega in his Ojibway Dictionary explains it as follows: "Winnipeg—Swamp, or, better, salt water, unclean water. The Indians call Lake Winnipeg the great water, the great sea, and use the same expression for the salt water of the sea." The Relation of 1640 is confirmed in that explanation by the Relation of 1656. But the Relation of 1660, while it admits that salt water is dirty water in Indian phrase, goes on to explain that the reason of the name was the frequency of sulphur springs in that region—which certainly is not true. Father Marquette was struck with the inappropriateness of the name, and when he passed there in 1673 wrote: " This bay bears a name which had not so bad a meaning in the Indian language, for they call it rather ' Salt Bay ' than ' Fetid Bay,' although among them it is almost the same, and this is also the name they give to the sea. This induced us to make very exact researches to discover whether there were not in those parts some salt springs, as there are among the Iroquois, but we could not find any. We accordingly concluded that the name has been given on account of the quantity of slime and mud there, constantly exhaling noisome vapours which cause the loudest and longest peals of thunder that I ever heard." The good father was beyond question mistaken; for the country has no such characteristics; in fact, the valley of the Fox River from Lake Winnebago to Green Bay is now the seat of some of the largest paper mills of the West, and in a country where water power is abundant such an industry as paper making would not be extensively established unless the water was pure. The name *puant* has no foundation in fact, and is a curious reminder of the persistent expectation in those days of finding the great sea of China and Japan in every extensive sheet of water reported by Indians to exist in the unknown and mysterious West.

To reach the "people of the sea" (*gens de la mer*), then, Nicollet paddled along the western shore of Lake Michigan, and keeping still to the right hand, turned into what is now Green Bay. There on the Menominee River, which falls in on the north shore of the bay, he met the

Indians called by the French *Les Folles Avoines,* by the English in after years Menomonees, an Algonquin word signifying wild rice (called wild oats by the French), for those Indians used it largely as food. They were of Algonquin stock and doubtless Nicollet remained a short time with them, for it is recorded that he sent one of the Hurons in advance to announce his approach to these people of strange speech. Then he pushed on to the head of the bay, where, at the mouth of Fox River, he found the Winnebagoes. His envoy had been well received and four or five thousand people came to meet him and young men were sent to carry his baggage to the village. They had heard of the wonderful white men and supposed them to be spirits. Nicollet donned his embroidered robe of Chinese damask and advanced, discharging a pistol in each hand. It was a Manitou wielding thunder and lightning, and the women and children fled in terror. The chiefs gave him a warm welcome and a course of feasting on a lavish scale, for one chief served up one hundred and twenty beavers at a single entertainment. The peace he was sent to arrange was soon negotiated and Nicollet had leisure to examine the country and become acquainted with the neighbouring tribes. He went up the Fox River, passed through Lake Winnebago and followed the upper river as far as the portage to the Wisconsin. Nicollet told Father Le Jeune that three days' more travel would have brought him to the sea, for the Algonquin word Mississippi means *great water,* not "father of waters," and, misled by the name, he thought he was only three days' distance from the south sea. Father Vimont wrote in 1640: "I have a strong conviction that this sea is part of that on the north of New Mexico and by it is a passage to Japan and China." There is no reason to believe that Nicollet passed into the Wisconsin River, but it seems clear that he stood upon the water-parting between the basins of the Mississippi and St. Lawrence. It is only a mile and a half wide.

After his voyage Nicollet returned to the Huron country, where the Jesuit Fathers had been labouring with some success. Abandoning their first idea of setting up a separate mission in each of the larger towns they decided upon one central establishment from which to work all their stations, and they chose a spot on the right bank of the river Wye, where it issues from Mud Lake to fall into Gloucester Bay, near the present city of Midland. There they built the residence or mission of Sainte Marie of the Hurons, fortified with palisades and flanked with bastions—an establishment of considerable extent, with a church, and buildings for various uses, and lodgings for sixty men. The three Jesuit priests, Brébeuf, Daniel, and Davost, who went up with Nicollet, were gradually increased to eighteen. There were, besides, four lay brothers and forty to fifty Frenchmen. Fifteen of the priests went out to their different stations, and those in residence carried on the services of the church with a ceremony which impressed the Indians. It was a busy community, for the fathers exercised a generous hospitality and provided for all wants by cultivating maize and procuring game and fish from the woods and waters around. Starving Indians clustered about it in time of scarcity, and were never refused food. It was a time of organisation, not of discovery, and during these years there is no record of any notable exploration, but the Jesuit Fathers were constantly adding to their knowledge, and extending their operations among neighbouring tribes.

In 1641, at a great "feast for the dead," held by the Nipissings, there was a great assemblage of people of different nations, and Fathers Pijart and Raymbault, who were there serving the mission of St. Esprit, made great effort to gain the good-will of all, and were invited by the Algonquins who lived at the Sault to visit their country. These people were afterwards known as the Sauteurs and the Ojibways. Fathers Raymbault and Jogues were selected for the attempt and left Ste. Marie of the Hurons in September. It took them seventeen days to paddle along the north shore of Lake Huron to the Sault. They found two thousand savages assembled

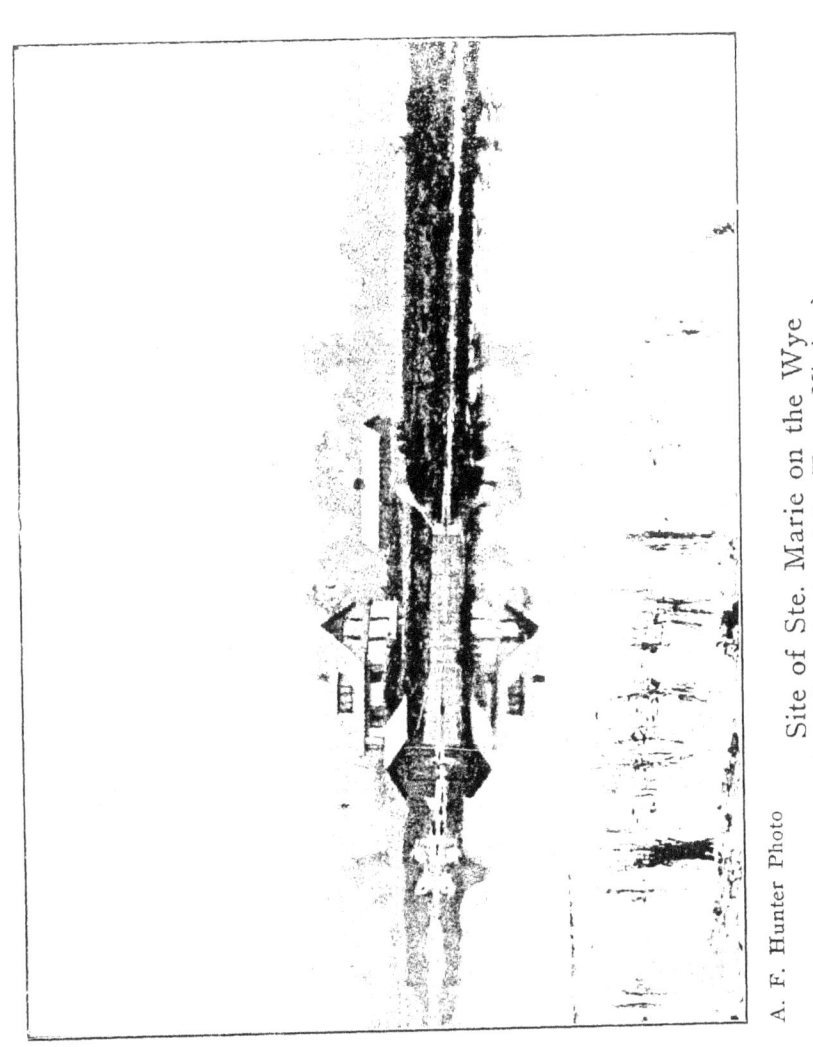

A. F. Hunter Photo

Site of Ste. Marie on the Wye
(The Central point of the Huron Missions)

EXPLORATION OF THE WEST

there and met people of many nations at a council. There they heard of the great nation of the Nadouessieux, now abbreviated to Sioux, who dwelt eighteen days' journey from the Sault across the lake (Superior) and upon a river cutting through the country. If Brulé had traversed the lake the information of the Jesuits would have been more precise, but they knew very little about it, and did not know that the river of the Sioux was the great water Nicollet had been in search of and had been within three days of reaching.

By this expedition and by Lalemant's narrative, embodied in Vimont's Relation of 1641, it will be seen that the Jesuits had grasped in idea the main feature of the geographical system of the lake region. Vimont writes of the Niagara River as the "famous river of the Neutral Nation," and continues: "This is that river by which our great Lake of the Hurons is discharged. It flows first into Lake Erie, or the Lake of the Cat nation, and at that point it enters the territory of the Neutral nation and takes the name of Onguiaaha up to where it is discharged into Ontario, or the Lake of St. Louis, from whence issues the St. Lawrence River, which flows past Quebec." This information would have been obtained by Fathers Brébeuf and Chaumonot, who went in 1640 on a mission, more perilous than any forlorn hope, to the Neutral nation, the fiercest and most intractable savages of the St. Lawrence valley. But no hint appears of the Falls of Niagara, which could not have escaped remark if they had been seen. The two priests could not have reached the river, for from the first they encountered the curses of every village they entered, and having suffered every kind of indignity and violence, barely escaped with their lives. It is not until 1648 that we learn of the Falls from Father Rageneau. After writing of Lake Erie he adds that it "passes on to precipitate itself by a fall of a frightful height into a third lake called Ontario, which we call St. Louis." Still, however, there is nothing to indicate that any white explorer had seen the Falls, and certainly if any missionary had walked along the Niagara River he would not fail to have left a record of a scene so remarkable and, in many respects, unique.

The storm, long blackening in the South and breaking out from time to time in intermitting flashes, now began to gather for its final outbreak. The devoted Brébeuf, with the mystical insight which often enlightens a lofty soul as the end of its earthly career draws near, saw it coming and rose to meet it with passion for a martyr's death. "*Sentio me vehementer impelli ad moriendum pro Christo,*" he wrote. The time was near, but had not come when, driven out of the Neutral country in the winter, the two priests were struggling back towards St. Mary of the Hurons, Brébeuf left his comrade to the sleep of exhaustion and went to pray in the neighbouring forest. Before he reached the shadow he looked up into the clear starlight and he saw a great bright cross moving swiftly towards him from the southeast—from the country of the Iroquois, and its meaning was borne in upon his soul. The following day they resumed their journey and as Brébeuf described the mystic cross, Chaumonot asked " Was it large?" " Large enough," replied the other, " to crucify us all." In the clear, thin atmosphere of ecstatic vision the boundaries of the physical and metaphysical overlap, and by some radiancy of the soul the supernatural becomes the natural. Who shall say that the light which irradiated the face of the protomartyr, Stephen, disdained the upturned visage of the solitary wayworn priest kneeling in earnest supplication at the edge of the dark, primæval forest?

From 1641 communication between Quebec and the upper country became increasingly difficult, for small war parties of Iroquois infested all the routes of travel. Montreal was founded in 1642, but no settler dared venture away from the fort to hunt or fish or clear the forest. The Mohawks prowled incessantly round the little settlement and the war whoop from the adjoining forest often startled Jeanne Mance and her devoted hospital sisters from their slumbers. A few months of peace supervened in 1645-46, and then, in 1648, the war broke out with increased intensity. In 1649 the Huron towns were taken, one after the other, by assault. The pitiless ferocity of the Iroquois warriors raged throughout the whole country of the Hurons, insatiable in massacre and torture. The Jesuit missionaries, Brébeuf and Lalemant, perished at the stake, after exhausting the fiendish ingenuity of Indian tortures. Garnier, Daniel, and Chabanel were tomahawked. The remains of the Huron nation were scattered among the neighbouring tribes and the triumphant Iroquois gloated over a wilderness depopulated from the palisades of the French fort at Montreal to the Strait of Michilimackinac. Champlain was right. It was well to send the missionaries to evangelise the Hurons, but the six-score light-armed soldiers he applied for would have been a solid nucleus around which the Hurons and Algonquins might have rallied and become a firm basis for the spread of civilisation to more distant tribes.

CHAPTER XIX

EXPLORATION RESUMED AND POSSESSION TAKEN FOR FRANCE

THE scene of interest now shifts, and for a few years exploration paused. The Huron country, formerly so populous, lay silent, and the forest began to grow over the ashes of the burned villages. The Huron church, planted with so great toil and hardship, was blasted; the banner of the Gospel was thrown down, and for a time paganism triumphed over the cross. It was a sore trial of faith to the Jesuit Fathers. As for their wild neophytes we must not despise them. Their Christianity may have been rudimentary, but their opportunity had been short. For sixteen centuries Christianity had been striving with the nations of Europe, and the result had not been so perfect as to lead us to expect more from the sixteen years of Huron missions. The cruelties of savage warfare were indeed appalling; but from the sack of Magdeburg in 1631 to the destruction of the Huron towns in 1649 is not a far stretch, either in time or in cruelty. Nature overflowed to cover quickly the scars made by the hate of man. The blood-stained soil was soon clothed with a dense mantle of forest, and when the English settlers a hundred and seventy years later cleared the land, undefined mounds and bone pits and relics of domestic utensils, or warlike weapons, alone witnessed to the tragedy of blood which had been enacted in that sylvan paradise.

It was a pious reflection of some of the good fathers and one that served to support the strain upon their faith, that Providence, in permitting the Huron nation to be scattered, designed to scatter also the seeds of Christianity and to open up the western tribes to the influence of the

EXPLORATION RESUMED

Gospel. So at least it turned out; for, subsequently, in following up those remnants who went westward, the Jesuit Fathers found the paths which led to the "great water" nearly reached by Nicollet in 1634. In 1639 they dreamed of it as the avenue to the Vermilion Sea of the Southern Ocean and, in 1641, Jogues and Raymbault stood for a short time upon its threshold at the Sault.

The tide of massacre had swept up close to the palisades of St. Mary on the Wye. There were forty Frenchmen within the fort, who would have sold their lives dearly, waiting hour after hour with strained attention for the impending assault. A party of Christian Hurons, after inflicting severe loss on the Iroquois, had been overborne until scarcely twenty were left. The enemy's scouts began to peer through the outskirts of the surrounding forest, while all through the night the priests within the chapel put up incessant supplication, especially to St. Joseph. The day dawned—it was St. Joseph's own festival—when they found that an uncontrollable panic had seized the Iroquois, who were retiring with their prisoners. They had lost a hundred of their best warriors in the last battle and they did not care to attack a garrison of forty desperate Frenchmen armed with fire-arms. In those days, as in all times of supreme trial, the supernatural seemed very near, and in the sudden retreat of the Iroquois the good fathers recognised the influence of an unseen power. They knew that respite would be short, and, moved by the entreaties of the remaining Hurons, they set fire to their fort—to the chapel where they had found the support which had sustained them in all their trials, and to all the buildings, and retreated to an island off the northern point of Nottawasaga Bay, which they called St. Joseph's Island, but which now appears as Christian Island on our maps. There they built a fort and around it gathered about three hundred families of Hurons; but the island was small and all communication with Quebec was cut off. During the winter famine drove a swarm of starving savages in upon the fort to be fed by the charity of the fathers. No one dared to set foot upon the mainland, for Iroquois war parties infested the whole region. Urged by the chiefs to lead them to a place of safety, the Jesuits resolved to abandon all the missions in the West, and taking with them about three hundred souls—the remnant of their flock—they started on a melancholy retreat down the Ottawa. "With tears" (writes the narrator of 1650) "we left the country which we loved, around which all our hopes had centred and which, reddened by the blood of our glorified brethren, promised to open up to us also the road to Heaven and the gate of Paradise." All the way was marked by traces of Iroquois triumph. The Nipissings had been massacred. The Algonquins of Allumette Island were slaughtered or dispersed. The retreating Hurons were completely cowed and, refusing to stop even at Montreal, hastened to the shelter of the guns of Quebec. They settled first on the Island of Orleans; but even there, a few years later, the Mohawk scalping knife reached them. At last they removed to Lorette, on the St. Charles, near Quebec, where to this day a few individuals represent in their earliest home the people who, under Donnacona, first greeted the French under Cartier.

In the West the work of destruction went on. The powerful Neutral nation was scattered. The Erie nation was annihilated. Tradition tells of more than a thousand fires alight at one time and in each fire a stake to which was bound a writhing Erie. The picture may be somewhat overdrawn as to the number at one time, but it is in the main true, and there is nothing in Dante's Inferno more horrible. The Hurons and their near relatives, the Tobacco nation, long wandered in search of a safe retreat. A large band of them fled to the Manitoulin Islands and from thence to Michilimackinac, but Iroquois war parties sought them out. They went to the islands at the mouth of Green Bay of Lake Michigan, but found no safety. Hunted thence they fled to the territories of the Illinois and the Sioux, upon the Mississippi, and from thence they retired up the St. Croix and Black rivers. At last they found refuge at Chequamegon Bay

EXPLORATION RESUMED 315

in the southwest corner of Lake Superior. There, within reach of the head-waters of the Mississippi, they dwelt until their renewed arrogance provoked the Sioux to drive them out.

In 1653, when the whole colony of New France was in despair from the incursions of the Iroquois, to the surprise of all the Onondagas made proposals of peace, and the exploration of the western country recommenced with the reviving fur trade. In 1654 two young Frenchmen left for the far West and the Relation of 1656 chronicles their return with fifty loaded canoes and two hundred and fifty savages. Their names have not been recorded, nor the localities they visited; but from the names of the tribes mentioned, it is clear that they had been on Lake Michigan, on the Fox River, and probably on Lake Superior. They brought messages from distant nations asking for missionaries. Thirty young Frenchmen started to return with them, but their courage failed them when they heard of the dangers on the road. Fathers Druillettes and Garreau, with a lay brother and three other Frenchmen of their party, persevered until they fell into an ambuscade of Mohawks, who mortally wounded Father Garreau. The Algonquins escaped in the night, leaving all the Frenchmen behind. The Iroquois were at peace with the French, but not with the Hurons and Algonquins. The Mohawks carried Father Garreau to Montreal, where he died, and, after the custom of their people, they made their apology by giving a present, and the haughty savages took care that it was a small one.

The way to the west was opened up again by two fur-traders, whose daring enterprise places them among the chief of western pioneers. Médard Chouart, called after some property he had, Sieur des Groseilliers, had been in the employ of the Jesuits and, with them, had shared the dangers and excitements of the Huron missions and become familiar with the Ottawa route and the Huron waters. In 1646 he left their service and began trading on his own account with the Indians and, in 1647, he married, as his first wife, Hélène, daughter of Abraham Martin, whose name has been perpetuated in history in the " Plains of Abraham," the theatre of the struggle between Wolfe and Montcalm. Three Rivers was then the focus of the fur trade, and in 1651 the Radisson family came out from France and settled there. Two daughters came and one son, Pierre Esprit Radisson—whose life and adventures, written two hundred years ago, and only recently discovered and published, surpass in interest the creations of any writer of romances. He had not been long in Canada when he was captured by Mohawks while hunting near Three Rivers. He was tied at the stake for burning, and after suffering the preliminary tortures of having some of his finger nails torn out and being a target for the arrows of the village youth, he was adopted by a Mohawk woman and became a member of her family and a favourite in the tribe. He escaped in company with some Algonquin captives, and when he had nearly reached home, was again captured. Although three Mohawks had been killed in his flight his adopted relatives again saved him when at the stake. A second attempt succeeded. He got away to the Dutch post at Orange (Albany) and was taken to Holland, from whence he returned to Canada.

The Jesuits had opened a mission among the Onondagas, and in 1657 two of the fathers were sent to strengthen it, and with them went a small party of Frenchmen. Radisson could not resist the opportunity, and his knowledge of the Iroquois language and customs made him a welcome addition to the party. As the spring approached the Jesuits became aware that the Iroquois were preparing to massacre the whole mission. Their position was difficult. The fort was built on Onondaga Lake in the heart of the Iroquois country; a small stream led into the Oswego River, which, after a course of about thirty-five miles, falls into Lake Ontario. The French dissembled their suspicions, and, in the loft over their fort, built canoes. When the spring sun opened the river they made a great feast, and invited the

EXPLORATION RESUMED

whole village—and here we may conceive that Radisson's Mohawk experience was especially useful. It was a religious feast savouring dangerously of paganism, and savage ceremonial imperatively required that everything presented should be eaten. The lives of the party depended upon it, and never in the Indian country was hospitality so profuse—maize, hogs, bustards, ducks, turtles, eels, carp, and everything else that could be thought of were brought in, while the savages solemnly ate until even they could eat no more. In vain did they beg for surcease. The French urged upon them their religious duty, and even soothed their gastronomic efforts by playing on some musical instruments they had. At last, gorged like boa-constrictors, the Indians fell back, their eyelids closed over their bulging eyeballs, and they slept the sleep of repletion. When the last man dropped the French got their canoes, and by the time day dawned, and the savages recovered, they were far down the Oswego River. A fortunate snowfall obliterated their tracks, and to the puzzled savages it seemed as if the Frenchmen had flown away in the night. The episode is Homeric—it is Ulysses escaping from the cave of Polyphemus; but this plot was far better designed, and better executed.

Radisson arrived at Three Rivers the same spring, and found his brother-in-law Chouart preparing for a voyage to the great lakes. It was another opportunity for adventure not to be resisted. Chouart had heard from the Indians of new tribes in the further West, and these he was intent on discovering. This voyage was the beginning of a joint career, which united the brothers-in-law (for Chouart had married Radisson's sister Marguerite for his second wife) in a loyal and warm partnership of adventure and friendship throughout their lives. In the middle of June, 1658, they started westward with twenty-nine Frenchmen in the party, and a number of savages. They had to take up a few more at Montreal, but as Iroquois spies were watching all movements there, they got them away as quietly as possible. On the lake above they overtook a party of boisterous young Frenchmen who were making a picnic of passing through a country infested by Iroquois. The natural result followed. The straggling and disorderly party were attacked suddenly, a number were killed, others were captured, and the rest got back as best they could to Montreal. Chouart and Radisson were, however, made of different stuff. They escaped westwards, and, with their own Indians, hurried up the Ottawa with a speed which outstripped pursuit until they reached Lake Nipissing (Lake of the Castors), where they could rest. From thence they passed down French River to the " bay of crystal water, full of islands, and abounding in fish," which we at once recognise as Georgian Bay. There the party divided; those for the Sault went west-north-west, and the rest went south.

Chouart and Radisson were not yet ready to explore the North. They went with the south-bound party, and, in a course of many days, they made very nearly a circuit of Lake Huron. They coasted along the pleasant shores of the deserted paradise of Jesuit hope, and saw the clearings of its former population. They penetrated to the south of the lake, and noted its freedom from islands; then returning northwards they stayed for a while on one of the Manitoulin islands. The sheet of water cut off by islands from the " great lake of the Hurons," they call the " Lake of the Staring Hairs." It included what is now known as the north channel, and was named from the *Cheveux Relevés,* or Ottawas, who lived on the Manitoulin Islands. Some Iroquois were traced lurking round, and Radisson won the heart of his hosts by leading a war party and bringing home eight dead and three living of the prowlers. The dead, he calmly writes, were eaten, and " the living burned with a slow fire to the rigour of cruelties," which, he adds, " comforted the desolate " relatives of slain Ottawas. While staying with the Ottawas some Pottawatomies arrived, and the two adventurers went with them to their home at the mouth of Green Bay on Lake Michigan. This was the " Baie des Puants," on the " Lac des Puants," or, to

EXPLORATION RESUMED

use once for all the names of Radisson's narrative—"the small Lake of the Stinkings" on the "great Lake of the Stinkings," an undeservedly disagreeable name applied, as already explained, by a persistent philological freak to a charming region. There they made the acquaintance of the Mascoutins, or "Nation of Fire," as the name was mistranslated.

During the whole winter of 1658, and the spring of 1659, the two brothers-in-law wandered at their will from their camp at Green Bay, up the Fox River, and over Wisconsin and the adjoining territories, and saw many sedentary nations, living in villages, all of whom were kind and hospitable. They met some people of the Sioux, a great nation of the West, and of the Crees, a roaming nation of the North, whose summer wanderings extended to the shores of the great salt water "Sea of the North" (Hudson's Bay). They visited the great sea (Mississippi), fourteen years before Jolliet and Marquette, and described it to one of the Jesuit fathers as a beautiful river, great, wide, and deep, comparable to the great river St. Lawrence. Especially were they pleased with Michigan, "the delightfullest lake of the world," "uncomparable," "finer than Italy, as to climate, and more delightful the farther south one goes." The philanthropy which "consoled the desolate" at the north of the lake breaks out in a more legitimate form in Radisson's lament that the starving poor of Europe cannot be brought out to a land so fertile, and abounding in game. The poor of Europe came two hundred years later, for the crowded streets of Milwaukee and Chicago are now vociferous in every European tongue, and, though the game has long since been exterminated, the fields of maize are more productive than ever. So passed the summer, and, as the fall came on, the two adventurers retired up the lake. They passed through the Strait of Michilimackinac, and we read with startled resentment the name "Strait of the Stinkings," applied to the beauty-spot of the northern waters. They did not stay at the Sault, but passed up Lake Superior to Chequamegon Bay, that part of the south shore where the head-waters of affluents of the Mississippi approach the lake. There they established their headquarters, and from thence they explored over a large portion of the present State of Wisconsin. They were the first white men known to have paddled upon Lake Superior beyond the Sault or Strait of St. Mary.

Around this central point of Indian life the two adventurers moved during the winter of 1659-60. Iroquois raids had driven the Saulteurs (or Sault Indians) there, and there also were remnants of the Tobacco nation of the Hurons, and many Ottawas. Thither also came the Crees, bringing intelligence of their summer wanderings on the shores of the northern sea. Radisson went on snowshoes into the interior, and down one of the streams leading into the Mississippi. Here his narrative reverts to his previous visit to that river. He identifies it by calling it the "great river," where the Hurons and Ottawas had taken refuge—"the forked river," of which one branch went south to Mexico, and the other (the Missouri) to the west—the first notice of the Missouri. As the summer of 1660 approached the two traders prepared to go down to the settlements, and, after many difficulties arising from the terror of Iroquois hostility existing even in that remote region, they got away with a party of five hundred savages, and, after some encounters on the Ottawa, reached Montreal and Three Rivers, in the month of August, 1660.

The region about the head-waters of the Mississippi was thus revealed in this adventurous expedition. The voyageurs not only had been over the Wisconsin portage, but had been over the southern water-parting of Lake Superior, and gone down streams flowing south-westward until they reached the great river (Mississippi) itself. They had visited the extreme south of Lake Michigan, and explored beyond its western water-parting. They had seen much, but they had not seen the "Bay of the North"; they had heard of it from the Crees, and they resolved to rest at Three Rivers for a year, and say as little as possible about their travels until they could succeed in reaching its shores. The objective point of their next expedition was to be Hudson's Bay, passing thither by way of Lake Superior. It is perfectly clear from the Relation of 1660 that the Jesuits at that time knew nothing of the lake beyond the Sault, nor of the Bay, beyond what they had gathered from Indian reports. They were confident that the Southern Ocean joined the Bay of the North by means of a connecting water at the west, and that thus the sea leading to Japan and China was only a few days' journey from Lake Superior.

In the summer of 1661 Chouart and Radisson prepared their outfit for their new enterprise, and applied to the Governor for a license to leave; but, although he had only just arrived, the Baron d'Avaugour had already learned to consult his own private interest in public matters, and he refused to allow them to leave unless they took with them two of his own servants, and gave them half the profits of the venture. Chouart resented the injustice of being compelled to impart to green hands the experience of a lifetime of danger, and to divide his profits with two useless men, raw from France, who had never seen a canoe or an Indian; and he, together with Radisson, escaped in the night from Three Rivers, and by concerted arrangement met on the river a party of savages, Saulteurs and Nipissings, who were about to return to their homes.

Once more the two brothers-in-law were in the midst of the wild life they loved. Above Montreal, on the Ottawa, the Iroquois lay in wait, as usual, and, in a number of skirmishes and fights, owing to the skill in Indian warfare of the two white leaders, the Iroquois got the worst of it. They lost ten killed, and were shut up in a fort. The two traders, whose object was trading, not fighting, seized the opportunity, and started with all speed up the river, taking with them four Iroquois prisoners to burn as soon as they got leisure. They did not slacken their speed until they reached Lake Nipissing, then, following down the French River and along the north shore of

Lake Huron, they arrived at the Sault, through which Lake Superior discharges its waters.

Game was plentiful at the Sault, and whitefish, then as now, were abundant, and the adventurers rested for a little while. What became of the Iroquois prisoners does not appear—probably they had been knocked on the head to lighten the canoes. The voyage was resumed by the way of the south shore of the lake, and it can be easily traced in Radisson's narrative. The long range of sand-dunes, the pictured rocks, the copper region, Keweenaw Bay, and its long projecting point, are fully described. They did not round the point, but crossed it near the base by a convenient portage always followed by the savages. At the Montreal River, now the boundary between Northern Michigan and Wisconsin, some of the savages went south to the portages for the Mississippi waters. Chouart and Radisson went on until they reached the present Chequamegon Bay, near the site of the present Ashland. There, on a convenient point, they built a trading fort. Three or four years later the Jesuits established there the mission of St. Esprit, and it became known as *La Pointe*. It is near the portages to the Chippewa and the St. Croix rivers, which fall into the Mississippi, near Lake Pepin, and the locality was the favourite resort of many tribes of savages from Lake Michigan, the Mississippi, and Hudson's Bay.

During the winter of 1661-62 they went through many experiences. They wandered over a portion of what is now the State of Minnesota. They made a long visit to a lake, the resort of eighteen tribes, and there they built a trading fort, and made it a centre of operations. There, also, a grand council was held, at which five hundred savages were present. The two traders went, by invitation, to visit the " Nation of Beef " (*Nation du Bœuf*), where they found seven thousand men, and they stayed there six weeks, then they returned to La Pointe on Lake Superior.

So far there have been only minor difficulties in the narrative, due mainly to the indescribably bad English

EXPLORATION RESUMED 323

which Radisson wrote. Some of the sentences might as well have been written in Cree; for, although the words taken separately may be English, taken collectively, they yield no intelligible meaning, but now comes a question which is supposed to have a political bearing. French writers maintain that Chouart and Radisson went to Hudson's Bay, which few English writers will admit. No political question is really involved, for they made no settlement there. That the English discovered and first wintered on the bay cannot be disputed—Hudson in 1610, Button in 1612, James in 1631, had wintered there, and, by them, and Baffin, and Bylot, the whole bay had been explored. If, however, the question be made to turn on first settlement, the priority of the English can easily be established also. When it is considered that Chouart and Radisson deliberately planned this voyage with Hudson's Bay as its objective point—that they openly stated that intention only a few weeks before their departure—that they subsequently led the English there, and were the first to suggest the formation of the Hudson's Bay Company, a presumption is created which in all fairness should guide the interpretation of Radisson's English.

Among the Indians resorting to La Pointe and the portages they had met a band of Crees, and had arranged to make them a visit the following year. They concealed their intention from the other Indians, and got away, in the spring of 1662, to carry out their design. They crossed the western end of the lake, and found, after some trouble, the camp of their Cree friends. They started at once for what they call the "great river," and "following it they came to the seaside," where "they found an old house all demolished battered with bullets." Apropos of the old house the Crees began to tell Indian yarns about two nations who had been there, and of the "peculiarities of European," but Radisson, in his peculiar English, says: "We know ourselves, and what Europe is, therefore in vaine they tell us as for that." All this points to Hudson's Bay as the place they had reached. Further indications lead to the same conclusion. "We passed that summer quietly coasting the seaside," writes Radisson, "and as the cold began we prevented the ice. We have the commoditie of the river to carry our things in our boats to the best place, where we are most bests." This means that they left the bay before the ice began to form, and chose for their return the most convenient river—which would be the Moose River. Further confirmation will be found in the statement, "We went further in the bay to see ye place that they weare to passe that summer. That river comes from the lake, and empties itselfe in ye river of Sagnes, called Tadousack, which is a hundred leagues in the great river of Canada as where we are in ye Bay of ye North." This passage determines the place they reached, and must, fairly, mean that, having reached the shore of the bay, they coasted to the outlet of a river which led to the Saguenay, that might be Rupert River, flowing from Lake Mistassini. From that lake there is a portage over the height of land to the head-waters of the Saguenay. Radisson adds: "We left in this place our marks and rendezvous," and to that place Chouart conducted Gillam in 1667. Somewhere near there Hudson wintered in 1610, and James in 1631. The old ruined house with bullet marks may thus be accounted for, and there was the first settlement on the bay. This view is incidentally confirmed by a passage in the Jesuit Relation of 1667, where it is recorded that a Cree Indian told Allouez that he had seen a ship on the bay and on its shore had seen a house made of boards and wood (sawn lumber) such as Allouez and the French used.

Doubtless there are difficulties in the narrative, for in another passage Radisson says: "We went from isle to isle all that summer," and "this place hath a great store of cows," meaning buffalo. These are notes pointing to the Lake of the Woods, or to Lake Nipigon, but in close succession he writes: "We promised them [the Crees] to come with such shipps as we invented." That cannot apply to any inland lake, for only at Hudson's Bay could

EXPLORATION RESUMED

they reach the Crees by ships. For these special reasons, and from the whole sequence of events the conclusion that Chouart and Radisson reached Hudson's Bay is irresistible, and when it is considered that Summit Lake discharges both ways, by the Albany River into Hudson's Bay, and by the Ombabike River into Lake Nipigon, which discharges into Lake Superior, it is apparent how easily the passage could be made.

There is no need to dwell upon the succeeding adventures of the two traders in this expedition. They returned to their fort on Chequamegon Bay on Lake Superior, and in the spring of 1663 prepared to descend to Three Rivers. They had great difficulty in persuading the savages to go down. The fear of the Iroquois was upon all the tribes. They succeeded at last, and in company with several hundred savages arrived at Three Rivers in the summer of 1663. There they fell into D'Avaugour's clutches, and from his injustice they appealed in vain to the courts of France. Their resentment led to the offer of their services to England, and brought on the formation of the Hudson's Bay Company. The remaining years of these remarkable men were full of adventures, but the story is beyond the scope of this volume. Radisson's narrative, in spite of its occasional obscurity, is generally clear enough. There are some transpositions, which show that it was in part, at least, written from memory, a few years after the events. In the vicissitudes of such a life as his it is not surprising if papers should have been lost, but the main facts of the discoveries are confirmed by other contemporary authorities, which give the reader confidence in the general truth of the narrative.

The Jesuit fathers could not forget their scattered flock in the distant west. We have seen how their attempt to pass up in 1656 had failed; but in 1660, when Chouart and Radisson returned, Father René Ménard, though fifty-five years old, and broken by hardships, resolved to go up with the returning Ottawas to the upper lakes. He left at the end of August in company with a few French traders. The Ottawas, who seemed to have been the most intractable ruffians of all the western savages, ill-treated him on the route; nevertheless he remained with them during the winter at a place on Lake Superior, he called Ste. Thérèse, supposed to have been on Keweenaw Bay. After eight months of hardship and semi-starvation, finding that the Ottawas were absolutely irreclaimable, he resolved to go to La Pointe (St. Michel, he called it), where some Hurons had taken refuge, and had sent to invite him. He started with one Frenchman and a party of Huron guides. The journey was long, and the Hurons abandoned him under the pretense of going to their village for food. The Frenchman, Jean Guerin, remained with him and they waited two weeks for the promised return of the Hurons until, their food running short, they repaired a canoe which they found hidden in the brush, and followed on. At one of the portages Guerin went ahead with a load, expecting the father to follow, but Ménard wandered into the forest and was lost. His companion searched for him in vain. Guerin succeeded in arriving at the Huron village, and a young Indian was sent in search, but without success.

The priest's body was never found. Some articles belonging to him were found among the Sacs, and, years after, his cassock and breviary were found among the Sioux, as objects of worship. Some suppose that the Keweenaw portage was the place of his death, but, in going over the particulars recorded in the Jesuit Relation of 1663, and in the memoir of Nicholas Perrot, it seems evident that when he arrived at La Pointe the Hurons had retired up one of the rivers into the interior. Perrot says they were on the Black River, and the father was following their traces.

It was late in 1663 when the news of Father Ménard's death reached Quebec, and, in 1665, Father Allouez went up to Ottawa to continue his work. The Indians had flatly refused to take him, although they willingly took some white traders; but he persisted in going. His

EXPLORATION RESUMED

canoe was wrecked and the Indians left him to starve, but an Ottawa chief, passing not long after, took him into his canoe and made him work his way by paddling. He did not stop at the Sault, but pressed on to Keweenaw Bay (Ste. Thérèse). After staying there a short time he decided that La Pointe was the most important Indian rendezvous on the lake, and, going by the portage through Keweenaw Point, he went there and founded the mission he called Saint Esprit upon a point of the mainland on Chequamegon Bay. A hundred and thirty years later, in 1765, Henry, the fur trader, established a post there among the Ojibways, and said it might be called the metropolis of that tribe. The lake affords abundance of food. In a short time his men took two thousand trout and whitefish. In winter they caught them by spearing, and the trout weighed on an average twenty pounds each.

It was a well-chosen spot. Allouez was a skilled linguist and could preach in six languages—a most important qualification at that polyglot post. There were two villages there—one of the refugee Hurons of the Tobacco tribe and the other of Algonquins. He built his chapel between the two, and began his labours among the shifting throng of Sacs, Foxes, Illinois, Crees, Sioux, Pottawatomies, Ojibways, and Saulteurs. The Nipissings had retired to Lake Nipigon (Alimebegong), in the country of the Crees, and Allouez visited them—the first missionary to touch the north shore of the lake. All these nations resorted peaceably to La Pointe. The country properly belonged to the Ojibways, but they, like the Sioux and Crees, though addicted to war, had not the truculence and cruelty of the eastern tribes. They did not even torture their prisoners. In fact, burning at the stake was a custom practised only by the semi-civilised Indians of eastern America, and the fully civilised nations of western Europe. The western tribes, after the Iroquois wars, adopted it to a limited extent in retaliation; but, though careless of life, they did not delight in cruelty for its own sake.

In such a centre of Indian life Allouez soon learned of the Mississippi from the Sioux and Illinois, and also of the populous nations on its banks. The field opened out before him and he went down to Quebec to obtain help. He stayed there only two days, and returned with another Jesuit, Father Nicholas, a lay brother, and four hired men. His active labours led him to the extreme western end of the lake to make a visit to the Sioux. He crossed to the north shore, went up to Lake Nipigon and thoroughly examined it around all its shores and islands. He was following the Nipissings, who took refuge there after the Iroquois war, although the region properly belonged to the Crees. For three years he laboured at La Pointe with indifferent success. Those of the Hurons who had learned something of Christianity in their old home on Lake Huron had relapsed into paganism. In full council he took off his shoes and " shook off the dust of his feet as a witness against them." He told them that the people of the Sault had sent to invite him, and he would leave them to their sins. They were impressed, but only for a short time. Allouez left them in 1669 to found the mission of St. François Xavier on the Fox River of Green Bay. There he spent the winter among the Pottawatomies, Sacs, Foxes, Winnebagoes, and Mascoutins, and in the spring he went up the river beyond the portage and saw the Wisconsin flowing to the southwest, to fall into " the great river called the Messi Sipi, only six days' journey distant." He prepared the way for Marquette and Jolliet by founding the first mission on Lake Michigan.

Meantime, at Quebec and Montreal, great changes were taking place. The King had sent out a very capable soldier, De Courcelles, as governor, and as intendant he had sent Talon, one of Colbert's most trusted scholars. He sent also the Marquis de Tracy as lieutenant-general with vice-regal powers, and, most important of all, he sent a regiment twelve hundred strong—the Carignan-Salières regiment of veteran soldiers, seasoned in the Turkish wars. They arrived in 1665, and, without losing time, De Courcelles, in January, 1666, marched an expedition, on snowshoes, to attack the Mohawks in their homes. In the summer the Marquis de Tracy invaded the Mohawk territory with a strong force, burned all their towns and destroyed all their standing crops and stores of provisions. The troops were the missionaries needed by the Mohawks. They were the peacemakers, and, for twenty years after, there was peace along the waterways of Canada, and the communications with the missions on the Great Lakes were unmolested. Champlain was justified. If France had sent him the six score men he asked for, before the power of her Huron and Algonquin allies had been broken, the Iroquois would never have attained such pre-eminence, hundreds of Canadians would have been saved from the scalping knife and the stake, and the French would have been entrenched in the country before the English had time to gather strength. At the peace commenced the era of the great expansion, and men like Frontenac and Talon began to dream of a great transatlantic France, extending from Hudson's Bay to the Gulf of Mexico, and crowding the English back upon a narrow strip of the seacoast.

The way was now open. Allouez once more went down to Quebec with earnest representations, and Father Dablon went up to the lakes, taking with him Father Marquette. In 1669 the Jesuits had three fixed stations in the West. The chief one was the mission of St. Mary at the Sault, the others were St. Esprit at La Pointe on Lake Superior, and St. François Xavier on Fox River of Green Bay in Lake Michigan. Father Dablon, who was the Superior of western missions, visited these stations, and in 1670, he and Allouez went to Green Bay and up the Fox River to the Mascoutins and doubtless stood upon the portage and saw the smooth current of the Wisconsin inviting them westwards. He saw that the Sault was the key of the West, and founded the residence on the south shore of the Strait just below the rapids. He and Marquette were there in 1669. Not long after he was recalled to Quebec, Allouez went to the Sault, Marquette to La Pointe, and Fathers Druillettes and André were sent to Green Bay. The results of these explorations are shown upon a map in the Jesuit Relation of 1670-71. It is doubtful if there ever have been so many exceptionally able men in power at one time in Canada as at this period. The Governor, De Courcelles, soon to be followed by Frontenac, the Intendant Talon, and Bishop Laval, were at the head of affairs. The Abbé de Queylus was Superior of the Sulpicians, the hot-headed Abbé Fénelon, and the ex-captain of cavalry, the Abbé Dollier de Casson, were missionaries. Jolliet, the versatile and good-natured Canadian, and La Salle, the intractable and reserved Norman, were on the eve of the discoveries which have written their names in history. The saintly Marquette, who is almost canonised throughout the Western States of the Union, had just gone to the Sault, and some of the most able of the Jesuit fathers, Druillettes, Dablon, and Allouez, were still active in their work. These men were to lift the veil which had hidden the West when the soldier, De Tracy, had swept the way clear of the hostile Iroquois.

In 1663 the company of religious enthusiasts who had founded the City of Montreal in 1642 and held it as a "Castle Dangerous," in spite of incessant Mohawk war parties, transferred to the Seminary of St. Sulpice their property and rights in the Island of Montreal, and five years later the Abbé de Queylus returned to Canada as Superior. He was not content to leave to the Jesuits a monopoly of mission work. The peace had opened up the lower lakes. The Ottawa route and the upper lakes had been made known by the Recollets and the Jesuits, and the south shore of Lake Ontario was occupied by Jesuit missions. The Sulpicians now inaugurated mission stations along the north shore of Lake Ontario, where Iroquois bands were establishing themselves. Their first post was on the Bay of Quinté (Kenté). A band of Cayugas had settled there and the Abbés Trouvé and Fénelon were sent to evangelise them. Shortly after

Fort of the Gentlemen of the Seminary of St. Sulpice at Montreal
From an old print—the two towers alone remain at present

EXPLORATION RESUMED 331

the Abbé Fénelon (a brother of the celebrated Archbishop) went to Gandaseteiagon, near the site of the present city of Toronto. It is laid down on a contemporaneous map at the lake terminus of the route to Lake Toronto, the present Lake Simcoe, and near a river which cannot be other than the Humber. Another mission was at Ganeraska, probably Bowmanville.

The zealous Superior heard the rumours of populous tribes in the far West, more tractable than the Iroquois, who were calling for news of the Gospel, and, in 1669, he despatched two Sulpicians, Dollier de Casson and Galinée, to discover some of them, and more particularly one in the southwest, of which he had heard from a captive given him by the Iroquois. They started from Montreal on July 6 with seven canoes and twenty-one men. With them was La Salle, of whom we shall hear later, and they had as guides two canoes of Seneca Indians. The Abbé Dollier de Casson had served under Turenne and was a priest of the most imperturbable good nature; his companion, Galinée, was in minor orders and had some skill in practical mathematics and cartography. His accounts of the voyage and map have been preserved and are of great geographical value because up to that time Lake Erie was almost unknown.

The route taken was up the St. Lawrence and across Lake Ontario to Irondequoit Bay (Karontogouat) near the mouth of the Genessee River. The Seneca towns were not far from there and the largest of them, which Galinée calls Seneca, was the first point on their voyage, for there they expected to obtain guides, and there the Jesuit Father Frémin had a mission. The town was six leagues from the lake shore where the Frenchmen encamped and there was much parleying, for the Indians were never in a hurry and the business had to be considered in council. They were unwilling that the expedition should go further, and it was delayed several weeks, waiting for a decision. At last, hearing from an Indian that there was an Iroquois town at the end of the lake, where they would be certain to find slaves of the western nations who could act as guides, the Frenchmen went on. They passed the mouth of the Niagara River and although they heard the roar of the cataract, they were content to accept the Indian accounts of it. It is almost incredible at this date, but Galinée says distinctly that they were in such haste to arrive at the Iroquois town they did not go to see "this wonder," and from the narrative it is clear that no Frenchman up to that time had described it or recorded a visit there. Even the Sulpician Trouvé, who told Galinée that he had heard the sound of the fall across the lake, does not seem to have visited it.

They arrived at a large sandy bay at the end of the lake at the outlet of a little lake, evidently near the present city of Hamilton. The village they were in search of was five or six leagues distant and the inhabitants being few were in fear of the French and begged that they might not be burned as were the Mohawks. Here the voyagers were more successful. The Indians gave them two slaves. One, a Shawnee from the Ohio, fell to La Salle, and the other, a Nez-Percé, from the upper Lake Huron, fell to the party of Galinée. At the Indian village they were amazed to find two Frenchmen on their way down from the upper lakes. It was a memorable meeting. Jolliet had been sent to Lake Superior with Jean Péré of Quebec to look for the copper mine, of which so much had been heard ever since Cartier's time, and was returning. In this little Indian village the two who were to be rival discoverers of the Mississippi met, and, with characteristic openness, Jolliet gave the others the results of his explorations and sketches of the routes he had been following. He had gone up by way of the Ottawa and on his return had persuaded the Ottawas to let him take back with him one of their Iroquois prisoners as a preliminary to a peace. This Iroquois had shown him the easier route down by Lake Huron and the Detroit River, but was afraid of the Niagara portage, because it was infested by war parties of the Andastes. Jolliet, therefore, went down Lake Erie only as far as the mouth of the Grand River. He did not see Niagara, but

EXPLORATION RESUMED

leaving his canoe on Lake Erie made a portage over to the head of Lake Ontario. He was the first to make a passage by way of Detroit, but while the upper lakes were all discovered, Niagara, the most remarkable point on the whole St. Lawrence system and the earliest to be talked about, was the last to be seen and described.

The rift in this ill-assorted expedition now began to appear. The enthusiastic priest, Dollier de Casson, heard from Jolliet of a populous tribe in the West, the Pottawatomies, who had asked for missionaries, and to them he decided to go—the readier because they were of Algonquin stock, and he could speak with them. It was true that the expedition had been designed to discover an unknown river, the Ohio, but he would go there by way of Lake Erie and this well-disposed tribe of savages. La Salle had other views. With characteristic reticence he dissembled them, and with an obstinacy equally characteristic clung to them. He was convinced that the way to the Ohio lay through the Seneca country; and in fact, it was through the Senecas he had first heard of it. He had been constrained by the authority of the Governor to take part in this expedition and it was repugnant to his nature to share responsibility with anyone. At the Iroquois village he pleaded illness and would not, or could not, proceed. Jolliet went on his way eastward down to Quebec, and the two priests went westward to Lake Erie with their party, over Jolliet's trail. Where La Salle went is a fruitful source of dispute.

It was October 1, 1669, when they started, and half the village turned out to carry the baggage and canoes of the Sulpicians over to the Grand River; but they had only three canoes for twelve people, and the water in the river was low and very rapid, so their interpreter and two Indians volunteered to walk over the trail and search for the canoe Jolliet had left on the lake. The men were never seen again, and it is probable they deserted. When the two priests arrived on the lake the waves, under a gale from the south, were rolling in as on an ocean beach. The season was getting late and they resolved to winter on the lake, so they ran up along shore inside of Long Point Bay to a place now known as Port Dover, in the county of Norfolk. They went a little way up the Lynn River to the junction of Black Creek and there settled down in what Galinée calls the "Earthly Paradise" of Canada. He writes: "There is assuredly no more beautiful region in all Canada. The woods are open, interspersed with beautiful meadows, watered by rivers and rivulets filled with fish and beaver, an abundance of fruits, and what is more important, so full of game that we saw there at one time more than a hundred roebucks in a single band." There, on the bank of the stream, in a nook among the trees, sheltered from the stormy lake, they built their cabin with a small chapel attached, where they said mass three times a week. It was an ideal life for an ecclesiastic. Galinée writes: "Monsieur Dollier often told us that that winter ought to be worth more for our eternal welfare than the best ten years of our lives." They were undisturbed all winter and unvisited save by an occasional Iroquois hunter in search of beaver.

In the spring of 1670 they started again, and after nearly six months of peace and plenty, their troubles commenced. One of their canoes was blown into the lake and some of the party had to walk along the trail, where they got entangled in the marshes. At last they all safely reached the portage at Long Point neck, and finding again Jolliet's canoe, which some Iroquois had been using, they launched upon the main lake westwards, camping at night upon the shore. When they arrived at Point Pelée they were very tired and left their packs upon the beach. They slept very soundly and during the night the wind rose and the rising water carried away some of Dollier's baggage, and would have stripped them clean if one of the party had not chanced to waken. Fortunately the canoes themselves had been carried up to higher land and were safe. Dollier's altar service was lost, and also the goods they had for use in payment for provisions. This accident destroyed in their view the object of their journey, for it put it out of their power to administer the

Junction of the River Lynn and Black Creek. The Earthly Paradise where Dollier and Galinée wintered

sacraments. After much deliberation they decided to give up the Pottawatomies and to return to Montreal with the Indians, who would be going down in the summer from the Sault St. Mary. This detour seemed to them very little longer and would enable them to see the country. They resumed their westward course, passed up the Detroit River, through Lake St. Clair and the St. Clair River, and into Lake Huron. At a sharp turn in the river they encountered a stone idol painted with red paint, the object of the veneration of passing savages. In some occult way they associated it with the loss of their altar service. It was, in their notion, a demon who objected to the opening of missions. " In short," says Galinée, " there was no one whose hatred it had not incurred." So they smashed it and sank the pieces in the deep river, and, adds the pious father, " God rewarded us immediately for this good action, for we killed a roebuck and a bear that very day." They were surprised to find that the water in Lake St. Clair was fresh, for Sanson on his map of 1656 had marked it " Lake of Sea-Water."

It must be noted that Galinée, both in his narrative and in his map, confused together Lake Michigan and Lake Huron. He writes that the fresh-water sea of the Hurons is called in Algonquin " Michigane," and his Lake of the Hurons is evidently the North Channel of that lake. They found no mission post at the Strait of Michilimackinac. At last they arrived at the Sault, where they found Fathers Dablon and Marquette comfortably settled in a fortified mission with a house and chapel and large clearings around for crops. They were received " with all charity." but their welcome is open to doubt, for their stay was very short. Galinée comments with freedom upon what he saw, and as he and Dollier were ecclesiastics, his remarks are of the nature of expert evidence. He says: " I saw no particular sign of Christianity amongst the Indians of this place, nor in any other country of the Ottawas," and he thinks that the fruit of the missions is rather for the French, " of whom there are twenty or twenty-five there, than for the Indians, of whom there are so far none sufficiently good Catholics to attend divine service at high mass or vespers." Too much importance must not be attributed to these comments, for there were serious differences at Quebec in those days between the Sulpicians and the Jesuits; nor should too much be expected from these poor savages; at the same time it is evident that while the published relations of the Jesuit missionaries had been too optimistic as regards the spiritual progress of the Indians, they had erred in the opposite direction in reporting the scarcity of food in the country. The abundance of fish at La Pointe has been noted, the whitefish at Michilimackinac were in astonishing numbers, and even to the present day the Great Lakes abound with fish. The countless streams are full of trout and the woods of game. The two Sulpicians had gone into this wilderness of anticipated hardships and had lived in a sportsman's paradise for six months, evidently much to their surprise, and they found the Jesuit mission very comfortably supplied. The Relations were by no means adapted to encourage immigration and that may help to account for their suppression a few years later. The two travellers left the Sault with hired guides on May 28 and arrived at Montreal on June 18, 1670, by way of the Ottawa River. The expedition did much to stimulate exploration. These two priests, not long out from France, had not only wintered in comfort and abundance, but had reached the extreme point of Jesuit missions and returned in safety.

Father Marquette, the sweet-souled hero of western discovery, had gone up to the Ottawa country in 1668 and in 1670 was at the Sault. From thence he went to the mission of St. Esprit at La Pointe. There the Illinois and other western and southern tribes fired his religious zeal by stories of the great water (Mississippi) and its teeming nations. The fugitive Hurons and Ottawas, who had settled at La Pointe and on the streams to the south, had been hospitably received by the Sioux; but, after a few years, growing arrogant with the possession of guns and iron weapons, they sought to drive their generous

EXPLORATION RESUMED

hosts away and obtain exclusive possession of the country. The indignant Sioux declared war, and with Indian ceremony before commencing hostilities, they sent back to Father Marquette all the religious pictures he had given them. The anger of that redoubtable nation—the Iroquois of the West—was too serious to face, and the Hurons and Ottawas, who never knew how to be quiet, had again to fly. Some beginning of a mission seems to have been made in 1670, probably by Father Allouez, upon the Island of Michilimackinac, and thither in 1671 went Marquette with the retreating Hurons. Father André with the Ottawas went to the Manitoulin Islands.

Michilimackinac is the name of a region, as well as of an island, and much confusion has arisen in consequence. It is applied properly to the holy island of Algonquin mythology in the middle of the strait leading out of Lake Michigan, and also to the northern and southern points of land which form the strait. Of late the northern point has been called Ancient Michilimackinac and the southern point Old Mackinac. It is a convenient distinction. In 1671 Father Marquette moved from the island to the north point of the strait and founded there the mission of St. Ignace. It was a more convenient location because a trail led directly across the peninsula to the mission at the Sault. At St. Ignace he erected a chapel and a mission post, and soon two villages gathered on either side, one of Hurons and the other of Algonquins. It speedily became the most important rendezvous of the fur trade in the Northwest and was besides the head of four missions. La Motte Cadillac was sent there by Frontenac as governor in 1694, but in 1701 he founded Detroit and, as he drew thither most of the Indians, Michilimackinac lost much of its importance. The French Government, in one of its fits of contraction, withdrew the garrison and no one was left there but a pack of wood-rangers (*coureurs de bois*) and traders who, being under no control, made a pandemonium of the place. There was not a Christian Indian left and the Frenchmen were a disgrace to the name. The scandalised missionaries, in 1705, set fire to their church and residence and retired in disgust to Quebec, and the post of Ancient Michilimackinac on the north side—St. Ignace of Marquette—was abandoned. This aroused the governor, Vaudreuil, and he persuaded Father Marest to return to the mission the following year and sent an officer, De Louvigny, to restore order. In 1712 the cold fit of the French court having passed off, orders were given to restore the post, and De Louvigny was sent up with a garrison. Then the fort was built on the south point, now known as Old Mackinac, or simply Mackinac, and that was the post given over to the English at the cession. If then La Hontan or Hennepin, or any other writer previous to 1712 be referred to, Michilimackinac means the point on the north still known as St. Ignace or Ancient Michilimackinac. If the reference be to Charlevoix' works, Henry's Travels, Pontiac's War, or any other matter later, the south point of the strait or Old Mackinac will be meant. That fort, was, however, also abandoned, and in 1780 the English built a fort upon the island. The last was the Fort Michilimackinac taken by the Canadians in 1812 and held until the close of the war, and it is now the only place known by the name. Thus the fact that the maps in Charlevoix' Travels and later works, place the fort and mission on the south point is reconciled with the earlier maps of Hennepin and La Hontan. Again it is clear that the fort and the mission on the south point were not identical, although there was a chapel inside the palisades. When the mission moved to the south shore, it was fixed about twenty miles westward from the fort, at a place across the point of land called L'Arbre Croche. On Charlevoix' map they are separately shown, and Henry, who was there in 1761, makes the matter very plain. The mission was at the Ottawa village of L'Arbre Croche and the missionary's house was halfway between it and the fort. These changes and the extended application of the name have led to much dispute.

The French Government had now adopted a definite policy concerning Canada and, in 1670, the Intendant

Talon prepared to take, on behalf of the French crown, full and formal possession of all the region of the western lakes together with the avenues opening up from them leading, as was confidently thought, in some way to the Great South Sea. Acting under his instructions, Daumont de St. Lusson went up the country and, while he was wintering on the Manitoulin Islands, Nicholas Perrot, who had been engaged as interpreter, was sent round the Indian country to summon representatives to attend the ceremony. The great assembly was held at the Sault Ste. Marie, upon a hill overlooking the Indian village, and nothing was omitted which might impress the minds of the savages. The principal chiefs of the Pottawatomies, Sacs, Winnebagoes, Menomonees, Foxes, Mascoutins, Kickapoos and Miamis were there from Lake Michigan. The Crees and Ojibways from the north, the Nipissings, the Beavers and many other tribes, fourteen in all, were represented. The Saulteurs were at home there, and the Hurons and Ottawas gave in their adhesion later; for they were engaged at that time in escaping from the Sioux, whom their insolence had provoked. The French were represented by the Jesuit fathers Dablon, Allouez, Druillettes, and André. Jolliet was present, and many others, traders and interpreters. A cross was erected and blessed, with all the ceremonies of the church, and the *Vexilla Regis prodeunt* was chanted by all the Frenchmen present—an ancient hymn of the Roman Church, familiar in English hymbooks as

> The Royal Banners forward go,
> The Cross shines forth with mystic glow.

Then, below the cross, an escutcheon bearing the arms of France was raised upon a cedar pole, and all chanted *Exaudiat*—the twentieth Psalm in Latin, the equivalent of the English " God Save the King." The Procès Verbal was then read, followed by shouts of *Vive la Roi* and a general discharge of fire-arms. Father Allouez then addressed the Indians in their own language and, with skilful ease, employed their own rhetorical style. He told them of the powerful King of France, who had ten thousand captains as great as the Governor of Quebec, who had beaten the Iroquois, and of the enormous number of his troops and ships. He pictured the air ablaze with his cannons, and the King, covered with the blood of his enemies, riding in the middle of his squadrons. He told them that the King ordered so many to be slain that he kept no count of the number of scalps, but only that the blood flowed in rivers. The salient points of this edifying discourse are preserved in the Relation of 1671. St. Lusson then followed in a less flowery style, and set forth the meaning of the ceremony, and told the assembled nations that they were all under the protection of this great King across the sea, of whom they had just heard. Then the *Te Deum* was chanted and a grand fusillade closed the proceedings. The Indians were profoundly impressed. The formal ceremony, the rich vestments of the priests, the chanting, the firing, and the shouting appealed to their innate love of ceremonial, and, in the sermon of Father Allouez and St. Lusson's address, with Perrot's embellishments in interpretation, they carried away matter for narration and discussion at the lodge fires of many tribes for long years to come. In such manner did France enter into possession of the head-waters of the great valleys of the St. Lawrence and Mississippi.

CHAPTER XX

JOLLIET AND LA SALLE—THE MISSISSIPPI VALLEY UNVEILED

THE period of Catholic puritanism passed away with the arrival of the troops, and men and women, being relieved of fear for their scalps, became less anxious concerning their souls. One of the pious sisters writes: "The golden age is over—the officers and soldiers have ruined the vineyard of the Lord." On the 10th of January, 1667, there was a ball at Quebec—the first ball. "God grant," prays the "Journal" of the Jesuit fathers, "that it may not be a precedent." Maisonneuve, the belated crusader who led a forlorn hope to found the city of Montreal in the debatable land, was retired to France in 1665—an impossible person under the new conditions. There was, however, no relaxation of orthodoxy. Huguenots might indeed go to Canada and pass through and trade in it, but they could not assemble to practise "their false religion," nor settle down to permanent residence. There was no attempt at persecution, although there were many of the reformed religion in the country.

The peace had opened up all routes to the upper lakes, and the active and capable intendant, Talon, together with Courcelles and Frontenac, the successive governors, thought of nothing so much as to develop the fur trade, discover the mines of copper in the far West, and open up the country in its full extent. The great river of the West had indeed been long since discovered near its mouth by Hernando de Soto, but the importance of his discovery was not recognised. The knowledge had been practically lost, and the Mississippi had been confused, upon the Spanish maps, with other large rivers falling into the Gulf of Mexico. Chouart and Radisson had, indeed, reached its upper waters, but they had not appreciated the magnitude of the river. That had been gradually revealed by the reports of the Indians who congregated at La Pointe and the Sault on Lake Superior, and at Green Bay on Lake Michigan. Father Dablon, in the Relation of 1671, gave a general review of the geography of the West which displays considerable knowledge of the great river and the Indians upon its upper reaches. He was in doubt, however, whether it discharged into the Gulf of Mexico or into the Vermilion Sea. Talon was determined to know its real outlet, and recommended Jolliet to Frontenac, the newly arrived governor, as the most suitable person for that purpose.

Jolliet was a Canadian by birth, born in Quebec in 1645, and had already been up to Lake Superior. While free from those salient peculiarities which are often associated with genius, he was endowed with great courage and enterprise tempered by good nature and common sense. He had been well educated by the Jesuits in Quebec, for he had intended to enter their order, and, indeed, had taken some preliminary steps towards the priesthood; but the woods and streams called him, and he adopted the life of an explorer and trader. His knowledge of mathematics was considerable, and after Franquelin's death he became royal hydrographer. On returning from his western explorations he married, in 1675, Claire, daughter of François Bissot, a Quebec merchant who had obtained the concession of an immense extent of coast on the north shore of the gulf. This drew his energies eastward, and in 1679 he explored the country up the Saguenay as far as Hudson's Bay. For this and for his western discoveries the Island of Anticosti was granted to him. He had an extensive fishing establishment on that island, and its destruction by the English impoverished him. He died poor, and the place of his death is unknown. It is supposed to have been somewhere on the Labrador coast. No explorer in Canada covered so extensive a field—from the Mississippi on the west to Hudson's Bay on the north and Labrador on the east.

Paul de Chomedey, Sieur de Maisonneuve, Founder of Montreal

JOLLIET AND LA SALLE 343

Frontenac had hardly arrived in Canada, in the autumn of 1672, when Jolliet was despatched on his memorable voyage. He reached Michilimackinac on December 8, 1672, and found Father Marquette (who had been designated as his companion) at the mission of St. Ignace. It was a happy combination, for Jolliet was a favourite of the Jesuits, and Marquette, ever since he had gone to La Pointe, had dreamed of such an expedition. He had been studying the Illinois dialect, and during the winter of 1672-73 he and Jolliet made plans and gathered information for the voyage. On May 17, 1673, they started with five men. It was a slight outfit for so important an enterprise, and the traders and Indians who thronged the sandy shore of the cove to see them off watched with doubtful minds as the two slight bark canoes rounded Point St. Ignace to the right and turned into the broad waters of Lake Michigan. The course was westwards until Green Bay was reached, where it turned to the southwest, and halfway up the bay Marquette stopped to preach to the Folles Avoines, or Menomonees, whose name still clings to the river which bounds Wisconsin on the northeast. The "wild oats" which formed their chief food grows abundantly in the marshes and in the shallow watercourses and innumerable small lakes of the Northwest. All the tribes of that region (Wisconsin and Minnesota) use it for food, but the French met it first in extensive use with this tribe. They were an Algonquin people, as indeed were all the surrounding nations excepting the Winnebagoes, and Marquette was master of all the dialects of Algonquin speech.

The voyagers continued their way to the Fox River at the head of the bay—a river with many falls and rapids, utilised in our day for many large mills. Allouez had already founded the mission of St. François Xavier at the first rapid of the ascent, still called De Père, from the fact that the Jesuit fathers' chapel was erected there. They made no stay, but pushed on to the town of the Mascoutins, the extreme limit up to that time reached by the French missionaries. Three nations, the Miamis, the Kickapoos, and the Mascoutins, dwelt there in harmony, and there the good father was encouraged by finding a large cross which Allouez, his predecessor, had planted in the middle of the town, and to which the natives had attached votive offerings. The Mascoutins are usually called, in the old French narratives, "the Fire Nation" (*Nation de Feu*) by a philological mistake similar to that pointed out in the case of the Puants. The real signification of the name is "prairie" nation, for in their country the French came upon the open prairie land. The word for fire, in Algonquin, is similar in sound to that for land bare of trees. A council was held and the voyagers stated the object of their visit and asked for guides. Two Miami Indians were given them, and on June 10 the Frenchmen resumed their journey up the Fox River. Through the maze of marshes and little lakes at the head of the Fox their guides led them to a point only twenty-seven hundred paces distant from an elbow of the Wisconsin, where that river turns to the southwest. The place is now occupied by a town called Portage, which extends to both streams. The savages helped them across with their baggage and canoes, and saw them safely away to the southwest, alone on their adventurous journey. The country was very beautiful and moose and deer were numerous; but all their skill as canoemen was taxed, for the river, though wide and quiet, abounded with sandy shallows. After paddling about forty leagues the two canoes glided out into the broad Mississippi at a place now marked by the town of Prairie du Chien.

The voyagers were now over the threshold of the great central basin of the continent and were floating on the current of a grand and beautiful stream—floating southwards—but whither? Was it to the Vermilion Sea (Gulf of California), as Frontenac told Jolliet would be probable, or to the Gulf of Mexico? It was necessary to know, for profound and far-reaching results would follow if this were indeed an avenue to the great South Sea and the spice islands of Cathay.

It is not within the scope of this volume to follow the

wondering Frenchmen down the ever broadening river of the West; nor to dwell upon the bands of bison and flocks of turkeys which took the place of the game of the St. Lawrence valley. They noticed the great river from the west, known afterwards as the Missouri, and the stream from the east, which La Salle knew as the Ohio. They began to think the river they were floating on would carry them to the Gulf of Mexico, but that great turbulent western stream they thought would surely lead them to the Vermilion Sea. They had no time to follow it up, for it was necessary first to ascertain the outflow of the Mississippi. They communicated with the Indians, whom they found to be Illinois, and they floated down from tribe to tribe, with many adventures, until they reached the river Akamsea (Arkansas), which they were told was ten days' journey from the sea. They took the latitude and concluded that they were not more than three days distant from the north shore of the Gulf of Mexico, into which they then became certain that the great river discharged. They knew that if they fell into the hands of Spaniards they would be imprisoned, or more likely killed, and the fruits of their discovery would be lost; so they turned their canoes northwards and soon found the difference between floating down the Mississippi and stemming its current. On the return voyage they learned from the Indians of a better route. They ascended the Illinois, and branching northwards into the Des Plaines River they came to the portage at the Chicago River—one of the cardinal points of the hydrography of the continent, for there the brim of the two great river basins is almost obliterated. On the west and south Lake Michigan is bounded by a low rim of rock which, in the glacial age, had been worn through and a channel had existed connecting the two great basins. In the course of ages the channel had been filled and the only barrier to the lake was a long, low ridge of glacial drift from six to ten feet higher than the lake level. The distance between the ridge and the lake margin varied, and between them the Chicago River flowed with a fork from the north and a fork from the south. These unite in the centre of the business part of the present city into a short stream, not a mile long, opening into the lake, and formed in early times a shelter harbour in the low, reedy marshland. There canoes bound to the southwest turned in from the lake to seek the portage. Dablon, in August, 1674, describing the place from Jolliet's lips, writes that it is a harbour very convenient for "receiving vessels and sheltering them from the wind." Jolliet and Marquette were on the return voyage northward, and followed up the Des Plaines to its nearest point of approach to the southern fork of the Chicago River, which would be at a place now known as Summit, about four miles outside the city limits. The distance across the portage varied with the season from four to nine miles, and in a wet season it might even be possible to paddle a canoe from one water to another, for the south fork of the Chicago River rises in a swamp which communicates with the Des Plaines. Many changes have resulted from the making and winning of land in building a great city, but such were the natural features of the site before the city was founded. Jolliet's account of it is in Father Dablon's narrative. He writes again: " We could go with facility to Florida in a barque and with very easy navigation. It would only be necessary to make a canal by cutting through but half a league of prairie to pass from the foot of the lake of Illinois [Michigan] to the river St. Louis [Des Plaines]." Jolliet's idea has been carried out during the last few years in the great Sanitary and Ship Canal connecting the south fork of the Chicago River with the Des Plaines River at the present town of Joliet, and the curious traveller may see, in the heart of the great city which strides across the portage, the water running in a steady current from the lake a mile behind him towards the Gulf of Mexico, sixteen hundred miles distant. In 1673 the seven Frenchmen carried their canoes over the low ridge and launched them into St. Lawrence water, bearing with them the secret of the West.

From the Chicago portage the voyagers pursued their way along the shore of Lake Michigan. Once more they lifted their canoes from the water to cross the portage at Sturgeon Bay and cut off the promontory which forms the eastern side of Green Bay. At last, after 2800 miles of travel, they arrived at the first rapids of the Fox River—at the mission station of St. François Xavier. It was late in September—too late to go down to Quebec that year, and the travellers needed rest. Marquette had in the meantime been transferred to this station and had reached the end of his journey. It was well; for the hardships he had gone through had implanted the beginnings of the disease which was soon to carry him off. Jolliet was eager to report to Frontenac at Quebec, but now there was nothing to be done but to rest and prepare an account of their discoveries. In the spring of 1674 Jolliet started, but his canoe upset in going down the Lachine Rapids, near Montreal, and all his maps and papers were lost. With difficulty he escaped. His crew and a young Indian he was bringing down were drowned. Father Marquette's report and map were sent in usual course to his Superior, and have survived. It is upon those records that authentic knowledge of the details of the voyage rests.

The remaining life of the gentle-souled Jesuit was short. All through the summer of 1674 he struggled with disease, but in October he thought he was well enough to start for the Illinois country, where he intended to found a mission. The winter set in and his progress was slow. It was December before he reached the Chicago portage, and there he had to spend the winter in a little hut erected by his attendants. In the spring of 1675 he succeeded in reaching the chief town of the Illinois tribe where, to the assembled people, he preached the Gospel with great power and with the earnestness of a man whose end was near. Then he set his face homewards to the mission of St. Ignace of Michilimackinac and his men followed up the eastern shore of the lake to avail themselves of the northward current. When his time drew near they stopped at the mouth of a river where now stands the city of Ludington, and his attendants put up a slight shelter of bark, under which they placed the dying priest. About midnight he passed away. His men heard his voice in the darkness, as he gave thanks that he had been permitted to die as a missionary of the Gospel of Christ to the heathen. Without a struggle, his last sleep came quietly upon him, and in the morning his men buried him there in the forest wilderness on the lake shore and marked his grave with a cross. He was not forgotten; for a year later some Kiskakon Indians, hunting on the shores of the lake, went to see the grave of "their father." They disinterred the body, and after the custom of their people dissected and washed the bones and dried them in the sun, and reverently, as if of a dead kinsman, placed them in a box of bark. Other Indians joined them and a procession of thirty canoes carried the remains of the priest to the resting place of his choice on the Strait of Michilimackinac and delivered them to Fathers Nouvel and Pierson. They were buried on June 9, 1677, in the chapel he had built. Thirty years after, when, as has been related, the station was abandoned, all the buildings, including the church, were burned lest they should be desecrated, and when a new establishment was ordered it was made upon the opposite side of the strait. In the stir of trade and military activity which followed, the site of the old mission was neglected and the landmarks forgotten until, in recent years, St. Ignace became a railway town and an intelligent interest in its past history arose. In 1877 the foundations of Marquette's church were discovered, and in a vault the bark casket was found containing the remains brought by the savages two hundred years before. An insignificant pillar with an inscription was erected to mark the spot and a small square surrounds it, open to the sandy beach where the canoes were pulled up in early days. Opposite the Island of Michilimackinac is in full view; across the strait, on the right, is the site of the second fort and mission and the main channel to Lake Huron, and to the left the coast leads along the Detour passage into Lake Superior. It is a quiet spot, only disturbed when the huge ferryboat arrives to transfer a railway train across the strait.

Father Marquette, so far as the respect and sympathy of the West can extend, is already canonised; but the pilgrim to St. Ignace de Michilimackinac must content himself with the natural features of the place, for although

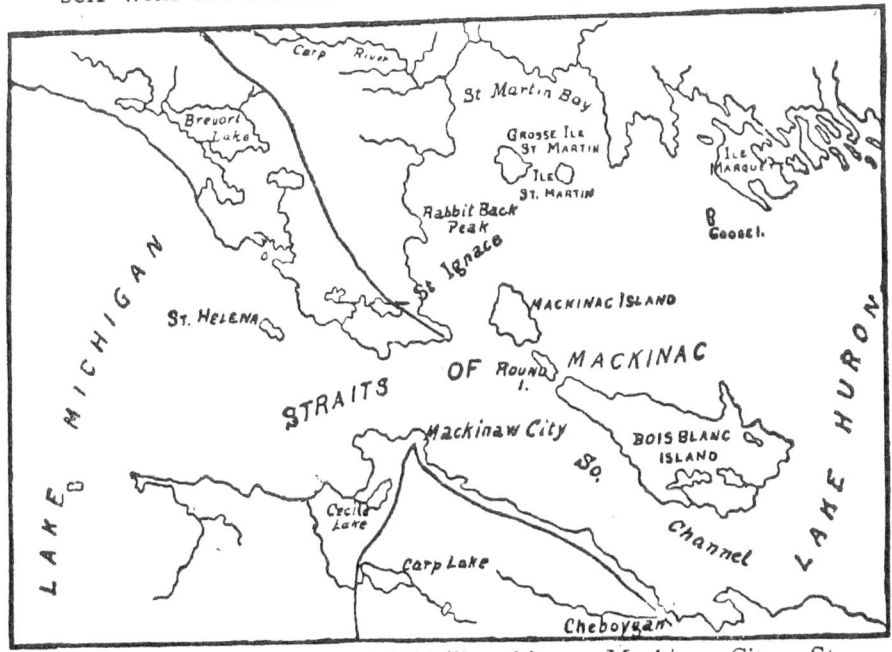

Sketch Map of Strait of Michilimackinac. Mackinac City. St. Ignace = Ancient Michilimackinac = Old Mackinac. Mackinac Island = Michilimackinac, where the present Fort is situated. See p. 337.

the inscription on the little monument asserts that it covers the relics of the good priest, the assertion is not generally accepted to its full extent. A high authority states that some of the relics are shown at the Jesuit college named after Marquette, in Milwaukee. Popular imagination loves to adorn the memory of its favourites, and although Jolliet was the chief of the expedition, his leadership has been obscured by veneration for the humble and saintly Jesuit and sympathy for his early death.

It has already been related that when Jolliet was on his way down from his voyage with Péré to Lake Superior in search of copper mines, he met at the portage from the head of Lake Ontario to the Grand River the party of Sulpician priests in company with La Salle, and that La Salle, under the pretext of illness, turned back. That incident was the beginning of a series of independent enterprises which completed the exploration and definition of the St. Lawrence basin on the southwest.

In the year 1667 Robert Cavelier, better known from a property he held in France as La Salle or de La Salle, arrived in Canada. He was of a good Norman merchant family. His brother, Abbé Jean Cavelier, was at the time in Canada as a priest of the Seminary of St. Sulpice at Montreal. La Salle was well educated, for he had intended to enter the Jesuit order and had been trained in their schools, but had changed his mind and determined to seek his fortune at Montreal—then the portal of western adventure. He was only twenty-three years old, but his character was formed—self-reliant, proud, reticent, persevering, and indomitable. No enterprise appalled him by its magnitude and no complication of misfortune could crush him. He was not amiable, nor had he the power of attaching men to himself by sympathy, or of awakening enthusiasm in his followers; yet he won the respect of the Indians and was the object of the unbounded friendship and fidelity of one Frenchman to so remarkable a degree that to find a parallel to the devotion of Henri de Tonty to La Salle we must go back to the history of Jonathan and David. The distrustful and taciturn La Salle was no David, yet he had the power of impressing men high in rank with the importance of his schemes. In carrying out his plans, however, he had not the necessary personal magnetism which secures obedience, fidelity, and aid, for no man can carry out a great enterprise singlehanded. The fickleness apprehended by Galinée at the commencement of the voyage was rather intractability than inconstancy.

La Salle was a favourite of the Seminary of St. Sulpice,

JOLLIET AND LA SALLE 351

and as seigneurs of the island of Montreal they gave him, in the year of his arrival, a grant of land west of the city, just at the head of the rapids—Sault St. Louis, or Lachine Rapids of to-day. There was at that time no road, save the trail beside the river, and there were no settlers. It was prairie on the lower level, and where the land rises at the entrance to the present canal the forest came down to the waterside. La Salle commenced clearing, built a house for himself and obtained a few settlers; but the broad avenue of Lake St. Louis led his thoughts far away into the mysterious west. Some Seneca Indians stayed with him during the winter of 1668-69 and told him of the Ohio, a great and beautiful river of the West accessible from their country. The course of his life was decided. He disposed of all his property and improvements and applied the proceeds to a new enterprise. He presented to the Governor, De Courcelles, his plan of exploration, and the Governor persuaded him to join his expedition to that of Dollier de Casson and Galinée. The united party started from the lake shore opposite his own seigniory on July 6, 1669.

It is clear that at the start all were of one mind and that their object was to discover the Ohio of the Senecas. For that reason they went straight to Irondequoit Bay, near the Genessee River, and to the chief town of the Senecas. It is also clear that at the portage where they met Jolliet MM. Dollier and Galinée changed their minds, while the defection of La Salle indicates that his purpose was unaltered. The Ohio of his aim was not in the direction whence Jolliet had come, but was a river which took its rise three days' journey from the chief town of the Senecas. They parted on the last day of September, 1669, and from that time until August 6, 1671, when he signed a notarial deed at Montreal, La Salle's movements are unrecorded and unknown. Some of his men deserted and returned to Montreal, and from that day the seigniory of La Salle was called Lachine (China), in derision, and the name extends to the whole town and parish to this day—an unconscious tribute to the memory of a great explorer. In this interval of unrecorded activity the discovery was made which some have maintained to have been the Mississippi, but which beyond all reasonable doubt was the Ohio.

That controversy should ever have arisen on a matter so plain is one of the many unaccountable things in American history. La Salle never claimed the discovery of the Mississippi; nor did his patron Frontenac ever claim it for him. On the contrary, in Frontenac's despatch to the French Government, dated November 14, 1674, he reported that Jolliet had recently returned and had discovered a great river flowing from north to south, and had followed it to within a few days' journey of the Gulf of Mexico, and had sent a map of the country discovered. All the contemporaneous maps are clear upon the point and subsequent vague expressions of detraction cannot weigh against the mass of positive evidence. No amount of speculative argument can dispose of the fact, recorded in the registers at Quebec, that in 1680 the intendant, Duchesneau, and the governor, Frontenac, concurred in a grant to Jolliet of the Island of Anticosti in consideration of this very discovery "which the said Sieur Jolliet has made of the country of the Illinois, whereof he has given us the plan on which was drawn the map which we sent two years ago to Monseigneur Colbert." Although Jolliet's first maps and papers were lost, he presented a map to Frontenac in 1674, showing his discoveries. The Mississippi is called La Rivière Buade, after Frontenac's family name. The chief facts are set forth upon the map in a signed letter. There are several later maps by Jolliet extant, on some of which the discovery of the Ohio is ascribed to La Salle. These are dedicated to Colbert. An official memoir, attached to a despatch from M. de Denonville to the French government on November 6, 1687, states the real facts simply and precisely as they have been elucidated after long controversy. "The year after, in 1672, the Mississippi river was discovered, as well as the Illinois Chaounanons and other tribes unknown to the Europeans by Sieur Jolliet

JOLLIET AND LA SALLE

and the Jesuit Father Marquette, who reached the thirty-second degree, planting the Royal arms and taking over, in the king's name, the newly discovered countries. A few years later Sieur de La Salle pushed his discoveries farther onward, as far as the sea, taking possession everywhere by planting the Royal Arms." The subject is exhaustively discussed by Parkman ("Discovery of the Great West"), and Harrisse ("Notes pour servir") summarises the question conclusively. It is not, however, necessary to suppose with Parkman that La Salle, after turning back, went to Onondaga to get guides to the portages from Lake Erie. The Genessee River flows through the Seneca country, and from it there is a portage to the head-waters of the Allegheny, which at the "Forks" unites with the Monongahela to form the Ohio. This last was the river "three days' journey distant," which the Senecas described to La Salle. It was the route of Iroquois war parties to the southwest. As Harrisse tacitly intimates, it was not necessary to go to Lake Erie to reach the Ohio. All the available evidence goes to show that La Salle on that occasion went down the Ohio as far only as the falls at the present Louisville, and that he did not reach the "great river"—the Mississippi.

As has been shown, La Salle was certainly back in 1671 from his obscure voyage; for in August of that year he was raising money in Montreal. He must have been concerned in new enterprises connected with the fur trade, for he was again in Montreal on December 16, 1672, signing an obligation to make certain payments either in cash or in furs. We may conceive of his spending time also in acquiring the Indian languages and in maturing his ambitious scheme for opening up the West.

The new governor, the Count de Frontenac, arrived in the autumn of 1672 and in him La Salle found a spirit responsive to any daring enterprise. The scheme which was visionary to the merchants of Montreal and Quebec was sober reason to Frontenac, and in 1673, while Jolliet and Marquette were on their journey to the Mississippi, Frontenac took the first step by building a fort at the outlet of Lake Ontario on the site of the present city of Kingston. He had acted on the recommendation of La Salle in selecting the site, and early in the spring had sent him to Onondaga to invite the Iroquois chiefs to meet him in council at the site selected. The governor went up the river with an escort of four hundred men and with a military pomp and circumstance which deeply impressed the Indians. Sixty of the leading chiefs of the Iroquois confederacy attended the council. The territory was theirs and they knew well the importance of the move; but Frontenac carried them by imposing ceremonies; and partly by blandishments, partly by effrontery, disarmed their opposition. The fort was traced by his engineers and half built before the speeches were over. La Salle, who became a firm partisan of the governor, was left in command. He was now established in an important trading post on the margin of the West, and it became evident that his plans would interfere with the business of the merchants of Quebec and Montreal and traverse the designs of the Jesuit fathers. Hence arose a bitter and sometimes unscrupulous opposition, which in the end thwarted his enterprise.

The following year La Salle, provided with strong recommendations from Frontenac, went to France, and in 1675 he was successful in obtaining a patent of nobility and a grant of the seigniory of Fort Frontenac upon the condition, among others, of repaying the cost of its establishment. All the conditions were faithfully carried out; a nucleus of settlers began to form, bands of Indians began to resort to the post, Recollet friars were stationed there to attend to their spiritual needs (for neither La Salle nor Frontenac liked the Jesuits), and vessels began to appear upon the lake. A firm basis for advance was established.

It was time for the next step, and in the autumn of 1677 La Salle again went to France upon the advice of the governor. He succeeded in enlisting the support of Colbert, Seignelay, the Prince de Conti, and other influential noblemen, and obtained authority to establish, at his own cost and risk, not only two, but as many posts in the West as he wished. He made large purchases of goods for the Indian trade, and in July, 1678, sailed from La Rochelle in company with Henri de Tonty, whom the Prince de Conti had strongly recommended as his lieutenant. No time was lost after his return. La Motte was sent on in November to the Niagara River to build a fort, and with him was Father Hennepin, one of the Recollet friars stationed at Fort Frontenac. At the end of the year La Salle arrived. He succeeded in obtaining the consent of the Seneca tribe for the fort he purposed building, but not without much difficulty, for his enemies had sown suspicion in their minds.

We have seen that, on account of the long-continued hostility of the Iroquois, communication with the West had been carried on by way of the Ottawa, and although the existence of a great fall interrupting navigation between lakes Erie and Ontario was known, there is nothing on record to show that such knowledge had any other basis than Indian report. Hennepin was the first European to describe the Falls of Niagara. There have been changes since his day, made by the retrocession continually going on, but Hennepin's description is fairly correct save that his ill-regulated imagination interpolated three mountains into the locality and exaggerated the height of the fall to over six hundred feet. It is really 158 feet on the Canadian and 167 on the American side. At that cardinal point the entire drainage water of the upper St. Lawrence basin falls to the lower plain over an escarpment stretching across the country to Lake Huron. The waters, in the erosion of long ages, have eaten away the rock and have formed a ravine or trough now seven miles in length back from the edge of the escarpment. Hennepin supplements his description by a bird's-eye view of the falls and the upper level of country as far as Lake Erie. It is drawn from memory, and he has placed the *Griffon* on the distant Lake Erie, but nevertheless the drawing conveys a fair, if rough, idea of the locality and proves that he really saw it. The party landed on the eastern or American side, and passing a few miles up the river erected a storehouse near the present Lewiston at the foot of the escarpment; not, however, without having first examined the opposite, or Canadian, side as far up as the Chippewa River. If anything had previously been known of the place there would have been no need of prospecting for the shortest and most convenient portage.

La Salle, with Tonty, sailed in a brigantine from Fort Frontenac late in December, 1678. His iron determination sought to overrule all inclemencies of season. He passed by the south shore to make a conciliatory visit to the Iroquois. He got from them permission to build a vessel on the upper lake, to carry supplies over the Niagara portage, and under the pretext of erecting a blacksmith's forge to build a fort at the mouth of the river. Proceeding onwards his vessel got becalmed, and impatient at the delay he and Tonty landed and proceeded on foot. The vessel was wrecked in a sudden storm and all the supplies but the anchors for the projected ship were lost. It was the first of a long series of misfortunes. La Salle's enemies were already beginning to corrupt his men.

Shortly after his arrival La Salle selected a suitable place above the falls to build his vessel. The controversy which at one time existed as to the precise locality of his shipyard was decided by the research of Mr. O. H. Marshall, of Buffalo. Halfway between Tonawanda and the town of Niagara Falls a small stream called Cayuga Creek falls into the Niagara River, and at its mouth is a small, low island (Cayuga Island) separated from the shore by a narrow channel of the main river, locally called the " little river," into which the creek discharges. The little village at the place is now called La Salle. It is at the foot of Grand Island in a spot where the water is quiet, being sheltered by Grand Island and Cayuga Island, from the main current of the river. There stocks were prepared, trees were felled in the adjoining forest, planks and timbers were sawn and shaped, and on January 26, 1679, was laid the keel of the first

Notman Photo. Montreal

Niagara, from Falls View

ship to sail upon the upper lakes. Within the memory of old residents the spot has been known as "the old shipyard," for the United States Government in the early part of the nineteenth century built some vessels there for service on the upper lakes. It was on the mainland just above the mouth of the creek. In May the vessel was launched and named the *Griffon* and floated in the Cayuga channel, safe from the jealousy of the suspicious Senecas, who had attempted to set her on fire. At her prow was a carved griffin, for the supporters of the arms of Frontenac were griffins, and five small cannon formed her armament. On August 7, 1679, she passed out into Lake Erie and spread her sails over its almost unknown waters.

The loss of the brigantine had seriously interfered with La Salle's plans, and as soon as the construction of the *Griffon* was well under way he left his faithful lieutenant in charge, and in the depth of winter, with only two men as attendants and a dog to draw his baggage, started on snowshoes for Fort Frontenac to arrange for supplies to replace the outfit lost in the wrecked vessel. These, as soon as the lake opened, were sent forward in another brigantine and carried up the steep and long portage. It was a weary and laborious task, but at last everything was ready. La Salle, Hennepin, and another Recollet friar, thirty-two of a crew in all, were on board, as, with a salvo of cannon and chanting *Te Deum,* they started on their voyage westward. On St. Clare's Day, August 12, they reached the shallow water of Lake St. Clair, and by careful sounding got through safely and launched out into Lake Huron, where they encountered a gale which staggered even the imperturbable La Salle. At last they reached Michilimackinac and dropped anchor in the quiet cove of St. Ignace. There the *Griffon* became the centre of a swarm of canoes, and the amazed savages of the two villages of Ottawas and Hurons were startled by the novel sound of cannon. The vessel proceeded on her course into Lake Michigan and anchored at one of the islands at the entrance of Green Bay. Here a quantity of furs had been collected by an advance party of La Salle's men, and, adding the furs collected by himself, he loaded all upon the *Griffon* and sent her back to appease his clamorous creditors. It was a fatal error, for the ship was never again heard of. Some trifling wreckage alone indicated that she had foundered in a gale which came on not long after her departure. The pilot was an incompetent who had already twice imperilled the ship. All on board perished, and with them went down the furs which would have satisfied La Salle's creditors—as well as all the surplus supplies sent back to be stored at Niagara. La Salle himself continued his voyage up the lake with four canoes and fourteen men, but before he had gone far he had to take refuge from the same storm in a small bay, where he was detained five days. Resuming his route he went up the lake and passing the Chicago portage went round by the south to the eastern shore, to the mouth of what Hennepin calls the Miami River, now known as the St. Joseph. There he waited until his party was reunited by the arrival of the detachment of Henri de Tonty. He passed the time in building a fort, called the Fort of the Miamis by Hennepin. It must be distinguished from a later fort of the same name built on the Maumee River at the portage to the Wabash—a shorter route by Lake Erie to the Mississippi, afterwards much frequented. His party being reassembled, La Salle started up the river on December 3, and after some difficulty found the portage at a place now known at South Bend in Indiana. It was about four miles long, over level and marshy ground, and led to the head springs of the Kankakee River—an affluent of the Illinois. Hennepin calls it the Illinois; but in later years that name was restricted to the river formed by the union of the Des Plaines from the Chicago portage with the Kankakee from the St. Joseph portage. Here they first met the buffalo of the western prairies.

The year drew to a close as they reached the chief town of the Illinois. It was deserted, for all the people were away hunting buffalo, and it was not until January

4, 1680, that they came upon an inhabited town on Peoria Lake. The Indians, at first hospitable, were soon alienated by Indian emissaries, instigated by La Salle's enemies. He therefore removed a short distance further down the river and erected a fort, which he called Crèvecœur,—Heartbreak,—a name expressive of the ruin which stared him in the face, for he now realised the fact that the *Griffon* was lost. In spite of the jealous reticence of the Illinois Indians, he obtained information that his canoes could, without interruption of fall or rapid, pass down the Illinois River to the Mississippi, and that the tribes on its banks were friendly and hospitable. He deputed one of his men, Accault, accompanied by Father Hennepin as chaplain, to explore the river down to its junction with the Mississippi; he himself would return to Montreal to stay his falling fortunes and procure fresh supplies, and Tonty would take command at Fort Crèvecœur. On February 29, 1680, Hennepin started with two companions and on March 2 La Salle with four Frenchmen and a Mohegan Indian, who had been faithful in all vicissitudes, set his face eastward.

To those who are familiar with the explorations of the Hudson's Bay Company's officers, and the long journeys they were, and are, accustomed to make on snowshoes in the conduct of their ordinary business, it will not be surprising that La Salle set out to go on foot from Lake Peoria in northern Illinois to Kingston at the outlet of Lake Ontario. The difficulty of La Salle's journey was not the length of the way, nor the snow; it was that the winter was breaking up, the ice was rotten, the snow was melting, the spring rains were commencing, the morasses were treacherous, and, above all, the route lay through a region infested by war parties of implacable Iroquois. Travelling is scarcely possible under such conditions, and if La Salle's resolution ever failed him, it might well have failed when he bade farewell to the staunch De Tonty in his isolated post. They tried in vain to work their canoes up the Illinois against the drifting ice, and were compelled to abandon them and make their way across the streams and marshes of the sodden prairie round the head of Lake Michigan to the fort at St. Joseph, where La Salle found two of his men. Thence he struck across the south of Michigan to the Detroit River. Crossing it on a raft, he pushed on across the country to Lake Erie, where he made a canoe in which he reached the fort at Niagara, where his worst forebodings of the loss of the *Griffon* were confirmed, and to crown his misfortunes he learned of the wreck, at the mouth of the St. Lawrence, of a vessel from France laden with supplies for his enterprise. He was the only one of the party in health, and, leaving his sick companions, he took two fresh men and reached Fort Frontenac, on May 6, from whence he pushed on to Montreal.

While he was procuring fresh supplies at Montreal his men in the West, not expecting his return, were deserting to the Indians, plundering his stores of furs and wrecking his forts. Tonty's garrison had been fifteen men, but during a short absence most of them deserted, and having only three left besides the two Recollets, he decided to go to live in the great Illinois village. Meanwhile the indomitable La Salle, with fresh supplies and fresh men, started from Fort Frontenac on August 10 to rebuild his shattered enterprises. Passing by way of Toronto, Lake Simcoe, and Georgian Bay, he reached Michilimackinac and hastened on to St. Joseph, where he found the fort plundered and wrecked by deserters from his own garrison. Crossing the portage and paddling down the river he found to his dismay that the Iroquois had swept over the country, and the ghastly evidences of their cruelty were everywhere visible. The Illinois tribes had disappeared, their great town had been burned, and mutilated bodies were scattered around. Fort Crèvecœur was abandoned and no written sign left to tell of De Tonty's fate. La Salle searched among the dead bodies with painful scrutiny, but no trace of the Frenchmen could be found. The skulls scattered round were not French, for the scanty hair which the Iroquois and the wolves had left was the long coarse hair of Indians. Leaving a small guard for the baggage, La Salle, with four men, proceeded down the river, and as he went on the circumstances of the catastrophe began to be unravelled. The Illinois had retreated in a body, followed on the opposite bank of the river by the Iroquois. La Salle searched the opposing camps and examined the remains of every victim at the stakes for traces of the Frenchmen, but in vain. At last he reached the Mississippi, seven years after Jolliet and Marquette; and although his men offered to follow him down the river he was compelled to return by the exigency of his affairs, for this new calamity wrecked his whole enterprise. The steadfast mind of La Salle, however, was unshaken. The winter was approaching and he turned back to the St. Joseph River. A happy chance led him to take the northern fork of the Illinois, the Des Plaines River, and on the Chicago portage the quick eyes of the woodsmen detected a faint but indubitable trace of the passage of De Tonty's men. La Salle, undismayed by misfortune, spent the winter on the St. Joseph River in organising the scattered tribes against a repetition of Iroquois invasion. The deadly wars had broken up the nations. There were bands of Abenaquis and Mohicans—strangers from the Atlantic, Shawnees from the Ohio, Miamis of the locality, and Illinois returning from beyond the Mississippi to their ruined towns. Then, in May, 1681, he once more turned his face eastwards to seek the means to renew once more his shattered fortunes. On the way, at Michilimackinac, he met De Tonty and with renewed hopes they started for Montreal. Once more Frontenac's influence availed on his behalf, and his wealthy relatives lent their aid, and, although powerful interests in the colony were opposed to his undertaking and had even instigated the bloody ravages of the Iroquois, his resolution triumphed over every obstacle; and, as the autumn began to colour the foliage, he was once more at the Toronto portage with a well-equipped party on his way to Fort Miami on the St. Joseph River.

Success at last was near. Frost had rendered the narrow stream of the upper Kankakee unavailable, for it was December 21, 1681, when they started from St. Joseph. The still open lake enabled them to use canoes as far as the Chicago portage, and as they had to carry their canoes over the snow on sledges the portages on the Des Plaines made no delay. At Lake Peoria they put their canoes into open water, and on February 6, 1682, they dipped their paddles into the "great water"— the Mississippi. The remainder of the story and the tragic death of the explorers do not belong to the history of the St. Lawrence valley, nor does the scope of this volume include the romantic story of the Rock of St. Louis of the Illinois, and of De Tonty's heroic devotion to his leader and friend. La Salle continued down the Mississippi to the sea. His party divided and followed the three great branches of its delta, and La Salle issued out upon the Gulf of Mexico. On April 9, 1682, a pillar was erected bearing the arms of Louis XIV. and possession was taken of the region with the usual formalities. The great problem was solved, the task was achieved, and from the chilly shadows of the cliffs of the Saguenay to the steaming lagoons of the delta of the Mississippi the whole magnificent avenue of waters passed into the possession of France.

CHAPTER XXI

WESTERN EXPLORATION OF THE ST. LAWRENCE BASIN COMPLETED—HENNEPIN AND DULHUT

THE northeastern part of the State of Minnesota must be attentively studied by those who seek to understand the ground plan of the North American continent east of the basin of the Mackenzie River and the ranges of the Rocky Mountains. It is a plain, nowhere more than fifteen hundred feet above the sea, studded with lakes innumerable, connected with each other by a mesh of streams of all grades of magnitude, which are fed by countless marshes from whose spongy recesses issue forth the infant springs of great rivers. There, within the area of a few square miles, separated by insensible inequalities of ground, flow and interflow the tiny rivulets which, as mighty floods, issue out on the north into Hudson's Bay, on the east into the Gulf of St. Lawrence, and on the south into the Gulf of Mexico. A mazy region where in a bark canoe, if he knows the country, a man may go anywhere; and if he does not know it he will be forthwith hopelessly lost. Indian reservations still cover much of the region, for it is unsuitable for settlement or cultivation. In the southeast corner of the White Earth Indian Reserve are the springs of the Mississippi, and close to them the brooks which lead into the Red River of the North take their rise. The main stream of the Red River flows from Lake Traverse south of the source of the Mississippi, and the Minnesota River has its source differing only eight feet in level in Bigstone Lake adjoining. On the east, not far off, the St. Louis River, the ultimate source of the St. Lawrence system, takes its rise—separated by an obscure water-parting and falling into Lake Superior at Fond du Lac. South of that lake large affluents of the Mississippi reach up close to its shores, spreading out fanlike into small streams, sufficient in a region where drought is unknown, to float a canoe.

The St. Croix draws its water thus from the region near Fond du Lac, the Chippewa reaches close to Chequamegon Bay, near Ashland, and the Flambeau River, one of its affluents, rises very near the head of the Montreal River, all three drain their waters into the great river of the West.

This region must not be supposed destitute of food resources. Apart from the fact that the Great Lakes were then, as they are still, the source of most productive fisheries, the streams were full of fish, and, moreover, the whole network of streams, marshes, and lakes were the reedy water-fields where the wild rice, *zizania aquatica*, chiefly delights to grow and the wild fowl delight to feed. The plant is known by many names. The French called it *Folle Avoine* or *riz du Canada;* the English, among many other names, wild oats, wild rice, Indian rice, Canadian rice; the Indians used some derivative of the Algonquin word *Manómin*, signifying "good berry." The region most abounding in this valuable article of food extended across Wisconsin to Lake Michigan, and the rivers and lakes between Green Bay and Lake Superior were covered with this graceful reedlike plant. It is an annual, self-sown from the ripe grain shed into the water of a sluggish or gently flowing stream and falling upon a muddy bottom. It grows abundantly anywhere in Canada or the Northwest where the conditions are favourable. Mrs. Traill, a writer resident near Rice Lake, not far from Peterborough in Ontario, describes the rice beds as looking in the distance like green islands. She thus writes of their appearance in June: " Passing through one of these rice beds, where the rice is in flower, it has a beautiful appearance, with its broad grassy leaves and light waving spikes garnished with pale yellow-green blossoms delicately shaded with red-

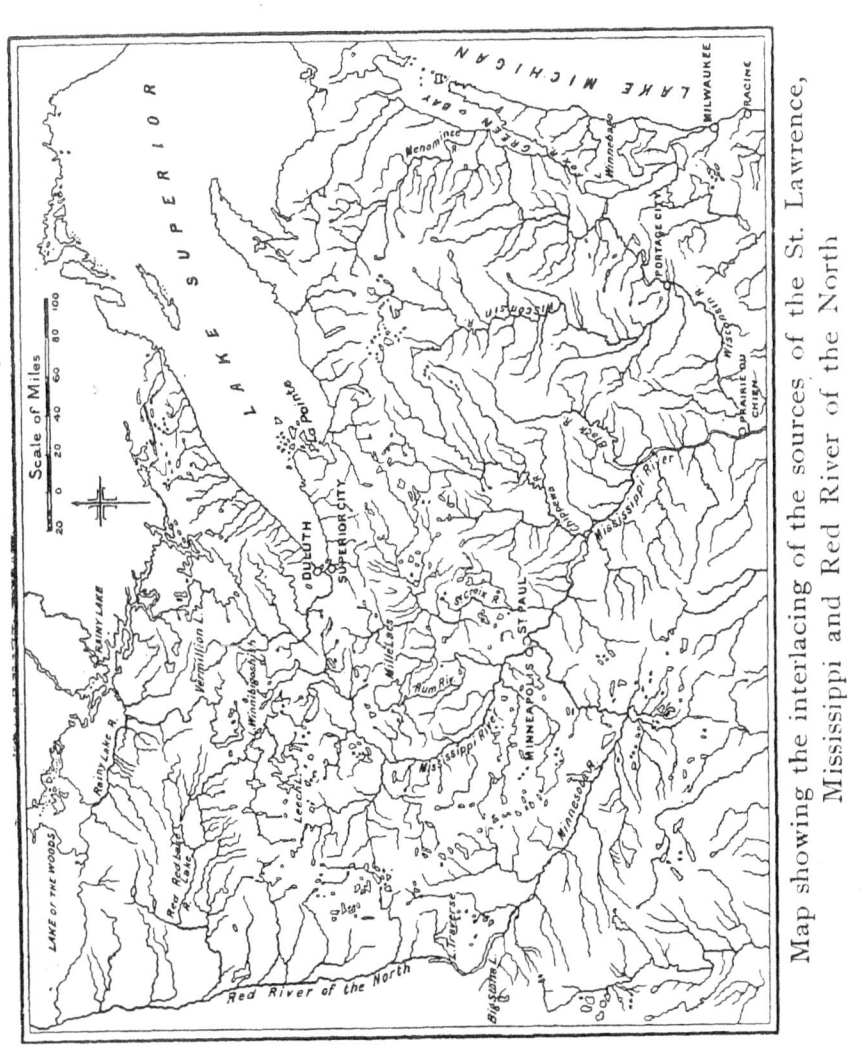

Map showing the interlacing of the sources of the St. Lawrence, Mississippi and Red River of the North

dish purple, from beneath which fall three straw-coloured anthers, which move with every breath of air or slightest motion of the water."

The Indians were not touched by such æsthetical considerations, and to them the possession of these rice fields was an economical question of prime importance, and on that account the Sioux (or Dakotas) contended incessantly with the Ojibways and Menomonees. The last-named people are the *Folles Avoines* of the French narratives, and their river, still called the Menominee, reaches far into the rice-producing region. As a food the wild rice is fully as nourishing as maize, or wheat, or any other of our cereals. It is collected by the women, who pole their bark canoes into the rice fields when the grain is ripe, and reaching out draw over the heads, on both sides, and beat out the grain into the canoe. It was the explorations of Nicollet, Radisson, Jolliet, Marquette, Allouez, and Perrot on the borders of this region which brought to the knowledge of the French the rice fields and the populous tribes dependent upon them for a large part of their food supply. The region extended over the divide between the St. Lawrence and Mississippi waters, and was the scene of the captivity of Hennepin and the enterprise of Dulhut.

We have seen that at the end of February, 1680, Father Hennepin started with two companions in a bark canoe from Fort Crèvecœur to explore the Illinois River to its junction with the Mississippi. He also had instructions, after reaching the great river, to explore its upper course. This he did, and in his first book he claims no more; but in his second book, published in 1698, he lays claim to the discovery and exploration of the Mississippi southwards to the sea, giving several palpably false reasons for having suppressed his claim until after La Salle's death. It is unnecessary to dwell upon the character of this vain and mendacious friar. His frauds have been sufficiently exposed. Not only did he claim to have preceded La Salle in exploring the river to the sea, but he asserts that Jolliet had not been upon the river at all, and had merely contented himself with remaining and trading among the Ottawas and Hurons. He represents Jolliet as having admitted this to him upon frequent canoe voyages they had made together—all of which is not only palpably false, but is glossed over with a disagreeable religiosity. Hennepin's discoveries extend from the mouth of the Wisconsin River to the Falls of St. Anthony, or, in more familiar terms, from Prairie du Chien to Minneapolis—and no farther. The expedition was really under the command of Accault, one of his two companions, although throughout the narrative Hennepin represents himself as having been the leader.

The voyage down the Illinois River was made without any incident of note. The current was gentle and the stream was deep. It flowed between low banks through a prairie country, where large herds of buffalo were seen feeding. On arriving at the Mississippi they found the ice still coming down, and were delayed until March 12, although in another place he stretches the time out four days more.

With unblushing effrontery Hennepin, in his second book, asserts that before going north he turned southwards and went to the mouth of the Mississippi. From the mouth of the Illinois it is a distance of 1293 miles to New Orleans, to which must be added the distance to the sea, which, although less then than it is now, could not have been less than 75 miles. To do this he must have paddled at the rate of over one hundred miles a day, and without stopping to sleep or eat. He states that he came to where the river forms a delta, and that he passed down the centre channel to a point where the water was completely salt, and that, passing further on, he reached the sea and finally landed on the east side at the mouth of the river. This point he attained on March 25. Then the details are added of the formal possession taken. The two men are represented as anxious to get back; they wanted to trade with the Indians, and were in terror of the Spaniards. He had not much time, but a cross was erected and Hennepin and his two companions kneeled and sang hymns proper to the occasion, such as the *Vexilla regis*. On April 1 they began their return voyage, and were captured by the Sioux, above the mouth of the Wisconsin, on April 12. The distance is 1861 miles, so that in ascending the current they made about 155 miles a day—much better time than in going down, and this in spite of the delay they made to repair their canoes and the precaution of travelling only by night as they neared the mouth of the Illinois for fear of being arrested by the garrison of Fort Crèvecœur. The description of the country and the details of the voyage are stolen from Father Membré's narrative of La Salle's discovery two years after, but Hennepin found it impossible to fit in the new piece, and his dates are therefore hopelessly muddled. Thus he says that when on the lower Mississippi near the sea, not having any wine he was unable to celebrate mass on March 23, Easter Day; but Easter Day fell on April 21 in that year, and, moreover, in his first narrative he reports having spent Easter at the Issati village, on Mille Lacs, at the head of an affluent of the Mississippi near Lake Superior. The dates of the pretended voyage are not only inconsistent with those of the first narrative, but in the second narrative itself are inconsistent with each other. This incident of Easter is cited because no Catholic priest could have been mistaken about that date. The story is a plain falsehood. Father Membré celebrated the first mass on the lower Mississippi with La Salle in 1682, and Easter fell, as he records it, on March 29 of that year. Hennepin, in concocting his fictitious voyage, omitted to consult the calendar.

It will be a waste of time to follow in detail this tissue of falsehood. The first narrative, published at Paris in 1684, contains no allusion to the apocryphal trip to the sea—indeed, it plainly says that he did not go there, although he thought of doing so. He was, however, beyond doubt upon the upper Mississippi, and his narrative does contain many facts confirmed from other sources. In a general description of the upper river, with which he introduces the story of his capture, while noting the streams now known as the Iowa and Minnesota, he observes that the tributaries from the east are more numerous than from the west. He indicates the Rock River and the Wisconsin leading to the portage to Green Bay, the Black River, and the Chippeway River. He mentions a river full of rapids (the St. Croix), by which there is a route to Lake Superior. He describes St. Anthony's Falls, at the present Minneapolis, named for St. Anthony of Padua, "in gratitude," he adds, "for the favours done me by the Almighty through the intercession of that great saint." Eight leagues beyond was the Issati (or Nadoussion) River, leading to Lake Issati, or Buade (Mille Lacs). This last river he called after St. Francis, a name which has been displaced by the vulgar appellation of Rum River. This is the extent of Hennepin's discoveries, for from the Wisconsin to the Illinois had been explored by Jolliet and Marquette. Returning now to the real voyage and adventures of Father Hennepin, the Frenchmen had issued out upon the Mississippi and had reached about as far north as the Wisconsin River, when, on April 11, they were suddenly surrounded and captured by a war party of a hundred and twenty Sioux on the way to attack the Miamis. The Indians refused the proffered peace pipe and carried them up the river. After the first excitement was over the prisoners were not in danger of their lives, for the western Indians were not bloodthirsty, like the Iroquois. That they were treated without any studied cruelty appears through Hennepin's exaggerated narrative. They were robbed of their goods, but they had the same food the Indians had. They were, no doubt, in great fear at first, for the Miamis had escaped and some of the Sioux who had lost relations were anxious to kill them. At Lake Pepin these homicidal feelings sought expression by weeping over the prisoners, a proceeding which will shock any notions of Indians derived from "Gertrude of Wyoming," or Cooper's novels.

"The stoic of the woods—the man without a tear,"

HENNEPIN AND DULHUT

wept and howled all night with many companions in distress, and in memory of that impressive ceremony Hennepin called the place the Lake of Tears (Lac des Pleurs). On other occasions when the Indians were overcome by the remembrance of their departed friends, Hennepin wiped away their tears " with a wretched handkerchief he had left " and sought to assuage their grief by giving them presents. The leading chiefs always intervened when matters seemed serious, but the relations between the prisoners and these bereaved Sioux were for a long time strained. If this curious custom rested on Hennepin's evidence alone it would not be believed, but the same peculiarity has been recorded by other early writers, and Henry met with it at the Lake of the Woods among the Assiniboines, a Siouan people. At a council " several of the Indians began to weep and they were soon joined by the whole party." He adds: "Had I not previously been witness to a weeping scene of this description, I should certainly have been apprehensive of some disastrous catastrophe." The fur trader's nerves were steadier than the friar's. Henry inquired of the people why they always wept at their feasts, and was informed that such occasions brought back the memory of departed friends who had formerly been present at them and reminded them of the brevity of their own lives.

The party went steadily up the river, and when near the Falls of St. Anthony held a council to decide upon the fate of the Frenchmen. It resulted in their being adopted into different families. Hennepin was taken to the chief town of the tribe on the shores of Mille Lacs, and although he makes much moan over his hardships he was evidently treated by the Sioux as one of themselves. It was painful for him to see his embroidered chasuble paraded through the town on the shoulders of a naked Indian boy, but he was allowed to go about freely, explaining Christian doctrine in such scraps of Dakota as he could command. During his detention at Mille Lacs an embassy arrived from a distant western tribe, and Hennepin concluded from what they told him that there was no Strait of Anian, as laid down on the maps of the time, and that the land was continuous from Louisiana to China. He seems to have gathered from the same source information which led him to believe that large vessels might pass down by the rivers of the West into the Pacific Ocean and go to Japan and China without crossing the equator. In the interchange of presents with the deputies the friar's chasuble was utilised and the western Sioux carried it off to the plains of the Missouri.

The Indians started in July, 1680, for their summer hunt and the French went with them. Hennepin's companions do not seem to have had much respect for him, for they would not have him in their canoe, saying they had had enough of him. Accault preferred to stay among these good-natured savages, but Hennepin's imagination did not fail. He gave out that La Salle had promised to meet him at the mouth of the Wisconsin and he started thither with the other Frenchman. Some Indians went also to meet these "spirits," as they called the white men. There were, of course, no Frenchmen found there; but, while the Indians were hunting and moving up and down the river as the buffalo appeared, word came to the camp that a party of Indians who had been hunting towards the end of Lake Superior had met some "spirits," who were interested in hearing that there were white people among the Indians, and before long the Sieur Dulhut, with two Frenchmen, an Indian interpreter, and a Sioux guide, arrived at the camp. Hennepin was at once relieved from his disagreeable position, for Dulhut assumed a lofty tone and reproached the Indians with robbing and ill-treating "his brother."

He had come down over the portage to the St. Croix River from Lake Superior, where he had established a trading post. Dulhut's boldness and influence with these wild people is accounted for by his efforts among them at a great council on Lake Superior. He had been at the Indian town at Mille Lacs the previous year, 1679, and

HENNEPIN AND DULHUT

had planted there the arms of France. He did not come as a stranger; but with characteristic effrontery Hennepin, in his narrative, at once assumes the conduct of the whole party. He represents that as he had some knowledge of the language Dulhut begged that he would accompany him to the villages of the Sioux—"to which," adds the friar, " I readily agreed, knowing that these Frenchmen had not approached the sacraments for two years." After this there is no word of Dulhut, nor is the least gratitude expressed for his rescue. Dulhut, a captain of the King's troops and the most capable partisan leader in the West, is effaced, and with the pronouns " I " and " we " the boastful friar substitutes himself. Dulhut determined to return by Jolliet and Marquette's route up the Wisconsin, and Hennepin and his companions went with him. As Hennepin relates it, the season wore on and "*we* resolved to tell these people that, for their benefit, *we* would have to return to the French settlements; the grand chief of the Issati or Nadouessieuz [Sioux] consented and traced, in pencil on a paper *I* gave him, the route we should take for four hundred leagues. With this *we* set out, eight Frenchmen in two canoes." They returned by the Wisconsin and Fox rivers to Green Bay. The Jesuits had three missions there, but Hennepin, without mention of them, says mass and all the Frenchmen go to confession and communion. From Green Bay he went to Michilimackinac, and although he stayed there all winter at the mission of St. Ignace he utterly ignores the Jesuits and their missions. He reports that he preached every holy-day and on the Sundays of Advent, but says nothing of the mission church. He states that he found forty-two French traders there and that they begged him to give them the cord of St. Francis, which he did, making a suitable exhortation to each recipient. In his second book he admits having met Father Pierson at Michilimackinac, who, he says, had gone there to learn the language. There is not one word to indicate that Christian missionaries had ever been in that country. He left Canada shortly after the completion of his western voyage and never returned. A monastic Munchausen, devoid of the saving grace of humour, he fell into disgrace in France and was disfrocked. His books were, however, translated into many European languages and were widely read and believed until of late years, when Jared Sparks exposed the fraud.

Daniel de Greysolon, Sieur du L'hut, at the commencement of his adventurous career completed the circuit of exploration of the St. Lawrence basin in the Northwest. His name is spelled in as many ways as Shakespeare's. The name of the prosperous city at the head of Lake Superior is spelled Duluth, but the explorer generally spelled his name "Dulhut," and we shall not go far astray in following his example. He was of a noble family, as is clear from the fact that he was a gendarme of the King's Guard, but having connections in Canada he decided to seek his fortune there and procured a commission as captain in the troops of marine. His brother-in-law was De Lussigny, an officer of Frontenac's guard, and his cousin was La Salle's lieutenant, Henri de Tonty. He was in Canada in 1674, and having occasion to go back to France he arrived there in time to serve in his old regiment as esquire to the Marquis de Lassay and to take part in the bloody battle of Seneff, on August 11, 1674.

He returned to Canada shortly after and settled in Montreal, and set up what for those days was a handsome establishment, where also resided with him his younger brother, Claude Greysolon de la Tourette. He had long meditated a design to visit the country of the Sioux on the upper Mississippi and endeavour to arrange a peace which would open up to trade all the region contiguous to Lake Superior. In the autumn of 1678 he sold all his property in Montreal, and with his brother and three Indian guides left for the far Northwest. It was the commencement of a career of adventure. He went to the southwest shore of Lake Superior, across to the headwaters of the Mississippi, and down one of the streams, probably the St. Croix, until he reached the chief village of the Issati or Sioux. There on July 2, 1679, he planted the arms of France. That was a year before Hennepin's capture, and yet the friar records that Dulhut solicited him to act as guide thither. Other towns of the Sioux were also visited, and Dulhut gathered in September of the same year a great council at Fond du Lac, the extreme western end of Lake Superior. The Sioux from the upper Mississippi, the Assiniboines from the Lake of the Woods, and the Crees from Lake Nipigon were represented there and a peace was arranged. The following year, while exploring a river which led to the Mississippi, he heard of Hennepin's ignominious' captivity and hastened to rescue him, taking with him an interpreter—although Hennepin reports that Dulhut solicited him to act as interpreter.

To follow the adventures of Dulhut during the thirty years of his stirring life among the western Indians is beyond the scope of this volume. While it is true that Chouart and Radisson had already been in these regions, their stay was short and their observations imperfect. The Jesuits Allouez and Dablon had established missions on the southern shore of the lake, Marquette and Jolliet had reached the Mississippi from Lake Michigan, but Dulhut lived there and knew thoroughly all the region on the divide between the great lake and the great river, where no white man had previously been. He established his main post at the mouth of the River Kaministiquia—the chief portage, in after years, of the Northwest and Hudson's Bay companies and the site of the present town of Fort William. From thence he explored and traded, not only into the basin of the Mississippi, but with the Assiniboines around the Lake of the Woods and into the basin of the Winnipeg. On the north he had a post on Lake Nipigon, called La Tourette, after his brother, and from thence he traded with the Crees over the divide into the Hudson's Bay basin. He acquired immense influence among the Indian nations of the West, and more than once brought large contingents to the assistance of the governors of New France. The great Dakota nation had indeed been known before his establishment on the lake, but they had not previously been visited at their homes. He was a friend of Frontenac and therefore was hated by the intendant, Duchesneau, who stigmatised him falsely as a *coureur de bois* (bush ranger) and a lawless infringer of the royal ordinances. He, at the request of the Governor, Denonville, built in 1686 the first fort at Detroit and occupied it with fifty men of his own following. One daring feat has been specially recorded. In 1684 two Frenchmen were murdered, and he knew that the safety of the whites on Lake Superior depended on the punishment of the murderers. He arrested them in the midst of their people, tried them fairly, and shot two of them in the presence of five hundred savages. His own followers were a handful among these populous tribes, but his procedure was as bold and unhesitating as that of a patrol of mounted police at the present day.

He was the first to strike a return blow after the great massacre by the Iroquois on the Island of Montreal, and in 1695 he was in command at Fort Frontenac. A chivalrous, fearless, and tactful leader, he swayed the tribes of the Northwest and made the name of France respected on the divide around the lakes and over into the adjoining river basins. He died at Montreal in 1710 with the reputation of being the bravest officer who had ever served the King in New France.

With Dulhut closed the roll of daring and capable men who won for France the St. Lawrence valley to its utmost bounds. Churchmen and soldiers each in his own path fought and suffered and conquered—a brilliant and heroic band of whom any nation might be proud. They carried their lives ever in their hands and their daring was their safety. Their careers were crowded with picturesque adventure, and might have been the theme of novelist and poet were it not that the truth is stranger than fiction and there is nothing which imagination could add or improve.

CHAPTER XXII

EXPLORATION TO THE NORTH AND EAST—THE CIRCUIT OF THE VALLEY COMPLETED

THE great inland ocean of Hudson's Bay drains an area of three millions of square miles. Its basin not only bounds the St. Lawrence valley in its whole length on the north, but, outflanking it on the west, extends southwards and interlocks the head-waters of its rivers with the sources of the Mississippi. We have followed the progress of discovevery over the southern and western edges of the St. Lawrence basin and it now remains to retrace to the east the circuit of exploration along its northern border.

Champlain had scarcely founded Quebec when Henry Hudson, in an English ship, searched to the extremity of the great bay and spent the winter of 1610-11 at that part of it which reaches the farthest south towards Canada. In a map published in 1613 Champlain laid down " the bay where Hudson did winter " at the bottom of the present James Bay, but to him it was a bay of the northern ocean, "*Mare Magnum,*" extending round by the north to the Pacific Ocean; and in his last map, that in the voyages of 1632, the belief is still manifest. Button, Bylot, Baffin, and Fox followed. Button had wintered at the mouth of the Nelson River in 1612 and James at the mouth of Rupert's River in 1631, before Lake St. John on the Saguenay had been discovered or any permanent post had been founded west of Quebec. It is plain on James' map of 1633 that the English had by that time circumnavigated the bay, for the entire shore line is closed in; but Sanson's map of 1656 shows a small opening where a strait to the western ocean might lurk. To reach that supposed *Mare Magnum* at the north and so find a way to the West was the motive of Champlain's voyage up the Ottawa in 1613, and an explanation of the ready credence given to the impostor Vignau.

The natural development of the colony of New France was, as has been pointed out, retarded by the Iroquois war until the English colonies had time to grow strong. Not only did these truculent savages root up and destroy the Huron nation and extinguish the Jesuit missions in the West, but their war parties enveloped the eastern settlements and reached far to the north—to the upper St. Maurice, to Lake St. John, and even beyond the water-parting of Hudson's Bay. When, however, in 1665, the French Government waked up to its opportunities and sent out in quick succession Courcelles, De Tracy, Talon, and Frontenac, the colony began to extend on all sides. The Indian reports of vessels on Hudson's Bay were then taken by the government as signs of a new danger, while at the same time the fur traders began to feel the competition of the English merchants.

In the diplomatic discussions of later years the French Government put forth some claims which had no foundation in fact. It was confidently asserted, and the assertion is even now occasionally repeated, that in 1656 the Sovereign Council of Quebec authorised an expedition under Jean Bourdon, and that he went to Hudson's Bay and took possession for France. This is easily disproved. The Sovereign Council was not created until 1663, and the Jesuit Relation of 1658 records the fact that Bourdon's voyage was made in 1657, and also that he returned to Quebec on August 11 of that year and reported that on account of the ice he was unable to go along the Labrador coast further than lat. 55° N.—or five degrees south of the entrance to the bay. It was also asserted that a Canadian fur company in 1661 built a fort on Lake Nemiskau. That is abundantly disproved by Father Albanel's narrative of his voyage in 1672. It is on record that savages coming down from the north asked for missionaries; but that is proof that no missionaries had penetrated to their country, wherever it was. It was also claimed that in

1663 "a missionary, the Sieur Couture," was sent north with five men and that he planted the arms of France on the shore of Hudson's Bay. No record of such a thing exists. All that exists is a short permit of ten lines, dated May 10, 1663, by the Governor d'Avaugour to "Lieut. Couture" to be absent, with some savages from the north, for so long as he may deem it advisable in the public interest. No one in those days could be absent in the woods without a permit. Couture in the early part of his life was a "*donné*" of the Jesuits—a lay worker without pay. If he had been to the bay the Jesuits could not have been ignorant of it, as they unquestionably were, and any act so important would have been recorded. The closer the records are examined the more certain it will appear that, excepting Chouart and Radisson, as related in a previous chapter, Father Albanel, in 1672, was the first Frenchman to cross the height of land. Chouart and Radisson made no stay and Father Albanel found, at his arrival, the English flag flying on a vessel and buildings erected by the English; so that whether the title be claimed by discovery or possession, it must be awarded to the English.

It is a very remarkable fact that from Lake Mistassini on the east to the longitude of Lake Nipigon on the west, all the rivers north of the water-parting converge, like the spokes of a wheel, to James' Bay. The bay is very shallow, from the silt brought down by so many large and rapid rivers. The height of land is obscure, winding about and threading its way through myriads of small lakes and the interlocking sources of countless streams. Often the same lake gives rise to two rivers flowing in opposite directions. The height of the divide ranges only from 850 to 1350 feet above the sea level, but the country is rough and the portage routes used by the Indians were few. That from Lake Nipigon leads to a lake discharging both ways and issues upon the Albany River. The next towards the east is by the Michipicoton River on the east of Lake Superior and leads into the Moose River. One of these two, doubtless the first, Chouart and Radisson followed into James' Bay. The second is the route now generally used.

The next route is by the Ottawa, and there is no record of exploration to the north by that river until 1686, when an expedition started from Montreal to attack the English posts on the bay. It was in a time of profound peace and the English had no suspicion of danger; still, to take a body of a hundred men over such a route and bring them back without mishap was a very arduous task. The party consisted of sixty-eight Canadian militia and thirty soldiers. Three brothers of the Le Moyne family of Montreal, who subsequently won high distinction in the French service, were in leading positions, but De Troyes was in chief command. They assembled in winter on snowshoes at the head of the Long Sault on the Ottawa, where they made canoes, and as soon as the ice came down they proceeded up the river. Passing on the left hand the Mattawa route to Lake Huron, they went on northward to Lake Temiscaming, and thence by a chain of lakes and streams with short portages across the height of land into Lake Abitibi, 830 feet above the sea. They followed down the Abitibi River into the Moose River, and came out at the fort at its mouth, then called Hayes Factory, which they surprised, and then proceeded to seize the forts at Rupert's River on the east and at the Albany River on the west. The English were sent home in the arriving ships and French-Canadian garrisons were left in charge of the posts. A small post was established on Lake Abitibi as a connecting link. That the English were in effective possession of the bay is proved by the fact that they were holding, besides the captured forts, posts on the Severn and Nelson rivers. Under the rules of international law current at that period, and for a long time subsequent, the English had a valid claim as far as the height of land, and so it is formulated in the Royal Charter of 1670 to the Hudson's Bay Company. The French disputed it; but a hundred years later set up a similar claim to the whole valley of the Ohio. It is not the justice or equity of a pretension, but the power of the

EXPLORATION TO THE NORTH

nation making it, which renders a claim under international law so serious to the weaker party.

Thirty years previous to De Troyes' raid the Indians on the north and west, in order to escape the Iroquois war parties, frequently crossed from the head-waters of the Ottawa into those of the St. Maurice or Saguenay and came down to Three Rivers or Tadoussac. Although the St. Maurice is a large and important river it does not directly lead to any convenient route to the bay, but owing to the wide reach of its northern sources the post called Three Rivers at its mouth early became an important centre of the fur trade. Pont-Gravé had noticed the suitability of the place, and Champlain, and even Cartier, had ascended the river to the first rapids. There was no permanent post, however, at the mouth of the river until the town of Three Rivers was founded in 1634. Far up the river were the hunting grounds of the Attikamegues, or Whitefish Indians, a gentle and docile people, very amenable to instruction, though as apt to forget it; and at their solicitation Father Buteux, the Jesuit missionary at Three Rivers, ascended the river to the height of land. It was a long and laborious journey, but the good father was more than recompensed by the exemplary piety of his flock. He was absent from March 27 to June 18, 1651. He met many parties of savages, but the precise places visited are not easy to identify, for many of the missionaries were not as much interested in geography as might be wished, but the Shawinigan Falls may be easily recognised from his description. On his first voyage he had with him the Sieur de Normanville and two men. The poor savages besought him to make them another visit, and as a pledge of return he left his portable chapel to the care of the chief. He kept his promise at the sacrifice of his life, for he and a young Frenchman, his companion, were murdered at a portage by a war party of Iroquois. The territory to the height of land was reached, and two more martyrs were added to the honour roll of the Company of Jesus.

Yet farther to the east the Saguenay opens its gloomy

portals, leading the earliest sailors, by the profound depth of its waters, black with overshadowing mountains, to believe it to be an avenue to the western ocean. Nor can we wonder at their error, for the largest battle-ship of our days can pass fifty-seven miles up, and the tide rises twelve feet at Chicoutimi. A stern and savage wilderness it still is, but at Chicoutimi nature relaxes her frowning aspect, and in the basin of Lake St. John spreads out a broad region of fertile land. Beyond that is a vast wilderness unvisited save by wandering tribes of Indians, and unsettled save by trading posts of the Hudson's Bay Company.

The missionaries who laboured in the West suffered in their lifetime, but their names are honoured by millions, even of people who are strangers to their faith. Cities are named after them, monuments are erected and orations are made in their honour, but the names of those whose burning zeal spent itself in the regions beyond the Saguenay are little known, save to the special student. Although the statue of "a bearded athlete" in the Capitol at Washington may misrepresent to our eyes the outward aspect of the saintly Jesuit, the real Marquette is almost canonised in Wisconsin, and Brébeuf is still venerated at Quebec. There is a monument to Allouez in Milwaukee, but the names of De Quen, and Nonvel, and Laure, and De Crepieul are comparatively unknown. These last did not have to contend with the truculent Iroquois, the shifty Hurons, or the chivalrous Sioux; their flocks were the timid savages of the northern wilds whose arms were trained to ply the paddle rather than the tomahawk. To win the souls of these wandering savages François de Crepieul renounced the prospects of a brilliant career in France. He followed them to their hunting grounds, sharing their food and sleeping in the woods and in the snow—followed them in regions scarcely yet explored, and bore with them the hardships of the long winters of the northern wilds. For thirty years he laboured in the missions of Tadoussac and Lake St. John, and when at last, worn out, he went to die at Quebec, the

EXPLORATION TO THE NORTH 381

covered dwellings of civilisation had become strange and distasteful to him.

The Recollet Friar Dolbeau was the first to attempt to visit the northern Indians. He started in December, 1615, to winter with the Montagnais. How far he went does not appear, but his efforts were along the north shore of the River and Gulf of St. Lawrence rather than towards the interior. He was obliged to abandon the attempt, for, his eyes being weak, the smoke of the Indian lodges nearly blinded him.

It was not until 1647 that the upper Saguenay was explored. On July 11 of that year Father de Quen left Tadoussac to visit the nation of the Porc-epic (Porcupine nation), so named from the number of these creatures found in their country. His guides took him by Lake Kenogami and a short portage into a stream falling into Lake St. John, thus avoiding the heavy portages on the main river and especially the long and violent rapids at the discharge of the lake. The Indian name of Lake St. John is Piouagamik—the flat lake—and here the missionary was surprised to issue upon an immense plain surrounding a lake almost circular in shape. High mountains bounded the level landscape, excepting on the north, and many streams falling into the lake brought down numerous scattered tribes to its shores. The priest remained several days with the Porc-epics, who thronged round to welcome the first white man to visit their country. In 1652 he returned and the Indians built him a little church and house, where he commenced the mission of St. John. It was at the mouth of the River Metabetchouan. Father de Crepieul established the mission firmly in 1676 and made it a centre of evangelisation, and the merchants made it also a post of the fur trade. The broad clearings of the Jesuit mission still witness to the fertility of the soil, but the buildings are gone. When the English took Canada the whole northeastern region was forgotten. Under the name of the King's Posts (*Domaine du Roi*) it was successively leased to the Labrador Company, the Northwest Company, and, lastly, to the

Hudson's Bay Company, and was supposed to be a "great and terrible wilderness." The first settlers began to arrive upon Lake St. John in 1861, and it was not until 1868 that a missionary was sent there, where Father de Quen had preached in 1647!

This lake of the north, isolated on the map for so many years, has been the centre of many legends. It is remarkable on many accounts. Five large rivers and many smaller streams discharge into it, and in spring the melting snow raises its level twenty-five feet; for it has only one outlet—where by a double channel of foaming rapids the Saguenay drains its waters into the St. Lawrence, amidst scenery of wild and surpassing grandeur. Nothing can be more beautiful than the upper Saguenay when the hills between which it flows take on their autumn adornment of crimson and yellow. There is none of the depressing gloom of the lower river, for the woods clothing the hills are deciduous, and show as many colours as the sunset. The broad, level country round the lake produces bountiful crops of wheat and barley, and there also maize ripens and the tobacco plant flowers. The great tributaries open up the whole interior by their interlocking sources. On the west the St. Maurice and Ottawa and, on the north, Lake Mistassini are easily reached. From Lake Mistassini Rupert's River flows into Hudson's Bay and, from Rupert's River, there is ready transit to the East Main River, which latter stream flows also into the Bay on the west, but, on the east, leads to a portage to Lake Nichicun. From Lake Nichicun, the central point of the plateau of savage Labrador, Low, in 1892-94, explored the whole immense peninsula, until then a blank on our maps.

In this Lake St. John region the old scenes are still reproduced. In 1652 Father de Quen met a second time the converts he had taught there and at Tadoussac. It was Whitsunday, and the poor savages dressed the altar. They attended mass, and sang with their priest hymns in their language and the tunes they had been taught. Two hundred and thirty-six years later the writer witnessed,

Notman Photo

Grand Discharge Rapids, Lake St. John

at Pointe Bleue on the same lake, a similar service conducted by a priest of the Oblate Order. From all parts of the interior the Indians had assembled for their fall trade at the Hudson's Bay Company's post. Marriages and baptisms were performed, confessions were heard, and counsel given by the devoted missionary. At the service of the Benediction (*Salut*), kneeling before the altar, the men and women sang the church hymns responsively in Montagnais—the men in a deep bass and the women in a high treble, of a peculiar metallic quality not unpleasing, but like the high notes of a piano. It was an impressive service, for it vividly reproduced the scenes described by Father de Quen in the Relation of 1652, and many similar in the Relations of other years. The Jesuits are gone, and their buildings are gone, but some of their work in the hearts of these poor wild people has endured.

The Jesuit Relation of 1661 gives a clear statement of the views then prevalent concerning Hudson's Bay. Writing from Quebec the narrative says: "We have long known that, in our rear, we have the Northern Sea; that it is adjacent to the sea of China, and that only the gateway has to be found. There is that famous bay, first discovered by Hudson, who gave it his name, without reaping any other fame than that of having first opened the road which ends with unknown empires." All the previous winter a Nipissing chief had been telling the people of Quebec about the north, and especially of a general fair to be held the following summer, and to which the Indians of Quebec and Tadoussac had been invited. Such an opportunity of meeting the assembled tribes was not to be missed, and two of the most capable and experienced fathers—Gabriel Druillettes and Claude Dablon—were chosen for the expedition.

If any Canadian had previously visited Hudson's Bay these fathers must have known it; but the Relation is very definite on that point. The heading of the Journal of the expedition is "Journal of the *first* voyage made *towards* the Sea of the North." The voyagers say distinctly that they did not cross the height of land, but stopped at Lake Nekouba, the meeting place fixed, and from thence returned. The expedition started from Tadoussac on June 1, 1661, in forty canoes, and went up the Saguenay to Lake St. John by the usual route through Lake Kenogami. They rested a few days on the lake, which they describe, and add that "no Frenchman has passed beyond it." They then entered a country, which they say was, "up to now unknown to the French," and, on June 19 commenced the ascent of the Chamouchouan River. After much labour they at last reached Lake Nekouba, a central point in the northern wilds, where, write the voyagers, every year a sort of a fair is held, at which the northern savages meet to trade. It is worthy of remark that the only note of climate is that the party suffered from heat. The fathers, however, gave a very bad account of the land they passed through and complain of the smoke from forest fires. At Lake Nekouba the voyagers met representatives of eight or ten tribes, but even here the implacable Mohawks had penetrated and were haunting the portages. News came that they had killed many and had destroyed the whole tribe of the Escurieux. The assembly broke up in fear and scattered to their homes. The ubiquitous Iroquois checked the French advance on the north as they had in the far West. From Lake Nekouba to Lake Michigan is a long stretch, and yet that redoubtable confederacy was able to command it. Nothing could thenceforth hold the Indians of the party together, and the missionaries had to abandon the idea of going further, and returned to Tadoussac by the same route.

All had changed in New France by 1670. De Tracy and Courcelles and the regiment of Carignan-Salières had brought the Iroquois to terms, but in the meantime the English had become strong. In 1670 they were firmly established on Hudson's Bay and by the streams converging into James' Bay the news reached Quebec almost simultaneously from Tadoussac and Sault Ste. Marie, and produced a great sensation. The watchful intendant, Talon, learned from the Algonquins that two ships had been in the bay, and in 1671 selected Father Albanel, Denys de St. Simon, with another Frenchman and six Indians, to go to the bay and ascertain what the English were doing and to plant the flag of France on its shore. The party left Quebec for Tadoussac on August 6, 1671, where with much difficulty they procured a guide. Proceeding by way of Chicoutimi and Lake Kenogami they arrived at Lake St. John, where they found a party of Whitefish Indians from the source of the St. Maurice and some Mistassinis, who told them that there were two vessels trading on the bay and that there had been some conflict with the Indians. Albanel decided to send back to Quebec for letters of authorisation or passports, and in the meantime to pass the winter on the lake.

On June 1, 1672, the party started for the north. They went up the Chamouchouan to Lake Nekouba, the limit of the expedition of Druillettes and Dablon in 1661, and from thence to Lake Palistaskau, the summit, 1360 feet above the sea, where a little tongue of land separates two lakes discharging in opposite directions. The portage across is about half a mile. A party of Mistassini Indians endeavoured to stop the voyagers, but Albanel made presents and addressed them, exhorting them to carry their furs to Tadoussac and not to trade with the men on the bay, " who did not pray to God." On June 18 he arrived at Lake Mistassini, of which he was the discoverer, and coasted it until he found the Nemiscau (Rupert's River). He gives a good account of the lake and surrounding country. Even in that remote region they found an abandoned Iroquois fort. On June 28 they arrived at the shore of the bay, where they found a small sloop (hoy) flying the English flag, and two houses, but no people in them.

To quote the opinion of one of his own order, Father Albanel was more of a discoverer than a missionary, and he might have added more of a politician than either. Albanel entered into communication with the natives, and his own account will explain his subsequent difficulties with the English. He found that the savages, under the pretext of favouring the English, with whom they were accustomed to trade, were taking umbrage at his visit and were suspicious of his object. He writes: " To make them take a correct view of our action I determined to convince them that I was entirely disinterested in my visit, and that I had not come to carry on any trading or to enrich myself at their expense, or to the prejudice of the people with whom they were accustomed to deal—but rather to enrich them by giving them all we had brought so far." Then the politic father assembled all the chiefs and made an oration, giving them presents, telling them the benefits the French had bestowed on them by conquering the Iroquois, and that they had no motive in doing so but to constrain the northern tribes to pray to God in earnest. He adds: " I well know that it is for God alone to touch the heart; but these presents produced such an effect on the hearers that, under the influence of the Holy Ghost, which touched their hearts, they adopted the resolution to have themselves all instructed." Albanel was five days with the Indians, most of which time he spent in teaching and baptising some sixty-two persons, children and adults. He promised to return the following year, or to send someone in his place, and he says he left the Indians in tears. He returned by the same route and did not omit to plant the standard of France on Lake Nemiskau. He met none of the English, though he slept in their houses. From the complaints subsequently made by the Hudson's Bay Company he would seem to have pulled down the English flag he found flying on the bay. He left on July 5 and arrived at Tadoussac on August 1. The trained intelligence of the Jesuit records the physical peculiarities of James' Bay—the brackish water, its shallowness, and the incredibly long reflux of the tide. One observation is so apropos to present-day discussion that it may properly be quoted. After dwelling on the abundance of wild fowl and the plenty and variety of fruits, he writes:

EXPLORATION TO THE NORTH

"They are in error who have held this region, whether by reason of the intense cold, the ice and snow, or lack of wood suitable for building and heating, is uninhabitable. They have not seen these vast and dense forests, these beautiful plains and these wild prairies which border the rivers in various places covered with every kind of grass suitable for cattle. I can confidently say that on the fifteenth of June there were wild roses here as beautiful and fragrant as those at Quebec. The season seemed to me farther advanced, the air extremely mild and agreeable. There was no night during my visit; the twilight had not faded in the west when the dawn appeared in the east."

The Jesuit Relations put it beyond all doubt that Albanel was the first Frenchman to reach Hudson's Bay —excepting, as before explained, Chouart and Radisson. In the opening letter of the Relation of 1672 Father Dablon, the Superior of the missions, speaks of the "discovery" of the northern sea just made, and in that of 1671 he announces the departure of Albanel for that sea "which no Frenchman had hitherto reached." Albanel writes: "Hitherto this journey had been deemed impossible for the French, who had already thrice attempted it, but unable to overcome the obstacles in its way, had been forced to abandon it in despair of success."

It has been related in a former chapter how Chouart and Radisson were robbed by the Governor of Canada of the results of their northern voyage and were unable to obtain redress on appeal to France. They were not people to sit quiet under an injury so great. They transferred their services to England and made known to influential persons the resources of Hudson's Bay with such success that in 1668 two vessels were fitted out and sailed for the bay. The *Nonsuch*, commanded by a New England skipper, Captain Zachary Gillam, and carrying Chouart, arrived at the bay; the other, the *Eaglet*, with Radisson on board, had to put back. Chouart directed Gillam to the mouth of Rupert's River and there the party spent the winter of 1668-69. They returned to England in 1669, and in 1670 the Hudson's Bay Company was chartered and an expedition was sent out to establish posts upon the bay. The first governor, Charles Bayly, was sent in command and he built the first post at Rupert's River. These were the people who were on the bay when Albanel arrived.

Father Albanel did go back as he promised, but he does not appear to have been sent by ecclesiastical authority. He went armed with a letter from the Governor, Frontenac, addressed to the "Commandant for the King of Great Britain at Hudson's Bay." It was dated October 8, 1673, and, after setting forth the harmony existing between their respective monarchs and his own determination to maintain friendly relations with the English on the bay, Frontenac asks that the commandant will favour Father Albanel to the utmost of his ability. He gives no hint of the object of Albanel's visit.

Father Albanel left Quebec that year and wintered at some place north of the Saguenay, and on the route to Lake Mistassini Father de Crepieul met him in January and again in February, 1674, laid up in an Indian hut from the effects of a bad fall. The place of meeting was on a river which falls into the Saguenay on the north shore opposite Chicoutimi. Such a route to Lake Mistassini is laid down on Father Laure's map of 1733, and was better known by the Jesuit missionaries then than it is now. Nothing was heard of him in Quebec for some years; but from the Hudson's Bay Company's records it appears that he arrived at the bay on August 30, 1674, and presented his letters to the commandant. Suspicion was aroused by letters which he brought to Chouart, who was then at Fort Rupert. The result was that they sent him to England as a prisoner, charged with drawing away the Indians from the English alliance, with pulling down the English flag in the absence of the English, and with bringing letters to seduce Chouart from the service of the company. The petition in which these complaints are set forth is dated January 26, 1676, and further states that after Albanel had promised not to interfere again they had released him, whereupon he went to Paris, and

EXPLORATION TO THE NORTH 389

was then there with Chouart and Radisson planning new schemes to injure the company. The petition prays that the Ambassador to France be instructed to lay these complaints before the King of France with a view to prevent their schemes being carried out. The matter came to the King in council, and instructions were given in accordance with the petition. Albanel did return to Canada, but not to the Saguenay mission, and he troubled the company no more.

Not so, however, was it with the shifty Radisson. Whether tied by Mohawks to a stake for torture or outwitting the Onondagas at an " eat all " feast; whether with the Sioux on the Mississippi or the Crees on Lake Nipigon; with the Governors of New France or the Ministers at the French court, he was always superior to the occasion—a most interesting Canadian Ulysses, not to be overreached by courtier, merchant, or savage. The Hudson's Bay Company unwisely quarrelled with him and his brother-in-law, Chouart, whereupon they resumed their allegiance to France, and after a year or two of adventures in the Antilles in the service of France Radisson, in 1682, organised a Canadian company, and with two vessels started on July 11 to Hudson's Bay to found a post at the mouth of Nelson River. After two centuries of neglect such keen interest in Hudson's Bay seems strange to us, but it happened that others besides Radisson had fixed upon the same locality for a post, and when the French ships arrived they found that Captain Benjamin Gillam of Boston had preceded them by fourteen days. This Gillam must not be confounded with his father, Zachary Gillam, who was at the time in the company's service. Ten days later Governor Bridgar arrived with workmen and materials to build a fort in the same locality, and was warned off by Radisson. The details are too long to narrate; it will be sufficient to say that they all settled amicably down to winter on the Nelson River, and on the Hayes River, quite near. In the spring, however, Radisson got the better of both his competitors. He carried off Bridgar and Gillam to

Quebec and sent the rest of the English home. All this happened in time of peace, and therefore on arrival in Canada the prisoners were at once released, but Radisson had succeeded in establishing a French fort on the bay and had left a garrison there under the command of his nephew, young Chouart. In 1683 Radisson went to France and began to prepare another expedition, but suddenly in May, 1684, he again entered the English service and led out in the same year an expedition which captured the fort he had himself built and garrisoned, and also twenty thousand skins of furs belonging to the French Canadian company. This feat was the cause of De Troyes' expedition from Montreal in 1686, already narrated.

In relating these rapid changes it has been impossible to follow the course of events in strict order of time. Albanel's second expedition was in 1673-74. In 1679 Louis Jolliet, who with Father Marquette had discovered the Mississippi, went to Hudson's Bay by the Saguenay and Lake Mistassini. He was received kindly on account of his western discoveries, but he remained only a short time and returned the same way he went. He reported to Frontenac that the English had forts at the Rupert, Moose, and Albany rivers, and intended to extend their posts farther to the west, and also that they had a ship of twenty guns, and two barques to carry on their trade. They were, in fact, in possession of the bay they had discovered.

The region we are now considering is yet a wilderness. Chicoutimi is a thriving town, and during the last thirty years the valley of Lake St. John has been settled, but beyond that the country is wild. No cities have arisen in the tracks of the early explorers, nor are any likely to arise. On the north shore of the St. Lawrence from Isle aux Coudres eastward to Cape Cormorant stretched the *Domaine du Roi,* extending into the interior for an indefinite distance—at least as far as the height of land. That region was always leased as fur trading reserve, and the farmers of the revenue during the French *régime* from time to time secured it. After the conquest it was leased to the Northwest Company and their successors, the Hudson's Bay Company, until the provinces of Canada in 1867 were formed into one dominion and the lease expired. Under the French *régime* the country was penetrated by trading posts, and the same was the case under the Hudson's Bay Company, but a veil was drawn down over the whole territory and it was forgotten.

The region was known also to the French as the *Traite de Tadoussac,*—the Tadoussac trading post,—for Tadoussac was the point from which the trade was controlled. There, before Quebec was founded, a house was built by Chauvin,—the first house in Canada,—but the place was never more than a post under the French, and even now it is barely a village. It was, however, widely known as the " mission of Tadoussac," and a chapter of each annual Jesuit Relation was devoted to it, for it was the centre of the missions, not only to the northern tribes, but to the tribes along the north shore as far as the Esquimaux. When the Indians came down to trade their lodges clustered round the church and the few buildings of the post and the missionary catechised, preached, and baptised; but after a short time the trading was over and the Indians scattered to their hunting grounds in the far recesses of inner Labrador. In that way, and by often following the Indians in their migrations, the missionaries gained a knowledge of the north country, which was forgotten for a hundred years subsequent to the conquest.

Probably information concerning all this territory existed in the archives of the Hudson's Bay Company, but outside of their officers the whole region was an unknown wilderness, even to the Canadians themselves. Only those who were familiar with the Jesuit Relations and the old colony records knew the extent of what had been forgotten. In 1782 Michaux, the French botanist, reached Lake Mistassini with the intention of going to Hudson's Bay, but was unable to proceed farther. In 1860 the rivers Mistassini and Chamouchouan were surveyed by A. F. Blaiklock, and in 1870 a partial survey was made by the Geological Survey officers; but Lake Mistassini was either omitted from many of the modern maps or appeared in distorted shapes, although in Father Laure's map of 1733 it is laid down with its own very distinctive shape, divided into what are practically three long and narrow parallel lakes. There are a number of forgotten names laid down upon that old map besides the mission on Isle Ste. Croix on the lake. So little was known of the region by the general public that in 1880 a report was spread of an enormous lake, larger than Lake Superior, which occupied the interior of the peninsula of Labrador, and an expedition had to be fitted out in 1884-85 to survey the lake and dispel the absurd misconceptions then prevalent. Even then some newspapers persisted for a long time in asserting that only a bay of the prodigious sea of their imagination had been reached.

The coast of Labrador, inside the Strait of Belle-Isle, was, as narrated in earlier chapters, explored by Jacques Cartier, and it continued ever after to be the annual resort of fishermen and whalers from the western nations of Europe. In 1661 the Canadians began to take up the shore fisheries, and in that year a grant of a narrow strip along the north shore of the gulf was made to François Bissot of Quebec. The islands opposite, fringing the shore, were granted in 1679 to his son-in-law, Louis Jolliet, and a relative named Lalande. In the following year Jolliet received for himself a grant of the whole island of Anticosti. These grants extended along the entire north shore of the gulf from Cape Cormorant, a little east of Seven Islands, to Bradore Bay, within a few miles of the Strait of Belle-Isle. Jolliet spent some years in exploration there and in carrying on the fisheries. The Jesuits established mission stations at the mouths of the most important rivers, and often followed the savages up to their hunting grounds. In that way Father Bailloquet visited the Papinachoix on the upper Bersimis and was followed by Father Boucher. Father Nouvel, as early as 1664, had gone up the Manicouagan River to Manicouagan Lake, which he named Lake Barnabé. He had planned a journey to Hudson's Bay, but the Indians refused to take him. It may also be supposed that he knew, what we have only learned in 1895, that Summit Lake, the source of the Manicouagan, discharges also to the north by the Kaniapiskau River into Ungava Bay. In these expeditions the fathers must often have reached the edge of the central pleatau of Labrador. Father Nicholas in 1673 opened a mission at Seven Islands. That was the most eastern mission post established on the north shore.

On the south shore of the St. Lawrence, and in Acadia as far as the Penobscot, the missionaries were in constant communication with Tadoussac; and in the course of their duties were continually acquiring new information concerning the geography of the country. Father Druillettes in 1646 was the first Frenchman to penetrate, by way of the Chaudière River (opposite Quebec) and the Kennebec River, to the Atlantic seaboard, but, in 1640, an Englishman with a party of twenty Algonquins, in search of a passage to the northern sea reached Quebec by that route. He was sent to Tadoussac to return to England by way of France. The missions to the Etchemins in New Brunswick were carried on by the River du Loup, opposite Tadoussac. The route was over the portage to Lake Temiscouata and by the Madawaska into the St. John River. Miscou and Percé, at the mouth of Chaleur Bay, became favourite resorts for fishermen from France at a very early date. Restigouche and Nipisiquit, within the bay, were mission stations, as also were Richibucto and Miramichi on the gulf coast of New Brunswick. From the mouths of these rivers the interior of the country could easily be reached and traversed. The Recollets had not time before their exclusion to do more than touch at a few places. After their readmission in 1670 they resumed their work in Gaspé, but from 1629 to 1670 the missions were in the hands of the Jesuits and they had stations as far east as Ste. Anne on Cape Breton Island. Descriptions of the country round the gulf are contained in the Jesuit Relations from 1636 onwards.

Reaching far eastward towards Europe the grim ramparts of the Labrador coast tower steeply up against the lashing surf of the North Atlantic and the grinding ice thrown against them by the Arctic current bearing away the overflow of the polar ocean. We have seen in former chapters that this coast was well known to the earliest sailors on the western ocean. Whalers soon found that the cool waters of the Labrador current were the best hunting grounds for whales. Seals swarmed down on the ice fields, and at the beginning of the eighteenth century Canadians from Quebec began to establish sedentary fisheries along the coast beyond the Strait of Belle-Isle. These were checked by the English conquest, and for a while the government fluctuated between the French law of Quebec and the English law of Newfoundland. When in 1777 the first English settlers arrived at Hamilton Inlet, they found traces of French establishments, abandoned for years. Further to the north the Moravian Brethren established mission stations. They made the first attempt in 1764, and in 1771 founded their first settlement at Nain; afterwards extending their stations from Hopedale on the south (a little north of Hamilton Inlet) to Ramah, near Nachvak Inlet, on the north—from 55° 30' to 59° N. The Hudson's Bay Company about 1832 founded their post at Rigolet, at the head of Hamilton Inlet at the narrows leading into the long expanse of Lake Melville.

From this stern coast westwards approximately to a line drawn northwards up the Manicouagan River stretched the vast peninsula of Labrador, a blank upon the map until the last few years; and even still, over large areas, unexplored—an enormous tableland abounding in rock and moss and morass. The streams have cut no deep drainage valleys in the hard rock, but fall over the edges of the plateau in swift rapids or cataracts, barring the advance of explorers through their foaming channels. An explorer who in 1862 forced his way 120 miles up the Moisic River and got a peep over the edge of the plateau reported that "language fails to depict the awful desolation of the tableland of the Labrador peninsula." Since then we have learned more of that region and think somewhat better of it. It had to be taken in reverse to be understood, not stormed from the front, but entered from the rear by Lake Mistassini. The interior tableland is a network of streams and lakes, with rocks and morass in very truth, but also with many forests of subarctic trees. Even the wilderness relaxes its grimness when boldly faced, and a discovery of minerals would tame the unfinished giant-land of the Northeast as the Yukon and Alaska territories are being overcome at the Northwest.

The first attempt to penetrate this region was made by Mr. John McLean, an officer in charge of Fort Chimo, the Hudson's Bay post on Ungava Bay. In the winter of 1838 he started with a few men and succeeded in reaching the Hudson's Bay Company's post on Hamilton Inlet. He went across the country to Lake Michikamau and thence by the Northwest River. The journey being in the depth of winter the ice was an assistance in travelling, but the labour was great and the route was found impracticable as a means of regular communication. In 1839 he made another attempt—this time in summer, with canoes. He went by the George River, and passing to the west of Lake Michikamau crossed the divide into a tributary of the Hamilton or Grand River. Paddling carelessly down the stream the voyagers heard, one evening, the warning roar of a mighty cataract. They had come upon the Grand Falls, and McLean was the first white man to see them or even hear of them. It was, he writes, " one of the grandest spectacles in the world "; but he had to turn back, for not only the fall itself, but the succeeding thirty miles of rapids, had to be passed, and he could find no way round. The following year he heard from an old Indian at Ungava Bay of a chain of small lakes by which a portage around the falls and the canyon could be made. In 1841 he followed that route with success, and not only went down to Hamilton Inlet, but returned the same way. The following year he went again down to the coast, but as the post at Ungava was soon after abandoned for a few years, the route fell into disuse.

The Hudson's Bay Company a few years later established posts at Lakes Nichicun, Kaniapiscau, and Petitsikapau. These are key points upon the central tableland and unlock all the interior water courses. Whatever information the company acquired was not published. It remained for Mr. A. P. Low of the Canadian Geological Survey, in a series of arduous explorations extending from 1892 to 1895, to reveal to the world the geography of the inner peninsula. For the most of the time he was assisted by Mr. D. I. V. Eaton, who compiled the map accompanying his report. That the officers of the Hudson's Bay Company were acquainted with the geography of this region is evident from the fact that when at the H. B. Co. post at Lake Nichicun Low saw a manuscript map, made in 1842, showing the courses and connections of the great rivers upon the central plateau.

Meantime most exaggerated reports of the Grand Falls of the Hamilton, or Grand River of Labrador, had got abroad, and indeed are still abroad. In a standard gazetteer published as late as 1895 their height is given as "about 2000 feet," for McLean's book has been very little known and no other published information existed concerning them. Not long after McLean's visit a Mr. Joseph McPherson is said to have been conducted there by an Iroquois Indian attached to the Hudson's Bay post at Rigolet, and a missionary of the Oblate Order, Father Bebel, did really visit the Grand Falls about 1870, when following his wandering flock, but of this nothing was publicly known. At last in 1887 a bold attempt was made by an Englishman, Mr. R. F. Holme. Misled into supposing the distance from the sea to be not more than a hundred miles he ran short of food, and after a most laborious effort had to turn back at Lake Winokapau. Incited by these difficulties two American expeditions set out in 1891. One is known as the Bowdoin College expedition. It was under the direction of Professor Lee.

EXPLORATION TO THE NORTH

Four of the students went up the river without guides; the rest sailed further along the coast. One of the boats of the explorers was upset and the distance being unknown, while provisions were short, two of the party were obliged to turn back. The other two, Messrs. Cary and Cole, continued on a most difficult course along the river almost until they reached the cataract, but by an accident with their campfire in their absence their boat and outfit were burned and they had no alternative but to hurry back as fast as possible on foot over the whole distance.

The second expedition was undertaken by Mr. H. G. Bryant of Philadelphia and Professor Kenaston of Washington. They started on August 3 from the Hudson's Bay Company's post where the Northwest River falls in at the head of Lake Melville. None of the Indians around the post would go with them, for they have a superstitious dread of the falls, and believe that to see them will bring on an early death. They took with them a young Scotchman, resident at the post, and an Esquimau. Montague, the Scotchman, had been with Holme in his plucky attempt, and knew the lower river well. They hired at the post a strong river boat eighteen feet long, and towed their canoe at the stern. They slowly and laboriously worked up the river, for the most part by "tracking," for the current is strong and there are many rapids, until after three weeks' incessant toil they reached Big Hill. At that point commences the portage route round the canyon and the falls to the quiet water above. It was the portage which McLean had followed in 1841. The trail was very indistinct, for when Fort Chimo was re-opened communication by sea was preferred. After long search they found it, and leaving their heavy boat they started with their canoe through a circuit of small lakes. That was the reason they did not meet Messrs. Cary and Cole on their way back, for these two explorers followed the river bank as nearly as possible. On September 2 they arrived at the Grand Falls, having struck across from the upper lake, guided by a column of ascending mist and by the roar of the cataract. They were fortunate in being able to make measurements and take photographs of the falls, so that by their descriptions and those of Mr. Low a sufficiently accurate idea may be formed of this wilderness wonder.

Mr. Low entered upon the tableland by way of the Saguenay, Lake St. John, and Lake Mistassini. He examined the country down to Hudson's Bay by the upper Rupert River and the lower East Main River. He then followed up the East Main River to its source and made a portage to a stream falling into Lake Nichicun. From that lake he passed by a short portage into Lake Kaniapiscau and followed down by the river of that name into the Koksoak, which flows past Fort Chimo into Ungava Bay. From Fort Chimo he went round by sea to Rigolet on Hamilton Inlet. He passed the winter of 1893-94 at the Northwest River at the head of the inlet. From thence he went up the Hamilton River, visited the Grand Falls, and passed up the Ashuanippi Branch to Petitsikapau Lake. He then explored the southern or Attikonak branch to its head and crossed the parting to the Romaine River, flowing southwards. Finally he crossed over to the St. John River and followed it to the Gulf of St. Lawrence. It was a very remarkable exploration, and has a right to rank high in the geographical history of the country. From north to south and from east to west he cut through the very heart of the unknown region by routes for which, oftentimes, he could get no guides. His work opened up 289,000 square miles of territory and his report covers the geology, botany, and zoölogy of the country, not only explored, but examined. It was a journey in Labrador of 2960 miles by canoe, 500 miles with dogs, and 1000 miles on foot over a country bristling with difficulties and under a severe climate. Besides the main routes given above, the head-waters of the Manicouagan and Outarde Rivers were explored and careful examinations were made of the large central lakes which are the sources of the great rivers of the peninsula.

The Grand Falls mark a wide distinction in character

between the Upper and Lower Hamilton River. The upper river, like all other rivers on the great central tableland of Labrador, flows broadly on the surface between low banks fringed with a thick growth of brushwood. As it approaches the fall the river enters into a rocky channel, which gradually narrows. Down this trough the whole stream rushes in a steep descent, swirling in great waves twenty feet high, as the ever-narrowing walls compress it more and more, until as from a gigantic spout, only fifty yards in width, the whole river, of a volume as great as the Ottawa at Ottawa City, is projected into space over a fall 302 feet deep, to drop into a circular basin with steep walls of rock 500 feet high. Thence it flows away, at first at right angles, through a zigzag canyon eight miles long, cut straight down from the surface without any preparatory slope, where, hidden from sight save to an observer looking directly over, it rages boiling down a further descent of 260 feet. Thence it issues out into a valley deeply furrowed into the plain, from 500 to 800 feet below the general level, and with few intervals of quiet water rushes from rapid to fall and fall to rapid, until it discharges at sea level into the upper arm of the inlet called Lake Melville. The level of the river as it nears the fall is 1660 feet above the sea. Twelve miles below it has dropped 760 feet and it falls the remaining 900 feet down the remainder of its course to tide water. The total drop from the central plateau to the sea is indeed 1660 feet, the error has been in supposing that to be done all in one leap.

The story of exploration in Labrador closes with a tragedy, for hardly had the preceding lines been written when the news came by a courier, who reached the coast on March 18, of the death by starvation of Mr. Leonidas Hubbard, Jr., somewhere beyond Northwest River. Mr. Hubbard was the assistant editor of *Outing*, a well-known monthly magazine published in New York. He left for Labrador early in June, 1903. He had studied all that was known of the country, and determined to learn more of those parts of it which had not been explored.

He had made a *cache* of his provisions on the Northwest River, and with a companion and a guide had pushed forward, trusting to find game on the way. They found no game, and as starvation threatened the whole party they started to return to their *cache*. Hubbard's strength gave out and his companions had to leave him to hurry back for food. They reached the *cache* and hastened back, but though absent for a short time only they found Hubbard dead. He died on October 18, 1903. His companions made their way back to the coast with the body, but could not reach communication with the outer world until the following March.

We have now traced the course of discovery back to the points from whence it started—to Tadoussac, where Chauvin built the first house, to Labrador, which Cartier called the "land of Cain," and to Cape Breton Island, of which Cabot brought back such a glowing account. We have followed up the great avenue of waters to the west and reached the portals of another west, to be followed by yet another, before we reach the sunset. League after league our forefathers were tempted along their arduous course by the promise of the great Southern Ocean. The men whose names are now so often on our tongues died poor and unrewarded. We have entered into their labours and they have passed into their rest. All we can do is not to grudge an occasional recognition, by commemoration or monument, of lives so laborious and achievements so heroic.

CHAPTER XXIII

OCCUPATION OF THE ST. LAWRENCE VALLEY

THE era of discovery closed with the seventeenth century. The region of mystery moved westward, for the pathway of the two great rivers had been followed from the Gulf of St. Lawrence to the Gulf of Mexico. The movement was from Canada,—from Quebec and Montreal,—and the arms of France were planted at the sources as well as at the mouths of the St. Lawrence and Mississippi. But while these streams were the main arteries of the continent upon its Atlantic side and revealed the fundamental plan upon which it was constructed, a great deal remained to be done before the immense regions drained by their tributaries could be fully known and occupied. The eighteenth century was a period of conflict for the dominion of these two great valleys, and the struggle commenced when the outposts of France and England met upon the parting of their waters.

The physical conditions of the English and French colonies differed widely. For a long time the English settlers were hedged in by the Allegheny Mountains and by a barrier of broad and dense forests which concealed in their leafy recesses the springs of the westward-flowing streams. Gaps there were in " the endless mountains," and Indian war trails tunnelled the forest wilderness, but they were untravelled by the English and unknown, while the light French canoes glided everywhere along the interior waterways and their echoes rang with the speech of Norman France. Whatever may have been the strategic value of the great westward trails in the middle colonies, in Canada the streams were the roads alike in winter and summer, and the portages were the strategic keys which unlocked the whole northland.

Exploration along the lower lakes ceased for a time after the recall in 1682 of the Count de Frontenac. His incapable successors La Barre and Denonville irritated the Iroquios by abortive hostilities and tempted them by manifestations of weakness. To gratify a passing whim of the French court Denonville treacherously seized fifty-one Iroquois Indians and sent them to France to work in the galleys. They were neutral Indians residing on the Bay of Quinté and were on friendly terms with the garrison at Fort Frontenac. The colony paid dearly for this perfidy. The Iroquois with profound craft dissembled their resentment, until in the night of August 4, 1689, fifteen hundred warriors landed at Lachine and swept the Island of Montreal of every inhabitant up to the palisades of the forts. More than two hundred unsuspecting settlers were killed and scalped, and one hundred were carried away prisoners to the Iroquois towns. It is a dark and bloody day in the annals of Canada, long remembered as the "Massacre of Lachine." While the discouraged colonists were stunned by the suddenness and severity of the blow, Frontenac arrived for a second term of office—the one and only man who could rally them against the exultant Iroquois. He brought no troops, but he brought back thirteen of the captives—all who had survived the confinement and degrading labour of the slave galleys. With these he opened up negotiations.

Never did the colony stand in greater need, for the Iroquois raged like demons along the whole line of settlement and on the river and the lower lakes. Frontenac found to his disgust that the post at Niagara had been deserted and that Fort Frontenac had been abandoned and blown up. But the route by the Ottawa to the upper lakes was still available and the French traders at Michilimackinac and Sault Ste. Marie were not intimidated. The narrow streets of Montreal soon again swarmed with life. One hundred and sixty-five canoes laden with furs brought down Ojibways and Crees from Lake Superior, Hurons and Ottawas from Mackinac, and the

Quebec, about A.D. 1700

OCCUPATION OF THE VALLEY

Manitoulins, Pottawatomies from Lake Michigan, and Algonquins from Lake Nipissing, together with French fur traders and their men, and in the stir of reviving business the Montrealers with characteristic elasticity recovered their wonted spirits. A great council was held and the Count de Frontenac, a nobleman of the court of France who had held high command in the royal army and was Lieutenant General for the King, led the war dance, tomahawk in hand and whooping, in spite of his seventy years, with a vigour hardly surpassed by the wildest savage of them all. Then came the solemn war-feast, and two oxen and six large dogs assuaged the appetites of the Indian chieftains and tested the politic complaisance of their distinguished coryphæus. The fiery old governor soon rallied the forces of the colonists and his first care was to rebuild La Salle's Fort Frontenac. Then he carried the war across Lake Ontario into the Iroquois country, and although the Indians escaped into the forests he burned the Onondaga and Oneida towns and destroyed their stores of provisions for the winter. He died in 1698, and his successors reaped the benefit of his labours, for the Iroquois were so weakened by his attacks that after the peace of 1701 they ceased to be formidable. It was in fact with them as with the Romans of old whose policy they so singularly reproduced, the original stubborn fighting stock was reduced by incessant wars and the adopted stock did not possess the same stoical characteristics.

Peace with the Iroquois opened up again the routes to the west by the lower lakes—very fortunately for the colony, for the Fox Indians on the Michigan portages began to manifest an implacable hostility to the French, which closed the route by the Fox River and menaced the Chicago and Kankakee portages. La Salle had perished, but his projects survived and access to the Mississippi valley became the chief object of the Canadians. This was much more direct by Lake Erie and the Ohio than by the circuitous route through the Straits of Michilimackinac, for the main affluents of the Ohio approach very closely to the shore of the lake. Great cities now mark the river mouths leading to the portages, and great railways carry an enormous traffic along the old lines of canoe travel. These new routes were not discoveries, but they now began to be frequented and to draw away from the Ottawa route the main part of the western travel. Detroit began to supplant Michilimackinac as a centre of traffic, and the portages along the south shore of Lake Erie were developed successively. It will be convenient to review the results of exploration at the commencement of the new century and to trace along its western and southern margin the complete definition of the basin of the great river of Canada.

Commencing then on the north of Lake Superior, near the great double divide where the waters flow north, west, and south to James' Bay, Lake Winnipeg, and Lake Superior, we find that in 1683, acting under orders of Governor La Barre, the adventurous Dulhut had established a post on Lake Nipigon. It was a commanding situation, for from it the Indians descending to the English factories on Hudson's Bay could be headed off, and there he stationed his younger brother, Claude. Beyond this point the Winnipeg divide approaches Lake Superior and closes the St. Lawrence basin in on the west at a distance of only forty-five to sixty miles. Dulhut founded his main station at the mouth of the Kaministiquia River, now known as Fort William. A century later it was the headquarters of the Northwest and Hudson's Bay fur trading companies, for it was the key to the whole Northwest, and there the brigades of canoes met and crossed—some bound to Montreal over the waters of the lake, some to the Mackenzie River basin and the Arctic Ocean, and some to the Saskatchewan and the great south sea. There after business was over the barons of the fur trade held high carnival and exchanged experiences of perils by land and by water—perils of hunger, of hostile Indians, of rushing streams and of sealike lakes—true tales beyond the dreams of the wildest romancer. Now it is the shipping point upon St. Lawrence waters of the

Canadian Pacific Railway. From that point Dulhut swayed the Crees, Assiniboines, and Ojibways, and even reached the Sioux of the Upper Mississippi. At the extreme western end of the lake is the mouth of the St. Louis River, a small stream considered to be the source of the St. Lawrence.

South of the lake was the mission of La Pointe, on Chequamegon Bay, concerning which much has been said in former chapters. Although it was abandoned by Marquette and the Hurons the locality retained its importance as a centre of traffic, for it commanded the most convenient portages to the upper Mississippi. In later days the post of La Pointe was on Madaline Island, at the mouth of the bay. The American Fur Company built a post there in the beginning of the nineteenth century, and in 1835 Bishop Baraga re-established the mission of St. Esprit, intermitted for over one hundred and fifty years. Henry's post, however, was on the old site on the mainland, and though the position of the old La Pointe cannot now be precisely fixed, it must not be confounded with the comparatively recent La Pointe of existing maps. At the eastern end of Lake Superior is Sault Ste. Marie, concerning which enough has already been said, and from thence the route by the north shore of Lake Huron and French River, Lake Nipissing, and the Ottawa to Montreal was well known and had been frequented from the earliest days of the colony.

Sufficient has also been said of Michilimackinac, the gateway of Lake Michigan, and of the three main routes to the Mississippi from its shores. The route by Green Bay and Fox River, and that by the Chicago portage into the Des Plaines branch of the Illinois River, have been frequently mentioned. On the Illinois River Tonty held the fort of St. Louis during the absence and for some time after the death of La Salle. Passing round the end of the lake to its eastern shore was the third route, that by the St. Joseph River, which, as has been shown, was much used by La Salle. This stream divides into two branches; the eastern fork leads to an affluent of the Wabash and thence into the Ohio, and the southern leads to the Kankakee, a tributary of the Illinois. La Salle built his Fort St. Joseph at the mouth of the river, but in 1712 the French built another of the same name at the portage on the upper river near the present town of South Bend, Indiana. Although it commanded a network of interior communication, it soon was superseded by more direct routes to the Mississippi. There were usually missions at all established posts and the country around soon became well known.

All thoughts in Canada were now turned to the Mississippi. At the close of the seventeenth century it was known in its full extent. As early as 1689 Nicholas Perrot had forts on the upper river at the mouth of the Wisconsin and on Lake Pepin. The missionaries Montigny, St. Cosme, Davion, and Thaumur de la Source, starting from Michilimackinac and passing over the Chicago portage, went down in 1699 as far as the present Baton Rouge, establishing missions. In 1700 Father Gravier followed by the same route to the gulf, and in the same year Le Sueur went from the gulf up the river as far as the present St. Paul and some distance up the Minnesota River. In the same years (1699-1702) expeditions from France under Iberville and Bienville, two brothers of the Le Moyne family of Montreal, so celebrated in Canadian history, founded Biloxi and Mobile on the Gulf of Mexico to guard the mouths of the Mississippi. The mission priests from the posts on the Mississippi went down to visit the new settlers, and the chivalrous Tonty, abandoning by royal order his Fort of St. Louis on the Illinois, went down to another Fort St. Louis at Mobile, to die there in 1704. At many places along the river Canadians had settled among the Indians. The problem of its true source among the myriads of Minnesota lakes remained in dispute until very recent years, but when the eighteenth century opened the river was known in its whole course. It was to open more direct access to it that the south shore of Lake Erie was explored.

The foundation of Detroit marked the change. In 1686 Dulhut, under Denonville's orders, had established a temporary post there with a garrison of fifty men, but it was not until 1701 that La Mothe Cadillac made a permanent settlement and became the founder of the city. By his influence among the Indians and the post's proximity to the Erie portages it grew at the expense of Michilimackinac, and the southern waters of Lake Huron ceased to be frequented. This was the cause of the lateness of exploration and settlement in the Huron tract in Canada and on the peninsula of Michigan.

Following the geographical development of the country, we must cross the southern part of the peninsula of Michigan to the western shore of Lake Erie. There the City of Toledo, Ohio, at the mouth of the Maumee River, fifty-three miles east of Detroit, marks the entrance to the route by the Wabash leading by the Ohio into the Mississippi. This is the most direct and soon became the chief route of travel. It is important also from its extensive interior communications. The Maumee River is formed by two branches, the St. Mary and St. Joseph, uniting at the present Fort Wayne (Indiana), and a portage of eight miles at that point leads to a branch of the Wabash; but by following up the St. Joseph River a short portage leads to the other St. Joseph (for both rise in Hillsdale County, Michigan), and by that means a voyager could either pass down to La Salle's Fort at St. Joseph on Lake Michigan, or might carry his canoe into the Kankakee at La Salle's portage and so drop down into the Illinois. The route became so important that several forts were built upon it—Fort Miami at the Wabash portage, Fort Ouitanon, built in 1720, on the upper river, and Vincennes, nearer to the junction with the Ohio, founded perhaps as early as 1702, but certainly before 1709. In that year Bissot de Vincennes returned from the West to Montreal and sold out his interest in a seigniory on the Labrador coast.

Eastwards fifty-seven miles along the lake shore is the present city of Sandusky, not far from the mouth of a river of the same name, from the head of which, by a short portage, the Scioto River is reached. The next point to be noted is Cleveland, fifty-six miles further, at the mouth of the Cuyahoga, leading to a portage into the Tuscarawas and Muskingum rivers, draining into the Ohio. These two routes were not so much frequented as the others.

The Ohio divide approaches the lake shore closer and closer as it passes to the east, and French Creek, a branch of the Allegheny, rises near the site of the present city of Erie, Pennsylvania, ninety-five miles east of Cleveland, where the Island of Presque Isle makes an admirably sheltered harbour. This was a very important route, for it led down to the very spot where the English were beginning to cross the mountains into the Ohio valley. The Allegheny is the northern of the two main forks which unite to form the Ohio at the site of the present Pittsburgh, where in 1754 the Virginians built a fort which the French seized the same year and named Fort Duquesne. In that obscure spot in the North American woods originated the seven years' war which transferred to England the dominion of the St. Lawrence valley, and there, as a major in the service of the English king, George Washington struck the first blow in the fateful contest. Last of the Erie routes is the portage to Chautauqua Lake in the extreme west of New York State. The outlet of this beautiful lake is one of the sources of the Allegheny. It is only eight miles distant from the Lake Erie shore, but its level is 726 feet higher and the portage is steep. Fort Le Bœuf guarded the end of the Presqu'ile portage at French Creek, and Fort Venango at the junction of French Creek with the Allegheny River controlled both routes. On the lake shore Fort Presqu'ile was built in 1752. The portage by Presqu'ile was twenty miles long, but much less laborious than that by Chautauqua Lake. This route and that by the Wabash were the most used of all the routes to the Mississippi valley, as is evident by the number of forts guarding them. In the early part of the eighteenth

Quaint conceptions of Canada in A.D. 1715. The view of the Falls of Niagara in the background is adapted from Hennepin's book. In the front are beavers building a dam. Some are cutting down trees; others in a procession are carrying pats of clay on their tails

(From Herman Moll's Map)

OCCUPATION OF THE VALLEY 409

century the Ohio basin adjoining the St. Lawrence was well known to the French, and the English traders were beginning to pass over the mountains. To check their inroads the French Governor, La Galissonière, sent Céleron de Bienville with a party and a notary as witnesses to a renewal of possession of the whole region in the most formal way. He carried with him a number of metal plates engraved with the claims of France, which he buried at the chief points of his route. He went by the Chautauqua portage and passed down the Allegheny into the Ohio, which he followed to the Great Miami. He went up the last stream and made a portage to the Maumee and descended by it to Lake Erie.

We have seen in a previous chapter that La Salle erected a small post at the Niagara portage. That had been given up when in 1687 the governor, Denonville, after summoning to his aid in his inglorious Iroquois expedition all the French from the far West, ordered Dulhut, Durantaye, Tonty, and De Troyes to build and garrison a fort at Niagara. Garrison life did not suit such rovers, and one after another left. In 1688 the remainder of the garrison abandoned the fort by the governor's order, and the Senecas were once more relieved of the presence of white men at a place which they watched most jealously. Joncaire, a half-breed Seneca in the service of the French, settled there in 1721, and in that year Father Charlevoix on his journey up the lakes lodged in his cabin. In 1726 Joncaire got permission to build a fort, and the French held and strengthened it, for it was a most important strategic point and barred the English traders from the upper lakes. This the English resented, the more keenly inasmuch as, through their alliance with the Iroquois, they laid claim to an exclusive influence over their territory—such a claim as would now be set up in what is called a sphere of influence.

Following along the south shore of Lake Ontario, the Genesee River has already been indicated as the probable route of La Salle's first voyage down the Ohio. Charlevoix described it, in 1721, from descriptions of the French officers, and they evidently knew it in its whole length—not only the falls on its upper reaches, but the ultimate portage to the Allegheny. Both rivers rise in Potter County, Pennsylvania, and not far away the springs of the Susquehanna, flowing into the Atlantic, overlap. From the Genesee eastward the water south of the St. Lawrence divide ceases to flow into the Gulf of Mexico and drains by the Susquehanna, Delaware, and Mohawk rivers down the eastern slope of the Allegheny Mountains into the Atlantic. From Niagara to Lake Champlain—from the Seneca to the Mohawk towns—the great Iroquois trail passed, well known from the earliest days of the colony down even to our time, for the main road still follows it. The English as an offset to Niagara built a fort at Oswego, from whence they were extending their trade across Lake Ontario to Lake Huron by the Toronto portages. The French replied by building Fort Rouillé on the site of the present Toronto.

All these routes of access or exit to the valley of the St. Lawrence were of minor importance in comparison with the avenue by Lakes George and Champlain, and their outlet, the Richelieu River. That was the highroad between Canada and the English colonies to the south, and invading armies passed both ways during the constant struggle for empire, for a broad and deep navigable waterway extends the basin of the St. Lawrence far into the present United States. The heads of Lakes George and Champlain are close to the sources of the Hudson, and the water-parting is low. Large steamers may now ply from St. Johns on the Richelieu, only twenty-seven miles from Montreal, to Whitehall, in the State of New York. In the seventeenth century the river was known as Rivière aux Iroquois, for it led to the heart of the Mohawk country. The route was studded with forts, both English and French, and the whole region is rich in romantic and historical associations. Additional importance was attached to this route because it led to the Mohawk River. By following up the Mohawk to a short portage of over one mile the

OCCUPATION OF THE VALLEY 411

traveller could cross into Wood Creek, flowing into Oneida Lake, and from thence down the Oswego River to Lake Ontario. Fort Stanwix was built on the portage where the city of Rome now stands—a spot full of stirring historical associations, smothered under a venerable Old World name, meaningless there. Oswego on the lake shore was strongly fortified by the English. At the present time, when so much is said about expeditionary forces, it may be useful to recall the fact that Amherst in 1760 assembled his main army at Oswego by this route, and from thence went down the St. Lawrence with 11,000 men and 822 boats and batteaux to the attack of Montreal. This immense flotilla ran all the rapids of the river to Lachine, and though a few batteaux were wrecked the success of the expedition testified to the rare military skill of its leaders.

East of Lake Champlain the Connecticut River was the main avenue for French and Indian raids upon the back settlements of the English colonies. Otter Creek, which falls into Lake Champlain opposite Ticonderoga, was a common route, and Onion, now called Winooski River, was also followed. There were routes from the St. Francis River and Lake Memphremagog leading to the sources of the Connecticut, but they were laborious and used mainly by the Abenaqui Indians in their merciless war parties against the hated New Englanders.

The historic portage route from Quebec to New England has been mentioned in a previous chapter. It was up the Chaudière River opposite Quebec and through Lake Megantic to its source, then by a portage across the height of land to Dead River,—a branch of the Kennebec,—and down the Kennebec to the sea near the present Portland, Maine. The route was well known to the Jesuits, who served their coast missions by it, and Father Druillettes several times passed down that way on his errands to Boston. There was nothing surprising in Arnold's expedition to Quebec by that route in 1775. The portage had been " blazed " and could not have been missed. The feat has been greatly exaggerated in the books of history. Below Quebec there were many routes leading south to the sea. That chiefly followed was by the Rivière du Loup and a portage to Lake Temiscouata, from whence the Madawaska led into the River St. John. It was known from the earliest years of French discovery. The portage routes between Chaleur Bay and the St. Lawrence were well known also, but the peninsula of Gaspé was not explored. It is a rough mountain table-land, and until it was examined by Messrs. Macoun and Low of the Geological Survey, twenty years ago, little was known about the interior of that region.

In this chapter and the one immediately preceding, the water-parting of the St. Lawrence basin has been traced throughout its whole length and its relations to the adjoining river basins have been shown. When the French handed Canada over to the English Crown it was a definite and mapped country very much larger than it is now. The valleys of the Ohio and upper Mississippi—including the present States of Ohio, Indiana, Illinois, Michigan, Wisconsin, and Minnesota—formed part of it, for the whole region had been discovered from Canada and was governed from Quebec. After the conquest came the Indian war stirred up by Pontiac, and then followed the war of the American Revolution.

After the peace of 1783 those in the thirteen revolted colonies who had sided with the Crown were proscribed and their property was confiscated. Then began the settlement of the western part of Canada, now known as the Province of Ontario. The French grants extended as far as Coteau du Lac on Lake St. Francis, forty miles above Montreal; beyond that was a forest wilderness. The military posts existed, but there was not one settler until Detroit was reached. There were a few farms on the Detroit River, and west of that, excepting the military posts, was wilderness again. The great immigration commenced in 1783. The exiles with their families arrived on foot, bringing their scanty baggage on carts —some of them all the way from the Carolinas. They crossed Lake Ontario in open boats, coasting along the

The Town and Fortifications of Montreal
From an old engraving

OCCUPATION OF THE VALLEY 413

shore and camping at night. Then came the surveyors, who laid off township after township on the river, commencing where the French grants ended; continuing at the present Kingston and on the Bay of Quinté and extending their surveys rapidly westwards along Lakes Ontario and Erie as the loyalist regiments were disbanded. It was not exploration, it was settlement. The story of the struggle with the wilderness is too long to narrate. It is full of courage and devotion, but it does not fall within our scheme.

The loyalist settlers had been driven from the lands where were the roads and bridges they had helped to build. Everything was to be done over again, and they set bravely to work to tame the wilderness. Attempts were made to improve the channel of the St. Lawrence close to the shore as early as 1779. A little later the projecting points of the river banks were cut through and boats of light draught were "tracked up" at places where, in the French period, portages were necessary. Gradually these cuts were improved, and the present magnificent system of canals was evolved, until a chain of canals opened up, for vessels drawing fourteen feet, a stretch of 1274 miles of inland navigation; so that from the quay opposite Dulhut's old home in Montreal a steamer could pass, without breaking bulk, to Port Arthur at the head of Lake Superior, the headquarters of his busy life in the West. The last to be completed was the Sault Ste. Marie canal on the Canada side—a great work, consisting of one lock 900 feet long by 60 feet wide and with 20 feet depth of water. The route from Lake Simcoe to Lake Ontario which Champlain followed with the Huron war party is being rapidly improved by a system of works, and proposals are entertained for a series of canals to overcome the portages along the Ottawa and the French rivers to the Georgian Bay of Lake Huron, up which Champlain went, in 1615, on his visit to the Huron country.

In 1791 Upper Canada, now Ontario, was set off from the French province of Lower Canada as a separate government under English laws. The first survey of the harbour of the present Toronto was made in 1793. Two wigwams of Mississauga Indians were then the sole forerunners of the crowds which hurry along the streets of the busy capital of Ontario.

At the end of the portage where Jolliet and La Salle met the city of Hamilton now stands. The lakes are covered with steamboats and barges, railways run along the rivers and centre in the strategic points of the old portages, the forests are replaced by farms, and the lumbermen have to go up to the height of land on the north; but the process from the French times was one of survey and settlement. The story does not belong to geography, but to history, and in the pages of the historians it should be sought.

CHAPTER XXIV

OCCUPATION OF THE ATLANTIC COAST

IN previous chapters the discovery and exploration of the Acadian coast have been narrated up to the first settlement in 1604, by De Monts, Champlain, and Poutrincourt. The exploration of the coast, not only of the Atlantic, but of the Gulf of St. Lawrence, from the date of discovery was carried on continuously by the fishermen of Western Europe. One after another the bays and creeks and rivers were searched out, as prospects of a bountiful catch of fish and profitable trade with the natives presented themselves, until all of a sudden we find in Champlain's maps complete and fairly correct outlines of all the coast of Acadia and Newfoundland. While he had himself coasted nearly the whole of Acadia, Champlain made use of information derived from all sources. In his first map (1610) there is, however, no sign of Prince Edward Island; in the second, bearing upon it the date 1612, is a small, round island off the north coast of Nova Scotia, marked Ille St. Jean, and a legend states that the author had not visited that coast; but in the latest map—that of 1632—Isle St. Jean is laid down of full size and in correct position, although there is no record of Champlain ever having been there. These maps indicate that only between 1608 and 1632 the Island of St. John (Prince Edward Island) was recognised as separated from the mainland of Acadia.

The settlement of Poutrincourt at Port Royal was scattered and destroyed in 1613 by an English expedition from Virginia, and for nearly thirty years Acadia was the theatre of much romance and much history, but of little recorded exploration. The French, driven out of Port Royal, did not all leave Acadia, but some retired among the Indians and married Indian women. The attention of the English was, however, directed towards the country—or, to be precise, the attention of the Scotch—for in 1621 James I., as King of Scotland, with the concurrence of the Privy Council of Scotland, granted a charter to Sir William Alexander for an immense region, including all the present Maritime Provinces of Canada with the eastern part of the Province of Quebec. An abortive attempt was made in 1628 by Alexander's son to found a Scotch settlement at Port Royal. They built a fort on the site of Champlain's fort, but all that commemorates the attempt is the name Nova Scotia and the empty title, " Baronet of Nova Scotia," still borne by many noble families in Scotland. At the peace of St. Germain-en-Laye Acadia was restored to France and the Scotch settlers returned to Scotland, though it is maintained that a few of them remained with the Indians. The history immediately succeeding is confused. Biencourt, son and heir of the original grantee, Poutrincourt, transferred his rights to Charles de La Tour, to whose father, Claude de La Tour (who became an English subject and a Baronet of Nova Scotia), Sir William Alexander transferred a portion of what he considered his rights under the Scottish patent. The younger La Tour (Charles) had a post at Cape Sable, and held it for the French Crown against his father, notwithstanding which proof of loyalty the French King superseded him and sent out as Governor Isaac de Razilly, who founded a post at La Hève. In the meantime Charles de La Tour had removed his establishment to the mouth of the St. John River—the site of the present city of that name. When Razilly died, in 1636, he left his interests in Nova Scotia to d'Aulnay Charnisay, who was appointed by the French King. Private war ensued, and Charnisay besieged the fort at St. John, which in her husband's absence was bravely defended by Madame de La Tour. Treason led to the surrender of the fort and treachery led to the breach of the conditions of surrender. The garrison were all hanged, and the high-spirited lady was

View from the site of the old French Fort at Fo
across the Basin. Champlain's settlement

rt Royal (Annapolis)—looking down the river and
was on the opposite side and lower down

THE ATLANTIC COAST 417

forced to witness, with a rope round her own neck, the execution of her faithful servants. She died shortly after the indignity, and Charnisay was drowned five years later in the Annapolis River. It was he who transferred the settlement to the present site of the town of Annapolis. This quiet little town of to-day was a very storm centre in the seventeenth century. It was captured by Sedgwick in 1654 by the order of Cromwell—it was restored in 1668 by Charles II.; it was captured again by Phips in 1690 by order of William III., and was restored at the Treaty of Ryswick in 1697; it was captured again by Nicholson in 1710 for Queen Anne, and at last, in 1713, its destiny was settled at the Peace of Utrecht, when Acadia was ceded to the English Crown.

Among those who came to Acadia with De Razilly was Nicholas Denys, a man of different stamp—a man of peace, a coloniser and organiser. While Razilly lived at his post at La Hève Denys carried on a shore fishery at Port Rossignol (now Liverpool), but Charnisay was an impossible neighbour and Denys removed to the eastern end of Nova Scotia and established posts at Chedabucto (Guysborough), at St. Peter's and St. Anne's on Cape Breton Island, and at Miscou far up the gulf at the southern point of the opening of Chaleur Bay. At these posts he made clearings and plantations, and built forts for their protection. His thorough acquaintance with the country is manifest by the admirable situation of his establishments. At Miscou he secured the fisheries of Chaleur Bay, so productive that its Indian name was "sea of fish." At St. Peter's the Bras d'Or, which occupies the centre of the island, is separated from the outer sea by an isthmus only a mile wide, across which he made a road; and his post at St. Anne's, at the other end of the Bras d'Or, commanded the entrance from the ocean. Denys held his grant from the King of France. It was dated in 1654, and extended from Cape Canso in Nova Scotia to Cape Rosier in Gaspé. He wrote a volume, published at Paris in 1672 with a map, describing all the region. The coal of Cape Breton was first exploited by him—not a difficult task, however, for it crops out on the sea shore. Denys stands out an admirable type of organising coloniser in a period of confusion.

Under the French rule the Acadians had been overgoverned; but they prospered under the sleepy government of the little English garrison at Port Royal (Annapolis). Their clearings spread along the valley of the Annapolis River and the shores of the Basin of Minas and the head of the Bay of Fundy, but they never liked the English, whom they considered to be heretics, and they inspired the Indians with the same feeling. They dwelt in constant hope that the country would be again restored to France, and in the meantime they did as they liked and paid no taxes. At last the British Government decided to occupy Nova Scotia strongly, and in 1749 founded the city of Halifax. The expedition included all classes of society and artificers in all trades. The dreams of the Acadians received a rude shock, for they never expected the English to settle in Acadia, and indeed under the influence of the French in Canada and Cape Breton, and being very ignorant and simple in their isolation, they even doubted the right of the English to occupy the country. The pitiful story of the expatriation of the Acadians does not fall within the scope of this volume—it is long and difficult to narrate with justice, and full of sorrow and tears. Then came the recoil of Frontenac's and Vaudreuil's system of terrorising the English frontier by war parties of Indians led by Frenchmen. The aftermath of the bloody raids of Schenectady, Salmon Falls, and Casco, of Deerfield, Haverhill, and many other English settlements, fell upon this unfortunate people. The plan was conceived in Massachusetts and colonial troops carried it out.

The lands of the expelled Acadian French were slowly taken up, for the Micmac Indians scalped every Englishman who strayed outside the protection of the forts, but settlers came in after the peace of 1763, and after the Revolutionary War large numbers of loyalist refugees and disbanded troops settled in Nova Scotia. Lunen-

THE ATLANTIC COAST 419

burg was settled by Germans in 1753, Pictou and Antigonish by Scotch Highlanders about 1773. Colonel Robert Morse of the Royal Engineers wrote in 1784 a full description of Nova Scotia in its widest sense, including all Acadia. He found settlements dotted all along the shores of the peninsula and mainland, and since then the settlement of the province has steadily proceeded. There are unsettled parts in the interior, but as the peninsula is nowhere more than seventy-five miles across, and deep inlets indent the shores, and rivers and lakes lead into the interior, the country is well known to sportsmen and lumbermen and cannot be called unexplored. Similar conditions exist generally in all the provinces. Exploration was early completed. Everywhere the rivers and streams and lakes covered the forest wilderness with a network of roads and lanes of clear, bright water, and trails led from one cardinal point to another. As settlements progressed on the coast the lumbermen worked up the streams and cut the choice timber in the interior forests, floating it down to tide water. Every lumber firm had, and still has, "explorers" searching out good localities for the following year's cut, but the topography of the country in all its essential points was in the meantime well known, though not surveyed, nor always accurately mapped. Even yet there are discordances upon Canadian maps, for every provincial government and different departments of the Dominion Government make their own maps—there is no official central geographical authority as in England and other countries of Europe.

As appears in preceding chapters, the point of Cape Breton was the very first spot on the northeast coast of the continent known to Europeans. It was the point of discovery in 1497, and a well-known rendezvous for sailors after 1504. Sailors of all nations fished on the coast. Special harbours were preferred by each nation, as is clear from their old names. Thus St. Anne's Bay was resorted to chiefly by the French, the present Sydney harbour was known as la Baye des Espagnols, and the

Louisbourg of after times as Havre aux Anglais; Niganis, now Ingonish, was the site of an abortive Portuguese colony in 1521, and Mira Bay and River are names transferred from Portugal. Under the authority of King James' patent to Sir William Alexander, Sir James Stewart, Lord Ochiltree, in 1629, made an attempt to found a colony. He had sixty people with him, including women and children. He selected Baleine harbour, two miles west of the point of Cape Breton, for his settlement, and there he built a fort and forthwith proceeded to exercise authority. He had not been many months there when Captain Daniel of Dieppe seized the fort and hoisted the French flag. He deported the English settlers to England and France, razed the fort and carried off the guns and ammunition to Grand Cibou, where he established a post, which he called Ste. Anne—known after 1713 as Port Dauphin. After the Treaty of Utrecht had ceded Nova Scotia to England France determined to create at Louisbourg a western Gibraltar to guard the entrance of the gulf, a plan which was achieved with so much success that the English could not carry out any successful settlement in Acadia because of incessant intrigues carried on from thence among the Micmac Indians. In 1747 the New England troops, in conjunction with a British fleet, captured the stronghold which had been so long a thorn in their side. It was restored at the peace, and had to be taken again in 1758 by Wolfe before it was possible to attack Quebec. The island was made a separate government in 1784, and Sydney, the capital, was founded by the first governor, Des Barres, in 1785. Settlement was slow and the island was in 1820 annexed to the Province of Nova Scotia. It was thoroughly well known to the French, excepting the long mountainous prolongation to the north. The interior of that peninsula remained unexplored until within the last twenty years, when it was examined by an officer (Mr. Fletcher) of the Geological Survey.

The Province of New Brunswick was set off from Nova Scotia in 1784 and the city of St. John was founded

THE ATLANTIC COAST

in 1783, but, as we have seen, Champlain surveyed the harbour in 1604, and we have his chart with his soundings laid down upon it. La Tour built a fort there in 1635, and from that time to the conquest and cession of Canada there was always an establishment of more or less importance there. The River St. John is remarkable for navigability throughout its entire course. Only at one spot, the Grand Falls, two hundred and twelve miles from its mouth, is it necessary to make a portage. Its branches spread widely over the province and interlock with the head-waters of many important streams opening up the interior of what is now Maine, as well as New Brunswick, and giving access by several routes to the St. Lawrence. The whole province is singularly well watered, and in the French period, not only were there posts at the mouths of the rivers, but at cardinal points on their courses There was no formal exploration, but gradual advance along the streams. Among the grants registered at Quebec were a number of seigniories on the St. John River, as well as in other places in Acadia. There was a fort at the junction of the Nashwaak (near the present Fredericton), which the English besieged in 1696, and one at Jemseg, built first by the English in 1659, and strengthened by the French in later years. The country round the head of the Bay of Fundy was early settled and forts were built by the English and French. The concession to Nicholas Denys before mentioned ran along the New Brunswick coast on the Gulf of St. Lawrence, and at the end of the seventeenth century there were posts and grants at the mouths of the Richibucto, Miramichi, and Nipisiquit rivers, as well as at Miscou.

The deportation of the Acadians, the break-up of the French trade, and the withdrawal of all the little garrisons put back the development of this region until the outcome of the civil war among the English threw, in 1783, into New Brunswick a loyalist immigration, which really laid the foundation of the present province. To dwell farther upon the subject is beyond the scope of this volume. What occurred was settlement, for the exploration had previously been done. Parts of the interior are still wild—sacred to the moose and caribou, where the hunter and fisherman may leave behind all sign of civilisation, and where the rivers and portage trails are the only roads.

Prince Edward Island is the only completely occupied province of the Dominion. Although, as we have seen, Cartier coasted a part of its shore in 1534, he supposed it to be a part of the mainland, and so it remained on the maps for nearly a hundred years. We first hear of this Island of St. John (for there were others) in 1623, when the Basques, who for a time resisted the royal concessions to the companies trading and fishing in the gulf, seized one of Champlain's vessels and took it to a post they had fortified on the island for their own account. The island in 1661 was included with the Magdalen Islands in a concession made to the Sieur Doublet and others. After Louisbourg was founded attention was directed to the Island of St. John as a source of supply, and in 1720 it was regranted to a company of which the Count de St. Pierre was chief. The other islands in the gulf were again included, together with a post at Miscou. An attempt was made at colonisation, but although the fertility of the island was recognised, very little was done until 1733, when a fort was built and a garrison placed at Port La Joie, the present Charlottetown. The French Acadians were expelled from there also, and in 1769 the British Government granted the island to a number of proprietors. Settlement was slow at first, but about 1800 the current of settlers increased. The absentee proprietors clung in after years to their grants with great tenacity, and it was not until after confederation they could be compelled to sell out.

The islands in the gulf have been referred to incidentally in previous chapters. The Magdalen Islands were included in the grants first to Doublet and then to St. Pierre. The English Government granted them to Admiral Coffin in 1798, in whose family they have

THE ATLANTIC COAST 423

remained. They are inhabited by a contented population of fishermen. The Island of Anticosti, facing the estuary of the river, challenges attention from its size and position. It is 122 miles long and 30 miles wide, and until the last few years it was known only as one of the dangers of navigation in the gulf, and associated with gruesome stories of shipwreck and starvation. The coasts have long been accurately surveyed and charted, but the interior has been, until recently, unknown, and much of it is still unexplored. It was a favourite ground for hunting walruses, and Hakluyt records voyages thither, but the walruses have long since been exterminated. Jolliet made an attempt to settle there after the island was granted to him in 1680, and he wintered there with his family for several seasons, but in 1690 the English, under Admiral Phips, destroyed his establishments and ruined him. The property passed by inheritance through several generations until after the conquest, when some English people bought it, but none of them made any serious attempt to colonise or use the island in any way. It existed solely as a terror to sailors. At last in 1874 a company made an attempt at colonisation, but failed. No one would believe the island was good for anything but wrecking ships. After many abortive attempts to dispose of it, the island was in 1895 purchased for $125,000 by M. Henry Menier of Paris, and is now his property in fee simple. He is restocking it with game, bringing in settlers, establishing fisheries, leasing farms, making roads, and building mills for lumber, grain, and pulp. A village has started up at the place where M. Menier has fixed the seat of what is practically his government, and it has now been discovered that the thick matted brushwood along the coast is merely a screen concealing much good land and good timber. M. Menier has, in fact, a principality of 2600 square miles in extent—larger than Prince Edward Island—where, subject only to the public law of Canada, he is supreme. Attempts are now and then made to excite prejudice on account of M. Menier's nationality, but in vain, for he is redeeming a waste portion of Canada and making a wilderness into a home for a settled population. Such aliens are benefactors, and it will be time enough to fear M. Menier when he begins to rear fortresses and raise troops.

The island province of Newfoundland is a standing witness of the power of bad laws to retard the settlement of a fine colony. It is the oldest transatlantic possession of the British Crown, and it has been for hundreds of years the unfortunate subject of constant imperial legislation. Its early discovery has been sufficiently dwelt upon in previous chapters. At the beginning of the seventeenth century the coast line of the island was fully explored. Almost every harbour was then frequented by fishermen from Western Europe, and no more than that could be said at the close of the eighteenth century. Even yet the population is a fringe on the sea coast at the east and south, and it is only within the last few months that the foreign influence which for two hundred years kept the north and west coasts a wilderness, has, by a stroke of wise and happy statesmanship, been removed.

The dominant idea of all legislation from 1633 to 1800 regarding Newfoundland was that it should be a nursery of English seamen, and to that end the fishing industry was alone sanctioned. Every other interest was repressed. Such permanent settlers as there were were discouraged and more than once orders-in-council were passed to compel them to remove to another colony, by tearing down their homes. Buildings could not be erected without the permission of the governor, and vessels were forbidden to carry settlers to the island. The object was to make it a fishing station only, from which, when the season was over, all the inhabitants should return to England.

It is unprofitable to dwell upon such perversities of government excepting to explain the otherwise unaccountable fact that a large portion of the interior of Newfoundland is to this day unexplored. It is not sur-

THE ATLANTIC COAST 425

prising that a lake not laid down upon the maps should be announced as discovered in September, 1903. There are many blanks upon the map yet to be filled up, especially in the northern peninsula and in the southern part of the interior. Communication, until the railway was constructed, was almost solely by sea, and the first piece of ordinary road was not built until the year 1825.

The first attempt at exploration of the interior was made in 1822 by Mr. W. E. Cormack. He had arranged to have a companion from the colony with him, and a Micmac Indian as guide, but the governor opposed the attempt, and as the colonist held some civil appointment Cormack had to go with the Indian only, the governor, fortunately, having no hold on the Micmacs. Cormack started from the head of Random Sound, in Trinity Bay, September 3, and arrived at St. George's Bay, on the west coast, on November 2, having crossed the island on foot at its widest part. He found game plentiful, and in the ponds and lakes were geese, ducks, and fish in abundance. The woods were all furrowed with paths made by caribou in their migrations. There were marshes and barrens, but also green plains and good timber. No similar attempt was made until 1864, when a Geological Survey was instituted under Mr. Alexander Murray, and it has been successfully continued under his successor, Mr. James Howley, to the present day. Exploration has been directed chiefly to those parts of the island giving promise of minerals and along the valleys of the rivers, which all flow diagonally southwest and northeast across the centre of the island, and where the best land and timber are found.

The telegraph lines in connection with the ocean cables at Heart's Content on Trinity Bay do indeed cross the island to Port aux Basques, but they follow the heads of the great southern bays. A survey for a projected railway was made in 1875, and the route selected was not far from Cormack's track in 1822, across the broad southern portion of the island. Although no engineering difficulties were encountered, the project was not carried out, and in fact that part of the island gives little promise of resources to support a railway or to attract settlement. In 1882 railway building began with a line to connect the settlements along the east coast, and at last, in 1893, the Northern & Western Railway was commenced. It leads first to the north, touching the heads of the great eastern bays and serving the chief settlements; crosses the valley of the Gander to the Exploits River, which it follows westward for some distance, then strikes across the centre of the island to the head of Grand Lake and the Humber River, thus opening up the best part of the interior. The road follows the Humber to the head of the Bay of Islands on the west coast, and turning south it passes on to St. George's Bay, and thence to Port aux Basques on Cabot Strait, thus making a great semicircle through the heart of the island.

The unexplored regions lie to the north and south of the great river valleys which cross the centre of the island in a northeast and southwest direction. Along these valleys are the most promising regions. Large tracts of good land with fine timber are found there, and through them any movement towards settlement will proceed. What is known of the unexplored parts of the island indicates a plateau of no great height, abounding in lakes and ponds of all sizes connected by streams and with frequent marshes. There are large tracts of "barrens," bare of trees, but covered with caribou moss and interspersed with patches of stunted pines and larch. Great herds of caribou inhabit the interior and migrate to the south in the autumn to return in the spring to the north. When the fishing season is over the fishermen on the coast go up the deep inlets and the rivers to shoot the caribou on their migrations, and sportsmen from England and the United States resort to the island for the same purpose. Such excursions are made by men who do not concern themselves with geography, and there is, therefore, much knowledge of the country not recorded upon maps. To follow Cormack's track of 1822, or even the track of the railway survey of 1875, may be an

THE ATLANTIC COAST 427

arduous undertaking, but by the river valleys the island may be readily crossed. That so much should remain unexplored of that part of America which lies nearest to Europe is indeed surprising, until the history of the country is taken into account.

Our task is now achieved. From the landfall of 1497 we have traced, step by step, the progress of discovery and exploration into the heart of the Western World. It is a story of four hundred years. Its incidents, though of great interest and of vast eventual importance, for a long time attracted little attention in the great centres of civilisation and letters. Empires in the Old World have waxed and waned, but, in the New World, growth, feeble at first, has increased, and is increasing at a rate incessantly accelerating. We have passed from John Cabot's little vessel two thousand miles into the interior of the mainland he first touched, to the Sault of Lake Superior, where locks nine hundred feet long bear the monstrous craft which carry a traffic already larger in volume, if not in value, than the traffic through the Suez Canal between the hoary continents of Europe and Asia.

APPENDIX

LIST OF THE CHIEF WORKS CONSULTED OR REFERRED TO IN PREPARING THIS VOLUME

WORKS OF GENERAL REFERENCE

1. The Literature of American History. A bibliographical guide, in which the scope, character, and comparative worth of books in selected lists are set forth in brief notes by critics of authority. Edited for the American Library Association by J. N. Larned. 8vo, Boston; 1902.
2. A History of Ancient Geography among the Greeks and Romans, from the Earliest Ages to the Fall of the Roman Empire. By E. H. Bunbury. 2 vols., 8vo, London; 1883.
3. Géographie du Moyen Age, &c., &c. 5 vols. in four; 8vo, with atlas, oblong folio. By Joachim Lelewel. Brussels. 1852-57.
4. The Dawn of Modern Geography. A History of Exploration and Geographical Science. By C. Raymond Beazley. 8vo, London; 1897.
5. The Book of Ser Marco Polo, the Venetian; concerning the Kingdoms and Marvels of the East. Translated and edited with notes by Colonel Henry Yule. 2 vols., 8vo, second edition, London; 1875.
6. Fonti Italiani per la storia della scoperta del Nuovo Mondo. Raccolte da Guglielmo Berchet. 2 vols., folio, Rome; 1892.
7. Delle Navigationi et Viaggi. Raccolte da M. Gio. Battista Ramusio. 3 vols., folio, Venice, 1554-65.
8. Narrative and Critical History of America. Edited by Justin Winsor. 8 vols., imp. 8vo. Boston.
   This work is the joint production of a number of scholars, each writing on his own subject. It is especially valuable for the bibliographical and cartographical notes and appendices contributed by the editor.
9. Coleccion de los Viages y Descubrimientos que hicieron por mar los Españoles desde fines del Siglo XV. Por D. Martin Fernandez de Navarrete. 5 vols. in 4to, Madrid; 1825-37.

10. Historia general y natural de las Indias, islas y tierra-ferme del mar océano. Por el Capitan Gonzalo Fernandez de Oviedo y Valdéz. 4 vols., folio. Madrid; 1851-55.
11. Historia general de los hechos de los Castellanos en las Islas i Tierre firme del Mar océano. Éscrita por Antonio de Herrera—in eight Decades. 3 vols., folio. Madrid; 1726-30. Translation into French of the three first Decades by N. de La Coste. 3 vols., 4to, Paris; 1659-71.
12. Historia del Nuevo Mundo. Por J. B. Muñoz. Vol. I, Madrid; 1793.
13. The Principall Navigations, Voiages and Discoveries of the English nation made by sea or over land, . . . within the compasse of these 1500 years, &c., &c. By Richard Hakluyt. Edition by Edmund Goldsmid, 16 vols., 8vo. Edinburgh; 1885-90.
14. Diuers Voyages touching the Discoverie of America and the islands adjacent. Edited by Richard Hakluyt, 1582. Reprint, 8vo, London, 1850.
15. The Discoveries of the World from their first original unto the year of Our Lord 1555. By Antonio Galvano. Corrected, quoted, and published in England by Richard Hakluyt (1601). Reprinted with the original Portuguese text and edited by Vice-Admiral Bethune. 8vo, London; 1862.
16. The First Three English Books on America (1511-1555). Being chiefly translations, compilations, &c., by Richard Eden, from the writings of Peter Martyr of Anghiera, Sebastian Munster, the cosmographer, Sebastian Cabot of Bristol, with extracts from the works of other Spanish, Italian, and German Writers of the Time. Edited by Edward Arber. 4to, Birmingham; 1885.
17. America: Its Geographical History. By W. P. Scaife. 8vo, Baltimore; 1892.
18. The Discovery of North America: A critical, documentary and historic investigation, with an essay on the early Cartography of the New World, before the year 1536. By Henry Harrisse. 4to, London; 1892.
    Students of American history must always avail themselves of Mr. Harrisse's works, and should not fail to express their obligations to his exact and exhaustive researches. They cover the whole field of the history of the Western World.
19. Découverte et Evolution cartographique de Terre-Neuve et des pays circonvoisins, 1497-1501-1769. Essais de Géographie historique et documentaire. Par Henry Harrisse. 4to, London, Henry Stevens, Son & Stiles; 1890.
20. Historical and Biographical Notes on the Earliest Dis-

APPENDIX 431

coveries in America, 1493-1530, etc. By Henry Stevens. New Haven; 1869.
21. A History of the Discovery of Maine. By J. G. Kohl. With an Appendix on the Voyages of the Cabots, by M. d'Avezac. This work is Vol. 1 of the Documentary History of the State of Maine. 8vo, Portland; 1869.
22. The Early History of Cartography. By Charles P. Daly. 8vo. Address before the Am. Geog. Society, New York, 1879.
23. Lecture on American Maps. By J. G. Kohl. 8vo, Washington; 1857.
24. Les Monuments de la Géographie. Recueil d'anciennes Cartes Européenes et Orientales. Par E. F. Jomard. Imperial folio, Paris; 1854-56.
25. Die Entdeckung Amerikas, &c., &c. Text and Atlas. By F. Kunstmann. 4to and imperial folio. Munich; 1859.
26. Die Entdeckung Amerikas in ihrer Bedeutung für die Geschichte des Weltbildes. Text and atlas by Konrad Kretschmer. 4to and royal folio, Berlin; 1892.
27. Map of the World by the Spanish cosmographer, Alonzo de Santa Cruz, 1542. Reproduction in fac-simile edited by E. W. Dahlgren. Stockholm; 1892.
28. Fac-simile Atlas to the Early History of Cartography. By Baron A. E. Nordenskiöld; with English text rendered from the Swedish by J. A. Ekelof and Clements R. Markham. Folio, Stockholm; 1889.
29. Ensayo Biográfico del célebre navegante y consumado cosmógrafo Juan de La Cosa y Descripción é Historia de su famoso Carta Geográfica. Por Antonio Vascáno. 12mo, Madrid; 1892. With a fac-simile reproduction of La Cosa's map of 1500, of full size.
30. The Discoveries of America to the Year 1525. By Arthur James Weise. 8vo, London; 1884.
31. The Discovery of America. By John Fiske. 2 vols., 8vo, Boston; 1892.
32. The Life and Voyages of Christopher Columbus, together with the Voyages of his Companions. By Washington Irving.
33. Christopher Columbus, and How he received and imparted the Spirit of Discovery. By Justin Winsor. 8vo, Boston.
34. The Diplomatic History of America; its first chapter, 1452-1493-1494. By Henry Harrisse. 12mo, London; 1897.
35. The Line of Demarcation of Pope Alexander VI. in A. D. 1493 and that of the Treaty of Tordesillas in A. D. 1494; with an Inquiry concerning the Metrology of Ancient and Mediæval Times. By Samuel Edward Dawson.

432 APPENDIX

8vo, Ottawa; 1900. Trans. Roy. Soc. of Canada for 1899, and published separately.

36. Proceedings and Transactions of the Royal Society of Canada. Published annually since 1883. First series, 12 vols., 4to; second series (now current) in 8vo. Ottawa and Montreal.

Sections 1 and 2 (French and English History and Archæology) contain many important studies on the subjects of this volume.

CABOT AND CORTE-REAL VOYAGES.

37. Cabot Bibliography. With an introductory essay on the careers of the Cabots, based upon an independent examination of the sources of information. By George Parker Winship. London and New York; 1900.

This is an exhaustive work, leaving nothing to be desired. The notes are luminous and judicious.

38. A Memoir of Sebastian Cabot, with a Review of the History of Maritime Discovery. By Richard Biddle. 8vo, Philadelphia; 1831.
39. Presidential Address for 1897. By Sir Clements Markham. Geographical Journal, 1897; London.
40. John and Sebastian Cabot. Biographical Notice with Documents by Francesco Tarducci. Translated from the Italian by Henry F. Brownson. 8vo, Detroit; 1893.

This work contains extracts of the originals, in Latin, Spanish, English, and Italian, of all the references to the Cabot voyages scattered throughout the larger and rarer works.

41. Jean et Sebastian Cabot; leur origine et leurs Voyages. Etude d'Histoire Critique; suivie d'une Bibliographie et d'une Chronologie des Voyages au Nord-ouest de 1497 à 1550, etc. Par Henry Harrisse. Royal 8vo, Paris; 1882.
42. John Cabot, the Discoverer of North America, and Sebastian, his son: a Chapter of the Maritime History of England under the Tudors, 1496-1557. By Henry Harrisse. 8vo, London; 1896.
43. Papers by Samuel Edward Dawson in the Trans. Roy. Soc. of Canada.

The Voyages of the Cabots in 1497 and 1498. Vol. 12, 1st series.

The Voyages of the Cabots. A Sequel. Vol. 2, 2d series.

The Voyages of the Cabots. Latest phases of the controversy. Vol. 3, 2d series.

In the Appendix to Vol. 3 the legends on the Cabot map of 1544, as translated under the supervision of Dr. Charles Deane, are reprinted with the Spanish and Latin originals from Vol. 6. Series 2, Trans. Mass. Hist. Soc.

44. John and Sebastian Cabot, The Discovery of North America by. By C. Raymond Beazley. 12mo, London and New York; 1898.
45. Cabot's Discovery of North America. By G. E. Weare. 12mo, London; 1897.
46. Papers and Studies by M. d'Avezac in the "Bulletin de la Societé de Géographie," Paris, his introduction to the "Bref Récit" of the second voyage of Jacques Cartier (reprint by Tross), and his letter on the Cabot discovery of America addressed to the editor of Kohl's "Discovery of Maine," and published as a supplement thereto.
47. The Journal of Christopher Columbus (during his first voyage, 1492-93) and Documents Relating to the Voyages of John Cabot and Gaspar Corte-Real. Translated with notes and an introduction by Clements R. Markham. 8vo, London; 1893.

   This work contains the translations of the essential documents bearing upon the Cabot and Corte-Real voyages. In this volume, together with Nos. 40, 41, and 42, the original sources scattered through many rare and costly works are available.
48. Review of Historical Publications Relating to Canada. Edited by George M. Wrong. University of Toronto Studies in History. Published annually. 6 vols., 8vo, 1896-1903; Toronto.

   This publication is valuable in this connection, for it contains reviews by Canadian scholars of all recently published works on the history and exploration of Canada.
49. Etude sur les Rapports de l'Amerique et de l'Ancien Continent avant Christophe Colomb. Par Paul Gaffarel. 8vo, Paris; 1869.
50. Les Corte-Reals, et leurs Voyages au Nouveau Monde d'après des documents nouveaux ou peu connus, suivi de texte inédit d'un récit de la troisième expedition de Gaspar Corte-Real. Royal 8vo, Paris; 1883.

   This work is exhaustive of its special subject, for it contains all existing documents of importance relating to these voyages. They are given in the original Portuguese without translation. Translations of the most important will be found in No. 47.
51. La Part prise par les Portugais dans le découverte de l'Amérique. Par Luciano Cordeiro. Transactions of the Congress of Americanistes at Nancy in 1875. Paris; 1875.

52. Archivo dos Açores, vol. 12. Ponte Delgada, 1894, containing a paper by Ernesto do Canto on the Portuguese discovery of America. Also Vol. 4 of the same series, containing a memoir on the Corte-Reals by Do Canto.
53. Papers by H. Yule Oldham and J. Batalha Reis on Discoveries of America by the Portuguese prior to Columbus. Geog. Soc., Nov., 1894; Geog. Journal, March, 1895; April, 1895.

BASQUE, BRETON, AND NORMAN VOYAGES

54. Historia de la Provincia de Guipuzcoa. Por Don Nicholas de Soraluce. 12mo, Madrid; 1864.
55. Memoria acerca del origen y curso de las Pescas y Pesquerías de Ballenas y de Bacallaos, Asi que sobre el Descubrimiento de los Bancos e Isla de Terranova. Por Don Nicholas de Soraluce. 12mo, Vitoria; 1878.
56. Le Pays Basque. Par F. Michel. Paris; 1857.
57. Le Basque et les langues Americaines. Par M. Julien Vinson. Compte-Rendu du Congrès International des Americanistes; 1875. Paris; 1875.
58. Papers of the Rev. George Patterson in the Trans. Roy. Soc. of Canada.
    The Portuguese on the North-west Coast of North America. Vol. 8, 1st series.
    The Beothiks or Red Indians of Newfoundland. Vol. 9, 1st series.
    Sable Island. Vol. 12, 1st series.
    Last Years of Charles de Biencourt. Vol. 2, 2d series.
    Supplementary Notes on Sable Island. Vol. 3, 2d series.
59. Basques, Bretons, et Normands sur les côtes de l'Amerique de Nord pendant les premiéres années du XVIeme Siècle. Par Paul Gaffarel. Congrès des Americanistes. Sess. 7 à Berlin; 1890.
60. Histoire de Dieppe. Par M. L. Vitet. 2 vols., 8vo, Paris; 1833.
61. Les Navigations Françaises. Par Pierre Margry. 8vo, Paris; 1867.
62. Récherches sur les Voyages et Découvertes des Navigateurs Normands. Par L. Estancelin. Paris; 1832.
63. Documents relatifs à la Marine Normande et à ses armaments aux XVIe et XVIIe siècles pour le Canada, l'Afrique, &c. Recueillis, annotés et publiés par Charles et Paul Bréard. 8vo, Rouen; 1889.
64. Les Us et Coutumes de la Mer. 4to, Rouen, 1671. Containing Les Jugemens d'Oléron.
65. An Inquiry into the authenticity of documents concerning a

APPENDIX 435

discovery of America claimed to have been made by Verrazzano. Essay read before the New York Historical Society. By Buckingham Smith. 8vo, New York; 1864.
66. The Voyage of Verrazano. By Henry C. Murphy. 8vo, New York; 1875.
67. Notes on Giovanni da Verrazano and on a Planisphere of 1529, Illustrating his American Voyage in 1524, with a Reduced copy of the map. By James Carson Brevoort. 8vo. In the Journal of the American Geographical Society of New York for 1873, and also separately, New York; 1874.
68. Verrazano the Explorer; a Vindication of his Letter and Voyage by B. F. Da Costa. 4to, New York; 1881.

CANADIAN HISTORY: CARTIER'S VOYAGES, ETC.

69. Notes pour servir à l'Histoire, à la Bibliographie, et à la Cartographie de la Nouvelle France et des Pays adjacents, 1545-1703 (par Henri Harrisse). 8vo, Paris; 1872.
70. Histoire de la Nouvelle France. Contenant les navigations, découvertes, et habitations faites par les François és Indes Occidentales et Nouvelle France. Par Marc Lescarbot. Paris; 1612. Reprint, 3 vols., Paris; 1866.
71. Histoire et Description générale de la Nouvelle France et Journal d'un Voyage dans l'Amerique Septentrionale. Par le P. de Charlevoix de la Compagnie de Jesus. 3 vols., 4to, Paris; 1744. There is an English translation of this work by John Gilmary Shea, enriched with valuable notes. 6 vols., 8vo, New York; 1886.
72. Bibliotheca Lindesiana. Fac-simile of Three Mappe-mondes. With collations and notes by C. H. Coote. Atlas folio, London; 1898. (Harleian, Dauphin and Desceliers' Maps.) There is a paper by Harrisse upon this work. "Dieppe World Maps," Goettingen; 1899.
73. The Works of Francis Parkman: Pioneers of France; The Old Régime in Canada; The Jesuits in North America; La Salle and the Discovery of the Great West; Frontenac and New France. Boston.
    These are the titles of Parkman's works bearing upon the subject of this volume.
74. La Nouvelle France de Cartier à Champlain, 1540-1603. Par N. E. Dionne. 8vo, Quebec; 1901.
75. Historiæ Canadensis seu Novæ Franciæ libri decem ad annum usque Christi, 1656. Small 4to (Father Francis du Creux), Paris; 1664.
76. Histoire du Canada et Voyages que les Frères Mineurs

Recollects y ont faicts. Par le Frère Gabriel Sagard. 4 vols., 12mo, Paris; 1886.
77. Histoire Chronologique de la Nouvelle France ou Canada depuis sa découverte (1504) jusques en l'an 1632. Par la Père Sixte Le Tac, Récollect. Publiée pour la première fois d'apres le manuscript original de 1689 et accompagnée de Notes et d'un Appendice tout composé de documents originaux et inédits par Eug. Réveillaud. 8vo. Paris; 1888.
78. Cours d'Histoire du Canada. Par l'Abbé J. B. Ferland, 2 vols., 8vo, Quebec; 1861.
79. The History of Canada. By William Kingsford, 10 vols., 8vo, Toronto; 1887-98.
80. Histoire des Canadians-Français. Par Benjamin Sulte. 8 vols., 4to, Montréal; 1882-84.
81. New France and New England. By John Fiske. 12mo, Boston.
82. Historical and Descriptive Account of the Island of Cape Breton. By J. G. Bourinot. 4to, Montreal; 1892.
83. The Early Trading Companies of New France. A Contribution to the History of Commerce and Discovery in North America. By H. P. Biggar (University of Toronto Series of Studies). Royal 8vo, Toronto; 1901.
84. The Anticipations of Cartier's Voyages, 1492-1534. By Justin Winsor. From the Proceedings of the Massachusetts Historical Society. Cambridge, Mass.; 1893.
85. Voyages de Découverte au Canada entre les Années 1534 et 1542 par Jacques Cartier, le sieur de Roberval, Jean Alphonse de Xanctoigne, &c. Publiés sous la direction de la Société Littéraire et Historique de Québec. 8vo, Quebec; 1843.
86. Voyage de Jaques Cartier au Canada en 1534. Publiée d'après l'edition de 1598 et d'après Ramusio. Par M. H. Michelant. Documents indédits sur Jaques Cartier et le Canada communiqués. Par M. Alfred Ramé. 12mo, Paris; 1865.
87. Relation Originale du Voyage de Jacques Cartier au Canada en 1534. Documents inédits sur Jacques Cartier et le Canada. Publiés par H. Michelant et A. Ramé. 12mo, Paris; 1867.
88. Bref Récit et Succincte Narration de la Navigation faite en 1535-36 par le Capitaine Jacques Cartier aux Iles de Canada, Hochelaga, Saguenay, et Autres. Ré-impression de l'édition originale precedée d'une introduction historique. Par D'Avezac. 12mo, Paris; 1863.
89. Jacques Cartier; Documents Nouveaux recueillis par F. Joüon des Longrais. 12mo, Paris; 1888.

APPENDIX 437

90. Papers by Bishop Howley in the Trans. Roy. Soc. of Canada.
    Cartier's Course. Vol. 12, 1st series.
    The Old Basque Tombstones of Placentia. Vol. 8, 2d series.
91. Jacques Cartier; His Life and Voyages. By Joseph Pope. 12mo, Ottawa; (1890).
92. Jacques Cartier. Par N. E. Dionne. 12mo, Quebec; 1889.
93. Jacques Cartier and His Four Voyages to Canada. An essay with historical, explanatory and philological notes, by Hiram B. Stephens. Royal 8vo, Montreal (1890).
94. Papers by the Abbé Verreau in the Trans. Roy. Soc. of Canada.
    Les Fondateurs de Montréal. Vol. 5, 1st series.
    Jacques Cartier; Questions de Calendrier. Vol. 8, 1st series.
    Jacques Cartier; Questions de Droit et d'usage maritime. Vol. 9, 1st series.
    Jacques Cartier; Questions de Loi et Coutumes Maritimes. Vol. 3, 2d series.
    Samuel de Champlain. Vol. 5, 2d series.
95. Papers by W. F. Ganong in the Trans. Roy. Soc. of Canada.
    Jacques Cartier's First Voyage. Vol. 5, 1st series.
    Cartography of the Gulf of St. Lawrence from Cartier to Champlain. Vol. 7, 1st series.
    Dochet (St. Croix) Island. Vol. 8, 2d series.
96. Les Singularitez de la France Antarctique autrement nommée Amérique, . . . Par André Thevet. Small 8vo, Paris; Reprint, 1878.
97. La Cosmographie Universelle. . . . Par André Thevet. 2 vols., fol., Paris; 1575.
98. Papers by Paul de Cazes in the Trans. Roy. Soc. of Canada.
    Deux points d'Histoire—(1) Quatrième Voyage de Jacques Cartier. (2) Expedition du Marquis de La Roche. Vol. 1, 1st series.
    Les Points obscurs des Voyages de Jacques Cartier. Vol. 8, 1st series.
99. Papers by John Reade in the Trans. Roy. Soc. of Canada.
    The Making of Canada. Vol. 2, 1st series.
    The Basques in North America. Vol. 4, 1st series.

CHAMPLAIN VOYAGES AND COMMENCEMENTS OF EXPLORATION OF THE ST. LAWRENCE, ETC.

100. Œuvres de Champlain. Publiées sous le patronage de l'Université Laval par l'Abbé C. H. Laverdière. 6 vols., 4to, Quebec; 1870.
101. Voyages of Champlain. Translated by Chas. P. Otis. Edited

with memoir and notes by Edmund F. Slafter. 3 vols., sm. 4to. Boston (Prince Society); 1878-82.
102. Vie de Samuel Champlain, fondateur de la Nouvelle France (1567-1635). Par Gabriel Gravier. 8vo, Paris; 1900.
103. Papers by Benjamin Sulte in Trans. Roy. Soc. of Canada. Les Interprètes du temps de Champlain. Vol. 1, 1st series. Poutrincourt en Acadie. Vol. 2, 1st series. Le Golfe St. Laurent (1600-1625). Vols. 4 and 7, 1st series. Les Tonty. Vol. 12, 1st series. Pierre Boucher et son livre. Vol. 2, 2d series. La Guerre aux Iroquois, 1600-1653. Vol. 4, 2d series. The Valley of the Grand River. Vol. 4, 2d series.
104. Cartier to Frontenac. Geographical Discovery in the Interior of North America in Its Historical Relations, 1534-1700. By Justin Winsor. 8vo, Boston; 1900.
105. Le Journal des Jesuites, 1645-68. 4to, Quebec; 1871.
106. The Jesuit Relations and Allied Documents. Travels and Explorations of the Jesuit Missionaries in New France, 1610-1791. The original French, Latin, and Italian texts, with English translations and notes. Illustrated by portraits, maps, and fac-similes. Edited by Reuben Gold Thwaites. 73 vols., 8vo, Cleveland; 1896-1901.
107. Relations des Jésuites. Contenant ce qui s'est passé de plus remarquable dans les Missions des Pères de la Compagnie de Jésus dans la Nouvelle France. Québec, 3 vols., 8vo; 1858.
108. Relations Inédites de la Nouvelle France, 1672-79, pour faire suite aux anciennes Relations. 2 vols., 12mo, Paris; 1861.
  Cited by the name of the publisher, Charles Douniol. They are included in Thwaites' Series. See No. 106.
109. Les Jésuites et la Nouvelle France au XVIIme siécle. Par la R. P. Camille Rochemonteix. 3 vols., 8vo, Paris; 1895.
110. Relation Abrégée de quelques Missions des Pères de la Compagnie de Jésus dans la Nouvelle France. Par le R. P. F. I. Bressany de la même compagnie. Traduit de l'Italian. . . . par la R. P. F. Martin. 8vo, Montreal; 1852.
111. Etablissement de la Foy dans la Nouvelle France. Contenant l'histoire des Colonies Françaises et des découvertes, . . . avec une relation exacte des expeditions, &c., sous la conduite de Sieur de La Salle. 12mo, Paris; 1671.
  There is an English translation of the above by John Gilmary Shea, enriched with valuable notes. 2 vols., 8vo, New York; 1881.
112. Nouvelle Relation de la Gaspésie, qui contient les Mœurs et

APPENDIX 439

la Religion des Sauvages Gaspésiens. Par Chrestien Le Clercq. 12mo, Paris; 1691.
113. The Annual Reports on Canadian Archives, with Calendars of Documents, by Douglas Brymner, 1883 to 1902. Ottawa.
114. The First English Conquest of Canada. By Henry Kirke. 8vo, London; 1871.
115. Histoire de la Colonie Française en Canada. (By the Abbé Faillon.) 3 vols., imp. 8vo, Villemarie (Montreal); 1866.
116. Histoire veritable et naturelle du Canada. Par Pierre Boucher. 12mo, Paris; 1654.
117. Découvertes et Etablissements des Français dans l'Ouest et dans le Sud de l'Amérique Septentrionale, 1614-98. Par Pierre Margry. 6 vols., 8vo, Paris; 1879-88.
118. The Iroquois Book of Rites. By Horatio Hale. 8vo, Philadelphia; 1883.
119. Papers by Horatio Hale in the Trans. Roy. Soc. of Canada. An Iroquois Condoling Council. Vol. 1, 2d series.
120. League of the Ho-De-No-Sau-Nee, or Iroquois. By Lewis H. Morgan. New ed. with notes by Herbert M. Lloyd. 2 vols., 8vo, New York; 1901.
121. Paper by Sir Daniel Wilson in Trans. Roy. Soc. of Canada. The Huron-Iroquois of Canada. Vol. 2, 1st series.
122. The History of the Five Indian Nations which are dependent on the Province of New York in America. By Cadwallader Colden. 2 vols., 12mo, London; 1755.
123. The Traditional History and Characteristic Sketches of the Ojibway Nation. By G. Copway (Kah-ge-ga-gah-bowh), Chief of the Ojibway Nation. 12mo, London; 1850.
124. Origin and Traditional History of the Wyandotts. By Peter Dooyentate Clarke. 12mo, Toronto; 1870.
125. Mœurs des Sauvages Americains. Par le Père Lafiteau. 2 vols., 4vo, Paris; 1725.
126. Histoire de l'Amérique Septentrionale. Par M. de Bacqueville de la Potherie. 4 vols., 12mo, Paris; 1753.
127. Mémoire sur les Mœurs, Coutumes, et Religion des Sauvages de l'Amérique Septentrionale. Par Nicholas Perrot, publié pour la première fois par le L. P. J. Tailhan. 12mo. Paris and Leipzic; 1864.
128. History of Brulé's Discoveries and Explorations, 1610-1626, &c., &c., with a Biographical Notice by Consul Willshire Butterfield. 8vo, Cleveland; 1898.
129. History of the Discovery of the Northwest by John Nicolet in 1634, with a sketch of his life. By C. W. Butterfield, 12mo, Cincinnati; 1881.
130. Mélanges d'Histoire et de Littérature. Par B. Sulte. 12mo, Ottawa; 1876.

440 APPENDIX

131. History of Early Missions in Western Canada. By Rev. W. Harris. 12mo, Toronto; 1893.
132. The Country of the Neutrals. By Jas. H. Coyne. 8vo, St. Thomas; 1895.

EXPLORATIONS ON THE LAKES, ETC., ETC.

133. Papers by N. E. Dionne in the Trans. Roy. Soc. of Canada. Chouart et Radisson. Vol. 11, 1st series. Chouart et Radisson. Vol. 12, 1st series. Jean François de la Rocque, Seigneur de Roberval. Vol. 5, 2d series.
134. Voyages. Being an account of his Travels and Experiences among the North American Indians, 1652-84, by Pierre Esprit Radisson. With historical illustrations and introduction by Gideon D. Scull. Sm. 4to, Boston (Prince Society); 1885.
135. Annals of Fort Mackinac. By Dwight H. Kelton. 12mo, Detroit; 1888.
136. Mackinac; formerly Michilimackinac. . . . By John P. Bailey. 12mo, Lansing, Michigan; 1899.
137. Early Mackinac: a Sketch Historical and Descriptive. By Meade C. Williams. 12mo, St. Louis; 1901.
138. Exploration of the Great Lakes, 1669-70, by Dollier de Casson and de Bréhant de Galinée. A reprint of the original with an English translation and reproduction of the map with all the legends. By James H. Coyne. 8vo, Ontario Historical Society, Toronto; 1903.
139. Discovery and Exploration of the Mississippi Valley, with the Original Narratives of Marquette, Allouez, Membré, Hennepin, and Anastase Douay. By John Gilmary Shea. 2d ed., 8vo, Albany; 1903.
140. Louis Jolliet; Découvreur du Mississippi et du Pays des Illinois, Premier Seigneur de l'Ile d'Anticosti. Par Ernest Gagnon. 8vo, Quebec; 1902.
141. La Revue Canadienne. Vol. 9, containing a series of papers by Pierre Margry on Jolliet's life and voyages. 8vo, Montreal.
142. Father Marquette. By Reuben Gold Thwaites. 12mo, New York; 1902.
143. Lake St. Louis—old and new—illustrated, and Cavelier de La Salle. By Désiré Girouard. Imp. 8vo, Montreal; 1893.
144. The Ship-yard of the *Griffon*. By Cyrus K. Remington. 8vo, Buffalo; 1891.
145. Hulbert, H. H. Historic Highways of America. 10 vols., 12mo, Cleveland; 1903.
146. The Mississippi Basin. By Justin Winsor. 8vo, Boston.

APPENDIX 441

147. Nouvelle Découverte d'un très grand pays situé dans l'Amérique, entre le Nouveau Mexique et la Mer Glaciale, &c. Par le R. P. Louis Hennepin. 12mo, Amsterdam; 1698.
148. The Niagara Region in History. By Peter A. Porter, in The Harnessing of Niagara, Cassier's Magazine. 8vo, London; 1899; and published separately.
149. Publications of the Buffalo Historical Society. Volume 1, containing Marshall's paper on early Niagara. 8vo, Buffalo.
150. Old Trails on the Niagara Frontier. By Frank H. Severance. Second edition. 8vo, Cleveland; 1903.
151. Daniel de Greysolon Du L'Hut—a Gentleman of the Royal Guard. By William McLennan. Harper's Magazine, September, 1893.
152. Nouveaux Voyages de M. le Baron de Lahontan dans l'Amérique Septentrionale. 2 vols., 12mo, La Haye; 1703.
153. Collections of the State Historical Society of Wisconsin. Edited by Reuben Gold Thwaites. 8vo, vols. 1-16; Madison; especially vols. 5, 10, 11, 12, 14, 16, which contain exceedingly valuable papers on the French explorations of the west.
154. Minnesota Historical Society. Collections. 8 vols., 8vo, St. Paul; 1860-98. Volume 2, containing Early French Forts and Footprints in the Valley of the Upper Mississippi.
155. Travels and Adventures in Canada and the Indian Territories between the Years 1760 and 1776. By Alexander Henry. New ed., edited with notes by James Bain. 8vo, Toronto; 1901.
    The notes add much to the value of the edition.
156. Papers by the Rev. George Bryce in the Trans. Roy. Soc. of Canada.
    The Further History of Pierre Esprit Radisson. Vol. 4, 2d series.
157. The British Empire in America (by John Oldmixon). 2 vols., 8vo, London; 1741. Hudson's Bay in vol. 1.
158. An Account of Six Years' Residence in Hudson's Bay, . . . By Joseph Robson. 8vo, London; 1752. Appendix containing a short history.
159. The Remarkable History of the Hudson's Bay Company, &c. By Rev. George Bryce. 8vo, Toronto; 1900.

NEWFOUNDLAND AND LABRADOR.

160. The Golden Fleece, divided into three parts. . . . Transported from Cambrioll Colchos out of the Southern-

most part of the island called Newfoundland. By Orpheus Junior (Sir William Vaughan). Small 4to, London; 1626.
161. A Discourse and Discovery of Newfoundland, &c., &c. By Richard Whitbourne. 4to, London; 1622.
162. A History of Newfoundland, from the English, Colonial and Foreign Records. By D. W. Prowse, LL.D., with numerous illustrations and maps. Second Edition, 8vo, London; 1896.
163. Newfoundland; its History and Present Condition, &c., &c. By Rev. M. Harvey and J. Hatton. 8vo, Boston; 1888.
164. History of the Island of Newfoundland. By the Rev. Lewis A. Anspach. 2 vols., 8vo, London; 1819.
165. Narrative of a Journey Across the Island of Newfoundland. By W. E. Cormack. 12mo, St. John's, N. F.; 1873. (Reprint of original edition of 1836.)
166. Notes of a Twenty-five Years' Service in the Hudson's Bay Company. By John Maclean. 2 vols., 12mo, London; 1849.
167. The Grand Falls of Labrador. By Henry G. Bryant. Century Magazine, September, 1892.
168. Labrador; a Sketch of the People, Its Industries and Its Natural History. By W. A. Stearns. 12mo, Boston; 1884. The author resided on the coast for two years. The most generally useful book.
169. The Labrador Coast. Journal of Two Summer Cruises. By A. S. Packard. 8vo, New York; 1891.
170. Report of the Geological Survey of Canada for 1895, containing A. P. Low's account of his explorations. Ottawa.
This report contains a summary of all that is known of the interior of Labrador.
171. Holme, Randle F. Journey in the Interior of Labrador. Proc. Royal Geog. Soc., April, 1888.
172. Cary, Austin. Exploration in Labrador. Journal of the American Geographical Society. Vol. 24 (New York), No. 1 of 1892.
173. Guay, Monsiegneur Charles. Lettres sur l'Ile d'Anticosti. 8vo, Montreal; 1902.

INDEX

——, Marguerite 207-208
ABERCROMBIE, 259
ACCAULT, 359 366 370
AGNESE, 215
ALBANEL, 385-390 Father 376-377 385 388
ALEXANDER, 416 William 251 416 420
ALLEFONCE, Jean 217
ALLEFONSCE, Jean 219 244
ALLEFONSE, Jean 11 209 219
ALLOUEZ, 324 327-330 343-344 365 373 380 Father 326 330 337 339-340
ALPHONSE, Jean 201
ALPHONSE*V, King of Portugal 47
ANDRE, Father 330 339
ANGO, 81 Jean 89-90 95
ANNE, Duchess of Bretagne 118 Queen of? 118 417
ANTHOINE, Dom 153 185
ARGALL, 251
ARNOLD, 411
ASHEHURST, Thomas 69 75
AUBERT, 81 of Dieppe 90 Thomas 81 120
AUBRY, Abbe 249
AUDUBON, 149-150
AVA, Marquis of 45
AYALA, 30

BACON, Roger 4
BAFFIN, 42 323 375
BAILLOQUET, Father 392
BALBOA, 11
BANCROFT, 291
BARAGA, Bishop 405
BARBOT, 201
BARCELLOS, Pedro de 69
BARCIA, 90 96
BAREGA, Bishop 305
BAYLY, Charles 388
BAYONNE, 65
BEBEL, Father 396
BEHAIM, 8 10 Martin 8-9 60
BEJA, Duke of 48
BELLEFOREST, 94 152 188
BERNARDIN, Father 296
BIANCO, Andrea 10 62 66
BIDDLE, 25 60 68 Richard 14
BIENCOURT, 416 Jean de 244
BIENVILLE, 406
BISSOT, Claire 342 de Vincennes 407 Francois 342 392
BLAIKLOCK, A F 391
BOUCHER, Father 392
BOURDON, 376 Jean 376
BRADLEY, Thomas 37
BREBEUF, 298-300 302 308 310-311 380 Father 298 309 Jean de 298 300

444 INDEX

BREBEUF (Cont.) Missionary 295
BRETON, Guillaume Le 153
BRIDGAR, 389 Capt 389
BRION, Chabot de 193 210 Philippe Chabot de 95
BRULE, 292-294 296-297 299 301-302 309 Etienne 276 292
BRYANT, H G 397
BUADE, 352
BULL, Friar 38
BURLEIGH, Lord 226
BUSH, J 13
BUTEUX, Father 379
BUTTON, 323 375 Thomas 265
BYLOT, 323 375
CABOT, 2 7 10 15 17-26 28-29 31 33 35-37 40 42-44 46 48 51-53 57 59 61 63 71-72 74-79 82 84 87 92 99 114 211 218 223 225 251 400 John 13-16 22 25-26 29-31 35-38 40 45-46 69 74 79 218 427 Lewis 16 38 74 Sancius 16 38 74 Sebastian 11 15-16 28 30-31 38-41 43 45 62 70 74 76-78 85 87 99 101 218
CADILLAC, La Mothe 407 La Motte 337
CAMPBELL, of Inverawe 259
CANTINO, 35 49-51 55 68-69 92 Albert 49 53 Alberto 52
CANTO, Ernesto do 60
CARIGNAN-SALIERES, 384
CARLI, 93 Fernando 92
CARTER, John 37
CARTIER, 11-12 33 63 72 81 83-84 95 99 112 114 117-138 140-184 186-190 192-200

CARTIER (Cont.) 202-203 205-207 209-222 225-226 236-237 248 254 257 262 264 296 314 379 400 422 Catherine 126 Jacques 2 11 13 24-25 58 63 112 114 119 121-122 130 148 189 206 212 220 274 392 Jean 153
CARTWRIGHT, 149
CARY, Mr 397
CAVELIER, Jean 350 Robert 350
CELERON, De Bienville 409
CHABANEL, 311
CHABERT, 123
CHABOT, 152 Adm 120 193 210 Philippe de 119 134 151
CHAMBLY, 260
CHAMPLAIN, 3 12 21 95 98 106 113 161 165 181 188-190 196 215 220 222-223 233-239 241-247 249-276 279-290 292-297 300-302 304-305 311 329 375-376 379 413 415-416 421 Madame de 297 Samuel de 233
CHARLES, Emperor 81
CHARLES II, King of? 417
CHARLES IX, King of? 219
CHARLES V, 89-90 99 102 Emperor 88 100 192-193 196
CHARLES VIII, King of? 118
CHARLEVOIX, 81-82 96 122 155 166 185 188-189 201 251 338 409 Father 409
CHARNISAY, 416-417 D'aulnay 416
CHASTES, De 233 239-240 M de 234

INDEX

CHATEAUBRIAND, Madame de 153
CHATILLON, Marechal de 92
CHATON, 221
CHAUCER, 10
CHAUMONOT, 310 Father 309
CHAUVIN, 232 262 391 400 Pierre de 232 260
CHAVES, 102
CHEFD'OTEL, 228
CHOMEDEY, Paul de 270
CHOUART, 317-319 321-325 341 373 377 387-390 Helene 316 Marguerite 317 Medard 315
CHRISTIAN I, of Denmark 67
CLAUDE, Heiress of Bretagne 88
CLAUDE, Queen of France 88 118
CLEMENTS, Sir 65
COFFIN, Adm 422
COLBERT, 328 352 354
COLE, Mr 397
COLIGNY, Adm 89 92
COLUMBUS, 2-3 6 8 10-11 14-15 17-20 28 35-36 44 47 52 59 61 63-65 67 69 74 86 92 123 212-213 Bartholomew 16 Diego 8 Fernan 116
CONDE, Prince de 264 270-271 286
CONTARINI, Marcantonio 77
CONTI, Prince de 354-355
COO, Capt 82
COOK, Capt 145
COOPER, 368
COOTE, Mr 46
CORDEIRO, Antonio 60 Luciano 60
CORMACK, 425-426 W E 425
CORTE-REAL, 48-51 53 55-57 68-69 81-84 211 223 Galvano 49 51 55 Gaspar 48-49 51-52 60-61 83 Joao Vaz 48 60 Miguel 48 52-53 Vasqueanes 48 53
CORTES, 11
CORTEZ, 89 96
COSTA, Vasqueanes da 48
COURCELLES, 341 376 384 Gov de 351
COUSIN, Jean 67
COUTURE, 377 Lt 377 Sieur 377
CRAWFORD, Earl o f 213 Lord 213
CREPIEUL, Father de 388 Francois de 380
CROMWELL, 417
CUOQ, Father 188
D'AILLON, 298-300 Father 298-299 Jos de la Roche 298
D'AILLY, Cardinal 4
D'AUXILLON, Paul 201 205
D'AVAUGOUR, 325 Baron de 321 Gov 377
D'AVEZAC, 100 153 165
D'ETAMPES, Madame 153
D'OLBEAU, Father 295
DA COSTA, Dr 91
DABLON, 346 373 385 Claude 383 Father 329-330 335 339 342 346 387
DANIEL, 308 311 Capt 420
DAUPHIN, of France 118-119 192 214 217

INDEX

DAVION, Missionary 406
DAVIS, 43
DAVOST, 308
DE AGRAMONTE, Juan 81 84
DE CAEN, 287
DE CHASTES, 233 239-240 Aymar 233 M De 234
DE CHAVES, 102 111 Alonzo 102 112
DE COURCELLES, 328-329 Gov 330 351
DE CREPIEUL, 380 Father 381
DE ECHEVETE, 85
DE GOES, 49 Damian 49
DE LA SALLE, 350
DE LAET, 83
DE LASSEY, Marquis de 372
DE LOUVIGNY, 338
DE LUSSIGNY, 372
DE MEDINA, Pedro 124
DE MONTS, 222 241-253 255 260-261 263-264 287 415 Sieur 240
DE QUEN, 380 Father 381-383
DE RAZILLY, 417 Isaac 416
DE SAUSSURE, 251
DE TONTY, 359-362 Henri 350 355 358 372
DE TRACY, 330 376 384
DE TROYES, 378 390 409
DEAYALA, 37 Pedro 28-29
DEL CANO, 99 Sebastian 99
DELACOSA, Juan 28
DENAVARRETE, Martin Fernandez 64
DENONVILLE, 402 407 Gov 374 409 M de 352
DENYS, 81 417-418 Jean 81 120 Nicholas 417 421

DES BARRES, Gov 420
DES GRANCHES, 131 Catherine 126
DESCELIERS, 199 216-217 222 285
DESLIENS, 218 Nicholas 216
DESOTO, Hernando 341
DIAZ, 60
DOLBEAU, 296 Friar 381
DOLLIER, 334-335 351 De Casson 330-331 333 351
DON, Nicholas 81
DORNELOS, Juan 84
DOUBLET, 422 Sieur 422
DRAKE, George 226
DRUILLETTES, 385 Father 315 330 339 393 411 Gabriel 383
DU, L'hut Sieur 372
DU PARC, 262
DU PLESSIS, 296 Pacifique 296
DU PONT, Sieur 231-232
DUCHESNEAU, The Intendant 374 The Intendent 352
DUFFERIN, Marquis Of 45
DULHUT, 365 370-374 404-405 407 409 413 Claude 404 Sieur 370
DUPONT, 27
DUPONT-GRAVE, 232
DURANTAYE, 409
EAMES, Mr 66
EATON, D I V 396
ECHAIDE, 85 Juan de 65
ECHEVESTE, Mateas de 65
ECHEVETE, 85
EDEN, Richard 2 77
EDWARD VI, King of England 224

INDEX

ELIZABETH, Queen of
England 13 47 224-225
ELLIOTT, Hugh 75
EMERY, De Caen 300
EMMANUEL, King of Portugal
47-48 53 82
ESTIENNE, Robert 121
EUSEBIUS, 81
FADEN, 9
FAGUNDEZ, 84 114 211 227
Joao Alvarez 83
FAILLON, Abbe 184
FENELON, Abbe 330-331
Archbishop 331
FERDINAND, 84 King of? 30
85 King of Spain 38 64 of
Aragon 17 38-39 44 77
FERDINANDO, Simon 252
FERLAND, Abbe 122 184 208
FERNANDEZ, Francis 69
Francisco 69 75 77 Joao 75
FERRARA, Duke de 49 52-53
68
FLETCHER, Mr 420
FLORENTIN, Juan 90 96
FLORIN, 96-97 Juan 90 96
FLORIO, 122 John 121
FORMALEONI, 66
FOX, 375
FRANCIROY, 217
FRANCIS, 90 118 192-193
D'angoulesme 166 King of
France 95 97 119
FRANCIS I, King of France 88-
90 121 126
FRANQUELIN, 342
FREMIN, Father 331
FRONTENAC, 329-330 337
341-344 347 352-354 357 361

FRONTENAC (Cont.) 374 376
388 390 402 418 Count de
353 402-403 Gov 352-353
FROSMOND, Thomas 153
GABOT, Anthony (sic) 68
Sebastian (sic) 68
GAFFAREL, 60
GALINEE, 331-332 334-335
351
GALVANO, 100-101 109
Antonio 49
GAMA, Vasco da 47 60
GAMART, 81 120
GANONG, 137 140 Mr 122 W
F 122
GARNIER, 311
GARREAU, Father 315
GASPE, 393
GASTALDI, 219 250 Jacomo di
208
GILBERT, 225 251 Humphrey
82 225 227-228 252
GILLAM, 324 387 389
Benjamin 389 Zachary 387
389
GOMARA, 39 42 44 76 220
GOMEZ, 85 99-102 104-107
109-114 116 211 221 Stephen
11 44 64 85 93 98-100 110-
111 114
GONZALES, Joao 69 75 77
John 69
GORDON, Capt 43
GORGES, Ferdinando 252
GOSNOLD, Bartholomew 252
GRAVE, Francois 231-232
GRAVIER, Father 406
GREELY, 42
GRENFELL, Dr 25

GRENOLLE, 294
GREYSOLON, Claude 372
  Daniel de 372
GROSEILLIERS, Sieur des 315
GUAST, Pierre du 240
GUERCHEVILLE, Madame de 251
GUERIN, 326 Jean 326
GUILLIAUME, Le Breton 185
HAIES, Edward 82
HAKLUYT, 13 37-38 41 43 67 76 80 91 94-95 97-99 119 121-122 127-128 132 145 152 160 168 177 187 199-205 218-220 224-226 229 423 Richard 196 200
HARLEYAN, 213 216-217
HARRISSE, 53 60 81 100 108 194 196 205 213-214 250 353 Henry 48 Mr 68-69 76-77 103 215
HAYES, Edward 224
HENNEPIN, 338 355 357-359 365-371 373 Father 355 359 365 368
HENRY, 267 327 338 369 405 King 75 King of ? 260 Prince of Portugal 8
HENRY II, 214 217 King of ? 89
HENRY III, King of ? 219 221 227
HENRY IV, King of ? 227 233-234 262 King of France 240 249
HENRY V, King of ? 264
HENRY VI, King of ? 232
HENRY VII, King of England 35 69 77 88

HENRY VIII, King of England 39 41 74 77-80 88 97 224
HERRERA, 82 89-90 94 99 101
HOLME, 397 R F 396
HOMEM, 84 106 Alvaro Martins 60
HORE, Master 79
HOWE, Lord 259
HOWLEY, Bishop 122 126 James 425
HUBBARD, 400 Leonidas Jr 399 Mr 399
HUDSON, 323 375 Henry 236 375
HUERTAR, Job de 8
HUMBOLDT, 60
HUMPHREY, Sir 225
IBERVILLE, 406
INDIAN, Chkoudun 243 Domagaya 156 159-161 163-164 171 173-174 180 183 186 192 198 Donnacona 161-164 171 173-175 184 186-188 197-198 257 314 Hiawatha 277 Joncaire 409 Mahomet 277 Marsolet 295 Mary March 70 72 Membertou 245-246 Pocahontas 193 Pontiac 304 412 Taignoagny 156 159-161 163-164 171 173-175 180 183 186 198 Tessouat 268-269
IRENAEUS, Father 297
JACQUES, Christovao 97
JALOBERT, Mace 153 197
JAMAY, 296 Father 295
JAMES, 323 375 King of ? 420 Thomas 226
JAMES I, King of Scotland 416

INDEX

JEFFREY, 9
JOANNA, Queen of Spain 81 84
JOAO III, King of Portugal 96
JOGUES, 313 Father 308
JOHN, King of Portugal 69 of Nantes 204
JOHN II, King of? 47 King of Portugal 47
JOHN III, King of Portugal 92
JOLLIET, 12 319 328 330 332-333 339 342-344 346-347 349-353 361 365-366 368 371 373 392 414 423 Claire 342 Louis 390 392 Sieur 352
JOMARD, 213 217
JONCAIRE, 409
JOUEN, 196 206
KENASTON, Prof 397
KING, 29 56 69
KIRKE, Comm 295
KOHL, 48 51 60 72 77 100 106 213 250
KRETSCHMER, 115
L'HUT, Sieur du 372
LA BARRE, 402 Gov 404
LA COSA, 3 25-30 35 56 Juan de 53 64
LA GALISSONIERE, Gov 409
LA HONTAN, 338
LA MOTTE, 355
LA NOUE, 298-300
LA PIERRE, Sieur de 260
LA POTHERIE, 190
LA ROCHE, 82 227-229 248 Jean Francois de 194 Marquis de 227-228
LA ROCHELLE, 90 120 Florin de 90
LA ROQUE, Jean Francois de 194

LA SALLE, 330-333 345 350-352 354-362 365 367 370 372 403 405-407 409 414 Sieur de 353
LA SOURCE, Thaumur de 406
LA TOUR, 421 Charles de 416 Claude de 416 Madame de 416
LA TOURETTE, Claude de 372
LALANDE, 392
LALEMANT, 311 Charles 298
LALEMONT, 309
LALLEMANT, Father 65
LALLEMENT, Father 73
LAUDONNIERE, 94
LAURE, 380 Father 388 392
LAVAL, Bishop 330
LAVRADOR, 69 Joao Fernandez 69
LAZARO, Luis 84
LE CARON, 295-296 298 300 Father 272 275-276 295-296 299
LE JEUNE, 300 Father 307
LE MOYNE, 378 406
LE SUEUR, 406
LE TAC, Pere 166 189
LEE, Prof 396
LEIGH, Dr 75
LELEWEL, 67
LERY, Baron De 82
LESCARBOT, 71-73 107 120-122 149 157 160 165-166 176-177 181 184 188-189 196 201 206 210 220-221 227-228 239 243-244 246-247 249-250 254 278 285 Marc 246
LIMOILEU, Sieur de 210

LOCKE, Richard 95
LOK, 95
LONGRAIS, Jouon des 196 206
LOUIS XIV, King of France 362
LOUIS XII, King of France 118
LOUIS XIII, King of France 233
LOUISE, Queen of France 92
LOW, A P 396 Mr 398 412
LUCAS, Frederick A 149
MACKENZIE, 267
MACOUN, Mr 412
MADOC, Prince of Wales 67
MAGELLAN, 87 99-101
MAGGIOLO, 69 Vesconte di 95
MAIOLLO, Visconte de 27
MAISONNEUVE, 341 Sieur de 270
MAJOR, 60
MANCE, Jeanne 310
MAREST, Father 338
MARGARET, Queen of Navarre 208-209
MARGRY, 66
MARKHAM, Adm 43 Clements 65
MARQUETTE, 12 304 319 328-330 337 343 346-349 353 361 365 368 371 373 380 405 Father 306 329 335-337 343 349 353 390
MARSHALL, O H 356
MARTIN, Abraham 316 Helene 316
MARTINS, Fernan 47
MARTYR, 39-40 42 71 76 Peter 38-39 41-42 44 70
MASSE, Ennemond 298
MCLEAN, 395-397 John 395

MCPHERSON, Joseph 396
MEMBRE, Father 367
MENARD, 326 Father 326 Rene 325
MENIER, Henry 423 M 423-424
MERCOEUR, Duke de 228-229
MICHAUX, 391
MICHELANT, M 121
MONTAGUE, 397
MONTCALM, 316
MONTIGNY, Missionary 406
MONTMORENCI, Duke de 286 297 Seigneur de 236
MORSE, Robert 419
MUNCHAUSEN, 372
MURRAY, Alexander 425
NAVARRETE, 81
NICHOLAS, Father 328 393
NICHOLSON, 417
NICOLLET, 301-309 313 365 Jean 301 303
NOEL, 218 Jacques 218 220-221 Stephen 197
NONVEL, (sic) 380
NORMANVILLE, Sieur de 379
NOUVEL, Father 348 392
OCHILTREE, Lord 420
OLIVERIANA, 69
OVIEDO, 102 104-109 111 116
PARKHURST, 224 Anthony 148
PARKMAN, 120 204 208 278 353
PASQUALIGO, 50-52 54-55 68 92 Alvise 36 Francesco 36 Pietro 49 52 68
PECKHAM, George 38
PERE, 350 Jean 332

INDEX

PERESTRELLO, 8
PERROT, 326 340 365 Nicholas 326 339 406
PERTE, Thomas 78
PETIT-VAL, 122 127-128 132 145 Raphael du 121
PHILIP II, King of? 102 223
PHIPS, 417 Adm 423
PIERSON, Father 348 371
PIET, Irenaeus 297
PIJART, Father 308
PILESTRINA, Salvat de 114
PINELLO, 91
PINZON, Vincent 67
PIZARRO, 11
PONT-GRAVE, 223 232-236 239 241-242 244-246 251 253-255 257 260-264 270-271 283 379
PONTGRAVE, 232
PONTIAC, 338
POPHAM, John 252
PORTIERS, Diane de 153
POUTRINCOURT, 244 246-249 415-416 Baron de 250 Madame de 249 Sieur de 244
PRATO, Albert de 96
PREUDHOMME, Guillaume 95
PREVERT, 242 The Sieur 239 242 245 247 The Sieur of Saint Malo 238
PRING, 252
PROWSE, 79
PTOLEMY, 3 19
PUEBLA, Dr de 17 37
PURCHAS, 79 William 76
QUARTIER, 210
QUEYLUS, Abbe de 330

RADISSON, 316-325 341 365 373 377-378 387 389-390 Marguerite 317
RAGENEAU, Father 309
RALEIGH, 251
RALLEAU, 246
RAME, 196
RAMUSIO, 11 39 44 50 56 76 80-81 90-91 94 96-97 120-122 152 160 167 196 208 219-220 274
RAND, Dr 250
RAYMBAULT, 313 Father 308
RAZILLY, 416-417 Isaac de 416
REINEL, 57 Pedro 57 72 117
RIBAUT, 94
RIBEIRO, 80 102 250
RICHELIEU, 300-301 Cardinal 256 287 301
ROBERVAL, 194-197 200-207 209-211 217-219 225 227 248 251 Sieur de 194
RODERICK, Don 9
ROSS, John 144
ROUGEMONT, Philippe 173
RUT, 79 96 John 79 114
RUYSCH, 19 29 36 42-43 72
SAGARD, 294 296-297 Gabriel 296 Pere 189 267
SAINETERRE, 204-206 M de 201 203 205 Seigneur de 201 205
SAINT AUDEBERT, Seigneur de 246
SAINT BARTHOLOMEW, 219
SAINT COSME, Missionary 406
SAINT JUST, Baron de 244

INDEX

SAINT LUSSON, 340 Daumont de 339
SAINT PIERRE, 422 Count de 422
SAINT SIMON, Denys de 385
SANSON, 155 335 375
SANTA CRUZ, 102 104-105 111-113 116 Alonzo de 68 80 102
SAVALET, Capt 221
SCOTT, Edward 46
SEDGWICK, 417
SEIGNELAY, 354
SERVANT, Louis 263 265
SHEA, J G 184 190
SKOLNO, 10 67
SMITH, Buckingham 94 John 294
SOISSONS, Count De 264 286
SONCINO, 92 Raimondo da 23
SOUZA, 61 Francesco de 61
SPARKS, Jared 372
STEARNS, 127
STEPHEN, The Protomartyr 310
STEVENS, Henry 45
STEWART, James 420
STOW, 76-77
SULLY, 240 Duke of 231 240
SULTE, M 232
TALON, 328-329 341 376 Intendant 385 The Intendant 330 338-339
THAUMUR, De La Source 406
THEVET, 188 192 204 207-208
THIRKILL, Lanslot 37 Launcelot 45 Thomas 37
THLYDE, 15 Capt 15
THOMAS, John 69 75
THORNE, Robert 41 45 75-76
TONTUIT, Sieur de 260
TONTY, 356 360 405-406 de 360-361 Henri de 350 355 358 372
TOSCANELLI, 47
TRACY, Marquis de 328-329
TRAILL, Mrs 364
TROUVE, 332 Abbe 330
TURENNE, 331
VALLARD, 222
VAUDREUIL, 418 Gov 338
VAZ, Joao 61
VELASCO, 81 Capt 81
VENTADOUR, Duke de 286 297
VERASANUS, John 99
VERRAZANO, 81 91-99 114 118 211 215 217 251 Giovanni 97 Giovanni da 90 Giovanni de 95 Hieronimus de 94 Jean 101 Jerome 96 Juan 14 90 96
VERREAU, Abbe 91 193 206
VESPUCCI, 2 92 Amerigo 14
VIEGAS, 27 108 Gaspar 114
VIEL, 298 Nicholas 296 298
VIGNAU, 265 269-270 376
VIMONT, 305 309 Father 307
VINCENNES, Bissot de 407
VINSON, Julien 73
WALKER, John 252
WARDE, 77 Richard 69 75
WASHINGTON, George 408
WAYMOUTH, George 252
WEIMAR, 116
WHITBOURNE, Richard 148
WHYTFLIET, 220
WILLIAM, Fitz 78

INDEX

WILLIAM III, King of? 417
WINSOR, 60 213-214 Justin 184
WOLFE, 288 316 420

WOLFENBUTTEL, 116
WOLSEY, Cardinal 43 78
WYTFLIET, 84
ZALTIERI, 250

www.ingramcontent.com/pod-product-compliance
Lightning Source LLC
Chambersburg PA
CBHW060907300426
44112CB00011B/1378